Java on the Raspberry Pi

Develop Java Programs to Control Devices for Robotics, IoT, and Beyond

Greg Flurry

Apress®

Java on the Raspberry Pi: Develop Java Programs to Control Devices for Robotics, IoT, and Beyond

Greg Flurry
Austin, TX, USA

ISBN-13 (pbk): 978-1-4842-7263-3   ISBN-13 (electronic): 978-1-4842-7264-0
https://doi.org/10.1007/978-1-4842-7264-0

Managing Director, Apress Media LLC: Welmoed Spahr
Acquisitions Editor: Aaron Black
Development Editor: James Markham
Coordinating Editor: Jessica Vakili

Distributed to the book trade worldwide by Springer Science+Business Media New York, 1 NY Plaza, New York, NY 10014. Phone 1-800-SPRINGER, fax (201) 348-4505, e-mail orders-ny@springer-sbm.com, or visit www.springeronline.com. Apress Media, LLC is a California LLC and the sole member (owner) is Springer Science + Business Media Finance Inc (SSBM Finance Inc). SSBM Finance Inc is a **Delaware** corporation.

For information on translations, please e-mail booktranslations@springernature.com; for reprint, paperback, or audio rights, please e-mail bookpermissions@springernature.com.

Apress titles may be purchased in bulk for academic, corporate, or promotional use. eBook versions and licenses are also available for most titles. For more information, reference our Print and eBook Bulk Sales web page at http://www.apress.com/bulk-sales.

Any source code or other supplementary material referenced by the author in this book is available to readers on GitHub via the book's product page, located at www.apress.com/978-1-4842-7263-3. For more detailed information, please visit http://www.apress.com/source-code.

Printed on acid-free paper

To my wonderful wife Sylvia, who endured many months of a distracted husband who talked about "the book" whenever he considered it acceptable.

Table of Contents

About the Author

Greg Flurry, an IBM employee for 40 years, retired as a Distinguished Engineer in 2013. At IBM, his roles included research, product development, and client services. While at IBM, Greg authored over 50 articles in both IBM and non-IBM publications on topics ranging from "getting started" in Java programming to designing enterprise system architectures; he was granted over 30 patents worldwide.

After retiring, Greg explored robotics. He used the Raspberry Pi as the brain in autonomous robots, initially programming in Python. As the robots became more complex, he yearned for Java and professional development tools. In 2015, he began using Java and Eclipse on a workstation for robotics projects. In 2017, he began using Java on the Raspberry Pi, with NetBeans on a workstation, for robotics projects. Greg continues to use Java and NetBeans to build complex robotics systems based on the Raspberry Pi.

About the Technical Reviewer

Joshua Willman is a software engineer with more than 12 years of experience developing applications in Python, Java, and C++. His career has allowed him to participate in many different fields, from robotics, machine learning, and computer vision to UI development, game development, and more.

In recent years, his passion for programming and all things visual has allowed him to participate in numerous projects. These include designing educational courses for mobile robotics and computer vision using Arduino and Raspberry Pi, building GUI applications, and working as a solo indie game developer. He currently works as a freelance developer, a technical writer, and a content creator (learning web development in his spare time in order to build his own platform, redhuli.io). When he's not working, he enjoys tinkering on robotics projects and spending time with his wonderful wife and daughter.

He is also the author of two books with Apress:

- *Beginning PyQt: A Hands-on Approach to GUI Programming*

- *Modern PyQt: Create GUI Applications for Project Management, Computer Vision, and Data Analysis*

About the Technical Reviewer

Acknowledgments

This book was built on a foundation laid by many others. Some are obvious: the professional developers of Java, Raspberry Pi, NetBeans, and various devices. Some are not so obvious: the thousands of "volunteer" developers that form communities around these technologies, expanding the collective knowledge base with supplemental technology, books, tutorials, examples, recommendations, and troubleshooting tips.

I must especially thank one "volunteer" developer, Matt Lewis from the UK. Matt created *diozero*, the technology used in this book to provide Java access to devices connected to a Raspberry Pi. During my investigation of such technologies, he helped me learn diozero, and we became colleagues. As a result of our collaboration, he enhanced his already great technology; he reviewed two key book chapters; he wrote an important appendix. Without Matt's herculean efforts, the book would have been harder to write, harder to understand, and harder to apply to the real world.

CHAPTER 1

Motivations

This book primarily focuses on using the Raspberry Pi and Java for *robotics* projects and *Internet of Things* (IoT) projects. A secondary focus is remote code development using Apache NetBeans. I've found the combination of the Raspberry Pi, Java, and NetBeans to be a very powerful and productive means of developing robotics projects. I believe the combination applies to IoT projects as well. In this chapter, I'll discuss the *motivation*, in the context of robotics and IoT projects, for

- Using the Raspberry Pi as the *primary* provider of computing resources

- Using Java as the *primary* programming language

- Using Apache NetBeans for remote development of Java programs running on the Raspberry Pi

Before discussing motivations in depth, I want to emphasize something very important. Most of this book explores finding or creating support for the *devices* used in robotics and IoT projects. As a consequence, much of the device-related material applies even if you don't do remote development, don't use NetBeans, don't use Java, or don't use the Raspberry Pi.

That said, on to motivations!

Why the Raspberry Pi?

To understand why the Raspberry Pi is a great match for robotics and IoT projects, we must explore the needs of such projects. I won't delve too deeply into the definition of the term *robotics*, as it can have a broad or narrow scope, depending on context, and it is evolving. For example, to my grandson, a toy bird that waves its wings because a microcontroller drives two servos is a robot. To me, unless a system senses its environment and reacts to that environment *autonomously*, it is not a robot. To some, possibly now, and certainly within a few years, unless a system learns as it senses and reacts adaptively to its environment based on its informed experience (i.e., unless it includes artificial intelligence and machine learning), it cannot be a robot.

For the purposes of this book, *robotics always* implies

- *Sensors* to sample the environment in various ways

- *Actuators* that enable reacting to the environment

- *Intelligence* to interpret the output of the sensors and drive the actuators to achieve the desired goals

IoT is also loosely defined and still evolving. Fundamentally, IoT is about *things* (e.g., a door lock, a thermostat, or a refrigerator) communicating over the *Internet*. Things sense their environment and send data for analysis. The data gets analyzed to inform *people* and *things*, and zero or more *things* react, although it is not necessarily the *things* that did the sensing. As in robotics, artificial intelligence and machine learning are becoming an important aspect of IoT, but usually in the *cloud*, not in the *things*.

For the purposes of this book, *IoT* implies

- *Sensors* to sample the environment in various ways, *always*

- *Communication* to communicate over the "Internet," *always*

- *Actuators* that allow reacting to the environment, *sometimes*

Clearly there is overlap between the two disciplines. In fact, a *robot* may be a *thing*. Even if not a *thing*, for some robots, communication is just as important as it is for IoT projects. For example, a robot could cooperate with other robots, or leverage cloud services, like image processing or even artificial intelligence.

There are other common needs for robotics and IoT. Many robotics systems and some IoT systems are mobile, so wireless communication and small size and low weight are often considerations. Such systems must be battery powered. Some IoT systems are stationary but deployed in remote locations; these too require wireless communication and battery power. This book assumes projects that require wireless communications and battery power.

So, what makes the Raspberry Pi a good choice for robotics and IoT?

- All models support many types of *base I/O* used to interact with sensors and actuators (*devices*). The relevant base I/O types are digital input and output (a.k.a. GPIO), the UART protocol (serial port or just serial), and more complex serial protocols, that is, the Inter-Integrated Circuit bus (I2C[1]) and the Serial Peripheral Interface bus (SPI).

- Most models offer modern wireless communications technologies, that is, Wi-Fi, Bluetooth, and Bluetooth low energy (BLE).

---

[1] I2C is the most common acronym; I²C and IIC are sometimes used.

- All models support multiple operating systems and multiple programming languages.

- Various models offer a choice of memory and processing capacity, as well as physical size, to support a wide range of needs, from relatively simple controllers to desktop computing.

- All models have reasonably low power consumption.

- All models have quite good price/performance ratios.

- The user community is enormous, and supportive.

To be fair, there are competing products that have faster processors, more memory, better I/O capabilities, or a lower price. I, however, know of no product that comes close to the size of the Raspberry Pi community (over *40 million* have been sold as of May 2021). When you encounter a problem, you almost always find that someone, somewhere, has encountered the problem and addressed it.

So, for your project, you might find a competing product that seems a better fit. However, you will likely do more work, and find less support, than if you choose a Raspberry Pi.

The "Best" Raspberry Pi for Robotics

If your project focuses on robotics, the salient characteristics are low power consumption, base I/O capability, communications capability, and as much compute power as possible so that the Pi can provide the "brains" of the project. All modern Raspberry Pi families have the same base I/O capability but vary in other areas. In my opinion, at the time of writing, one of the three models of the Raspberry Pi 3 family is the best compromise between low electrical power consumption and high compute power.

You can find full descriptions of the models on the Raspberry Pi Foundation's website (see www.raspberrypi.org/products/). Table 1-1 shows a comparison of the salient features of the models. The table does not list equivalent features, such as base I/O, audio, camera, and display support.

Table 1-1. *Comparison of Raspberry Pi 3 models*

Feature	3B	3B+	3A+
CPU speed	1.2 GHz	1.4 GHz	1.4 GHz
RAM	1 GB	1 GB	512 MB
Wi-Fi	2.4 GHz	2.4 GHz and 5 GHz	2.4 GHz and 5 GHz
Bluetooth	BLE	Bluetooth 4.2 and BLE	Bluetooth 4.2 and BLE
Ethernet	100 base	Gigabit Ethernet over USB 2.0	NA
USB 2.0 ports	4	4	1
Size	56 mm x 85 mm	56 mm x 85 mm	56 mm x 65 mm
Cost (US$)	35	35	25

As you can see, models B+ and A+ have a superior CPU speed and better wireless communication features than model B. If you have a model B already, however, it is most likely acceptable. If you must purchase a Pi, either the model B+ or A+ would be a better option. The choice between the B+ and the A+ becomes a matter of the amount of RAM, physical size, and connectivity needed for the project, as well as the cost sensitivity of the project.

For the purposes of this book, all three models are equivalent. I will use a Raspberry Pi 3 Model B+ (Pi3B+). Chapter 2 shows you how to set it up.

> **Note**   You might wonder why I don't recommend a member of the
> Raspberry Pi model 4 family. At the time of writing, any Pi4, compared
> to the Pi3B+, cost more, required more power (thus bigger batteries),
> and required heat sinks or even a fan. Pi4 prices have decreased,
> though the other differences have not changed. If you wish to use the
> Pi4, the vast majority of the book's content regarding the Pi3B+ apply
> to the Pi4 as well.

The "Best" Raspberry Pi for IoT

If your project focuses on IoT, the salient characteristics are low power
consumption, base I/O capability, wireless communications capability,
and modest compute power. In my opinion, at the time of writing, only one
model, the Raspberry Pi Zero W (Zero W), is a candidate. It also is roughly
40% (30 mm x 65 mm) of the size and as little as 20% of the weight of a Pi3B+.

You do have one choice to make. You can purchase the Zero W with
(US$14) or without (US$10) the GPIO header populated with pins. If you
plan to connect only to I2C or SPI devices, or use only a few GPIO pins, you
might be better off getting the Zero W and soldering just the pins you need.
If you need a lot of GPIO pins or hate soldering, get the Zero WH with pre-
soldered header pins. Chapter 3 shows you how to set up a Zero W.

Why Java?

I admit that I have a difficult time being objective (no pun intended) about
Java. I started programming in Java when it was introduced in 1995. I'm
still programming in Java. My most ambitious robotics projects are mostly
written in Java, sometimes with a bit of C/C++ (for an Arduino) and Python
in the mix. That said, I shall try to be objective in the following discussion.

The Raspberry Pi supports a broad spectrum of programming languages. In fact, a primary goal of the Raspberry Pi is to enable people of all ages to learn how to program. Rather than try to compare Java to that spectrum, I will limit the discussion to what I'll term *professional grade* programming languages that target standalone programs, support multitasking, support robotics and IoT device access, support network access, are supported by professional grade development tools, etc. I claim that limits the choice of a programming language to Java, Python, or C/C++.

What are the criteria for the choice? There are a few; the ones I'll use, mostly in order of importance:

- Programmer productivity
- Performance
- Industry acceptance

Programmer Productivity

Programmer productivity is multifaceted, difficult to define precisely, and somewhat subjective to measure. I'll discuss what I think are the most compelling facets.

Object-Oriented Programming (OOP)

OOP is self-explanatory. While somewhat contradicting the goal of high performance, I consider the benefits of OOP well worth the trade-off. Those benefits include improved modularity, maintainability, quality, reusability, and flexibility – basically a huge boost for programmer productivity.

Java was designed from its inception to promote OOP and in fact mandates OOP. Python supports OOP but, in my opinion, does not emphasize it. Thus, while present in Python, OOP is better supported in Java.

C of course is not object oriented at all. C++ arrived prior to Java (although it was not standardized until 1998) and seems like an afterthought, in effect an object-oriented "wrapper" around C. So, my opinion is that while present in C++, OOP is better supported in Java.

Safety

Safety refers to the probability of introducing difficult to diagnose, or even dangerous bugs into a program. The benefits of a safer language mean less time debugging and less danger of crashing software or even hardware systems – in effect better programming productivity.

Python has some characteristics that I (subjectively) dislike as I feel they introduce the possibility of bugs. Python's loose or dynamic typing is the best example; I much prefer Java's static typing. Even Python's seemingly desirable use of whitespace as part of its syntax can introduce logic bugs, as it makes it more difficult for development tools to find errors before running; Java's admittedly more verbose syntax eliminates this problem. Thus, I claim Java is safer than Python.

C, in my opinion, is basically a "high-level machine language" that is very close to the system hardware and the operating system. You can do pretty much anything. That means that you are only an obscure bug (e.g., bad pointer arithmetic, an errant `memcpy`, or a missing `free` for a corresponding `malloc`) away from potentially crashing the program or even the entire system (I've done it!). C++ does little, if anything, to eliminate the hazards of C. Java prevents such hazards, so Java is much safer than C/C++.

Write Once, Run Anywhere

Java is famous for the promise of "write once, run anywhere." In the context of this book, that means you can write, and build, code and then run the executable on any platform – your Raspberry Pi, a macOS workstation, a Windows 10 workstation, or some Linux machine. And that promise is kept – except when platform specifics become involved. Obviously, you must use platform-specific base I/O when attaching robotics and IoT devices to the Raspberry Pi. However, my experience in robotics has been that maybe 10–20% of a project works with hardware, so as much as 90% of the project can be written and tested on a high-performance workstation rather than a Raspberry Pi. This can result in a very large increase in programmer productivity. I believe the increase would not be as large for IoT projects, however.

Python, as an interpreted language, enjoys the same advantages as Java in this area. Thus, Java and Python roughly tie.

C/C++, as compiled languages, do not compare to Java in this area. While it is possible to develop and test platform-agnostic code on a high-performance workstation, to make it run on a Raspberry Pi, the code must be copied to and compiled on the Pi. It is possible to cross compile for the Pi on the workstation and then copy to the Pi. In either case, it is prudent to test again on the Pi. This is an unpleasant hit to programmer productivity.

Libraries

While perhaps not as important in the context of robotics and IoT as the preceding productivity facets, Java's extensive collection of standard libraries is unrivaled by C/C++ or Python. You name it, Java likely has a standard library for it; to mention just a few, networking, database, security, cryptography, concurrency, and collections. C forces you to roll your own support or find a third-party library. C++ and Python have less extensive support than Java. Java's extensive set of libraries definitely give it the edge in programmer productivity in this facet.

Limitations

Are there limitations to programmer productivity when using Java? The answer is yes. To explain the limitations, we need to examine the idealized software architecture this book assumes for robotics and IoT projects; it is illustrated in Figure 1-1. The *Raspberry Pi OS* layer represents the OS and its kernel. The layer provides a low-level C API[2] for the Raspberry Pi's base I/O capabilities (GPIO, serial, I2C, SPI). The layer, naturally, knows nothing about specific devices.

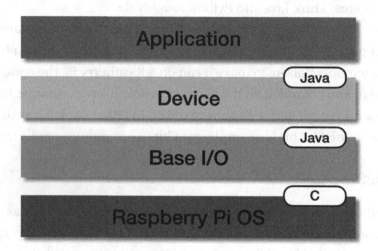

Figure 1-1. *Idealized software architecture*

The *Application* layer represents the *Java* application program(s) you write for your project. An application wants to use an API that presents an *abstraction* of a device; that is, an application cares only about *what* the device does, not about *how* it does it. Some examples:

---

[2] I am, for better or worse, using the modern definition of "API," which in effect means *any* programming interface, at the level of the application or anywhere else in a software stack.

- For an LED connected via GPIO, the application wants "turn on" or "turn off" – not "set GPIO pin 8 high" or "set GPIO pin 8 low."

- For a temperature sensor connected via I2C, the application wants to "read the temperature" – not "read 2 bytes from the device at address 0x42 on I2C bus 1 starting at register 0x0E, assemble a 14-bit value from the 2 bytes, apply compensation factors to produce the temperature."

The *Base I/O* layer represents a *base I/O library*, the "magic" code[3] that provides a *Java* API for the Raspberry Pi base I/O capabilities available via the C API of the Raspberry Pi OS layer. Fundamentally, the layer abstracts a Java programmer from the scary and difficult-to-use OS C API. Like the Raspberry Pi OS layer, the Base I/O layer knows *nothing* about specific devices; it simply offers a Java API for GPIO, serial, I2C, and SPI via a single base I/O library, or via multiple base I/O libraries.

The *Device* layer represents a *device library*. A device library knows *everything* about a device, both what it does and how it does it. A device library offers a high-level *Java* API to an application with the desired abstraction for *what* a device does. The device library leverages its device-specific knowledge to use the base I/O API provided by the Base I/O layer to implement the *how*. So, fundamentally, a device library allows the application programmer to focus on *what* the device does rather than *how* it does it.

You might ask at this point why there are two layers, Device and Base I/O, instead of one layer, between the Application and Raspberry Pi OS layers. One reason: reuse! Accessing the Base I/O C API from Java is nontrivial, and using that API can be nontrivial. Repeating that work for every device would be extremely counterproductive. Encapsulating that work in a Java base I/O library allows reuse across all devices and saves a lot of work and time, in effect improving programmer productivity.

---

[3] The "magic" includes the Java Native Interface (JNI) framework.

11

So, what are the limitations?

1. Java has no standard base I/O library providing access to the Raspberry Pi OS base I/O C interfaces. Given Java's "run anywhere" mantra, that is no surprise, but it inhibits device library development.

2. I've not found a manufacturer or vendor that offers Java device libraries for their devices. I think it is a matter of low demand. Most devices target a broad market, well beyond the Raspberry Pi. Further, the Java community is a small part of the overall Pi community.

Fortunately, the limitations are not insurmountable. The "Java for the Raspberry Pi" community is surprisingly large, skilled, dedicated, and active. I have found, and you can find, a base I/O library that supports your project's needs. In fact, you may find multiple options.

Once you've chosen a base I/O library or a set of base I/O libraries that work for your devices, it is sometimes possible to find a Java device library from a third party that you can use or adapt, especially for popular devices. If you can't find a Java library, you can almost always find a non-Java device library that you can port to Java on your base I/O library or libraries with what is almost always an acceptable amount of work. I'll discuss the subject in depth in Chapter 6.

The *conclusion* is that Java offers the best programmer productivity, followed by Python, then C/C++.

Performance

Performance is self-explanatory, and it is easy to be objective when discussing performance. For any task, the performance must be adequate to complete the task in a timely manner. My experience has been, however, that performance requirements are often difficult to predict accurately. As a result, you should generally pick the best performing language, unless that choice is contradicted by other criteria.

Java is the clear choice over Python. Comparison benchmarks (`https://benchmarksgame-team.pages.debian.net/benchmarksgame/ fastest/python3-java.html`) show that Java is almost always faster than Python 3 and in fact can run hundreds of times faster, depending on the benchmark.

C has a clear performance advantage over Java. Comparing benchmarks for C (`https://benchmarksgame-team.pages.debian. net/benchmarksgame/fastest/c.html`) to benchmarks for Java (benchmarks for Java (`https://benchmarksgame-team.pages.debian. net/benchmarksgame/fastest/java.html`), C runs up to six times as fast as Java. Those benchmarks show C++ is slower than C, but still is usually faster than Java.

Basically, if you want the utmost in performance, then C or even C++ is the best choice. Java is a much better choice than Python.

Industry Acceptance

Industry acceptance refers to how widespread the language usage is among *professional* programmers. A corollary is how attractive experience in the language might make you to potential employers.

For a long time, Java was the number one programming language worldwide among professional programmers. With the emergence of a number of new languages and changing requirements, the rankings have changed. Polls in October 2020 and December 2020 had C ranked first,

Java second, and Python third (C++ was fourth). A poll in November 2020 ranked C first, Python second, and Java third. Java will be an important and well-supported language for years to come. So, I'll consider the industry acceptance contest a tie, at least for the next few years.

The Verdict

Java offers much better programmer productivity than Python. Java is much faster than Python. Java is roughly as popular (among experienced programmers) as Python. Overall, Java wins over Python.

Java offers much, much better programmer productivity than C/C++. Java is slower than C/C++. Java is roughly as popular (among experienced programmers) as C (and more popular than C++). Overall, Java wins over C/C++.

The verdict: Java is the best *primary* programming language for *complex* robotics and IoT projects on the Raspberry Pi.

You might wonder why I include the adjective "primary" in the verdict. Neither Java nor the Raspberry Pi OS guarantees "real-time" behavior. It is common in robotics to find situations that require "real-time" or require parallel processing. In such situations, you can delegate tasks to a microcontroller like an Arduino that can perform tasks independent of the Raspberry Pi and better approach "real-time" behavior. Using an Arduino means using C/C++ as a secondary programming language.

You might also wonder why I included the adjective "complex." I have to be honest. There are IoT projects that are *not* complex (e.g., require only one or two sensors and require very little data processing). In such cases, you won't be writing or running a lot of code. Programmer productivity, performance, and popularity don't matter much. In such cases, Python can be a better choice, unless your Java environment is already in place.

Why Remote Development Using NetBeans?

Can you develop Java programs on the Raspberry Pi? The *short* answer is "yes." The *better* answer is "yes, but …." Consider the following factors:

- The complexity of your program
- The compute power and memory size of the Raspberry Pi running your program

Assume your program is a single class, with a few 10s of lines. Then, even with a Zero W that has modest compute power and only 512 MB of memory, you could *do everything on the Pi* and *do it manually*. That means

- Iterate between using a simple text editor to edit the class and using the javac command to compile the class to find simple syntax errors as well as more serious errors until you have something that can run.
- Use the java command to run the class.

Unfortunately, a single class for an interesting project of any sort is almost certainly unrealistic.

Assume the complexity increases a bit so that now you have multiple classes or must use libraries not included in the Java Runtime Environment (JRE) (and for robotics and IoT, you *will* need libraries). You could still *do everything on the Pi manually*. That now means

- Iterate between a text editor and javac *for each of the multiple classes*.
- Build the executable using the multiple classes, or one or more libraries, or both, using the jar command.
- Use the java command to run the executable.

This becomes painful and unproductive. Even for some IoT projects, this might be unacceptable.

The harsh reality of developing code for projects of even modest complexity motivated the emergence of integrated development environments (IDEs) for various programming languages long before Java. Modern, *professional grade* IDEs[4] in effect compile as you type so that you see syntax and other errors immediately, offer code completion, automate the build process, and allow you to run and debug the program within the IDE. Such IDEs deliver a huge increase in programmer productivity, and the vast majority of developers today use an IDE no matter the programming language or project complexity.

So, the answer is run an IDE on the Raspberry PI! Unfortunately, *no*! Consider some more harsh reality. All modern IDEs require a graphical user interface (GUI). A GUI requires a windowing system (often called a *desktop*) that supports GUI-based applications like an IDE. It takes a fair amount of CPU power and memory to support a desktop. You will see in Chapter 2 that the Pi3B+ provides reasonable support for a desktop; the same cannot be said for the Zero W.

Even worse, professional grade IDEs can require at least as much computing resource (CPU and memory) as the desktop. For example, NetBeans 12 (see Chapter 5) running on macOS consumes up to 4 GB of memory;[5] I believe other professional grade IDEs would be similar. I think it fair to say that even the Pi3B+, with its 1 GB of physical memory, would have trouble providing an adequate user experience. On a Zero W, forget it.

But, assume for a moment that you could reasonably run the desktop and an IDE on a Raspberry Pi (and you might well do so on a Pi 4 with 8 GB). Your project, when running, would compete with them for computing resources. As a result, you could never do realistic performance testing and might even experience random errors due to multitasking induced delays

---

[4] I do not consider the IDEs that come with the Raspberry Pi OS professional grade.

[5] NetBeans 8.2 had a memory leak and could consume as much as 12 GB of memory!

while running the IDE. That means to do realistic testing, you'd need to shut down at least the IDE and most likely the desktop as well. And if you need to fix a bug, everything has to be restarted. Painful!

The solution: *remote development*. What does that mean? In a broad sense, remote development means

- All code writing, compiling, and executable building take place in an IDE that runs on a workstation with adequate resources to deliver a productive and pleasant user experience.

- The executable (including all library dependencies when necessary) gets pushed from the workstation to the target system.

- The executable is run on the target system, without any extraneous programs competing for resources on the target.

In this book, I use a narrower definition of remote development where

- The IDE runs on a workstation.

- The IDE *automatically* pushes the executable to the remote target system.

- The IDE *automatically* runs the executable on the target system and connects to the running program to control and monitor execution and debug.

Thus, with remote development, the developer gets the best of both worlds – a professional IDE running on a capable workstation and the project executable running on the Raspberry Pi in a realistic environment.

Why NetBeans?

At the time of writing, depending on the organization or individual doing the assessment, the top three professional-grade cross-platform Java IDEs were Eclipse (`www.eclipse.org/eclipseide`), NetBeans (`https://netbeans.org`), and IntelliJ (`www.jetbrains.com/idea`). Eclipse is almost universally first, and either NetBeans or IntelliJ is second, and the other third. In the spirit of full disclosure, I started using Eclipse for Java development at its initial release in 2001; in 2014, I began using NetBeans as well as Eclipse; in 2017, I switched to NetBeans exclusively, solely based on its support for remote development on the Raspberry Pi. I must confess I've never used IntelliJ.

Fundamentally, of the three IDEs, only NetBeans supports my narrow definition of remote development "out of the box." Remote development with NetBeans is little different than local development. You can create multiple classes in multiple NetBeans projects and require multiple external jar files (libraries). At the click of a single button, NetBeans compiles all the classes, builds the executable, downloads the executable (and any dependent libraries as needed) to the Raspberry Pi, and runs and even debugs the executable. That said, there are limitations. However, I've found these limitations a problem only for some testing.

The bottom line is that remote development delivers a huge increase in programmer productivity. Further, only NetBeans supports a very efficient form of remote development "out of the box," delivering an additional increase in programmer productivity. I'll show you how to set up and use NetBeans in Chapter 5.

Note   If you are more skilled than I am, you can create NetBeans-like behavior in Eclipse and IntelliJ. Doing so involves fairly deep knowledge of the IDE and your chosen build tool, plus fair knowledge of script building for your workstation OS. I have not pursued this because NetBeans makes it unnecessary. That said, see Appendix A3 for an example of how it can be done.

Summary

In this chapter, I discussed the motivation for recommendations for several aspects of robotics and IoT projects:

- Using a Raspberry Pi for overall control, due to a great match of the requirements for such projects and the massive support network for the Pi

- Using Java as the primary programming language, due to its programmer productivity and performance

- Doing remote development, due to the programmer productivity gains, and using NetBeans, due to its best-in-class support for remote development, further increasing programmer productivity

The rest of the book assumes you want to use a Raspberry Pi, use Java, and do remote development using NetBeans. A preview of the content:

- Chapter 2 shows you how to set up a Pi3B+.

- Chapter 3 shows you how to set up a Zero W.

- Chapter 4 discusses remote computing techniques, most of which are relevant only to the Pi3B+.

- Chapter 5 shows you how to set up NetBeans.

- Chapter 6 explores options for Java base I/O support.

- Chapter 7 examines the choice for Java base I/O support in this book and also offers useful detail about the Raspberry PI base I/O capabilities.

- Chapters 8 through 14 look at support for specific devices used in robotics and IoT.

- Appendixes A1 and A2 discuss off-loading tasks to an Arduino.

- Appendix A3 examines the use of Maven as a build tool in NetBeans.

Enjoy!

CHAPTER 2

Raspberry Pi 3 Model B+ Setup

I assume you are reading this chapter because you are interested in building robotics projects using a Raspberry Pi 3 Model B+ (I'll use *Pi3* in the rest of this chapter) and Java. In this chapter, you will learn how to

- Choose the "best" operating system for the Pi3

- Install Raspberry Pi OS

- Configure Raspberry Pi OS for remote development

- Install Java on Raspberry Pi OS

Setup Considerations

Every Raspberry Pi project of course requires the "basics":

- A Raspberry Pi

- A microSD card for the file system storage

- A power source

During setup and some project development, you can provide power from an electrical outlet (via a suitable power supply) or a battery. During the setup approach I'll describe in this chapter, you will need to connect an

© Greg Flurry 2021

G. Flurry, *Java on the Raspberry Pi*, https://doi.org/10.1007/978-1-4842-7264-0_2

HDMI compatible monitor or TV, a USB keyboard, and a USB mouse. You won't need any of those during project development.

Choose the Operating System

What operating system (OS) should you use? The Raspberry Pi runs a number of operating systems. However, the default OS, formerly called Raspbian, now called *Raspberry Pi OS*, draws the vast majority of users and the vast majority of support available online. I recommend using it unless you have a very good reason to use another. All the material in this book assumes Raspberry Pi OS and has not been tested on any other OS.

There are three versions of Raspberry Pi OS:

- **Full** includes the core operating system, the *desktop* graphical user interface, and *lots* of useful tools and applications. It boots to the desktop by default.

- **Recommended** (a somewhat informal term) includes the core operating system, the desktop, and a *few* useful tools and applications. It boots to the desktop by default.

- **Lite** includes only the core operating system. It boots to a command line interface (CLI). You'll have to install any non-OS tool or application you need.

A foundation of this book is remote development, where all the heavy-duty tools run on a robust workstation, leaving the Pi CPU cycles and storage available for your project. So, in truth, **Lite** is almost certainly the correct choice for most projects. However

- I find the initial configuration after the first boot to be much, much easier using the desktop available in **Recommended** and **Full**. I'll show you how to turn off the desktop so that it does not consume memory or CPU cycles when you no longer need it.

- I find it sometimes useful to leverage tools included in **Recommended**.

For those reasons, for the Pi3, I suggest **Recommended** and will show you how to install and configure **Recommended**. Note the same instructions work for **Full** if you'd prefer that version.

Caution   The following operating system instructions should work for all models of the Raspberry Pi. I have tested only on a model 3B (designed circa 2015), a model 3B+ (designed circa 2017), and a model 1 (designed circa 2011). However, the latest versions of Java do not install on older systems like the model 1.

Load Raspberry Pi OS on the microSD Card

I'll first describe some options for getting the Raspberry Pi OS. Then I'll describe what I feel is the optimal approach.

Get Raspberry Pi OS

There are a few ways to acquire Raspberry Pi OS:

- You can buy a microSD card preloaded with NOOBS (New Out Of Box Software; see www.raspberrypi.org/ documentation/installation/noobs.md). This offers several operating systems, and you can install your choice.

- You can buy an empty microSD card and download NOOBS and write it to the microSD card on a workstation. Again, you can install your chosen operating system.

- You can buy an empty microSD card and then use the *Raspberry Pi Imager* tool to write the Raspberry Pi OS to the card on a workstation. I think this is the easiest way, and I will describe it in the following.

Image Raspberry Pi OS

The Raspberry Pi Imager (`www.raspberrypi.org/downloads`) is a great tool that downloads the Raspberry Pi OS image and writes it to a microSD card. You can get additional information about the tool from `www.raspberrypi.org/blog/raspberry-pi-imager-imaging-utility`.

You can download the tool for Windows, macOS, or Ubuntu. I use macOS, but I suspect the following description will be quite similar for the other operating systems.

On macOS, you download a `.dmg` file. It appears in the `Downloads` folder with a name similar to `imager_1.4.dmg`. Double-click it to bring up the installation dialog shown in Figure 2-1.

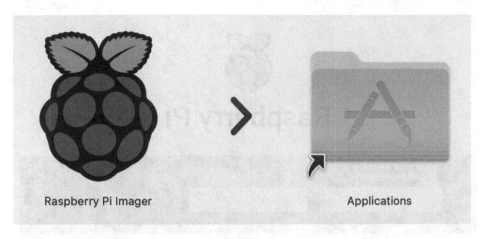

Figure 2-1. *Raspberry Pi Imager installer dialog*

Drag and drop the **Raspberry Pi Imager** icon to the Applications folder in the dialog to install the program. It takes just a few seconds to install.

To start the Raspberry Pi Imager, you can

- Go to a Finder window, and navigate to the Applications folder. Find the **Raspberry Pi Imager** icon. Double-click the icon.

- Press Command-space to bring up *Spotlight Search*. Type enough of the characters in "Raspberry Pi Imager" so that Spotlight finds the tool, and then hit the **Enter** key.

You will get a dialog asking if you really want to open the application (only the first time). If so, click **Open**. Figure 2-2 shows the Imager main dialog.

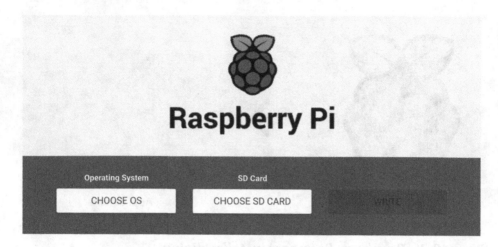

Figure 2-2. *Raspberry Pi Imager main dialog*

Click **Choose OS**. Figure 2-3 shows the dialog that allows you to choose the OS you want.

Operating System	X
Raspberry Pi OS (32-bit) A port of Debian with the Raspberry Pi Desktop (Recommended) Released: 2020-08-20 Online - 1.1 GB download	
Raspberry Pi OS (other) Other Raspberry Pi OS based images	>
LibreELEC A Kodi Entertainment Center distribution	>
Ubuntu Choose from Ubuntu Core and Server images	>
RetroPie Turn your Raspberry Pi into a retro gaming machine	>

Figure 2-3. *The Raspberry Pi Imager OS choice dialog*

Select, for the purposes of this book, the first choice, **Raspberry Pi OS (32-bit)**; this is what I called **Recommended** in the previous section (you can see that term in the description). This brings up the main dialog that now shows the chosen OS, as seen in Figure 2-4. At this point, you must make a microSD card available to your workstation if you haven't already done so.

Tip   Unless you expect your project to require a lot of file storage, I recommend a microSD card with a capacity of 16 GB or 32 GB. Larger than 32 GB will force you to reformat your microSD card before you can use it. Fortunately, Raspberry Pi Imager can reformat it. See `www.raspberrypi.org/documentation/installation/sdxc_formatting.md` for more information.

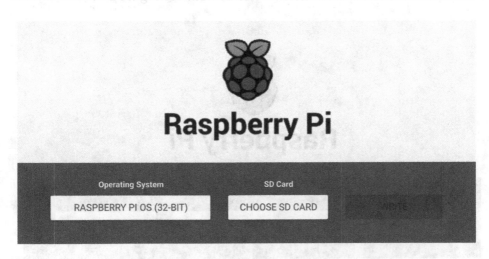

Figure 2-4. *The Raspberry Pi Imager main dialog; OS chosen*

Now you must choose the SD card to which Imager writes the chosen OS image. Click **Choose SD Card** to see the cards available. Figure 2-5 shows a microSD selection dialog similar to what you'll see. In this case, there is only one card available. If you have more than one microSD card mounted, click the one you want to use.

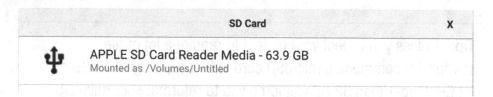

Figure 2-5. *The Raspberry Pi Imager SD card selection dialog*

Now you will once again see the main dialog showing the OS chosen, the SD card chosen, and an active **Write** button. See Figure 2-6.

Figure 2-6. *The Raspberry Pi Imager main dialog; OS and SD card chosen*

Click **Write** to start downloading and writing. You will get a *Warning* dialog that everything currently on the card will be erased. Just click **YES**. You will next get a prompt for your user password. Enter your password and click **OK**. You'll eventually see the main dialog again with a progress bar, as shown in Figure 2-7.

Figure 2-7.   The Raspberry Pi Imager writing dialog

The Raspberry Pi OS download and microSD card write actions take several minutes. The actual time depends on the size of the OS, the speed of your Internet connection, and the speed of the microSD card. Notice the **Cancel Write** button that you can use in case of an emergency. After writing finishes, the tool goes through a verification process that takes another few minutes. After verification, you should see the indication of success, shown in Figure 2-8.

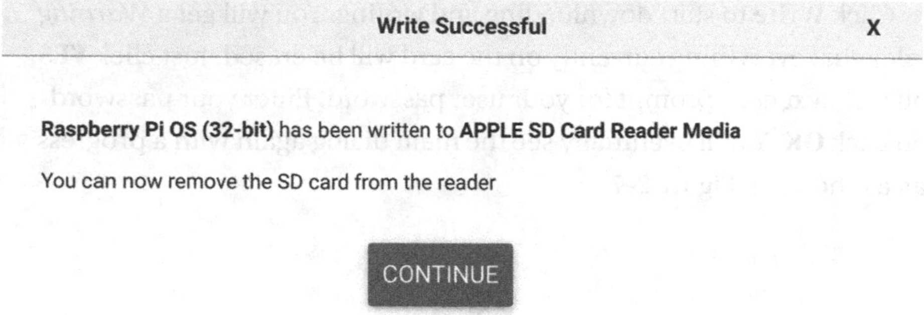

Write Successful	X

Raspberry Pi OS (32-bit) has been written to **APPLE SD Card Reader Media**

You can now remove the SD card from the reader

CONTINUE

Figure 2-8. *The Raspberry Pi Imager success dialog*

Click **Continue** to return to the main dialog (see Figure 2-5). From there, you can start the whole process again to write another microSD card. Or you can remove the microSD card and proceed to boot and configure the Pi3.

Tip The Raspberry Pi Imager does you a favor … maybe. The tool caches the OS image it downloads on your workstation file system. Thus, if you want to write the same OS to another SD card, you don't have to download the image again, so the overall task of imaging the microSD should run faster. Great! Unless you don't want to write the same OS again; if not, you have lost around 2 GB of your file system. The tool developers did not document where the OS gets cached, unfortunately. However, after an inordinate amount of sleuthing, I discovered that in macOS, you can find the cached image under (as this book is being written) ~/Library/Caches/Raspberry Pi/ Imager. On a Windows machine, it is supposed to be in c:\users\ your-username\AppData\Local, and on Ubuntu, it is supposed to be in ~/.cache. Find it, and you can delete it if you wish.

Boot and Configure Raspberry Pi OS

Prior to applying power to the Pi3, you must insert the microSD card into the microSD slot. Next, plug an HDMI cable into the Pi and then into an HDMI compatible monitor or TV. Next, plug a USB keyboard and mouse into the Pi3.

Finally, for power, you have the option of plugging in a wall adapter supplying 5V and 2.5A or using a power bank with similar specifications. While the initial boot and configuration can take a while, a battery should be just fine. I've frequently used a 10,000 mAh power bank for hours.

Note   It is possible to set up a Raspberry Pi without using a monitor, keyboard, and mouse. It is more complex. See Chapter 3 for a way to do it.

Initial Configuration

Once you've applied power to the Pi3, the magic begins to happen. The initial boot can take 10s of seconds to a couple of minutes. Eventually you'll see the desktop and *Welcome* splash as shown in Figure 2-9.

Figure 2-9. *Raspberry Pi OS desktop and Welcome splash*

The *Welcome* splash indicates the presence of a really nice configuration tool. It helps set up all the essentials in a way that I find much easier than using other configuration tools. Click **Next** in the *Welcome* splash to start configuration.

The first dialog you see allows you to set the proper locale, time zone, and keyboard. Figure 2-10 shows that, as has always been the case, the defaults are for the UK.

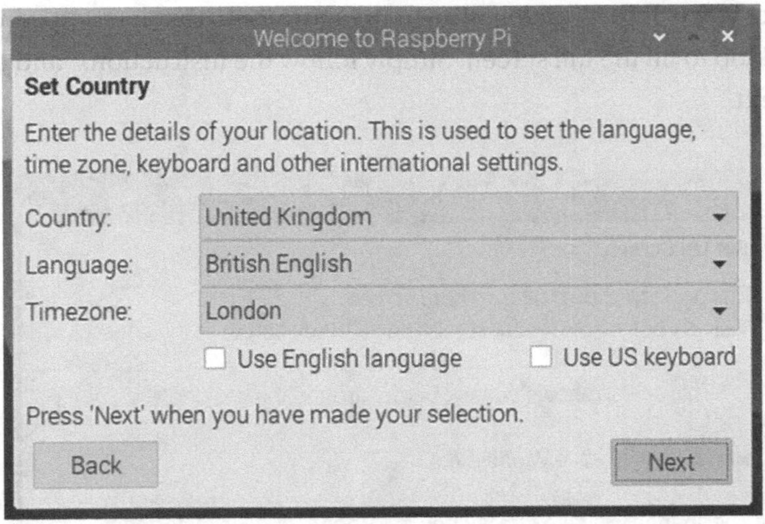

Figure 2-10. *Dialog for setting locale, time zone, and keyboard*

Since I live in the United States and pretend to read and write American English, I used the settings shown in Figure 2-11. Once you've made the appropriate settings for yourself, click **Next**.

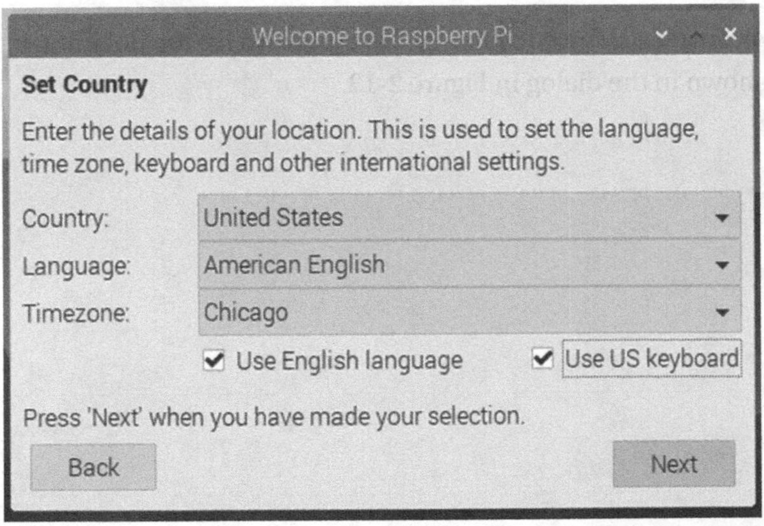

Figure 2-11. *Example settings for setting locale, time zone, and keyboard*

Next, you will see a dialog, shown in Figure 2-12, that lets you adjust the desktop to fill the full screen. Simply follow the instructions, and then click **Next**.

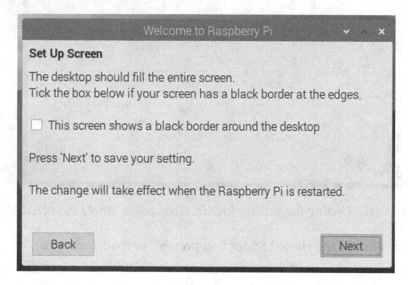

Figure 2-12. *Set Up Screen dialog*

Now you get a chance to change the password for the default user ID, "pi," as shown in the dialog in Figure 2-13.

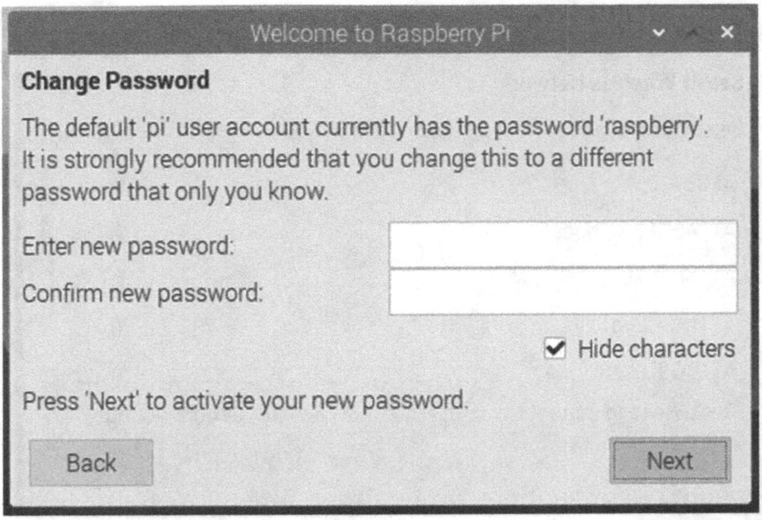

Figure 2-13. *Change password dialog*

If you don't want to change the password from "raspberry," leave the fields blank and click **Next**. If you want to change the password, I recommend you first uncheck **Hide characters** and then enter the new one into both text fields and click **Next**. If you do decide to change the password, you must use one with at least eight characters so that future setup steps will work. *Don't forget the password!*

Next, you get a chance to connect to a Wi-Fi network, as seen in Figure 2-14. You can skip this step if you connect to a network via Ethernet. Since this book assumes wireless communication, it is better to do it now.

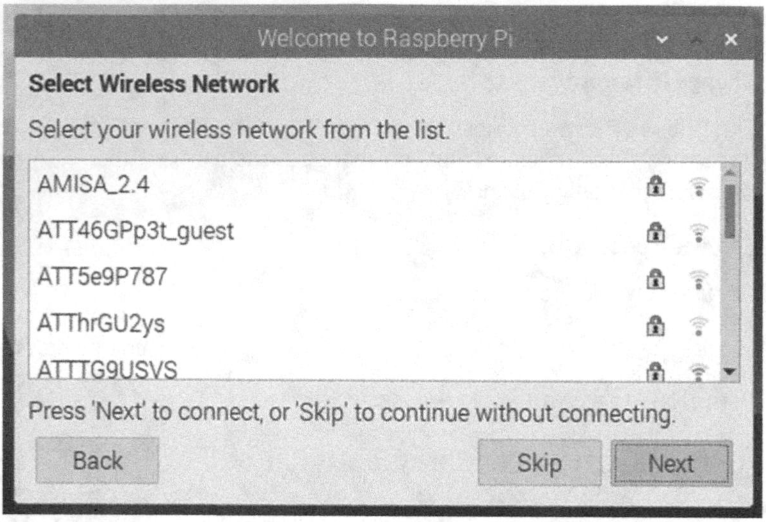

Figure 2-14. *Wireless network selection dialog*

Scroll through the list shown in the dialog to find your network, select it, and click **Next**. In the next dialog, shown in Figure 2-15, you can enter the password for the network.

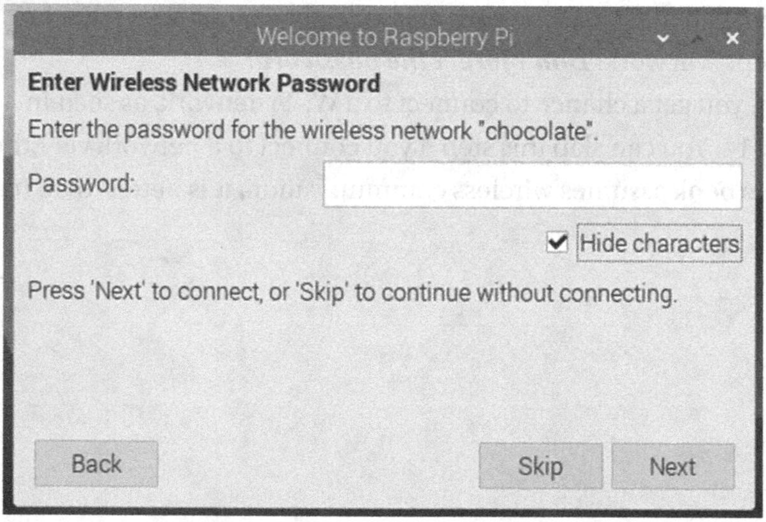

Figure 2-15. *Network password dialog*

As with the previous dialog, you can skip connecting to a Wi-Fi network, but you should connect. Once you've entered the correct password (unchecking **Hide characters** makes entering the correct password easier), click **Next**.

Now you'll have the opportunity to make sure the Raspberry Pi OS is up to date, as shown in Figure 2-16. Note that the OS cannot even check for necessary updates, much less do the updates, without a network connection. It is always a good idea to update, and I strongly urge you to do so! Click **Next**.

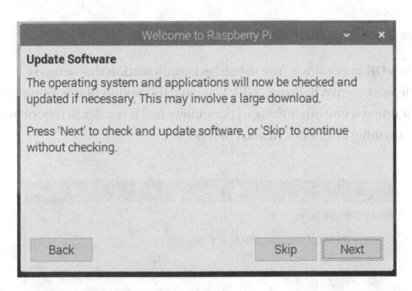

Figure 2-16. *Update Software dialog*

Now you will see a series of status messages while the OS reads the update list, gets the updates, downloads the updates, installs the updates, and finally finishes. Figure 2-17 shows the series.

Figure 2-17. *Raspberry Pi OS update messages*

Click **OK** to continue. You should get confirmation that setup is complete, as shown in Figure 2-18. You have the option of rebooting the OS now or doing some other things. I personally feel it is safer to reboot before doing anything else. Click **Restart** to reboot.

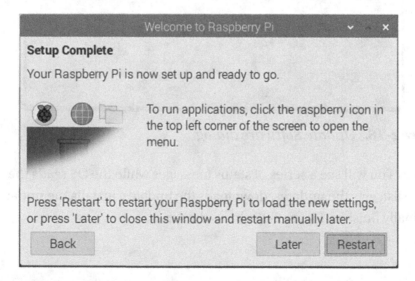

Figure 2-18. *Setup Complete dialog*

Congratulations! You've completed the initial configuration and have an up-to-date Raspberry Pi OS running!

Configure Remote Computing

You now have a Raspberry Pi system that you could use as a desktop computer, though you might find it disappointing for any significant activities. I will show you how to configure the Pi3 for headless operation, that is, no attached monitor/TV, keyboard, or mouse. Yet, you will have complete control of the system. This configuration is ideal for robotics or IoT systems and for remote development.

I assume at this point you completed the initial configuration described in the previous section, have rebooted, and can use the desktop to accomplish additional configuration. Bring up the desktop's *Raspberry Pi Configuration* tool via **Menu (Raspberry) ➤ Preferences ➤ Raspberry Pi Configuration**. You should see the dialog shown in Figure 2-19.

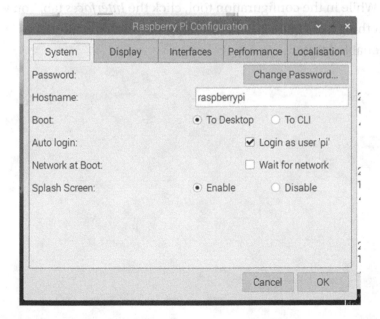

Figure 2-19. *Raspberry Pi Configuration dialog*

The configuration tool opens on the *System* tab. You need to change some of the defaults. I highly recommend that you change the *Hostname* if you have any expectation of having more than one Raspberry Pi connected to your network.

The *Boot* line controls the type of user interface loaded at boot time. As you have seen, by default, the OS boots up the desktop. It is modern and easy to use. As you can imagine, however, it takes up resources, in terms of CPU cycles and memory. The other option is CLI (the command line interface). It is harder to use but requires far fewer resources. Since you want to devote as much of the Pi3's resources as possible to your project, you want to boot to the CLI. Select **CLI**. *Do not* yet click **OK**.

Configure the Interface Capabilities

Now it is time to enable the Pi3 to interact with robotics and IoT devices via its various base I/O interfaces. Not all interfaces are enabled by default. While in the configuration tool, click the *Interfaces* tab. You will see something like Figure 2-20. The dialog shows all the interfaces and the current enabled state.

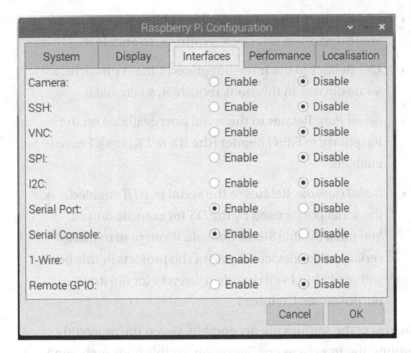

Figure 2-20. *The default settings for the Interfaces dialog*

The interfaces of interest are

- *Camera*: Relates to the Raspberry Pi Camera slot on the Pi3. The projects in this book don't leverage the camera, so I'll leave it disabled. If you plan to use the camera in your project, enable it.

- *SSH*: Relates to remote access to the Pi3 via the *Secure Shell*. You need this; it will be the primary means of interaction with the Pi! You ***must*** enable it.

- *VNC*: Relates to Virtual Network Computing. You will use this, but ironically, you want it disabled! This is because VNC, when running, also steals resources. See Chapter 4 for more on VNC.

- *SPI*: Relates to the Serial Peripheral Interface protocol. Some devices in this book require it, so enable it.

- *I2C*: Relates to the Inter-Integrated Circuit protocol. Some devices in this book require it, so enable it.

- *Serial Port*: Relates to the serial port available on the Raspberry Pi GPIO header (the RX & TX pins). Leave it enabled.

- *Serial Console*: Relates to the serial port; if enabled, the serial port is used by the OS for console output. You must disable Serial Console if you plan to use the serial port for devices. None of the projects in this book will use it, but I will disable it anyway for illustrative purposes; see Chapter 7.

The rest of the settings are acceptable. Given the preceding suggestions, the Interfaces configuration for this book is shown in Figure 2-21.

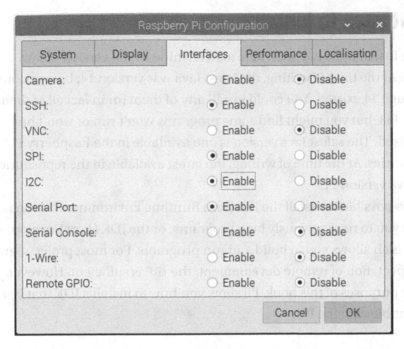

Figure 2-21. *Interfaces dialog with relevant interfaces enabled or disabled*

Once you've completed the task of enabling and disabling as needed for your project, click **OK** to confirm the configuration. You can close the configuration tool if you wish.

Install Java on Raspberry Pi OS

It is time to install Java on the Pi3. To get started with the installation, while in the desktop, start a terminal. Simply click the **Terminal** icon in the Launcher bar at the top left of the desktop.

What Java to Install?

Before installing, it is a good idea to determine which version of Java to install. At the time of writing, the latest Java was version 14, but versions 8 through 14 existed. You could install any of them (or in fact all of them) on the Pi3, but you might find some programs won't run or won't be optimized. The safest Java version is one available in the Raspberry Pi OS repositories. At the time of writing, the latest available in the repositories was Java version 11.

It is possible to install the JRE (Java Runtime Environment), which allows you to run previously built programs, or the JDK (Java Development Kit), which allows you to build and run programs. For most projects, given the expectation of remote development, the JRE is sufficient. However, for the purposes of this book, I'll show you how to install a JDK that is compatible with the Pi3.

Check for Prior Java Installations

At the time of writing, there appeared to be a bit of confusion about whether Java is included in the latest Raspberry Pi OS. My experience says it is not included; however, it is prudent to check. To do so, in the terminal, enter the `java -version` command to find the current default version of Java.

There are three possible responses:

1. `-bash: java: command not found`

2. `openjdk version "11.x.x" 202x-xx-xx`

3. something different

If you get the first response, you have to install Java. Skip to the next subsection.

If you get the second response, Java 11 is already installed, and you can skip the next subsection.

If you get the third response, you have more work to do. The "something different" means the OS has a different version of Java set as the default version. The OS defaults to the latest version installed unless the default has been changed. So, either Java 11 is not installed, or Java 11 is installed, and some other Java version is set as the default.

You can use the following command to diagnose the situation and change the default version:

```
sudo update-alternatives --config java
```

The response lists the Java versions installed. The default version is marked with a "*". The command also allows you to designate a different version as the default. If you see

```
/lib/jvm/java-11-openjdk-armhf/bin/java
```

in the list, type the number to the left of the string, and hit the Enter key. If you don't see that path in the list, you must install Java 11, in which case you have to read the following subsection.

After you have installed Java 11, if a later version of Java is the default, you'll have to use the update-alternatives command to make Java 11 the default.

Note   You can get more detail on the default Java version and how to manipulate it from https://phoenixnap.com/kb/install-java-raspberry-pi.

Install the JDK 11

The easiest way I've found to install Java is via the command line. To do so, in the terminal, enter the following command (it is a good idea, even though the system should be up to date):

`sudo apt update`

You should eventually see the following response:

`All packages are up to date.`

Now, for the good stuff, enter the following command:

`sudo apt install default-jdk`

After a few seconds, you'll be asked if you wish to continue. Enter "Y". After a few minutes, the installation finishes without any fanfare, simply returning the command line prompt.

Now, again enter the command `java -version`. The shell should now return something similar to the following:

`openjdk version "11.0.8" 2020-07-14`

If you get that response (or something similar), you can proceed to the next subsection. If not, you should start again in the previous subsection.

Finish Java Installation

For setting up NetBeans, in Chapter 5, you need to know the Java 11 install path. Enter the command

`sudo update-alternatives --config java`

You should see something like the following in the response:

`/usr/lib/jvm/java-11-openjdk-armhf/bin/java`

You can either *remember this path* or run the command later.

Finish Pi3 Setup

Now you need to find the IP address of your freshly configured and connected Pi3. Hover the mouse pointer over the Wi-Fi icon on the right side of the desktop menu bar. You should see a popup similar to that shown in Figure 2-22.

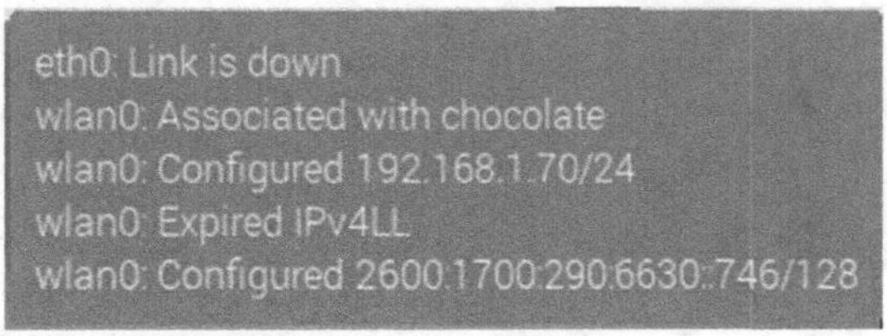

eth0: Link is down
wlan0: Associated with chocolate
wlan0: Configured 192.168.1.70/24
wlan0: Expired IPv4LL
wlan0: Configured 2600:1700:290:6630::746/128

Figure 2-22. Network pop-up

The first line confirms that no Ethernet connection exists. The second line shows the name of the Wi-Fi router to which the Pi is connected. The third line shows the IP address. *You need to remember the IP address*.

Now you should shut down the Pi. Some aspects of the new configuration will not take effect until the next reboot. For example, the desktop will still run until you reboot. To shut down, use **Menu (Raspberry) ➤ Logout**. You'll see the *Shutdown options* dialog. Click **Shutdown**. You may see an *Authentication* dialog; if so, enter the password for "pi" and click **OK**. After several seconds, the green LED should quit blinking; at that point, the Pi has shut down.

Once the system is shut down, it is safe to remove power. You should do so. Then disconnect the monitor/TV, the keyboard, and the mouse. From this point on, nothing but remote computing!

Tip   I discovered the latest version of Raspberry Pi OS includes a screen capture tool. It is called Scrot. To capture the entire screen, you simply press the PrtScr key on the keyboard. By default, Scrot stores the .png files it produces in the user's home directory. I took all the screenshots used in this section using Scrot. You can find out more from `https://magpi.raspberrypi.org/articles/take-screenshots-raspberry-pi`.

Summary

In this chapter, you've

- Learned about choosing the proper Raspberry Pi operating system for robotics

- Installed and configured the operating system to produce a functional computer based on the Pi

- Further configured the operating system to support the needed interfaces and to support remote computing

- Installed the right version of Java

Congratulations! Your Raspberry Pi 3 Model B+ setup is complete! In Chapter 4, you'll learn how to control the Pi3 from your workstation. In Chapter 5, you'll learn how to set up NetBeans for remote development on the Pi3.

CHAPTER 3

Raspberry Pi Zero W Setup

I assume if you are reading this chapter, you are interested in building IoT projects using the Raspberry Pi Zero W (I'll use Zero in the rest of this chapter) and Java. In this chapter, you will learn how to

- Choose the "best" operating system for the Pi

- Install the Raspberry Pi OS

- Configure Raspberry Pi OS for remote development

- Install Java on Raspberry Pi OS

Setup Considerations

The steps involved for the Zero are the same as for the Raspberry Pi 3 Model B+; however, some are executed differently. Likewise, the "basics" of a Pi, a microSD card, and power source are the same. The Zero, however, makes it somewhat difficult to attach a HDMI monitor or TV, a USB keyboard, and a USB mouse, unless you have the proper connectors. So, in this chapter, I'll show you how to do a "headless" setup, which is not a bad thing to understand in any case.

© Greg Flurry 2021
G. Flurry, *Java on the Raspberry Pi*, https://doi.org/10.1007/978-1-4842-7264-0_3

Choose the Operating System

The considerations are similar to those for the Raspberry Pi 3 Model B+. The Raspberry Pi OS is the best choice for the operating system (OS). The interesting decision is between the **Lite**, **Recommended**, and **Full** versions described in Chapter 2. It is possible to make a case for installing **Recommended**, but I recommend **Lite**. So, I will show you how to install and configure **Lite**.

Load Raspberry Pi OS on the microSD Card

I described the options for getting the Raspberry Pi OS in Chapter 2. In this chapter, I'll jump to using the Raspberry Pi Imager. If you don't have it installed on your workstation, see Chapter 2.

Write Raspberry Pi OS

Start the Raspberry Pi Imager (see Chapter 2 for details). You will get a dialog asking if you really want to open the application (only the first time). If so, click **Open**. Figure 3-1 shows the Imager main dialog.

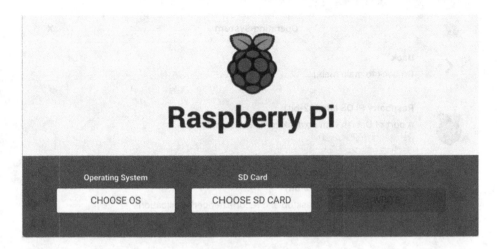

Figure 3-1. *Raspberry Pi Imager main dialog*

Click **Choose OS**. Figure 3-2 shows the dialog that allows you to choose the OS you want.

	Operating System	X
	Raspberry Pi OS (32-bit) A port of Debian with the Raspberry Pi Desktop (Recommended) Released: 2020-08-20 Online - 1.1 GB download	
	Raspberry Pi OS (other) Other Raspberry Pi OS based images	>
	LibreELEC A Kodi Entertainment Center distribution	>

Figure 3-2. *The Raspberry Pi Imager OS choice dialog*

Select, for the purposes of this book, the second choice, **Raspberry Pi OS (other)**. This brings up a pop-up shown in Figure 3-3.

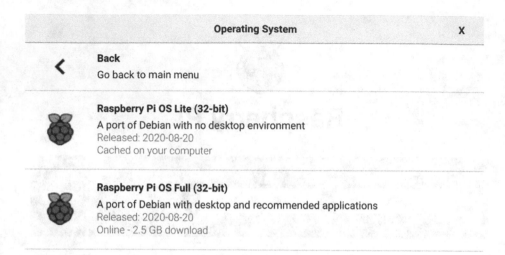

Figure 3-3. *OS selection*

You will see choices for Raspberry Pi OS **Lite** and **Full**. For the purposes of this book, click **Raspberry Pi OS Lite (32-bit)**. You'll again see the main dialog that now shows the chosen OS, as seen in Figure 3-4. At this point, you must make a microSD card available to your workstation if you haven't already done so.

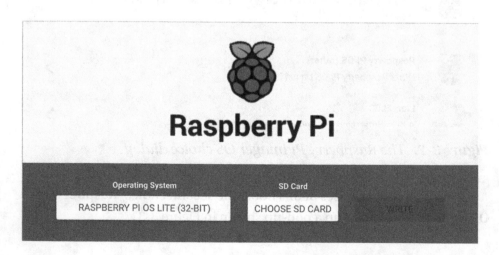

Figure 3-4. *The Raspberry Pi Imager main dialog; OS chosen*

Now you must choose the SD card to which Imager writes the chosen OS image. Click **Choose SD Card** to see the choices. Figure 3-5 shows a microSD selection dialog similar to what you'll see. In this case, there is only one card available. If you have more than one microSD card mounted, click the one you want to use.

Figure 3-5. *The Raspberry Pi Imager SD card selection dialog*

Now you will once again see the main dialog showing the OS chosen, the SD card chosen, and an active **Write** button. See Figure 3-6.

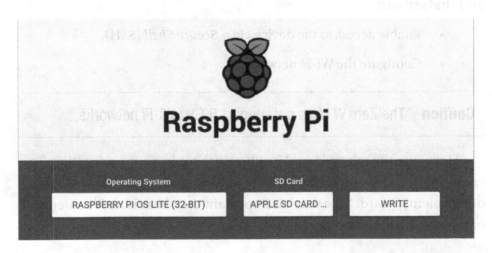

Figure 3-6. *The Raspberry Pi Imager main dialog; OS and SD card chosen*

After you click the **Write** button, the Raspberry Pi Imager downloads the OS, writes it to the microSD card, and verifies the write. Do not remove the microSD card until you see a dialog indicating success. For more detail, see Chapter 2.

Tip   See the **TIP** in Chapter 2 regarding caching of the OS image done by the Raspberry Pi Imager.

Finish the Bootable microSD Card

Since we are doing a "headless" setup, the Zero has no monitor and no keyboard attached, and you cannot simply insert the freshly written microSD card into the Zero and boot. You must first take some additional and vital actions:

- Enable access to the device via a *Secure Shell* (SSH).

- Configure the Wi-Fi network.

Caution   The Zero W *does not* support 5 GHz Wi-Fi networks.

Make sure the microSD card is still accessible by your workstation. To enable SSH, you simply create an empty file named ssh in the root folder of the microSD card. Note that it is important that there is no file extension or type for the file name.

Tip   To create an empty file with no extension on macOS, open a Terminal, navigate to the folder where you want the file, and enter the command `touch <fileName>`. To do so on Windows, open Notepad, create a new file, then click **Save as**, navigate to the folder where you want the file, and enter "<fileName>"; the quotation marks eliminate the extension.

To configure the Zero so it can connect to your Wi-Fi network, create a file named `wpa_supplicant.conf` in the root folder of the microSD card. Then edit the file with the text editor of your choice so that it has the content shown in Listing 3-1.

Listing 3-1. `wpa_supplicant.conf`

```
country=<2 letter ISO 3166-1 country code>
ctrl_interface=DIR=/var/run/wpa_supplicant GROUP=netdev
update_config=1

network={
  scan_ssid=1
  ssid="<WIFI LAN name>"
  psk="<WIFI LAN password>"
}
```

The **<2 letter ISO 3166-1 country code>** identifies your country (see www.iso.org/obp/ui/#search). For the United States, it would be "**US**"; for the United Kingdom, it would be "**UK**"; and so on. The **<WIFI LAN name>** is the name of your Wi-Fi network, and the **<WIFI LAN password>** is the password for that network. Note that what appears to be the second and third line in Listing 3-1 should really be a single line.

Now you are ready to boot and configure the Zero.

Boot and Configure Raspberry Pi OS

Prior to applying power to the Zero, you must insert the microSD card into the microSD slot. For power, you can use a wall adapter supplying 5V and 1.2A or more; you can also use a battery/power bank with the same specifications. Make sure you plug the power supply into the micro-USB connector marked "PWR IN."

After you've applied power, the initial boot should take around 90 seconds. If all goes well, the green LED eventually stops blinking and stays lit. That is the indication the Zero has finished booting.

Caution   I've noticed that when connected to an idle Zero, at least some power banks decide to shut off. I believe this is because the Zero draws less than 150 mA when idle. You might want to power the device with a wall supply during development.

Find the IP Address

The next thing you must do is find the IP address for the Zero. The simplest way is via a *terminal emulator*. On macOS, the terminal emulator is called Terminal; on Windows 10, the equivalent is also called Terminal. I'll just use the generic word *terminal* to refer to both. Open a terminal on your workstation and enter the command ping raspberrypi.local. The response contains the IP address. This works if the Zero is the only device on your Wi-Fi network with the hostname raspberrypi.

If the Zero is not the only device on your Wi-Fi network with the hostname raspberrypi, you can use the configuration tool for your wireless router to find the Zero's IP address. Basically, you must direct a browser to 192.168.1.1 or 192.168.1.254, or a similar address (see your wireless router's documentation). Poke around until you find a list of devices connected to the network. You should then be able to identify your Zero and determine the IP address.

Connect to the Zero

The simplest and most used means of connecting to the Zero is the *Secure Shell* command (ssh) issued from a terminal on your workstation. Open a terminal and enter the command

```
ssh <IP address> -l pi
```

where <IP address> means the IP address of your Zero that you determined earlier. After you enter the command, the terminal may warn you about the "authenticity of [the] host"; if so, simply type yes to continue. You will be prompted for a password; the default password for user pi is raspberry. Once you've entered the password, you should see the Zero respond as shown in Figure 3-7.

```
Linux raspberrypi 5.4.51+ #1333 Mon Aug 10 16:38:02 BST 2020 armv6l

The programs included with the Debian GNU/Linux system are free software;
the exact distribution terms for each program are described in the
individual files in /usr/share/doc/*/copyright.

Debian GNU/Linux comes with ABSOLUTELY NO WARRANTY, to the extent
permitted by applicable law.

SSH is enabled and the default password for the 'pi' user has not been changed.
This is a security risk - please login as the 'pi' user and type 'passwd' to set
 a new password.

pi@raspberrypi:~ $
```

Figure 3-7. *Initial Raspberry Pi OS ssh response*

Update and Upgrade Raspberry Pi OS

The first thing I suggest doing after connecting to the Zero is updating and upgrading the OS. To do so, you enter the following two commands in the terminal:

```
sudo apt-get update -y
sudo apt-get upgrade -y
```

The update command takes a reasonably short time to complete. It prints a few lines of feedback. When it finishes, you'll see the following line before the next command prompt:

```
Reading package lists... Done
```

The upgrade command can take a long time. The Zero is not a fast device, plus the overall time is impacted by your network speed and the speed of your microSD. The command prints hundreds of lines of feedback. What you see may be different, but when I upgraded, the last line before the next command prompt follows:

```
Processing triggers for libc-bin (2.28-10+rpi1)
```

You must reboot to ensure everything takes effect. Enter the command sudo reboot to reboot. Of course, you will have to enter the ssh command again in a terminal to reconnect to the Zero after it finishes rebooting.

Additional Configuration

Now it is prudent to do additional configuration. To start the Raspberry Pi Configuration tool, enter the command sudo raspi-config. You will see the configuration tool main dialog as shown in Figure 3-8 (the details may differ). You can navigate in the tool dialogs to highlight options using the tab key and the arrow keys on the keyboard. When you've highlighted the desired action, simply hit the Enter key.

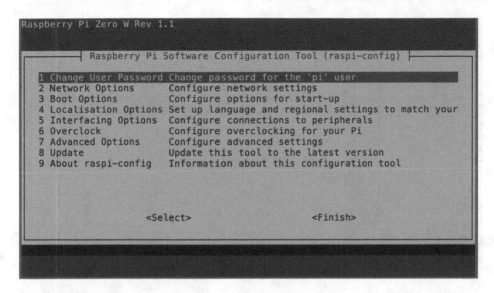

Raspberry Pi Zero W Rev 1.1

Raspberry Pi Software Configuration Tool (raspi-config)

```
1 Change User Password  Change password for the 'pi' user
2 Network Options        Configure network settings
3 Boot Options           Configure options for start-up
4 Localisation Options   Set up language and regional settings to match your
5 Interfacing Options    Configure connections to peripherals
6 Overclock              Configure overclocking for your Pi
7 Advanced Options       Configure advanced settings
8 Update                 Update this tool to the latest version
9 About raspi-config     Information about this configuration tool
```

<Select>   <Finish>

Figure 3-8. *Raspberry Pi OS Configuration Tool main dialog*

Note in Figure 3-7 the suggestion to change the password for user pi. Assuming you are working on a completely local network, I consider that optional. If you wish to do so, serendipitously, it is already highlighted when the configuration tool starts. To change the password for user pi, simply hit Enter. You'll see a dialog to confirm you are about to change the password for user pi. Hit Enter. You will leave the tool dialog and go back to the shell to enter and then reenter the password. When you've done that, you'll return to the tool with a confirmation that the password change succeeded; hit Enter. You'll again see the main dialog in Figure 3-8.

Another optional configuration is to change the hostname. I recommend doing so. To change the hostname, in the main dialog navigate to **Network Options** (use the down arrow), and then hit Enter. You'll see the Network Options dialog, shown in Figure 3-9.

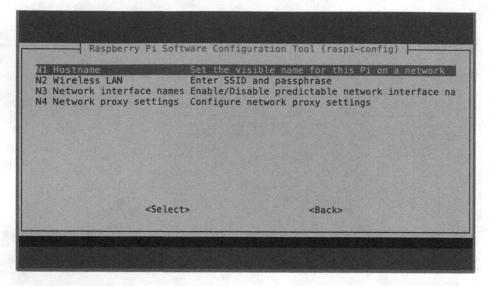

Figure 3-9. *Raspberry Pi OS Configuration Tool Network Options dialog*

You will see that **Hostname** is already highlighted, so simply hit Enter. You will see a dialog that describes what is legal and what is not legal in a hostname; simply hit Enter. Now you will see a dialog that allows you to type in a new host name. Do so; then hit the tab key or down arrow key so that **<OK>** is highlighted, and then hit Enter. You'll again see the main dialog shown in Figure 3-8.

Next, you'll configure **Localisation Options** (a.k.a. Localization Options in the United States). Navigate to the option, and then hit Enter. You'll see the dialog in Figure 3-10.

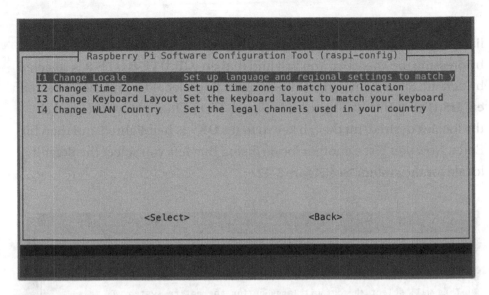

Figure 3-10. *Raspberry Pi OS Configuration Tool Localization Options dialog*

You should change the locale; the option is already selected, so just hit Enter. You will see the locale selection dialog shown in Figure 3-11.

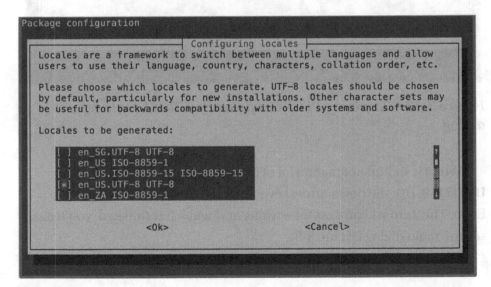

Figure 3-11. *Raspberry Pi OS Configuration Tool Locale dialog*

The selection box contains a list of locales. You can scroll through the list using the up and down arrow keys. You can select or deselect a locale by pressing the spacebar. You will find that **en_GB.UTF-8 UTF-8** is selected by default. Since I am in the United States, I deselected it and then selected **en_US.UTF-8 UTF-8** (as shown in Figure 3-11). Once you've selected all the locales desired, hit the tab key so that **<OK>** is highlighted and then hit Enter. Now you'll see another locale dialog that lets you select the default locale for the system. See Figure 3-12.

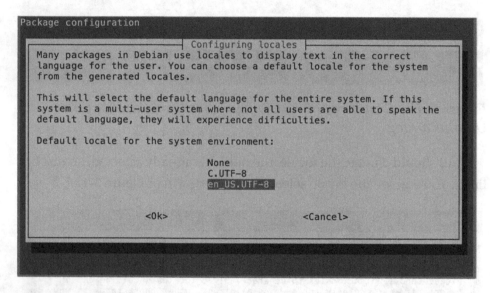

Figure 3-12. Raspberry Pi OS Configuration Tool Locale default dialog

While it should not make a lot of difference, the best choice is **en_ US.UTF-8**. Use the down arrow key to highlight that option, and then Enter. The Zero will process for a while, and when it is finished, you'll again see the main dialog (Figure 3-8).

Now you'll change the time zone so that the Zero knows the correct time for your location. Again, select **Localisation Options**, and you'll see the dialog shown in Figure 3-10. Now highlight and select **Change Time Zone**. You'll see the dialog shown in Figure 3-13.

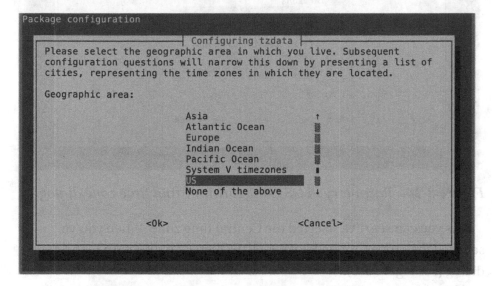

Figure 3-13. *Raspberry Pi OS Configuration Tool time zone dialog*

You need to select the proper geographic area for yourself. I chose the **US** option. Hit Enter to proceed. Next, you'll see a list of time zones relevant for the geographic area, in my case, those relevant for the United States. See Figure 3-14.

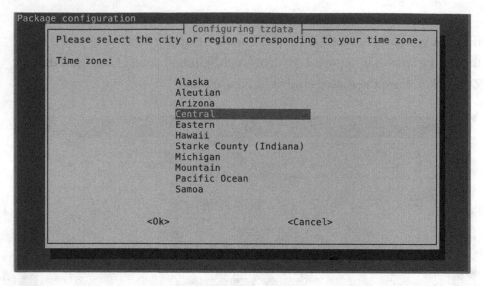

Figure 3-14. Raspberry Pi OS Configuration Tool time zone dialog

As you can see, I've selected the Central time zone. When you've selected the proper option for yourself, hit Enter. You'll return to the main dialog (see Figure 3-8).

Configure the Interface Capabilities

Now it is time to enable the Zero to interact with external devices via its various interfaces. While in the Configuration Tool main dialog, select **Interfacing Options**. You will see something like Figure 3-15. The dialog shows all the interfaces.

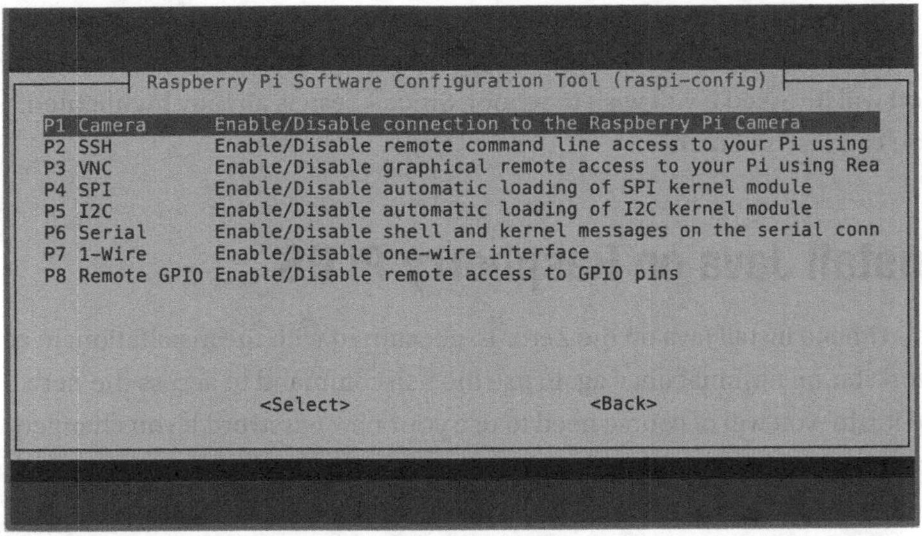

```
┌─┤ Raspberry Pi Software Configuration Tool (raspi-config) ├─┐
P1 Camera      Enable/Disable connection to the Raspberry Pi Camera
P2 SSH         Enable/Disable remote command line access to your Pi using
P3 VNC         Enable/Disable graphical remote access to your Pi using Rea
P4 SPI         Enable/Disable automatic loading of SPI kernel module
P5 I2C         Enable/Disable automatic loading of I2C kernel module
P6 Serial      Enable/Disable shell and kernel messages on the serial conn
P7 1-Wire      Enable/Disable one-wire interface
P8 Remote GPIO Enable/Disable remote access to GPIO pins



              <Select>                         <Back>
```

Figure 3-15. *Raspberry Pi OS Configuration Tool interfaces dialog*

The interfaces of interest are the same as discussed in Chapter 2. The initial configuration of the interfaces is the same as shown in Figure 2-20, with one exception; you've already enabled SSH. Some IoT devices in this book require SPI or I2C, so enable both. The serial port is not used, so you need do nothing with it; if you plan to use the serial port, you must disable the Serial Console.

To enable SPI, highlight **SPI** and hit Enter. You'll be asked if you want to enable it. Make sure **Yes** is highlighted and hit Enter. You'll get a message that SPI is enabled; simply hit Enter. You'll be returned to the main dialog shown in Figure 3-8.

To enable I2C, in the main dialog select **Interfacing Options**, highlight **I2C**, and hit Enter. You'll be asked if you want to enable it. Make sure **Yes** is highlighted and hit Enter. You'll get a message that I2C is enabled; simply hit Enter. You'll be returned to the main dialog shown in Figure 3-8.

Now is a good time to reboot so your new configuration takes effect. In the main dialog, use the tab key to highlight **<Finish>**, and then hit Enter. You will be asked if you wish to reboot. Since **<Yes>** is already highlighted, you can just hit Enter.

Install Java on Raspberry Pi OS

It is time to install Java on the Zero. To get started with the installation, in a workstation terminal once again use the `ssh` command to access the Zero. To log in, you will of course need to use your new password if you changed from the default "raspberry."

What Java to Install?

To ensure consistency between robotics (see Chapter 2) and IoT projects in this book, you want to install Java version 11. Sadly, the Raspberry Pi OS repository implementation of Java 11 *does not work on the Zero*! The repository implementation of Java 11 requires a more modern processor architecture than that used in the Zero. The repository implementation of Java 8 should work, but for compatibility with the Raspberry Pi 3 Model B+ configured in Chapter 2, you need Java 11.

Fortunately, Azul (`www.azul.com/`) provides a JRE (Java Runtime Environment), which allows you to run previously built programs, and a JDK (Java Development Kit), which allows you to build and run programs, for several versions of Java on several processor architectures. Even more fortunately, they are free for noncommercial use.

You can determine what JRE and JDK versions are available for the Raspberry Pi Zero by going to the Azul download page (`www.azul.com/downloads/zulu-community/?architecture=x86-64-bit&package=jdk`). At the time of writing, the page contained a filter capability to narrow the choices; see Figure 3-16.

Figure 3-16. Azul JDK/JRE download filter

I achieved the best results with the filter combination shown in Figure 3-16. Note in particular the *Architecture* filter. As shown in the figure, I set it to the proper value for the Raspberry Pi; note that the "HF" designation indicates hardware floating-point capability. At the time of writing, the resulting table produced by the filter contained only packages for JDK 8, JDK 11, and JDK 13. Obviously, you will want JDK 11.

Check for Prior Java Installations

At the time of writing, my experience indicates Java is not included in the latest Raspberry Pi OS. It seems possible that the reason is the default Java version does not work on all Raspberry Pi models. In any case, it is prudent to check. Please refer to Chapter 2, subsection "Check for Prior Java Installations," for details.

Install the JDK 11

It is a good idea, even though the system should be up to date, to check if the OS needs updating. To do so, in the terminal, enter the following command:

```
sudo apt update
```

You should eventually see the following response:

```
All packages are up to date.
```

Now you must create a folder for the JDK, and then navigate to that folder. Enter the following commands:

```
sudo mkdir /opt/jdk
cd /opt/jdk
```

Now in your workstation browser, go to the Azul download page and find the row in the table corresponding to JDK 11. See Figure 3-17.

Figure 3-17. *Azul JDK/JRE download row for JDK 11*

Hover your mouse cursor over the download icon (a little cloud with the text "**.tar.gz**" to the right of it) on the right side of the row. Right-click (on macOS, that is Ctrl-click or two-finger click) the icon to bring up an actions pop-up. Click **Copy Link**.

Now in the terminal, enter the command `sudo wget` followed by pasting the link you copied. For example, the command (in the terminal, the command should be a single line) I used was

```
sudo wget https://cdn.azul.com/zulu-embedded/
bin/zulu11.41.75-ca-jdk11.0.8-linux_aarch32hf.
tar.gz
```

It takes a few minutes to download the JDK. There is a progress bar to let you know the command is working.

When the download finishes, you need to find the name of the file downloaded. Use the `ls` command to do so. Copy the name of the file. Then enter the command `sudo tar -zxvf`, and paste the file name into the terminal. For example, the command (again, all on a single line) I used was

```
sudo tar -zxvf zulu11.41.75-ca-jdk11.0.8-
linux_aarch32hf.tar.gz
```

The command will take several minutes to extract all the files. There is no progress bar, and on occasion it seems to stall. Just be patient.

When the command finishes (you'll see a new command prompt), it is a good idea to do some cleanup. The `tar.gz` file is very large, so you should delete it. To do so, you can use the following command:

```
sudo rm *.tar.gz
```

Now you need to create symbolic links for the java and javac commands (javac is optional, since it is unlikely to be used). First, find the name of the directory the tar command created. Use the ls command to do so. Copy the name of the directory. Use the following commands (again, single lines) to create the symbolic links:

```
sudo update-alternatives --install
    /usr/bin/java java <name of the directory you
    copied>/bin/java 1
```

```
sudo update-alternatives --install
/usr/bin/javac javac <name of the directory
you copied>/bin/javac 1
```

Again, you should be able to paste the directory name into the terminal. For example, the commands I used were

```
sudo update-alternatives --install
/usr/bin/java java /opt/jdk/zulu11.41.75-
ca-jdk11.0.8-linux_aarch32hf/bin/java 1
```

```
sudo update-alternatives --install
/usr/bin/javac javac /opt/jdk/zulu11.41.75
    -ca-jdk11.0.8-linux_aarch32hf/bin/javac 1
```

Now enter the command

```
java -version
```

The shell should now return something similar to the following:

```
openjdk version "11.0.8" 2020-07-14 LTS
```

For setting up NetBeans, in Chapter 5, you need to know the Java 11 install path. Enter the command

```
sudo update-alternatives --config java
```

You should see something like the following in the response:

```
/usr/bin/java
```

You can either remember this path or run the command later.

Summary

In this chapter, you've

- Learned about choosing the proper Raspberry Pi operating system for IoT

- Installed and configured the operating system to produce a headless computer based on the Raspberry Pi Zero W

- Further configured the operating system to support the needed interfaces

- Installed the right version of Java

Congratulations! Your Raspberry Pi Zero W setup is complete! Chapter 4 pertains primarily to the Raspberry Pi 3 Model B+, so feel free to proceed to Chapter 5. In Chapter 5, you'll learn how to set up NetBeans for remote development.

CHAPTER 4

Set Up the Workstation

In the previous two chapters, you configured a Raspberry Pi to support robotics and IoT projects written in Java and to enable remote computing. In this chapter, I'll show you how to set up your workstation for remote computing and how to connect the workstation to the Pi. You'll set up two forms of remote computing:

- Secure Shell (SSH) for command line control for both the Raspberry Pi 3 Model B+ and the Raspberry Pi Zero W

- Virtual Network Computing (VNC) for desktop control for the Raspberry Pi 3 Model B+

Remote Computing with SSH

The simplest and most used means of connecting to a Raspberry Pi is the secure shell (ssh) command issued from a terminal emulator. If you read Chapter 3, this section is somewhat redundant, and you can skip it; if not, continue reading. On macOS, the terminal emulator is called Terminal; on Windows 10, the equivalent is also called Terminal. I'll just use the generic word *terminal* to refer to both.

© Greg Flurry 2021
G. Flurry, *Java on the Raspberry Pi*, https://doi.org/10.1007/978-1-4842-7264-0_4

To connect to the Raspberry Pi from your workstation, open a terminal. Enter the `ssh` command in one of two forms:

```
ssh <IP address> -l <username>
ssh <hostname> -l <username>
```

The "IP address" is that of the Pi you wish to control; this form will always work because IP addresses must be unique within the network domain. Similarly, the "hostname" is that of the Pi you wish to control; this form only works if your Pi has a unique hostname within the network domain. The command in effect logs you into the system with the "username." The system will prompt for the password for "username"; you set the password during the Raspberry Pi OS configuration. Figure 4-1 shows the results of using `ssh` with an IP address to get to the Raspberry Pi 3 Model B+ (Pi3) configured in Chapter 2.

```
Last login: Tue Sep 15 10:57:07 on ttys002
GregFlurrysMBP:~ gregflurry$ ssh 192.168.1.70 -l pi
pi@192.168.1.70's password:
Linux raspberrypi 5.4.51+ #1333 Mon Aug 10 16:38:02 BST 2020 armv6l

The programs included with the Debian GNU/Linux system are free software;
the exact distribution terms for each program are described in the
individual files in /usr/share/doc/*/copyright.

Debian GNU/Linux comes with ABSOLUTELY NO WARRANTY, to the extent
permitted by applicable law.
Last login: Tue Sep 15 16:30:15 2020
pi@raspberrypi: ~ $ 
```

Figure 4-1. *Terminal shell with the ssh command highlighted*

Success! You can see the prompt from the Pi3 as the last line in Figure 4-1. You can now enter all the commands available in the OS. You have in effect complete control over the Pi3 while sitting at your workstation.

Note   On older versions of Windows, and Windows 10, you can use PUTTY instead of Terminal. PUTTY is a free, open source, ssh client for Windows.

Remote Computing with VNC

Virtual Network Computing (VNC) provides a client/server architecture for remote computing that allows you to interact with the Raspberry Pi OS desktop. The VNC server runs on the Raspberry Pi, and the VNC client runs on your workstation. The VNC server is already installed on the Pi3, as it is part of the **Recommended** OS installation. Since you configured VNC as disabled, the VNC server won't be started when the Pi3 boots. No worries; you can start and stop it whenever you need to do so.

Start the VNC Server

In the terminal you opened earlier, enter the command vncserver. You will get a lengthy response that indicates the server is running, as shown in Figure 4-2. Note in particular the last line of the response. It shows the full address you need to use with the VNC client. In this case, it is 192.168.1.70:1.

```
● ● ●                 ⬆ gregflurry — pi@raspberrypi: ~ — ssh 192.168.1.70 -l pi — 80×24
RealVNC and VNC are trademarks of RealVNC Ltd and are protected by trademark
registrations and/or pending trademark applications in the European Union,
United States of America and other jurisdictions.
Protected by UK patent 2481870; US patent 8760366; EU patent 2652951.
See https://www.realvnc.com for information on VNC.
For third party acknowledgements see:
https://www.realvnc.com/docs/6/foss.html
OS: Raspbian GNU/Linux 10, Linux 5.4.51+, armv6l

Generating private key... done
On some distributions (in particular Red Hat), you may get a better experience
by running vncserver-virtual in conjunction with the system Xorg server, rather
than the old version built-in to Xvnc. More desktop environments and
applications will likely be compatible. For more information on this alternative
implementation, please see: https://www.realvnc.com/doclink/kb-546

Running applications in /etc/vnc/xstartup

VNC Server catchphrase: "Split trick ballad. Legend truck infant."
              signature: 8a-6d-5e-09-60-b1-58-90

Log file is /home/pi/.vnc/raspberrypi:1.log
New desktop is raspberrypi:1 (192.168.1.70:1)
pi@raspberrypi:~ $ ▏
```

Figure 4-2. *Confirmation that the VNC server is running*

Get and Start the VNC Viewer

The VNC server on the Pi3 comes from the company RealVNC. You will need to get a compatible client for your workstation, and the compatible client also comes from RealVNC; you can download it from `www.realvnc.com/en/connect/download/viewer`. On macOS, the installation is simple. The download is a `.dmg` file. Simply double-click it and you'll get the installer shown in Figure 4-3. Drag and drop the VNC Viewer icon to the Applications folder icon to start the installation; you may be prompted for a password.

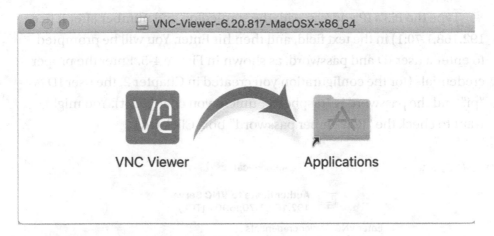

Figure 4-3. *VNC Viewer installation*

Now you can start the VNC Viewer on macOS by clicking its icon in the
Applications folder, or by doing a Spotlight search using the characters
"vnc." When the tool starts the first time, you will be asked (at least on
macOS) if you really want to open it; you know you do, so click the **Open**
button. Figure 4-4 shows the viewer the first time you run it.

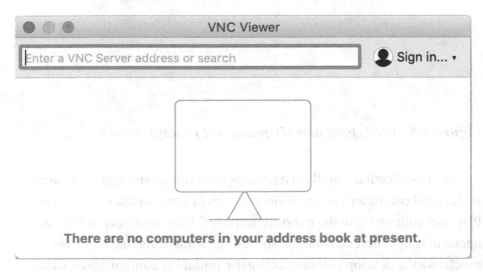

Figure 4-4. *VNC client initial open*

Type the Pi3's IP address, with the semicolon and number after it (e.g., 192.168.1.70:1) in the text field, and then hit Enter. You will be prompted to enter a user ID and password, as shown in Figure 4-5. Enter the proper credentials (for the configuration you created in Chapter 2, the user ID is "pi" and the password is "raspberry" unless you changed it). You might want to check the "Remember password" box. Click **OK**.

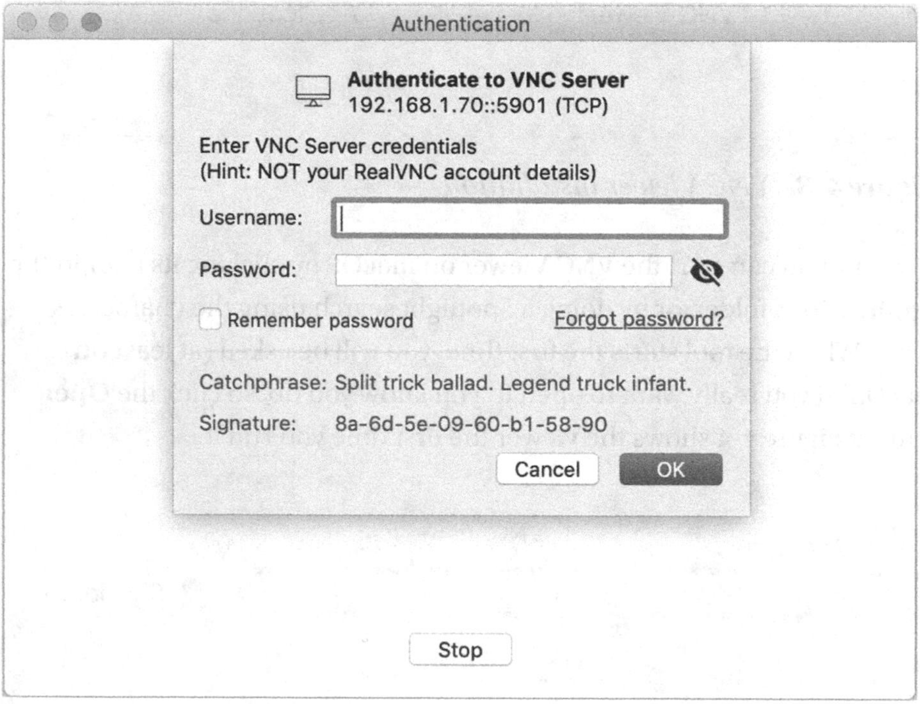

Figure 4-5. *VNC client user ID/password prompt*

After verification, you'll get a prompt from the server regarding "access to the local computer's accessibility features to send media keys such as Play and Volume Up to the remote computer." I say deny access, but your needs may be different. Now you should see something that looks very much like the desktop you saw during the initial Pi3 configuration, as in Figure 4-6.

Figure 4-6. *The Raspberry Pi OS desktop via VNC Viewer*

You can now do anything from the VNC Viewer that you could if you were using the Pi3 directly via a monitor, keyboard, and mouse. Explore. Try some things. Have fun.

Tune the VNC Server

There are some things you can do to tailor the VNC server's appearance to suit your preferences. I'll discuss two of them: the appearance of the cursor and the size of the desktop.

Change the Cursor

While you were playing in the VNC server version of the desktop, you may have noticed that the cursor is an "X" instead of an arrow. If you like it, fine; ignore the rest of this subsection. I prefer an arrow for the cursor, and I'll show you how to make the cursor an arrow.

First, you must terminate the connection between the viewer and the server. Move the cursor to the top middle of the client window. A menu will drop down. Move the cursor to the **X** and click it. You'll get a pop-up asking if you really want to close. Confirm.

Now return to the terminal connected to the Pi. Enter the following command to kill the VNC server:

```
vncserver -kill :1
```

The ":1" refers to the specific server you started earlier (the number may differ). You won't get any confirmation, but the server is no longer running.

To change the server cursor to an arrow, you first need to copy a VNC server configuration file from its system location to user pi's home folder and then modify the cursor shape in the copy. In the terminal, navigate to the .vnc folder using the command cd ~/.vnc. Now copy the configuration file to that folder using the following command (the ending "." is important, as it indicates the current folder is the target of the copy; the space between "xstartup" and the "." is also important):

```
cp /etc/vnc/xstartup .
```

Now you have to edit the copy of xstartup. You can use any available editor, but I prefer nano for its simplicity. To edit the file, enter the command nano xstartup. You should now see the xstartup file in the editor. It looks something like Figure 4-7.

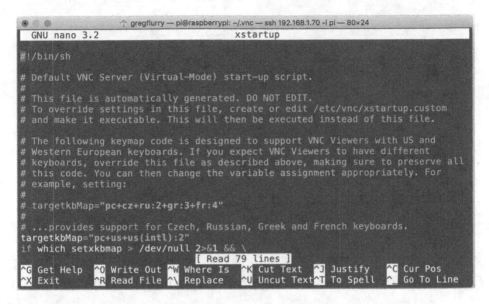

Figure 4-7. *Results of opening* xstartup *with the editor* nano

Now you need to find the line that says

xsetroot -solid grey

You can do so in nano by pressing Ctrl-w and typing "xsetroot" (without the quote marks) at the prompt. Hit Enter to start the search. Now enter the additional text so that the line reads as follows:

xsetroot -solid grey -cursor_name left_ptr

Save the edited file by pressing Ctrl-o; at the prompt, simply hit Enter; you should see a confirmation the file was written. Exit nano by pressing Ctrl-x.

Now, using the vncserver command, start the server again. Return to the VNC Viewer window. Its appearance should be different, as shown in Figure 4-8, because the viewer remembers the connection you established earlier.

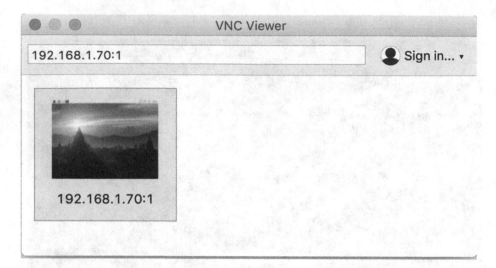

Figure 4-8. *VNC Viewer showing previously configured connection*

All you need to do to reestablish the connection is double-click the icon representing the Pi3 at address 192.168.1.70:1. Note that the viewer will remember multiple connections. When the desktop appears, you should see an arrow for the cursor.

Changing the Desktop Size

Let's say you don't like the size of the VNC desktop on your workstation. Fortunately, you can change the size when you start the VNC server. If you want to change the size, you must first kill the server as described earlier. Then you can start the VNC server with a command similar to the following:

```
vncserver -randr=640x480
```

This command produces a Pi desktop window size of 640 pixels wide by 480 pixels high on your workstation. You can use different sizes, for example, 1024x768, but I have not experimented enough to know the limits.

Tip   My experience suggests that vncserver remembers the size entered. So, if you are satisfied with a particular size, you don't have to enter it again.

Summary

You've now

- Learned how to use ssh from a terminal emulator

- Installed the VNC Viewer

- Learned how to start and stop the VNC server on the Raspberry Pi

- Learned how to connect the VNC Viewer to the VNC server

- Learned how to tailor the VNC server to fit your needs

Fundamentally, you now have two ways of remote computing with a Raspberry Pi (assuming the desktop is installed). Fantastic! Proceed to Chapter 5 to set up NetBeans for remote development.

CHAPTER 5

Remote Java Development with NetBeans

In this chapter, I'll show you the basics of remote Java development with NetBeans. I'll teach you how to install NetBeans and configure it for remote development. The configuration works on the Raspberry Pi 3 Model B+ set up in Chapter 2 and the Raspberry Pi Zero W set up in Chapter 3. I'll discuss how to

- Determine which NetBeans is "best"

- Determine which Java version is "best"

- Install Java

- Install NetBeans

- Configure remote development in NetBeans

- Run and debug remotely

Choose NetBeans and Java Versions

For the purposes of this book, the best NetBeans is the latest "long-term support" (LTS) release. At the time of writing, that was NetBeans 12.0.

© Greg Flurry 2021
G. Flurry, *Java on the Raspberry Pi*, https://doi.org/10.1007/978-1-4842-7264-0_5

NetBeans not only supports Java development, it is itself a Java application. NetBeans 12.0 can run on Java version 11 up to Java version 14. You will need one of those versions installed on your workstation to run NetBeans 12.0.

Previous chapters showed you how to install Java 11 on the Raspberry Pi. You must have the same version of Java on both your Raspberry Pi and your workstation for optimal remote development. That means you need to install Java 11 on your workstation.

Install Java 11

You must first download JDK 11 for your workstation operating system from the Oracle download page (`www.oracle.com/java/technologies/javase-jdk11-downloads.html`). It is important to understand that under the current licensing, the download is free for personal or development use. That said, you may have to create an account prior to downloading.

Note   The minor and security version numbers you find for the JDK 11 you download could be different than that shown in this chapter and used in this book (11.0.8). As long as your Raspberry Pi versions and workstation have the same numbers, everything should work fine.

For both macOS, and Windows 10, you can download an *installer* that does most of the work for you. I'll show the process for macOS using the installer; for Windows, it should be very similar.

To perform the installer download, look for the "macOS Installer" row in the table on the download page. Click the link on the right side of that row. It is at this point you may be asked to either create an account or register, and if so, just do it. It takes some time to perform the download. Once the macOS `.dmg` file is downloaded, on macOS, go to the `Downloads` folder and double-click the file. You will see the window shown in Figure 5-1.

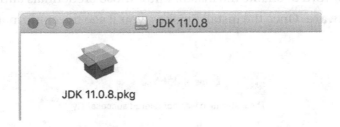

Figure 5-1. *JDK installer package*

Double-click the `.pkg` icon to start the installation. First, you see the *Introduction* panel as shown in Figure 5-2.

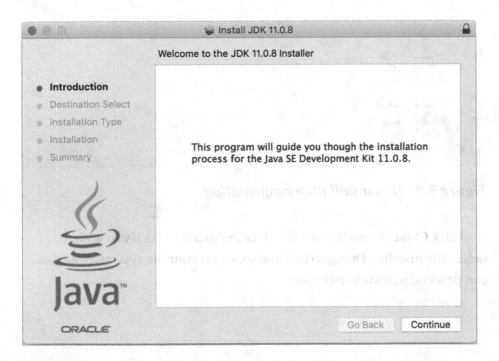

Figure 5-2. *JDK installation dialog*

Click **Continue**. You'll see the *Installation Type* dialog, but you can't do anything other than quit the installation, go back to the *Installation* panel, or continue. Click **Install**. You will be prompted to enter an administrative ID and password to enable the install. Enter those credentials and click **Install Software**. Once the install finishes, you'll see the confirmation in Figure 5-3.

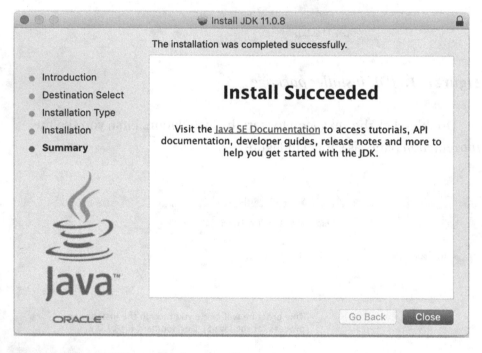

Figure 5-3. JDK installation confirmation

Click **Close** to end the installer. It conveniently asks if you wish to delete the installer. Doing so will free space on your file system. Now you can proceed to install NetBeans.

Install NetBeans 12.0

First, you must download NetBeans 12.0 from the Apache NetBeans download page (`https://netbeans.apache.org/download/nb120/nb120.html`). You can find an installer for macOS, Windows, and Linux. Click the proper link to start the download of the one you need. Once the download completes, on macOS, double-click the `.dmg` file in the **Downloads** folder. You'll next see the installer package as shown in Figure 5-4. Double-click the `.pkg` icon to start the installation.

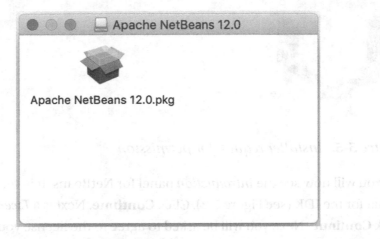

Figure 5-4. NetBeans installer package

Now the installer asks if you really want to install the program; see Figure 5-5. Click **Continue**.

Figure 5-5. *Installer request for permission*

You will now see the *Introduction* panel for NetBeans. It is very similar
to that for the JDK (see Figure 5-2). Click **Continue**. Next is a *License* panel.
Click **Continue**. Next, you will be asked to agree to the license you almost
certainly did not read. Click **Agree**. Next, you'll see the *Installation Type*
panel, shown in Figure 5-6.

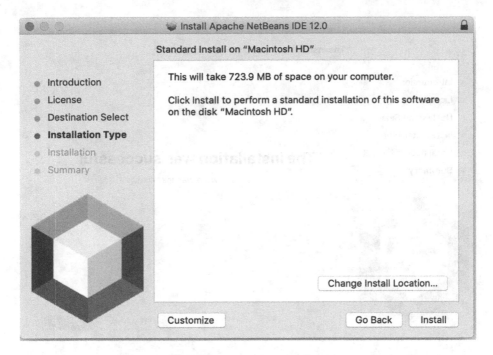

Figure 5-6. *NetBeans installer Installation Type panel*

NetBeans 12.0 allows you to develop in a number of programming languages. By default, in addition to the Base IDE, the install includes Java SE, Java EE, HTML5/JavaScript, and PHP. You obviously need Java SE. You can choose what to install by clicking **Customize**. You can save a lot of storage by not including the others, but I chose to install all of them; who knows what the next project will require? I recommend using the default install location, but you can change that by clicking **Change Install Location**. After all that thinking, click **Install**. You will be prompted for an administrator ID and password. Enter the credentials and click **Install Software**. Once the install finishes, you see the confirmation in Figure 5-7. Click **Close** to end the installer. Note that this installer does not delete the .pkg or .img file. You will have to do that manually if you wish to free up the space on your file system.

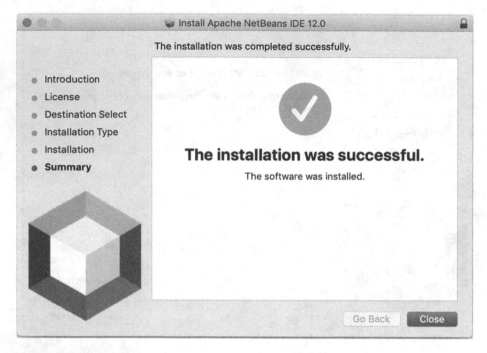

Figure 5-7. *NetBeans 12.0 installation success confirmation*

Test the NetBeans Installation

Now you can open NetBeans 12.0 on macOS by opening Spotlight search and typing characters in the string "Apache NetBeans 12.0" until it shows up and then hit Enter. NetBeans initializes itself and then displays the window in Figure 5-8.

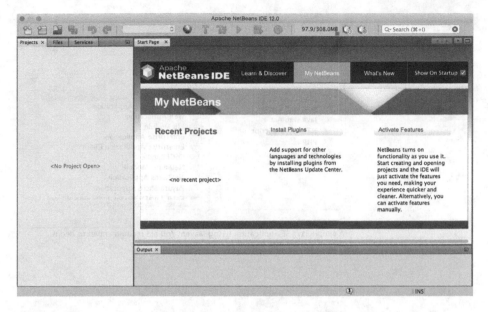

Figure 5-8. *NetBeans 12 initial window appearance*

Now you can create a test. In general, I won't try to give a tutorial on NetBeans development or Java, but I'll address some basic concepts.

In the NetBeans toolbar, click the **New Project** icon, the folder-looking icon (second from the left in the toolbar). You'll see the *New Project* dialog shown in Figure 5-9.

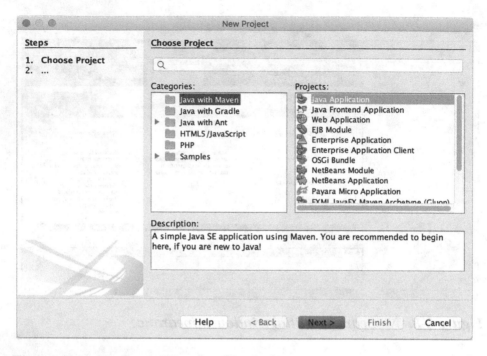

Figure 5-9. *NetBeans New Project dialog*

Note from Figure 5-9 that in NetBeans 12, the default project management/build tool is *Maven*. Maven *does not* support my definition of remote development "out of the box." The *Ant* tool *does* support it. Since one focus of the book is simple, yet efficient remote development, this book uses Ant, and in this chapter, I'll show you how to develop with Ant.

Tip   Maven does a better job of automating other development tasks. With some work, Maven can approximate "Ant style" remote development. See Appendix A3 for details. Before reading Appendix A3, I recommend that you at least browse the rest of this chapter as well as Chapters 6, 7, and even 8, to establish sufficient context.

To get started with Ant, in the *New Project* dialog (Figure 5-9), click **Java with Ant**, then click **Java Application**, and then click **Next**. You will see the *Name and Location* dialog, shown in Figure 5-10, which lets you enter the name of the project ("FirstTest" in this example) and application (or main class), manage the location of the files (I recommend not changing the default unless you really need to do so), decide whether to create a main class (in this case yes), and enter the package name (for this test, the default is fine). When you have finished entering the information to your satisfaction, click **Finish**.

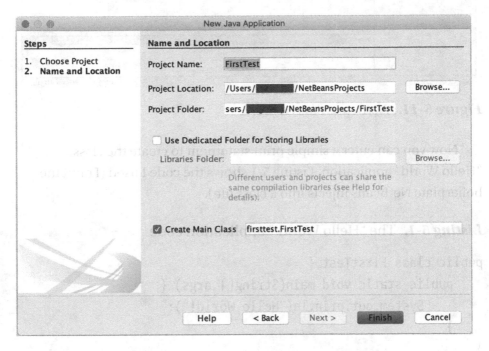

Figure 5-10. *NetBeans New Project dialog: entering project name (and main class name), location, and package name*

NetBeans creates the project and opens the class editor for the main class, which is FirstTest in my example. You'll see something like Figure 5-11.

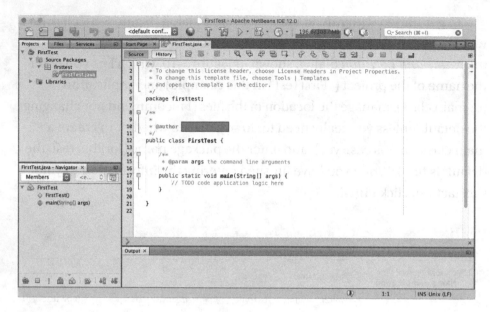

Figure 5-11. *NetBeans class editor*

Now you can enter a simple print statement to create the classic "Hello World" application. Listing 5-1 shows the code I used (I omit the boilerplate NetBeans injects into a class file).

Listing 5-1. The "Hello World!" application code

```
public class FirstTest {
    public static void main(String[] args) {
        System.out.println("Hello World!");
    }
}
```

Run the code by clicking the **Run** icon (the green right-pointing arrow in the middle of the toolbar). Assuming all is well, you should see the following in the NetBeans *Output* pane, which is below the editor:

```
run:
Hello World!
BUILD SUCCESSFUL (total time: 1 second)
```

Success! You've installed and tested NetBeans.

Configure the Raspberry Pi As a Remote Platform

Now you'll configure NetBeans to recognize the Raspberry Pi as a platform for remote development. In the NetBeans menu bar, select **Tools ➤ Java Platforms**. You will see the *Java Platform Manager* pop-up window shown in Figure 5-12.

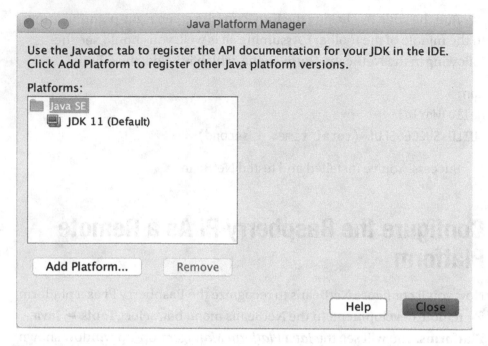

Figure 5-12. *NetBeans Java Platform Manager*

Notice the only current platform is the JDK 11 local on the workstation.
Click **Add Platform** so you can add a Raspberry Pi. Figure 5-13 shows
the *Add Platform* dialog. By default, you'll add another local JDK. In
this situation, you want to add a Pi, so select the **Remote Java Standard
Edition** option, and then click **Next**.

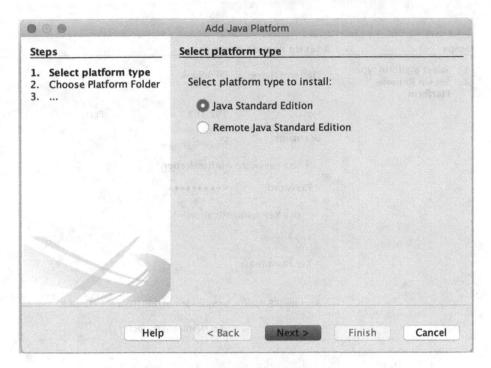

Figure 5-13. *NetBeans Add Java Platform dialog*

Now, you will see the *Set Up Remote Platform* dialog shown in Figure 5-14. You must enter a *Platform Name*. It should be something relatively unique. I have on occasion developed project components on three remote systems simultaneously, and in such cases, unique names are mandatory. You must enter the *Host* IP address or hostname for the remote Pi; you should use the address or name determined in Chapter 2 or Chapter 3, unless you are dealing with another Raspberry Pi. You must enter a user ID; for the purposes of the book, use "pi." The easiest *Authentication* type is password, so make sure **Use Password Authentication** is selected and enter the password you created in Chapter 2 or Chapter 3.

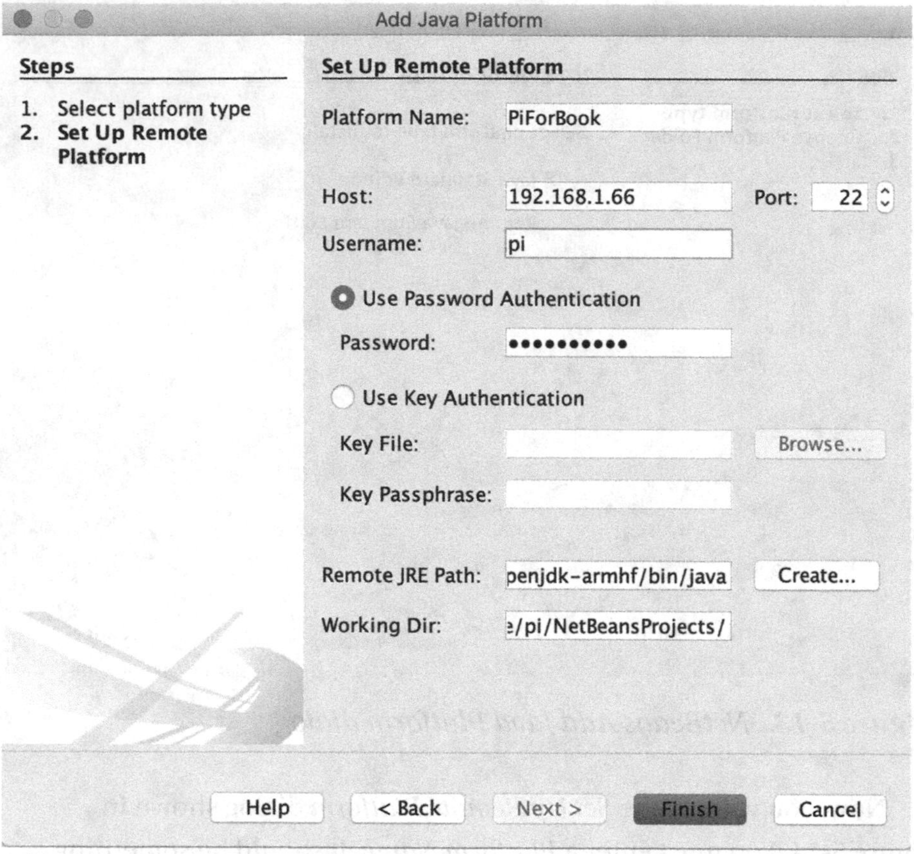

Figure 5-14. *A completed Set Up Remote Platform dialog*

A very key field in the dialog is the **Remote JRE Path**. You should use the path discovered in Chapter 2 or Chapter 3. If you don't remember it, the best way to find that path is go to a terminal with a ssh session to the Pi and enter the following command:

```
sudo update-alternatives --config java
```

The response should be something similar to the following:

```
/usr/lib/jvm/java-11-openjdk-armhf/bin/java
```

Enter that string, minus "/bin/java," into the *Remote JRE Path* field. You can change the remote *Working Directory*, but I find the default to be just fine. When you have completed the dialog, it should look similar to Figure 5-14. Click **Finish** to create the remote platform. NetBeans can take several seconds to do so. When finished, you will once again see the *Java Platform Manager* with the newly created remote platform information displayed. See Figure 5-15.

Figure 5-15. *NetBeans Java Platform Manager with remote platform*

Notice the **Test Platform** button in the *Java Platform Manager*. You can try it if you wish, but immediately after creating the new remote platform, it is unnecessary. However, it can be useful for a remote platform you haven't used for a while or to which you have made changes that might impact the configuration. Now you can click **Close** to close the *Java Platform Manager*.

Test Remote Development

Now you will run the FirstTest program created previously on the Raspberry Pi. In the NetBeans *Projects* pane, right-click (on macOS, that is Ctrl-click or two-finger click) the **FirstTest** project to bring up the *Project Properties* dialog. Under *Categories*, click **Run** to view the runtime properties of the project, shown in Figure 5-16. Click **New** to the right of the *Configuration* field. In the resulting *Create New Configuration* pop-up, enter a name for the configuration and click **OK**. The name can be anything. Click the drop-down icon on the right of the *Runtime Platform* field. From the list in the pop-up, select the remote platform you created earlier (**PiForBook** in this example). Click **OK** to save the properties.

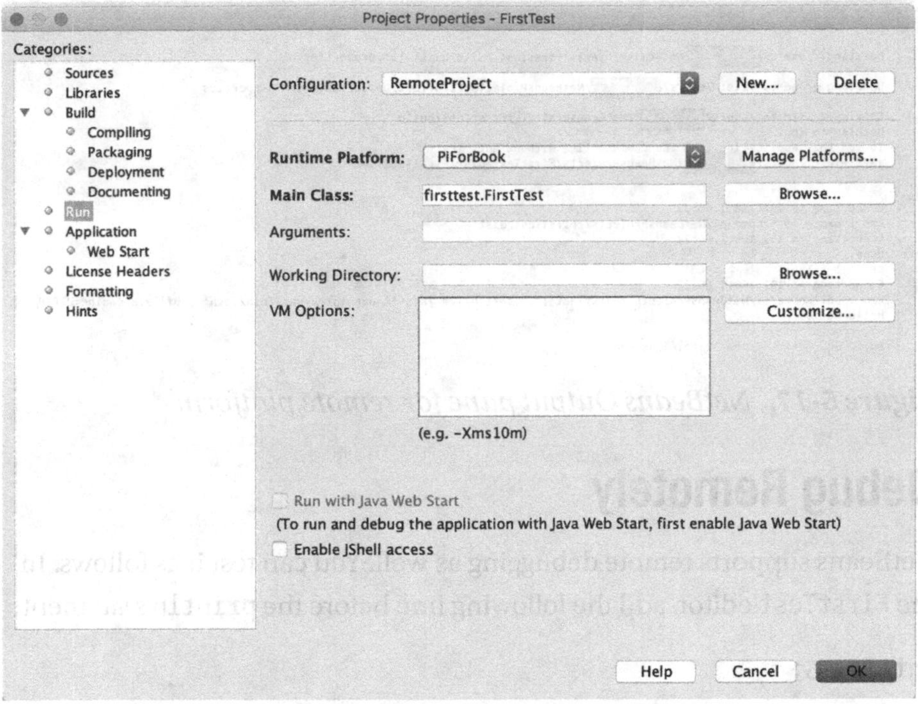

Figure 5-16. *NetBeans Project Properties (Run)*

Now run the project again. This time in the NetBeans *Output* pane, you will see something similar to Figure 5-17. Note the communication with the Pi to create a folder to store the resulting jar file on the Pi, download the jar file, run the jar file, and retrieve the output to display. It worked! Congratulations, you are developing remotely!

Figure 5-17. *NetBeans Output pane for remote platform*

Debug Remotely

NetBeans supports remote debugging as well. You can test it as follows. In the FirstTest editor, add the following line before the println statement:

```
int i = 5;
```

Now click the line number for the println statement. The entire line highlights in red. Click the **Debug** icon in the main menu bar; it is the icon immediately to the right of the **Run** icon. Sadly, the debug attempt might fail! At least it fails unless a suspected bug has been fixed by the NetBeans developers. If it works, great; you can skip the next subsection. If it fails, fear not; continue reading.

Fix Remote Debug

I initially assumed this to be a common problem, with an easily discoverable solution. I was wrong. However, I sleuthed around and cobbled together a solution. To fix the problem (at least this worked at the time of writing)

1. Click the **Files** tab to the right of the **Projects** tab.

2. Expand the **FirstTest** project.

3. Expand `build.xml`.

4. Scroll down until you find the `debug-remote` element.

5. Double-click `debug-remote`; an editor for it opens in the editor panel.

6. Search for the string "debug-args-line"; you will find two occurrences; the important one is in the element with the name "`-debug-remote-passwd`".

7. In that element, inside the sub-element `<remote:runwithpasswd/>`, delete the string `${debug-args-line}`.

8. Save the file and close the `run-remote` editor.

Now click **Debug** again. It should work. Unfortunately, there is a caveat. I have not discovered how to fix this problem system-wide. So, in every new NetBeans project you wish to debug remotely, you will have to apply the fix described in this subsection.

Successful Debug

When debug works, you should see the `println` statement turn green, indicating the debugger has stopped at that line, prior to executing it. See Figure 5-18.

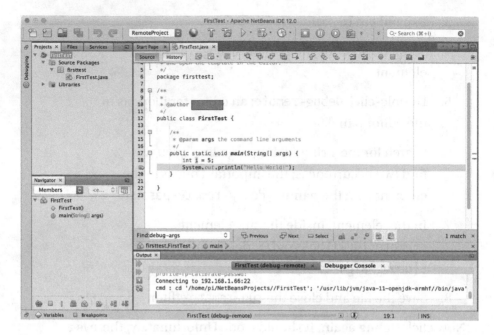

Figure 5-18. *NetBeans debugging*

Now you can debug code running on the Raspberry Pi!

Examine Variables While Debugging

When debugging, in the Output panel, you can now see sub-panels, the normal output and the Debugger Console. When debugging, you generally need to look at variables. To do so, click **Variables** at the lower left of the NetBeans window (see Figure 5-18); the *Variables* pop-up appears; it covers the Output pane. You can now look at variables; in particular, you can see that variable i has a value of 5.

You may not want the *Variables* pop-up to cover the Output pane. To make *Variables* another tab in the Output pane, click the "double window"-looking icon at the lower left of the NetBeans window shown in Figure 5-18. Now the Output panel appears like Figure 5-19 (I did the same thing with Breakpoints that I did with Variables).

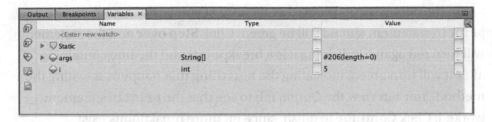

Figure 5-19. *NetBeans Output pane with Output, Breakpoints, and Variables tabs*

The Debugger Menu

Debugging is worth a bit more discussion. First, Figure 5-18 shows only a portion of the debug menu due to the size of the NetBeans window at the time I took the screen capture. Figure 5-20 shows the icons for the most useful debugger controls.

Figure 5-20. *NetBeans debugger controls*

From left to right, the controls are

- *Finish*: Terminates the debug session

- *Pause*: Pauses the debug session

- *Continue*: Runs until the next breakpoint

- *Step over*: Runs a single statement

- *Step over expression*: Runs a single expression

- *Step into*: Enters a method

- *Step out*: Runs to statement after method returns

105

In the debug session started previously, if you've done nothing else, the `println` statement should still be green. Click **Step over** and the statement will turn red again (indicating it is a breakpoint) and the line containing "}" after it will turn green, indicating the next thing that happens is exiting the method. You can view the *Output* tab to see that the `println` statement worked. Click **Continue** to finish, since no more breakpoints exist.

Run on the Raspberry Pi Without NetBeans

It is great that you can now use NetBeans running on your desktop to develop a Java program and then run and debug that program on the Raspberry Pi. At some point, however, you will want to run the program on the Pi without NetBeans involved. There are few reasons I've encountered:

- You don't need or want NetBeans "in the way" when your project is "in production" or even for some testing.

- Unfortunately, though it is not a surprise, the remote program running on the Pi cannot receive keyboard input.

- I've discovered that highly formatted console output (e.g., that produced by `System.out.format`) does not render properly.

In this section, I'll describe some ways to run your program on the Pi without NetBeans involvement. A later section will describe additional ways.

When you ran or debugged your program on the Raspberry Pi using NetBeans, NetBeans downloaded the program to the Pi. Earlier, when you configured the Pi as a remote platform, you had to identify the folder (or directory in NetBeans terminology) into which NetBeans saves the downloaded program in the form of a jar file (see Figure 5-14). The default folder is `/home/pi/NetBeansProjects` for user pi. In that base folder, NetBeans creates a specific subfolder that has the same name as the project. NetBeans places the jar in a subfolder called dist. For the preceding example project, the full path is /home/pi/NetBeansProjects/ FirstTest/dist.

To run the program on the Pi, first ssh to the Pi from a workstation terminal. Then enter the following command (on a single line):

```
java -jar /home/pi/NetBeansProjects/
FirstTest/dist/FirstTest.jar
```

You will see the results of the execution in the terminal. See Figure 5-21.

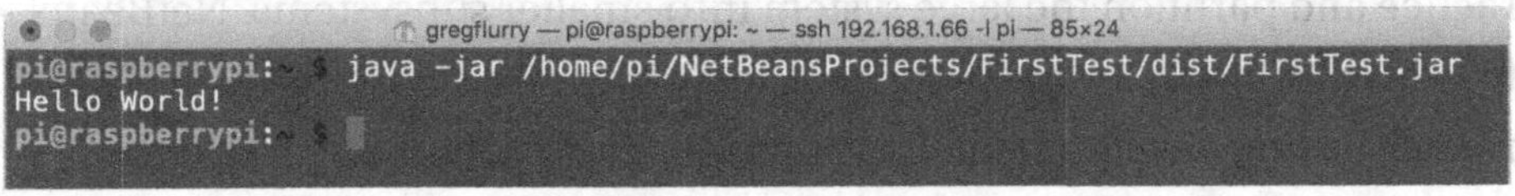

Figure 5-21. *Execution of the program without NetBeans (first way)*

You can also use a slightly different approach to accomplish the same thing. First, in the terminal, change the working directory (via the cd command) to the location of the jar file. Then enter the command

```
java -jar FirstTest.jar
```

You will get exactly the same behavior. See Figure 5-22.

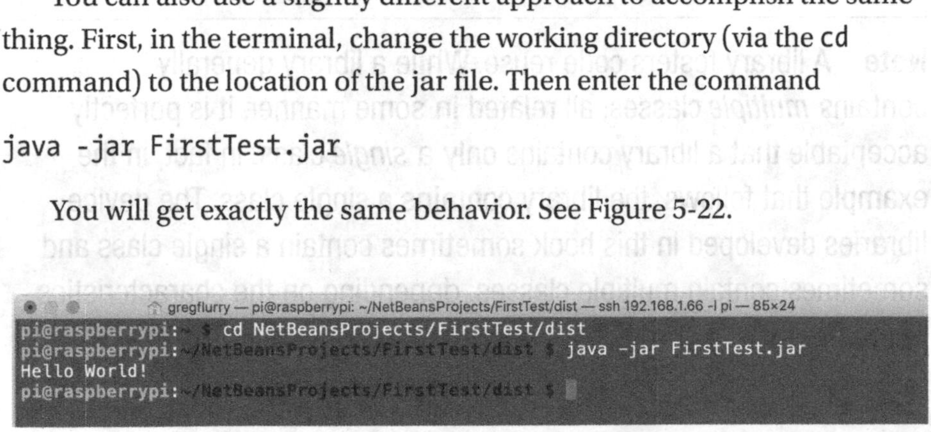

Figure 5-22. *Execution of the program without NetBeans (second way)*

These techniques work because information in the jar file identifies which main class in the jar to execute. That information comes from the NetBeans project *Run* property called *Main Class*. You can see and set the value for the project of interest in the *Project Properties* dialog; NetBeans kindly set that automatically when creating the **FirstTest** project containing the main class FirstTest (see Figure 5-16).

Leverage NetBeans in Complex Projects

While developing complex *system* projects, I follow a classic development practice and partition the large system into smaller subsystems. NetBeans offers great support for the practice, and I always create multiple NetBeans projects during development. For example, I might have one NetBeans project that supplies a "device library," a second that provides a "data processing library," and a third that contains applications that use the "device library" and the "data processing library."

Note   A library fosters code reuse. While a library generally contains *multiple* classes, all related in some manner, it is perfectly acceptable that a library contains only a *single* class. In fact, in the example that follows, the library contains a single class. The device libraries developed in this book sometimes contain a single class and sometimes contain multiple classes, depending on the characteristics of the device.

Create and Test Libraries

To explore the implications, you'll create a new NetBeans project for a simple library and test the library:

1. As you did for the **FirstTest** project earlier, in NetBeans, click the **New Project** icon in the menu bar.

2. Click **Java with Ant** in the *New Project* dialog.

3. Click **Java Class Library** in the *New Project* dialog.

4. Click **Next** in the *New Project* dialog.

5. In the *New Java Class Library* dialog, enter the name of the library; in this example, I'll use "LibraryTest".

6. Click **Finish** in the *New Java Class Library* dialog. You should see the new project appear in the NetBeans *Projects* pane.

7. Right-click **LibraryTest**, hover over **New**, and click **Java Package**. You'll see the *New Java Package* dialog.

8. Enter the desired package name; in this example, "org.addlib".

9. Click **Finish** in the *New Java Package* dialog. You should see the new package under the **LibraryTest** project.

10. Right-click **org.addlib**, hover over **New**, and click **Java Class**. You should see the *New Java Class* dialog.

11.   Enter the desired class name in the *New Java Class*
dialog, in this example, "AddThem", and click **Finish**.
You'll see the editor for the AddThem class. The
NetBeans window should appear similar to
Figure 5-23.

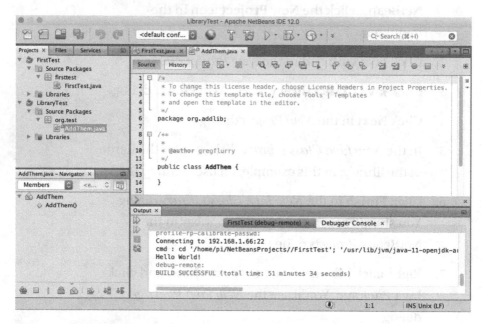

Figure 5-23. *NetBeans window for a new library class*

The new class needs a constructor with a parameter and a single
method with a parameter. The method will add its parameter to that from
the constructor and return the result. Enter the code in Listing 5-2 to
complete AddThem.

Listing 5-2. The AddThem class

```
public class AddThem {
    int base;
    public AddThem(int base) {
```

```
        this.base = base;
    }

    public int addIt(int it) {
        return base + it;
    }
}
```

After you've added the code to AddThem, notice the change in the Projects panel. Since the project is designated as a library, NetBeans does not expect to find main classes in the Source Packages. The expectation is that you'll want to test the library classes, so NetBeans kindly adds a Test Packages folder for test classes, as well as Test Libraries for classes associated only with testing. See Figure 5-24.

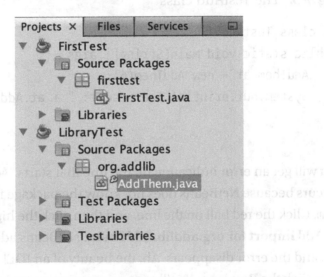

Figure 5-24. *Test Packages and Libraries in Projects panel*

These artifacts are intended to support JUnit test programs (beyond the scope of this book), but you can create simple test cases of your own. It is important to understand, however, that when NetBeans builds the jar file for the library, *it does not include any of the test classes or test libraries*! That is a very good thing, as you don't want test cases cluttering a library jar file. It also means, however, that the test cases would never get downloaded to the Raspberry Pi, so, for example, you cannot test a device library using a test case in a test package on the Pi.

Now you'll create a simple main class to test the single class in the library. Expand **Test Packages**; you will see **<default package>**. For the purposes of this book, that is a fine place to put the main class for testing the library. Right-click *<default package>*, hover over **New**, and click **Main Class**. In the resulting *New Java Main Class* dialog, enter "TestAdd" in the *Class Name* field, and then click **Finish**. You'll see the editor for the class. Complete the class so that it looks like Listing 5-3.

Listing 5-3. The TestAdd class

```java
public class TestAdd {
    public static void main(String[] args) {
        AddThem at = new AddThem(6);
        System.out.println("The result: " + at.AddIt(5));
    }
}
```

You will get an error indication on the line that starts "AddThem at". This occurs because NetBeans does not know the package name for AddThem. Click the red ball on the line, and then click the highlighted option **Add import for org.addlib.AddThem**. NetBeans adds the import for you, and the error disappears. Ah, the beauty of an IDE!

Now click the **Run** icon. You'll see an error pop up saying the project has no main class set. If you examine the project **Run** properties, you'll find that you can't set TestAdd as the *Main Class*; you can't even find it in the dialog! This is related to the earlier jar file discussion; since the test packages never appear in the jar file, they can't be runnable classes.

But you can run TestAdd! In the *Projects* pane, right-click **TestAdd**. In the pop-up, click **Run File**. In the Output pane, you'll see

```
The result: 11
```

It works! Not only can you run the test program, you can also debug it. In the pop-up mentioned, click **Debug File** instead of **Run File**.

The library is written and tested. Time to use it. Before using it, however, recognize that TestAdd ran on your workstation, not on the Raspberry Pi. This is extremely important. You can do a lot of testing of hardware-independent code on your workstation. Java's "write once, run anywhere" characteristic really proves valuable for this situation.

Caution   The *device libraries* we develop in later chapters are *not* hardware independent and must run on the Raspberry Pi. Thus, you must use a different testing approach. See Chapter 8 for details.

Use Libraries

I'll now show you how to use the library created previously. To illustrate some additional points, you'll create a new program (main class) in the **FirstTest** project that is already configured to run on the Raspberry Pi.

1. Right-click **Source Packages** under **FirstTest**.

2. Hover over **New** and then click **Java Package**.

3. In the *New Java Package* dialog, enter the package name in the *Package Name* field; for the book, enter "org.lib.user", and then click **Finish**.

4. Right-click *org.lib.user*, hover over **New** in the pop-up, and click **Java Main Class**.

5. In the resulting *New Java Main Class* dialog, enter
    the class name in the *Class Name* field; for the book,
    enter "LibTest", and then click **Finish**. As with other
    classes, NetBeans creates a skeleton and opens the
    class in the editor pane.

6. Complete the class so that it looks like Listing 5-4.

Listing 5-4. The LibTest class

```
public class LibTest {

    public static void main(String[] args) {
        AddThem at = new AddThem(6);
        System.out.println("The result: " + at.AddIt(5));
    }
}
```

As with TestAdd mentioned earlier, you will get an error indication on
the line that starts "AddThem at". Click the red ball on the line. You'll find
the option **Add import for org.addlib.AddThem** does not appear! That is
because NetBeans doesn't know where to find a library that contains the
right AddThem (there could be more than one).

You must tell NetBeans what library contains the proper AddThem class.
To do so, right-click the project **FirstTest**, and then click **Properties**. In the
resulting *Project Properties* dialog, under *Categories*, click **Libraries**. You'll
see the Libraries properties as shown in Figure 5-25.

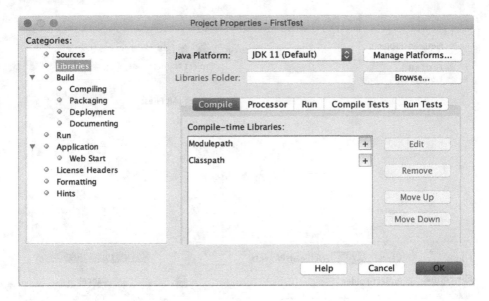

Figure 5-25. *NetBeans project properties for Libraries*

Now click the + to the right of *Classpath*. In the resulting small
pop-up, click **Add Project**. You'll now see the *Add Project* dialog shown
in Figure 5-26. Click **LibraryTest**, and then click **Add Project JAR Files**.
You'll return to the *Project Properties* dialog. Click **OK**.

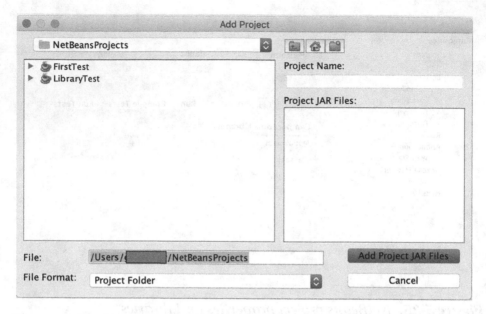

Figure 5-26. *NetBeans Add Project dialog*

Return to the TestAdd editor. Click the red ball. Now in the pop-up, you will see the desired option **Add import for org.addlib.AddThem**. Click the option and NetBeans will add the import from the library for you and the error disappears!

Now click the **Run** icon. You'll see that the main class FirstTest ran on the Raspberry Pi. That's obviously not what you want. There are two ways to run LibTest. If it is something you are going to run once or twice, simply right-click **LibTest** in the *Projects* pane and click **Run File**. Note that the pop-up also contains a **Debug File** option, so you can debug the same way. The second way is more interesting, and I'll cover it in the next section.

Choose Which Program to Run from NetBeans

What if you want to run LibTest over and over? Then you want to use the **Run** icon. I'll show you how to configure NetBeans to enable that.

First, right-click **FirstTest**, and select the project **Properties**. Under *Categories*, click **Run**. See Figure 5-16. Look at the entry in the field next to *Main Class*. You see that NetBeans is configured to run FirstTest. To pick another main class to run, click **Browse** to the right of the *Main Class*. You'll see a pop-up with a list of main classes in the project, with firsttest.FirstTest selected. See Figure 5-27.

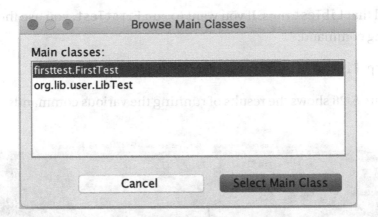

Figure 5-27. *NetBeans Browse Main Classes dialog*

In the dialog, click org.lib.user.LibTest and then click **Select Main Class**. In the *Project Properties* dialog, click **OK**. Now when you click the **Run** icon, LibTest runs!

Run the Chosen Program on the Raspberry Pi Without NetBeans

An earlier section showed you how to use the `java -jar` command to run the main class identified in a previously downloaded project jar file. If you have more than one main program you want to run in a single jar file, you have to use a different form of the `java` command.

In the previous section, you created a project with two main classes, `FirstTest` and `LibTest`. You configured NetBeans to run `LibTest`; thus, in a remote terminal, when you enter the following command

```
java -jar FirstTest.jar
```

you find that `LibTest` runs. If you want to run `FirstTest`, you use the following command:

```
java -cp FirstTest.jar firsttest.FirstTest
```

Figure 5-28 shows the results of running the various commands.

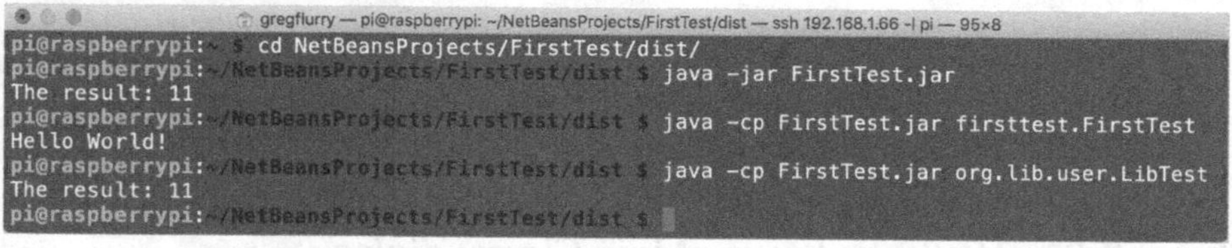

Figure 5-28. *Remote terminal with various java command results*

In general, you should use the second form described previously:

```
java -cp <jar>.jar <package>.<main class>
```

where

- `<jar>` refers to the jar file NetBeans created and downloaded (note that this name is the same as the NetBeans project name).

- `<package>` refers to the package name for the main class you want to run.

- `<main class>` refers to the name of the main class you want to run.

Just Download with NetBeans

In the sections above, you learned that NetBeans can download a project to the Raspberry Pi and then run or debug the program designated as the main class in the jar file. Subsequently, you can run one of many programs (main classes) in the same project on the Pi without NetBeans.

You also learned that if the main class you want to run is not the main class designated to run in the jar file, you can fix that. But what if you get lazy (like me) and simply want to use NetBeans to download an updated project and then run the program you want on the Pi?

It's easy. In the project, you create a "dummy" main class, one that does nothing except indicate that download succeeded (a little bit redundant). You designate it as the main class to run when you click the **Run** icon. For the example project **FirstTest**

1. Right-click **Source Packages** under **FirstTest**.

2. Hover over **New**, and click **Java Main Class**; you'll see the *New Java Main Class* dialog.

3. In the *Class Name* field, type a main class name, for example, "Dummy"; in the *Package* field, type a package name, for example, "dummy", and click **Finish**; at this point, if you want to add code to print something when Dummy runs, you can do so, but it is not necessary.

4. Bring up the **FirstTest** *Project Properties* dialog.

5. Under *Categories*, click **Run**.

6. On the right of the *Main Class* line, click **Browse**; you'll see the *Browse Main Classes* dialog (see Figure 5-27 for an example).

7. You should see dummy.Dummy in the list of main classes; click it and click **Select Main Class**, and you'll return to the *Project Properties* (Run) dialog.

8. Now click **OK**.

Now click the **Run** icon. In the *Output* pane, you won't see the output of FirstTest or LibTest because neither ran; Dummy ran, and it does *nothing*. What you'll see in the *Output* pane is just the following:

```
run-remote:
BUILD SUCCESSFUL (total time: 3 seconds)
```

Of course, if you inject a println statement into Dummy, you will see what it prints. And of course, you can still use a ssh terminal to run FirstTest and LibTest on the Raspberry Pi from the command line.

Summary

In this chapter, you've

- Installed Java on the workstation

- Installed NetBeans on the workstation

- Configured your Raspberry Pi as a remote platform in NetBeans

- Learned how, using NetBeans, to build, run, and debug complex Java programs from both the workstation and a Raspberry Pi in multiple ways

Now you have the tools in place to develop robotics and IoT projects using Java and the Raspberry Pi. In Chapter 6, you'll learn about considerations for developing device libraries for the devices used in robotics and IoT.

CHAPTER 6

Device Support in Java

If there is no struggle, there is no progress.

—Frederick Douglass, 1857

In Chapter 1, I mentioned the challenge of finding or creating device libraries for your devices when using Java on the Raspberry Pi. That challenge occurs at two levels:

1. Finding *base I/O* libraries for various forms of base I/O, that is, digital I/O (a.k.a. GPIO), serial, I2C, and SPI upon which devices libraries can be built

2. Finding or creating *device* libraries for your devices, which require one or more forms of base I/O

In this chapter, I'll discuss

- Finding base I/O libraries

- Selecting the base I/O library, or libraries, for your project and for this book

- Getting base I/O libraries into NetBeans

- Finding device libraries

- Porting non-Java device libraries to Java

© Greg Flurry 2021

G. Flurry, *Java on the Raspberry Pi*, https://doi.org/10.1007/978-1-4842-7264-0_6

Find Base I/O Libraries for Java

For any given project, the set of devices could require some combination of GPIO, serial, I2C, and SPI. Sadly, there is no centralized source that provides pointers to information about base I/O for Java on the Raspberry Pi. Or, perhaps more accurately, I cannot find it if one exists. So, to find the information, you must use a search engine. It can be difficult to produce immediately useful results. For example, if you want to find support for serial I/O, you might use the search terms "serial," "Java," and "Raspberry Pi." You will no doubt find a few candidates, for example, *Pi4J*, *RxTx* (a.k.a. *RXTX*), *jSerialComm*, *usb4java*, *jRXTX*, and *jSSC*. Sometimes, after that "first-order" search, you have to follow a trail of links before you find all the candidates. For example:

- Follow down Pi4J and you'll find it to be a wrapper around the *wiringPi* library (written in C).

- Follow down jRXTX and you'll find it to be an "easier-to-use" wrapper around *RxTx*.

But you are not done yet. I've found that sometimes, for unclear reasons, you have to search for other base I/O types to get a complete picture. So, for example, even if you are not interested in I2C, you probably should search for it and then follow down a new trail of links to see if you turn up anything else. Do so, and you'll turn up a lot of references to Pi4J. You will also turn up references to *device I/O* (a.k.a. DIO) and *diozero*. Pi4J, DIO, and diozero all support *everything*: GPIO, serial, I2C, and SPI. You might also have to look for I2C support in C and find *pigpio*, which supports everything. Dig into pigpio, and you'll find there is a Java "wrapper" for pigpio called *pigpioj*. I think you can see my point; generally, you have to do a quite broad, exhaustive search to get a complete picture.

Select the Best Base I/O Library

When you find multiple options for a type of base I/O, there are a few criteria for selecting the "best." Not necessarily in priority order, I suggest

- Functional coverage

- Performance

- Support

- Ease of use

Functional Coverage

Functional coverage raises the question "Does it do everything I need to do, and if not, what compromises are necessary?" Some examples:

- The Raspberry Pi has two forms of serial I/O: USB serial via the USB ports and TTY serial via the RX/TX pins on the GPIO header. usb4java supports only the USB ports, while others mentioned earlier support both forms.

- Some GPIO libraries offer support for pull-up and pull-down resistors for digital I/O; some don't.

Usually, you can determine functional coverage from documentation. However, I've found that testing is sometimes necessary. For example, in 2017, testing showed Pi4J I2C support could only do block reads starting at register address 0, forcing the use of the underlying wiringPi in some situations.

Performance

Performance is actually two pronged. The first question is "Does the option work reliably?" For example, testing jRXTX in 2017 indicated it worked but behaved erratically; I never determined why. Clearly not the best choice.

The second question is "Does the option work fast?" You certainly don't want to waste time or resources. If one option performs a task much faster than others, it is likely the best choice. For example, testing Pi4J serial and jSerialComm in 2017 showed that jSerialComm was much faster than Pi4J (or that I could not configure Pi4J correctly).

You should gather from this discussion that you must be prepared to not only test that a library works reliably but that it works with adequate performance in your project.

Support

Support is a somewhat ambiguous catchall. There are a few things to consider. Any library you find was created by and may be supported by an individual, a team of individuals, or an organization. Generally, the larger the creating and supporting entity, the better.

The current status and nature of the support is critical. You should probably be wary of using a library that has not been updated for a few years or has no visible support channel. For example, as of October 2020

- jSSC did not appear to have been updated since 2013.

- I found no updates to, and indeed no mention of, RxTx since 2017.

- The author of wiringPi had deprecated it, which, in effect, deprecated the then current version (1.2) of Pi4J.

- usb4java was actively supported as late as 2018.

- jRXTX appeared to have active support and updates.

- jSerialComm appeared to have active support and updates.

- DIO appeared to be little used.

- diozero had active support and updates.

- pigpio had active support and updates, as did the pigpioj wrapper.

- Pi4J 2.0 was under construction.

So, fair warning, what I find and recommend for the purposes of this book may change by the time you read the book. You should do your own research.

Another consideration is the user community size. The bigger the better, though this can be difficult to determine (a search engine can help). A large user community offers more opportunity for finding usage examples and getting help with unusual use cases or anomalous behavior. A large user community is no guarantee of "best," however. Pi4J appears to have the largest user community of any base I/O library, but remember, the current version should be considered deprecated (not only is the underlying wiringPi library deprecated, some parts of Pi4J 1.2 do not work on Java version 9 or greater).

Ease of Use

Ease of use is subjective and ambiguous and can include many aspects. For example, ideally, to use the library, you can acquire a single jar file and you are done. Some libraries achieve that. On the other hand, some can require you to build C code on the Raspberry Pi, install other code on the Pi, mess with Java permission files, or other activities that eat into the time you can spend on your project.

Another aspect was touched on earlier. Some libraries support more than one type of I/O. If all the types you require are all satisfied by a single library, that option could be "best," unless contraindicated by other criteria. Life is simpler with a single library; for example, you have a single source of documentation and a single contact point for support issues.

127

Other aspects include the presence and quality of documentation, existence of code examples, and the complexity of the API. All of these can impact how quickly you can get up and running with a library.

The Base I/O Choice for This Book

For better or worse, this book is mostly a set of individual device-focused projects rather than a single project. In part, the approach is due to the difference between robotics projects, which usually require several devices, and IoT projects, which often require just one or two devices. In part, it is due to the desire to demonstrate all forms of base I/O for the Raspberry Pi. So, for the purposes of the book, I will look for a library that supports *all* base I/O capabilities available on the Raspberry Pi, that is, GPIO, serial, I2C, and SPI.

Without a lot of tedious details, at the time of writing (late 2020), a filtering of available "all-in-one" libraries supporting all types of base I/O based on functional coverage, relative performance, support, and ease of use produced only two viable candidates:

- pigpioj (see `https://github.com/mattjlewis/pigpioj`)

- diozero (see `https://www.diozero.com`)

It is at this point where the final decision gets very interesting. Figure 1-1 shows the idealized software architecture applicable for this book, and the related text describes the nature of the architecture's four layers. We'll use that architecture to compare the candidates. I assert that when comparing pigpioj and diozero, there is no need to consider the Application layer because you'll *always* have to write the programs in the Application layer.

A Look at pigpioj

Figure 6-1 shows the software architecture of Figure 1-1, minus the Application layer, when using pigpioj. With pigpioj, the base I/O layer consists of two sub-layers. The *pigpio* sub-layer represents the pigpio C library that *exposes* a base I/O API in *C*; pigpio *uses* the more primitive Raspberry Pi OS C API for base I/O. The *pigpioj* sub-layer *is* the pigpioj "wrapper" for pigpio. The pigpioj sub-layer *exposes* the Java base I/O API you use to create device libraries; it *uses* the pigpio C API.

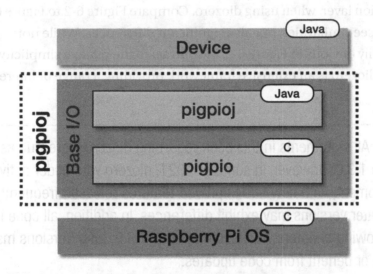

Figure 6-1. *Software architecture with pigpioj*

The Device layer represents the device libraries you find or write. They *expose* device-specific APIs to applications. They *use* the pigpioj base I/O API.

The combination of pigpio and pigpioj provides an interesting feature – *remote I/O*. That means you can run your application on a different computing platform but perform the I/O on the target Raspberry Pi. This of course is an alternative to remote development with NetBeans. See the pigpioj documentation for details.

A Look at diozero

Figure 6-2 shows the software architecture of Figure 1-1, minus the Application layer, when using diozero. Compare Figure 6-2 to Figure 6-1 and you see similarities, but also significant differences. While not necessarily obvious in Figure 6-2, in contrast to the relative simplicity of pigpioj, diozero is an extensive framework providing a range of interesting features.

Note   All statements in this book regarding diozero were true as of version 1.3.0; however, in summer 2021, diozero was under active development, with new and improved features released frequently. Thus, later versions may exhibit differences. In addition, all code in the following chapters was tested against 1.3.0; later versions may require or benefit from code updates.

In Figure 6-2, first note the *Single Board Computer OS* layer. The layer represents one of several single board computers (SBCs), including the Raspberry Pi. That's right; diozero works on the Raspberry Pi and also works on similar SBCs like the Odroid C2 and BeagleBone Black. You can find more about the supported SBCs in the diozero documentation.

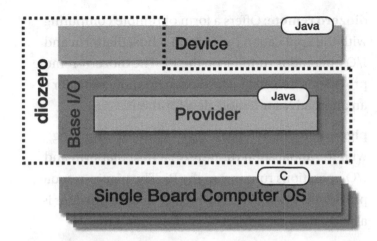

Figure 6-2. *Software architecture with diozero*

With diozero, the base I/O layer consists of the diozero *provider*. The diozero provider adapts, to the extent possible, the underlying SBC base I/O capabilities to provision the base I/O API exposed by the base I/O layer. The provider *exposes* the Java base I/O API you use to create device libraries. It *uses* the more primitive SBC OS C API for base I/O.

The provider concept represents perhaps the most interesting feature of diozero. The provider implements the well-known *service provider pattern* (see www.javapedia.net/Design-Patterns/1593). This means different providers can be used with *no change to higher layers*. As a result, you can write a device library, and it works across multiple providers and multiple SBCs (within the bounds of the base I/O capabilities of the SBCs). diozero supports providers that are *universal* and work on *any* SBC and providers that are *SBC specific*. In diozero version 1.3.0, there are four providers for the Raspberry Pi:

- **Built in:** Offers the optimal choice of function and performance within the bounds of the Pi base I/O capabilities. The built-in provider is universal.

- **pigpio:** Uses the pigpio C library. The pigpio provider is Pi specific.

- **diozero remote**: Offers a form of remote computing with the application running on a host platform and I/O operations running on the Pi. The diozero-remote provider is universal. The diozero-remote provider is an alternative for remote development.

- **pigpio remote**: Offers a form of remote computing with the application running on a host platform and I/O operations running on the Pi. The pigpio-remote provider is Pi specific. The pigpio-remote provider is also an alternative for remote development.

You can find more about the providers for the various SBCs in the diozero documentation.

In Figure 6-2, the Device layer represents device libraries with their exposed device APIs; they use the base I/O layer (a.k.a. Provider) API. Another great feature of diozero is that it includes a broad set of device libraries that you *don't* have to write! Of course, if diozero does not support your device, you can use the base I/O programming interfaces to create a device library. The best of both worlds! You can find the list of supported devices in the diozero documentation.

Note   This subsection describes only the aspects of diozero relevant to the Raspberry Pi and similar SBCs. diozero supports other computing platforms as well, for example, the Arduino and the Particle Photon. See the diozero documentation for more detail.

Evaluating the Choices

Now I'll use the four criteria mentioned previously to evaluate pigpioj and diozero to choose between them.

Functional Coverage

pigpioj gives you a robust base I/O layer for creating device libraries on the Raspberry Pi. That's it.

diozero gives you

- A robust *base I/O* layer for creating device libraries

- *Multiple providers, supplying differing characteristics,* for the base I/O layer

- An *existing set of device libraries,* for devices such as an LED, a button, environmental sensors, motor controllers, and even IMUs

- Support for *additional computing platforms,* for example, Odroid C2 and BeagleBone Black

Clearly diozero has much superior functional coverage.

Performance

As mentioned, pigpioj is a thin wrapper on pigpio. Thus, the performance is as good as you can get in Java for what pigpio does.

One of the providers offered by diozero is pigpio. The diozero built-in provider offers GPIO performance roughly seven times that of the pigpio provider, with I2C, SPI, and serial performance of the two providers roughly equal. Thus, it is certainly reasonable to claim that diozero offers superior performance.

Support

If you read the documentation for pigpioj and diozero carefully, you'll notice the libraries were created by the same individual. So, support is likely a tie. On the other hand, diozero is a much more comprehensive endeavor, and thus, support is perhaps more difficult to provide on a timely basis.

Ease of Use

As for ease of use, pigpioj is pretty good. You have to install pigpio on your Raspberry Pi before attempting to use pigpioj; doing so is quite simple, however. You have to acquire the pigpioj jar file on your workstation. To build and run applications, you must add the jar file to your NetBeans project(s).

Using pigpioj comes with a caution, however. The underlying pigpio library must be run with root privileges. Thus, you have to run your Java application as superuser via the sudo command. As a consequence, your application could unintentionally cause havoc. While not likely, it is possible.

The ease of use for diozero is pretty good as well. You have to acquire three or four jar files depending on the provider you use. To build and run applications, you must add the jar files to your NetBeans project(s). As you will see in the following, NetBeans makes that easy.

Both pigpioj and diozero support all base I/O in their Base IO layer, that is, GPIO, serial I/O, I2C, and SPI. Documentation for diozero is a bit better and naturally more extensive. While neither base I/O programming interface is difficult to use, I find the diozero API a bit easier to use, but just as effective. diozero also offers some useful convenience methods and functions not available in pigpioj.

Altogether, the two roughly tie for this criterion, though I feel diozero has a slight edge.

The Final Choice – diozero

As far as support and ease of use, there is no strong distinction between pigpioj and diozero. However, diozero can greatly outperform pigpioj in GPIO. The functional coverage of diozero, with its numerous compelling features, far exceeds pigpioj. Thus, the device libraries developed in this book use diozero. Of course, you could choose differently.

Keep in mind that unless you are adamant about keeping your base I/O options open, you only need the library or libraries required to support your project's devices. While diozero is a great choice for the book due to its extensive framework and admirable performance, a key factor in that choice is support for *all* base I/O. If you need only one specific form of base I/O, for example, serial, diozero is quite likely at least a fine candidate, but you might want to do your own assessment against other candidates.

Caution   I want to emphasize that diozero does not target robotics or IoT. It is a general-purpose framework supporting base I/O capabilities for *any* sort of device.

Configure diozero in NetBeans

Now diozero is identified as the base I/O library for the book; I'll show you how to make diozero available to NetBeans so that for your projects, you can either use existing device libraries from diozero or develop device libraries with diozero.

I mentioned in Chapter 5 that I discovered only the Ant project management/build tool supports efficient remote computing in NetBeans "out of the box." Thus, I'll show you how to get set up for Ant-based projects.[1]

First, you need to download the required diozero jar files. The easiest way is to get the diozero "distribution ZIP" file, which contains *all* the diozero JAR files plus *all* JAR files for diozero dependencies, plus the dependencies for the dependencies, and so on.

---

[1] As I mentioned in Chapter 5, with some work, Maven can approximate "Ant style" remote development. See Appendix A3 for details. If you decide to use Maven, you can skip the rest of this chapter.

Before downloading, you have to consider what version of diozero you want to use. Unless you have a really good reason not to do so, you should use the latest release (the highest version number). I've found three easy ways to download the distribution ZIP file for released versions of diozero. First, bring up the diozero documentation (`https://www.diozero.com`). If you want the latest diozero release, select **Creating Your Own Application** in the navigation panel on the left. Click the link called **diozero-distribution ZIP file** (just below the XML listing) to download the latest distribution ZIP file immediately. If you think you might want an earlier diozero release, after you bring up the documentation, scroll down until you see the section *Maven Dependency/Download Link*. The section describes two ways for finding and downloading the distribution ZIP for all released versions of diozero.

Download the distribution ZIP for your chosen version using one of the ways mentioned earlier. You'll download a file named something like `diozero-distribution-i.j.k-bin.zip`, where `i.j.k` stands for the version number, for example, 1.3.0. You may have to unzip the file; on macOS, it was automatically unzipped, and all the included JAR files placed in the folder `Downloads/diozero-distribution-i.j.k`. If you are using Windows, downloading and unzipping (if necessary) should result in a subfolder (with the same name) full of JAR files.

The distribution ZIP contains many more JAR files than you really need. In this book, you'll only use the built-in provider.[2] That means of the dozens of JAR files downloaded, you'll only need three:

- diozero-core-i.j.k.jar (includes the built-in provider; it depends on the next two)

- tinylog-api-m.n.o.jar and tinylog-impl-m.n.o.jar (the version number of these two is the same; the number will likely be different than the version number of diozero core)

---

[2] Appendix A3 is an exception. It uses a remote provider.

Now you create an *Ant Library* to use in diozero projects. In NetBeans, click **Tools** in the menu bar. Click **Libraries** in the pop-up; you'll see the *Ant Library Manager* dialog shown in Figure 6-3.

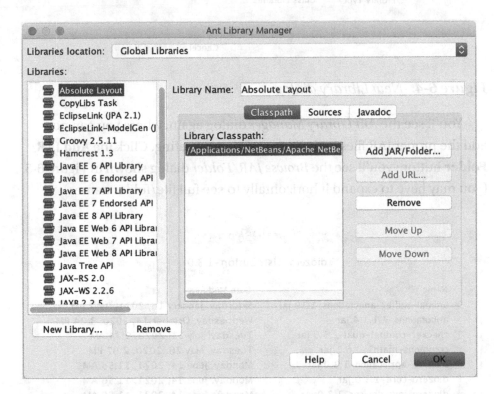

Figure 6-3. *NetBeans Ant Library Manager dialog*

Click the **New Library** button; you see the *New Library* dialog (Figure 6-4) that allows you to give the new library a name; you can see that I used "DIOZERO," but you can use anything that is unique. When you've entered the name, click **OK**.

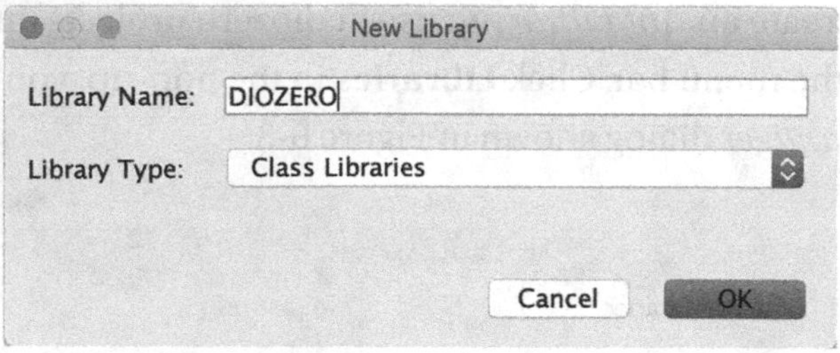

Figure 6-4. *New Library dialog*

You'll see the *Ant Library Manager* dialog again, where you can now add the proper JAR files to the library you are creating. Click the **Add JAR/Folder** button; you'll see the *Browse JAR/Folder* dialog shown in Figure 6-5 (you may have to expand it horizontally to see full file/folder names).

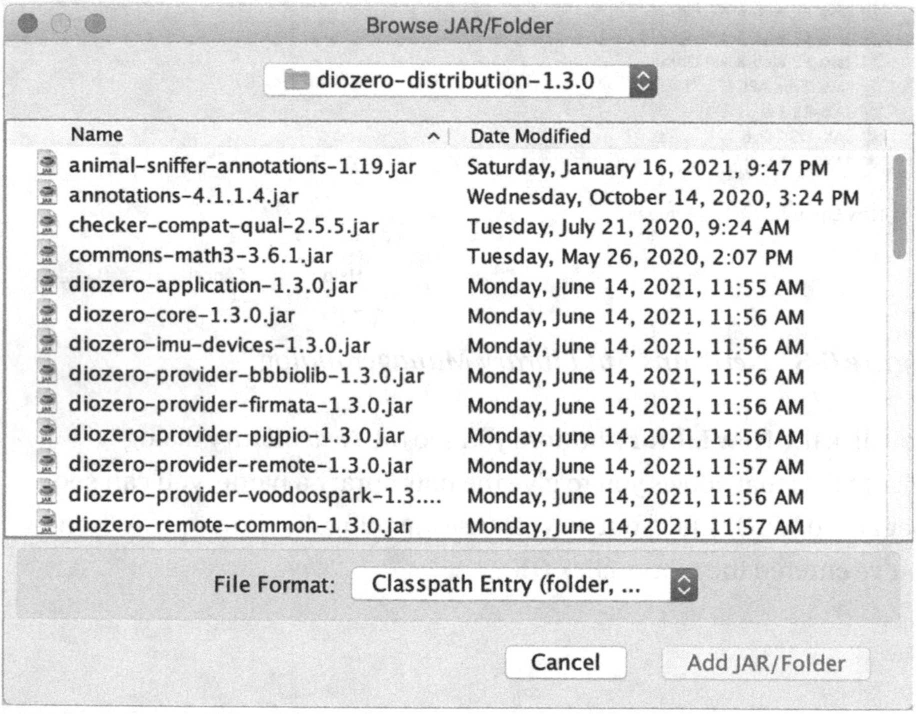

Figure 6-5. *Browse JAR/Folder dialog*

Navigate to the folder containing the JAR files you just downloaded. Select the three JAR files mentioned earlier, and click **Add JAR/Folder**. You'll see the *Ant Library Manager* dialog again, with the JAR files you just added to create the library DIOZERO; see Figure 6-6.

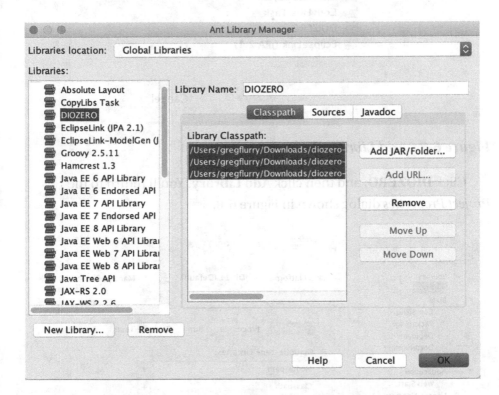

Figure 6-6. *Ant Library Manager dialog with DIOZERO library*

Click **OK** to create the DIOZERO library. The *Ant Library Manager* dialog closes and the library is ready to use.

Now we'll look at adding the DIOZERO library to a project. It is very similar to the process of adding a *project* library, as described in Chapter 5, so I'll cover only the differences. First, open the project properties and click **Libraries**, and you'll see the dialog shown in Figure 5-25. Now click the + to the right of *Classpath*. In the resulting small pop-up, click **Add Library**. You'll now see the *Add Library* dialog shown in Figure 6-7.

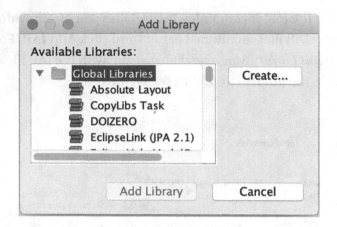

Figure 6-7. *Add Library dialog*

Click **DIOZERO**, and then click **Add Library**. You'll return to the *Project Properties* dialog shown in Figure 6-8.

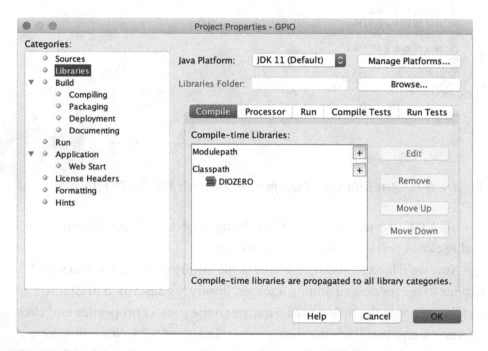

Figure 6-8. *Result of adding DIOZERO library to project*

You'll need to also set *Build* ➤ *Packaging* ➤ *Copy Dependent Libraries* property for the project. Click **OK**. Now you can write an application that uses some of the device libraries included in diozero, or you can write your own device library using the diozero base I/O API, or maybe both! The next section helps you decide what to do and how.

Find (and Port) Device Libraries

You have acquired a shiny new device for your project. How do you find support for it? Remember a search engine is your friend. A good approach is

- Check the diozero device library list for your device (see `https://www.diozero.com` and `www.javadoc.io/doc/com.diozero/diozero-core/latest/com/diozero/devices/package-summary.html`).

- Search the Internet for a Java device library for your device that uses the diozero base I/O layer.

- Search for Java device libraries that use other Raspberry Pi providers of base I/O support, for example, Pi4J or pigpioj.

- Search for Java device libraries more generally. The search should pick up support on other computing platforms as well as the Raspberry Pi.

- Search for a non-Java library for your device from the seller, the manufacturer, or anywhere else.

- Implement a library for your device from scratch.

You could find yourself in one (or more) of several situations. The following subsections discuss the situations more or less in order of desirability.

Before examining the situations, I must mention a couple of points. The first point is an important reality. Even in the best of situations, there may be *requirements differences* that could mandate work on your part. Sometimes a device library surfaces *too little* of the device's capability; for example, an IMU library might not support the FIFO common in such devices. Sometimes a device library *does too much*; in one of my projects, I used only the gyroscope z-axis from a 9-axis IMU. Sometimes, sadly, you find "*lazy programming*"; in one example, the developer coded console output in the case of errors instead of a more robust approach. No matter the situation, you must *always* be prepared to fix such requirements differences yourself, unless your project works fine with them present.

The second point is an important opportunity. In Chapter 1, I asserted you should consider yourself lucky to find *one* library for some devices. If you do find one library, or even multiple libraries, you can choose to port, or you can choose to start from scratch. The latter could be a better choice depending on the device complexity, the language in which an existing device library is written, how much of an existing library you really need to use, and other factors. One thing you should always consider, however, is actually *running* an existing library if you have the necessary resources. You can simply check that the device actually works the way you expect. You can compare the behavior or results from the existing library to your library as you create it. If you have the ability, via an IDE, you can debug to allow you to more deeply understand the existing library.

With those two points in mind, we'll now look at the possible situations.

Java Device Library and diozero Base I/O

There are two cases for this situation:

- You find a device library included in diozero.

- You find a non-diozero device library that uses diozero base I/O.

In these highly desirable cases, you need to do no work! Well, no work besides addressing the requirements differences mentioned earlier.

If you don't find either of these cases, you should check if diozero provides a device library for a device similar to yours. Classes of devices often share some common characteristics. Depending on the differences between the diozero-supported device and your device, you might be able to adapt that library (e.g., change I2C addresses, register addresses, control constants). At a minimum, you might be able use it as guidance.

Tip   There is a way to ensure you end up in this fortuitous situation. Prior to choosing devices for your project, examine the devices supported by diozero and use them where possible. No work!

Java Device Library and Non-diozero Base I/O

In this situation, you find a Java device library that uses a *non-diozero* base I/O library. The device library might target the Raspberry Pi or a different SBC. The most likely base I/O library is Pi4J due to its popularity and its coverage of all base I/O. Other possibilities include pigpioj for all base I/O and jSerialComm for serial.

For all possibilities, it should be reasonably straightforward to port the device library to the diozero base I/O API. All the design and a large majority of the code should port with no modification. You obviously have to understand the semantics and syntax of both the non-diozero and diozero base I/O APIs so that you can translate between them. There are two basic choices for porting:

- You can replace calls to the non-diozero base I/O API with an appropriate combination of logic and calls to the diozero base I/O API.

- You can create adapter methods that mimic the non-diozero base I/O API in its interface and encapsulate the appropriate combination of logic and calls to the diozero base I/O API. You can even group such methods in a class. This is desirable if you need multiple device libraries that use the same non-diozero base I/O API.

I must express a warning about this situation, however. The Java device libraries I've found tend to be embedded in a larger framework. Sometimes it is easy to ignore the larger framework and use the majority of the library; sometimes it is not. Just be cautious about the effort involved if alternatives exist.

C/C++ Device Library

There is a good chance you can find a C/C++ device library that uses a C/C++ base I/O library. My experience suggests the most common form of device libraries will be Arduino C++ libraries, due to the massive popularity of the Arduino. These are typically referenced on the device vendor's website, on the manufacturer's website, or both. You can sometimes find device libraries that use pigpio or wiringPi. These almost always come from individuals or small teams that have no affiliation with the vendor or manufacturer.

In general, much of the C/C++ design and implementation should be usable; you can port almost with copy/paste (especially C++). On the other hand, porting now includes

- Understanding the non-diozero base I/O API as well as the diozero base I/O API

- Dealing with the syntactic differences between C/C++ and Java (e.g., class definition, addresses and pointers, malloc/free)

- Handling differences is variable types; for example, there are no unsigned types in Java, but they exist in C/C++

None of these items is a lot of effort, but in total, this situation obviously requires more work than most pure Java situations. The amount of work involved depends on the complexity of the device, the competence of the C/C++ library developer (e.g., comments in the code), your knowledge of C/C++, and perhaps other factors.

Python Device Library

There is a chance that you can find a Python (or some variant) device library that uses some Python base I/O library, primarily because Python is the default programming language for the Raspberry Pi. There are a few base I/O libraries for Python; the most popular appear to be RPi.GPIO and gpiozero. There is also a Python wrapper for the C pigpio library; like pigpioj, the Python pigpio library (yes, it has exactly the same name as the C library) exposes exactly the pigpio interfaces.

With Python, the design should be usable, but obviously you have to port Python syntax and semantics to Java. You'll face all the issues of porting a C/C++ library, and the pain may be exaggerated (think loose typing vs. strong typing). Unless you are well versed in Python, porting a

Python device library will require more work than a C/C++ library and thus more work than Java situations. That said, porting a Python library likely takes less work than starting from scratch.

No Device Library

If you find no suitable library after all the searching, you obviously have to do all the work. In some ways, this is liberating. You have a clean slate, and you can design and implement precisely the capability you need from your device. You don't need to worry about understanding a non-diozero base I/O API. You don't have to worry about translating between languages.

Perhaps the biggest difference from the other situations is that you must become extremely well educated about your device (i.e., read the datasheet – at least twice), but that is not necessarily a bad thing. You should search for application notes for the device and anything else that might help you interpret the sometimes-terse datasheet for the device. Remember that you might be able to get guidance by looking at device libraries for similar devices.

Summary

In this chapter, I discussed device support for Java on the Raspberry Pi, covering

- The search techniques for finding support for base I/O capabilities

- The criteria for selecting the best of the candidates for *your* project

- The base I/O choice for *this book*, namely, *diozero*

- The configuration of NetBeans for development with diozero

146

- The search techniques for finding device libraries

- The effort involved in porting those libraries to Java, if needed, and to use your chosen base I/O library, if needed

- The effort when you can find no library

Now you are armed with some techniques and guidelines that allow you to deal with any situation. In Chapter 7, we'll look in a bit more detail at the diozero base I/O API. After that, we'll find or create some device libraries!

CHAPTER 7

The diozero Base I/O API

In this chapter, you'll learn more about the diozero base I/O API you'll use in this book to create Java libraries to support your devices on the Raspberry Pi. We'll cover

- Some useful utilities provided by diozero

- Physical connectivity between devices and a Pi

- Some background on Pi base I/O capabilities

- Highlights of selected diozero base I/O API classes

- Guidelines for developing device libraries and applications that use the diozero base I/O API

For more detail on the diozero base I/O API, you should read the diozero Javadoc (`www.javadoc.io/doc/com.diozero/diozero-core/latest/index.html`).

diozero Utilities

diozero includes sample applications that demonstrate many of its features. You may not find formal documentation for all of them, but you can find the source code for all of them on the diozero GitHub

© Greg Flurry 2021
G. Flurry, *Java on the Raspberry Pi*, https://doi.org/10.1007/978-1-4842-7264-0_7

(https://github.com/mattjlewis/diozero/tree/main/diozero-
sampleapps/src/main/java/com/diozero/sampleapps).

Among the most interesting samples are some *utility* applications
that deal with the base I/O capabilities. I'll discuss specific utilities in the
relevant sections in the following. You can find some of them documented
at www.diozero.com/utilityapps.html. To use a utility, you must have
the diozero-sampleapps-<version>.jar and jansi-<version>.jar in
your classpath. You can find these jars in the diozero distribution ZIP (see
Chapter 6). You can run a utility on the Raspberry Pi using the command

java -cp <classpath> com.diozero.sampleapps.<utility>

where <classpath> includes diozero-sampleapps-<version>.jar and
jansi-<version>.jar and <utility> is the class name of the utility.

Connect Devices to a Raspberry Pi

The devices covered in this book connect to a Raspberry Pi via its USB
ports or its general-purpose input/output (GPIO) *connector*, which is
described here: www.raspberrypi.org/documentation/usage/gpio/.
There are some extremely important points made in that reference:

- Several pins on the connector supply 5V, 3.3V
  (a.k.a. 3V3), or ground.

- The remaining pins in the connector can be configured,
  at a given time, to offer simple digital input or simple
  digital output. Some configurable pins can be used for
  other purposes as well, for example, serial, I2C, or SPI.

- Any particular capability requires one or more
  individual pins in the connector (e.g., I2C requires
  two pins).

- The Raspberry Pi is a 3.3V system. That means output pins produce a maximum of 3.3V and a minimum of 0V (ground). That means that input pins are *3.3V tolerant*; attaching to a source that produces more than 3.3V likely destroys the I/O chip or even the Raspberry Pi!

There are two diozero utilities relevant to base I/O in general. The first, GpioDetect, identifies the GPIO chips on your Raspberry Pi. The following two lines show the results when I ran GpioDetect on a Pi3B+:

```
gpiochip0 [pinctrl-bcm2835] (54 lines)
gpiochip1 [raspberrypi-exp-gpio] (8 lines)
```

Of particular interest is the BCM chip; note "bcm2835" in the report. It is somewhat curious since www.raspberrypi.org/documentation/hardware/raspberrypi/ says the Pi3B+ uses the BCM2837B0. Searching through various links on that reference (and links to links) shows that from a GPIO perspective, the Pi3B+ has the bcm2835 *architecture*. Thus, you can use BCM2835 documentation to find detailed information about base I/O capabilities. Running GpioDetect on a Zero W produces a single line

```
gpiochip0 [pinctrl-bcm2835] (54 lines)
```

The Zero W does use the BCM2835, so the report makes sense (it does not have a second chip) and confirms the two Raspberry Pi models share the same base I/O architecture. Nice!

The second utility, SystemInformation, describes the pinout for your Raspberry Pi, plus other system information. Figure 7-1 shows the results of running SystemInformation on a Pi3B+.

```
Local System Info
Operating System: raspbian "10 (buster)" "10"
I2C buses: [1]
CPU Temperature: 40.78

Native Device Factory: DefaultDeviceFactory
Board: Raspberry Pi 3B+ (RAM: 1,024,000 bytes)

Header: J8
+-------+----------+-------+----------+-------+----------+----------+-------+
+ GP# + |    Name + gpiod + Physical + gpiod  + Name     + GP# +
+-------+----------+-------+----------+-------+----------+----------+-------+
|       |       3v3 |   :   |  1 || 2  |   :   | 5v       |          |
|   2   |      SDA1 |  0:2  |  3 || 4  |   :   | 5v       |          |
|   3   |      SCL1 |  0:3  |  5 || 6  |   :   | GND      |          |
|   4   | GPIO_GCLK |  0:4  |  7 || 8  |  0:14 | TXD1     |    14    |
|       |       GND |   :   |  9 || 10 |  0:15 | RXD1     |    15    |
|  17   |    GPIO17 |  0:17 | 11 || 12 |  0:18 | GPIO18   |    18    |
|  27   |    GPIO27 |  0:27 | 13 || 14 |   :   | GND      |          |
|  22   |    GPIO22 |  0:22 | 15 || 16 |  0:23 | GPIO23   |    23    |
|       |       3v3 |   :   | 17 || 18 |  0:24 | GPIO24   |    24    |
|  10   |  SPI_MOSI |  0:10 | 19 || 20 |   :   | GND      |          |
|   9   |  SPI_MISO |  0:9  | 21 || 22 |  0:25 | GPIO25   |    25    |
|  11   |  SPI_SCLK |  0:11 | 23 || 24 |  0:8  | SPI_CE0_N|     8    |
|       |       GND |   :   | 25 || 26 |  0:7  | SPI_CE1_N|     7    |
|   0   |    ID_SDA |  0:0  | 27 || 28 |  0:1  | ID_SCL   |     1    |
|   5   |     GPIO5 |  0:5  | 29 || 30 |   :   | GND      |          |
|   6   |     GPIO6 |  0:6  | 31 || 32 |  0:12 | GPIO12   |    12    |
|  13   |    GPIO13 |  0:13 | 33 || 34 |   :   | GND      |          |
|  19   |    GPIO19 |  0:19 | 35 || 36 |  0:16 | GPIO16   |    16    |
|  26   |    GPIO26 |  0:26 | 37 || 38 |  0:20 | GPIO20   |    20    |
|       |       GND |   :   | 39 || 40 |  0:21 | GPIO21   |    21    |
+-------+----------+-------+----------+-------+----------+----------+-------+

Header: P5
+-------+--------------+-------+----------+-------+--------------+-------+
+ GP# + |        Name + gpiod + Physical + gpiod  + Name         + GP# +
+-------+--------------+-------+----------+-------+--------------+-------+
|  54   |        BT_ON |  1:0  |  0 || 1  |  1:1  | WL_ON        |  55   |
|  56   |  PWR_LED_OFF |  1:2  |  2 || 3  |  1:3  | GLOBAL_RESET |  57   |
|  58   | VDD_SD_IO_SEL|  1:4  |  4 || 5  |  1:5  | CAM_GPIO     |  59   |
|  60   |    SD_PWR_ON |  1:6  |  6 || 7  |  1:7  | SD_OC_N      |  61   |
+-------+--------------+-------+----------+-------+--------------+-------+
```

Figure 7-1. *SystemInformation results for a Pi3B+*

Tip The web page https://pinout.xyz also provides a very useful guide for understanding the Raspberry Pi GPIO connector pinout.

diozero SerialDevice

This section provides a brief introduction to the diozero base I/O API for serial capability via the `SerialDevice` class. It supports communication with serial devices that can be connected to a USB port on the Raspberry Pi or to the relevant UART pins on the Pi GPIO header. You can find more documentation at `www.javadoc.io/doc/com.diozero/diozero-core/latest/com/diozero/api/SerialDevice.html`.

Background on Raspberry Pi Serial I/O

Before digging into `SerialDevice`, I'll offer some useful background on serial I/O in the context of the Raspberry Pi. An important point about serial I/O *in general* is that it is *point to point*; that means that once a serial device is connected to a Pi on a serial port, the Pi can communicate *only* with that device via that port.[1] Given the simplicity of point-to-point communication, serial I/O on the Pi is a bit more complex than you might expect. The web page `www.engineersgarage.com/microcontroller-projects/articles-raspberry-pi-serial-communication-uart-protocol-serial-linux-devices/` covers serial I/O in general, as well as specifics for the Pi. The web page `www.raspberrypi.org/documentation/configuration/uart.md` offers more detail about *UART*-based communication on the Pi. The web page `www.raspberrypi.org/documentation/hardware/raspberrypi/usb/README.md` has some specifics on USB-based communication on the Pi.

Some important highlights from the references:

- All Pi families use only two UART types: the PL001 and the mini UART.

---

[1] You'll see an exception to that generalization in Chapter 8.

- Different Pi families have different numbers of serial UARTs. The Pi 3 and Pi Zero families both have two UARTs (one of each type).

- All families designate one UART as *primary*; it drives the RX/TX pins on the GPIO header.

- All families designate one UART as *secondary*; it drives the Bluetooth controller on models that support Bluetooth. The Pi 3B+ and the Pi Zero W support Bluetooth.

- The primary UART gets assigned to the Raspberry Pi OS console. If you wish to use the primary UART to communicate with devices, you must *disable* the console. Chapters 2 and 3 describe how to do so.

- The UARTs have *device files* in the Raspberry Pi OS file system. For the Pi 3 and Pi Zero W, the primary UART device file is /dev/ttyS0, and the secondary UART device file is /dev/ttyAMA0. On both systems, the device file /dev/serial0 is a symbolic link to /dev/ttyS0, and the device file /dev/serial1 is a symbolic link to /dev/ttyAMA0.

- USB devices can have a *hardware* or *software* controller.

- USB devices with hardware controllers have a device file in the Raspberry Pi OS file system of the form /dev/ttyACM<n> where <n> is a number, for example, /dev/ttyACM0.

- USB devices with software controllers have a device file in the file system as /dev/ttyUSB<n> where <n> is a number, for example, /dev/ttyUSB1.

USB device file naming deserves elaboration. The Raspberry Pi OS assigns device file *numbers* to USB devices *dynamically*. You *cannot* assume the OS always assigns a USB device the same device file number. For example, if you boot your Pi with no USB devices connected, plug in USB device A, and then plug in USB device B, device A gets assigned /dev/ttyACM0 and B gets assigned /dev/ttyACM1 (assuming both have hardware controllers). If you unplug both devices, then plug in B, and then plug in A, *B* becomes /dev/ttyACM0 and *A* becomes /dev/ttyACM1. This makes device identification problematic.

The good news is that there are ways to accommodate this dynamic behavior. One approach forces the operating system to assign the same device file each time it sees the device; see www.freva.com/2019/06/20/ assign-fixed-usb-port-names-to-your-raspberry-pi/ and https:// bnordgren.org/seismo/RPi/RPi_com_port_assignment.pdf. I must warn you that I have not tried this approach because diozero enables what I feel is a better approach; I'll discuss it later in this chapter.

The fact that the serial devices are managed by the OS has an important benefit. Once the device gets opened by an application, any further attempts to *open* that device will fail. That is good in that it prevents other applications from interfering with device use by the initial application. The operating system *cannot* prevent different threads within an application process from *using* the device and interfering with each other; doing so is up to the developer of the application to handle such concurrency issues. Unfortunately, Java concurrency in general is a subject *beyond the scope* of this book.

Constructors

SerialDevice has two constructors. Both constructors require a deviceFilename parameter that refers to the device file of a serial device. The previous subsection discussed the dynamic nature of how the operating system assigns device files for USB devices. A later subsection describes the diozero support for determining what device file to use for a specific USB device.

The simplest constructor requires only the deviceFilename parameter. It uses default values for additional configurable serial characteristics.

The second constructor allows tailoring all configurable serial characteristics: baud rate (default is 9600), data bits per *word* (default is 8), stop bits (default is 1), and parity (default is none). diozero provides a set of predefined constants (via SerialConstants) for use in the constructor. See the Javadoc for details.

SerialDevice and several other key classes in the API also provide what amounts to a convenience constructor with a nested Builder class. Builder implements a "builder" design pattern[2] and allows you to supply only the characteristics that differ from the default values. For example, using SerialDevice.Builder, you could specify only the baud rate. Nice!

Read and Write Methods

SerialDevice exposes three read methods:

- read has two forms:

  - The first reads a single byte, but returns an int; the byte read is the least significant byte in the int if the read succeeds; the int is negative if the read fails.

  - The second reads bytes to fill the byte array parameter; it returns the number of bytes actually read.

- readByte() reads a single byte and returns it as a byte.

---

[2] See https://dzone.com/articles/design-patterns-the-builder-pattern.

It is extremely important to understand that the `SerialDevice` read methods are *blocking*, with *no timeout*. That means that if you attempt to read from a serial device and it does not send the number of bytes you expect, the read method will *never return*.

`SerialDevice` also exposes a `bytesAvailable` method that returns the number of bytes waiting to be read. You can use this method to create non-blocking reads; you can find a crude example in Chapter 8 (see Listing 8-8).

`SerialDevice` exposes two `write` methods:

- `writeByte` writes a single byte.

- `write` writes an array of bytes.

Chapters 8 and 10 use `SerialDevice`.

Support for Device Identity

A previous subsection mentioned the problem caused by dynamic assignment of device files for USB serial devices. diozero offers support for mapping from unique device-specific information to the device file needed for a `SerialDevice` constructor.

`SerialDevice` has a static method `getLocalSerialDevices` that returns a list of `DeviceInfo` instances. The list includes *all* valid serial devices, including any USB-connected device, the Bluetooth device, and the serial port on the GPIO header (if the console is disabled) whether anything is connected to the GPIO RX/TX pins or not.

A `DeviceInfo` instance contains useful *identity* information about a *USB*[3] serial device derived from the device itself via the operating system. The individual fields are accessible via getter methods. To me, the most useful fields are

- `deviceFile`: The device file for a serial device, for example, `/dev/ttyACM0`. You use it in a `SerialDevice` constructor, as discussed earlier.

- `usbVendorId`: A unique hexadecimal number, for example, `1ffb`, for the device *vendor* or *manufacturer*; USB devices only.

- `usbProductId`: A unique (to a vendor/manufacturer) hexadecimal number for the *device*; USB devices only.

- `manufacturer`: Human-readable text that identifies the device *vendor/manufacturer*; USB devices only. This field is sometimes not available from the OS information, in which case the value of `usbVendorId` is copied.

- `description`: Human-readable text that identifies the *device*; USB devices only; a non-USB device produces "Physical Port."

For USB devices, the combination {`usbVendorId`, `usbProductId`} *is unique*. As a result, I'll call the combination the *USB device identity*. The combination {`manufacturer`, `description`} *should be unique* and thus can also be considered the USB device identity. While the device file for a particular device *can vary*, the USB device identity *does not vary*. This means that once you know the USB device identity for a device, you can get the device file for the device (the value of `deviceFile`) from the associated `DeviceInfo` instance.

---

[3] For non-USB devices, a `DeviceInfo` instance usually contains nothing regarding identity.

The information from getLocalSerialDevices is so useful I decided to create a utility library to help with USB device identity. How to start building the utility library? As with any new diozero-based project, you must create a new NetBeans project, package, and class; configure the project for remote development on your Raspberry Pi; and configure the project to use the DIOZERO library. In summary, you must

1. Create a new NetBeans "Java with Ant" project. You can create either a "Java Application" or a "Java Class Library"; the former is better.

2. Create a new package in the project.

3. Create a new Java main class.

4. Set the *Runtime Platform* in the project properties to your Raspberry Pi.

5. Add the requisite diozero jar files using the DIOZERO library.

6. Make sure you set the *Build* ➤ *Packaging* ➤ *Copy Dependent Libraries* property for the project.

See Chapter 5 (section "Test the NetBeans Installation") for details about steps 1–4 and Chapter 6 (section "Configure diozero in NetBeans") for details about steps 5 and 6.

I'll call my project **Utility**, my package org.gaf.util, and my class SerialUtil. Listing 7-1 shows SerialUtil. The method printDeviceInfo does just what the name implies.

Listing 7-1. SerialUtil

```
package org.gaf.util;

import com.diozero.api.SerialDevice;
import java.util.ArrayList;
import java.util.List;
```

```java
public class SerialUtil {

    public static void printDeviceInfo() {
        List<SerialDevice.DeviceInfo> devs =
                SerialDevice.
                    getLocalSerialDevices();
        for (SerialDevice.DeviceInfo di : devs){
            System.out.println(
                    "device name = " +
                    di.getDeviceName() + " : " +
                    "device file = " +
                    di.getDeviceFile() + " : " +
                    "description = " +
                    di.getDescription() + " : "+
                    "manufacturer = " +
                    di.getManufacturer()+ " : "+
                    "driver name = " +
                    di.getDriverName() + " : " +
                    "vendor ID = " +
                    di.getUsbVendorId() + " : "+
                    "product = " +
                    di.getUsbProductId());
        }
    }

    public static void main(String[] args) {
        printDeviceInfo();
    }
}
```

Tip You can find the actual source code for all *code* listings in this chapter and the rest of the book in the book's code repository (see the front matter for the location). You may find an error in a code listing, but the source code was fully tested.

Run SerialUtil and you'll see something similar to Listing 7-2, assuming you have some USB devices attached. When I ran the application, I had three USB devices attached to a Raspberry Pi 3B+ and the console disabled.

Listing 7-2. Output of SerialUtil.printDeviceInfo

```
device name = ttyACM1 : device file = /dev/ttyACM1 :
description = USB Roboclaw 2x15A : manufacturer = 03eb : driver
name = usb:cdc_acm : vendor ID = 03eb : product ID = 2404
device name = ttyACM0 : device file = /dev/ttyACM0 :
description = Pololu A-Star 32U4 : manufacturer = Pololu
Corporation : driver name = usb:cdc_acm : vendor ID = 1ffb :
product ID = 2300
device name = ttyACM2 : device file = /dev/ttyACM2 :
description = Pololu A-Star 32U4 : manufacturer = Pololu
Corporation : driver name = usb:cdc_acm : vendor ID = 1ffb :
product ID = 2300
device name = ttyS0 : device file = /dev/ttyS0 : description =
Physical Port : manufacturer = null : driver name = bcm2835-
aux-uart : vendor ID = null : product ID = null
device name = ttyAMA0 : device file = /dev/ttyAMA0 :
description = Physical Port : manufacturer = null : driver name
= uart-pl011 : vendor ID = null : product ID = null
```

Table 7-1 shows the most useful fields of each instance of DeviceInfo in Listing 7-2. I've reordered the list slightly.

Table 7-1. *Results from the list of DeviceInfo*

deviceFile	manufacturer	description	vendorId	productId
/dev/ttyACM0	Pololu Corporation	Pololu A-Star 32U4	1ffb	2300
/dev/ttyACM1	03eb	USB Roboclaw 2x15A	03eb	2404
/dev/ttyACM2	Pololu Corporation	Pololu A-Star 32U4	1ffb	2300
/dev/ttyS0	null	Physical Port	null	null
/dev/ttyAMA0	null	Physical Port	null	null

One of the USB devices (/dev/ttyACM0) is the Arduino "command server" described in Appendix A1. Another (/dev/ttyACM2) is the Arduino Lidar Unit (built with a "command server") described in Appendix A2 and used in Chapter 10. Another (/dev/ttyACM1) is a dual DC motor controller used in Chapter 8. /dev/ttyS0 represents the serial port on the GPIO header (nothing attached). /dev/ttyAMA0 represents the Bluetooth controller.

Note that it is easy to distinguish the motor controller from the "command servers" and the other devices because the USB device identity {usbVendorId, usbProductId} is unique. Further, note the manufacturer field for the motor controller; it is the same as the usbVendorId, indicating there is no guarantee it will be "human readable."

Note the two "command servers" have the *same* USB device identity. They cannot be distinguished using their USB device identity alone! In such situations, you must use features of the device itself to distinguish one *instance* from another. I assert that if a device designer anticipates multiple instances of that device present in a system, such features must exist. In effect, the device must have what can be considered a *device instance ID*.

Such a situation means there are two types of identity involved in resolving the device file required by the diozero SerialDevice constructor:

- The *USB device identity*: This is unique *only* if a single instance of a USB device is connected to a Raspberry Pi.

- The *device instance ID* for the device: This should always be unique for devices sharing the same USB device identity and is needed *only* if the USB device identity is not unique.

That means there can be two phases to *identity verification*. First, find all device files with the desired USB device identity; if there is only one, then that device file can be used in the SerialDevice constructor; phase two is not needed. Second, for any device file matching the USB device identity, construct a SerialDevice and determine the device instance ID, and then compare it to the desired device instance ID.

Identity verification is important enough that I decided to add support for it to SerialUtil. Listing 7-3 shows the findDeviceFiles method. It fundamentally performs the first phase of identity verification. Specifically, it examines all serial devices and returns a list of device files that match the USB device identity given in the parameters. I'll demonstrate the use of findDeviceFiles in Chapters 8 and 10.

Listing 7-3. findDeviceFiles

```
public static List<String> findDeviceFiles(
        String vendorID, String productID) {
    ArrayList<String> deviceFiles =
            new ArrayList<>();

    List<SerialDevice.DeviceInfo> dis =
            SerialDevice.getLocalSerialDevices();
    for (SerialDevice.DeviceInfo di : dis) {
        if (vendorID.equals(di.getUsbVendorId())) {
            if (productID.equals(
                    di.getUsbProductId())) {
                deviceFiles.add(di.getDeviceFile());
            }
        }
    }
```

```
    }
    return deviceFiles;
}
```

Tip   To find the USB device identity for your devices, you can use
`SerialUtil` (see Listings 7-1 and 7-2). You can use the diozero utility
application `SerialDeviceDetect` (see `https://github.com/`
`mattjlewis/diozero/blob/main/diozero-sampleapps/src/`
`main/java/com/diozero/sampleapps/SerialDeviceDetect.`
`java`); its output is similar to Listing 7-2 (sadly, I wrote `SerialUtil`
before I knew `SerialDeviceDetect` existed). You can also use the
Linux command `udevadm info --query=property --name=`
`/dev/tty<.>` where `<.>` implies the rest of a device file name in the
system; examples include `/dev/ttyACM0` and `/dev/ttyUSB0`.

---

diozero I2CDevice

This section provides a brief introduction to the diozero base I/O API for
I2C capability via the `I2CDevice` class. It supports communication with *I2C
devices* that can be connected to the Raspberry Pi via the relevant pins on the
GPIO header. You can find more documentation at `www.javadoc.io/doc/`
`com.diozero/diozero-core/latest/com/diozero/api/I2CDevice.html`.

Background on Raspberry Pi I2C

Before digging into `I2CDevice`, I'll offer some useful background on I2C
I/O in the context of the Raspberry Pi. Unlike serial, I2C is a *bus*, and
you can connect *multiple I2C devices* to an I2C bus. The I2C standard
allows for multiple *master* devices, which can initiate an interaction, and
multiple *slave* devices, which can respond to an interaction. The Pi can

be a master, but as far as I can tell, the Pi does *not* support a multi-master configuration. Further, as far as I can tell, the Pi cannot be a slave (see www.raspberrypi.org/forums/viewtopic.php?t=235740). In any case, I2CDevice works as an I2C master.

Since multiple I2C slave devices can exist on an I2C bus, each I2C device *must have* a theoretically *unique address*. The I2C standard allows for seven-bit or ten-bit addresses. The Pi supports both. That said, the vast majority of I2C devices use a 7-bit address, allowing 128 unique device addresses (the device datasheet will indicate the length of the address). This can lead to I2C device address conflicts. One source is conflicts among the hundreds or even thousands of *different* I2C devices manufactured. Another source occurs when a project requires multiple instances of the *same* I2C device. See https://learn.adafruit.com/i2c-addresses for some possible solutions.

The fact that there can be device conflicts led some manufacturers to include what is often called a "who am I" register on their devices. Reading the register and checking the value can provide an extra layer of device verification.

Raspberry Pi families have different numbers of I2C buses. For example, the P3B+ and Pi Zero W used in this book have two I2C buses. The two buses are named *i2c-0* and *i2c-1*. Only i2c-1 is intended for general use; i2c-0 is for access to the EEPROM on Pi "HATs" (see https://learn.sparkfun.com/tutorials/raspberry-pi-spi-and-i2c-tutorial/i2c-0-on-40-pin-pi-boards). This book will use only bus i2c-1.

Note A Raspberry Pi 4 has more I2C buses, but only i2c-1 is enabled by default. You can enable more; see www.raspberrypi.org/forums/viewtopic.php?t=271200).

---

diozero includes a utility for helping diagnose I2C address issues. I2CDetect finds all I2C devices attached to an I2C bus. Figure 7-2 shows the results of running I2CDetect on a Zero W with two I2C breakout boards attached to i2c-1. One of the boards contains two I2C devices, resulting in three I2C devices in total.

```
     0  1  2  3  4  5  6  7  8  9  a  b  c  d  e  f
00:      -- -- -- -- -- -- -- -- -- -- -- -- -- --
10: -- -- -- -- -- -- -- -- -- -- -- -- -- -- 1e --
20: -- -- -- -- -- -- -- -- -- -- -- -- -- -- -- --
30: -- -- -- -- -- -- -- -- -- -- -- -- -- -- -- --
40: -- -- -- -- -- -- -- -- -- -- -- -- -- -- -- --
50: -- -- -- -- -- -- -- -- -- -- -- -- -- -- -- --
60: -- -- -- -- -- -- -- -- -- -- -- 6b -- -- -- --
70: -- -- -- -- -- -- 76 --
```

Figure 7-2. *Results of running I2CDetect*

An I2C bus is considered a *low-speed* bus, at least compared to SPI (see the next section). The I2C standard (www.nxp.com/docs/en/user-guide/UM10204.pdf) says the clock speed can be from 0 Hz to a maximum defined by the *category*, which, for bidirectional transfers, can be

- *Standard mode*: 100 kHz; circa 1982

- *Fast mode*: 400 kHz; circa 1992

- *Fast-mode plus*: 1 MHz; circa 2007

- *High-speed mode*: 3.4 MHz; circa 2000

The closest thing I can find to *official* documentation for I2C bus speeds available on the Pi is www.raspberrypi.org/documentation/hardware/raspberrypi/bcm2835/BCM2835-ARM-Peripherals.pdf. Page 28 of that document suggests compliance with the January 2000 specification (2.1) which implies standard, fast, and high-speed mode compliance. However, the document mentions only fast mode (page 28) and a "default" speed of 100 kHz, or standard mode (page 34). Page 34 also describes the clock divider register (CDIV) which determines the speed of the I2C bus. CDIV can be set to any even number between 2 and 65534, resulting in potential speeds between ~2289 Hz and 75 MHz. Clearly anything beyond 3.4 MHz is out of spec. It is possible that anything beyond 400 kHz won't work.

Obviously, all I2C devices support standard mode. Many also support fast mode. You can find devices that support high-speed mode and fast-mode plus. In any case, it is safe, if potentially inefficient, to leave the I2C bus speed at the default of 100 kHz (see your device's datasheet).

You can change the I2C speed if you wish. To do so, on your Raspberry Pi, edit (as root)[4] the file /boot/config.txt; find the line that says

dtparam=i2c_arm=on

then edit the line so that it looks as follows:

dtparam=i2c_arm=on,i2c_arm_baudrate=NNNNNN

where NNNNNN represents the desired speed in Hz. Save the file and then reboot. With the right Pi model, the right OS version, and luck, your I2C bus will run at the desired speed.

Finally, it is important to understand that with I2C, all devices on the bus are always looking for their address, and so all get clocked at the same speed. That means that the maximum speed of the bus is limited by the slowest device on that bus.

Constructors

I2CDevice has several constructors. All constructors require the following two parameters:

- controller: This selects the I2C bus to use; per the earlier discussion on the Raspberry Pi, you *must* identify i2c-1; you can use the constant I2CConstants. CONTROLLER_1 to do so.

---

[4] You can use the simple editor nano. See Chapter 4 for some instructions.

- **address:** This indicates the I2C address for your device; you should be able to find it in the device's datasheet.

Additional parameters on some constructors allow you to define other characteristics (consult your device's datasheet for the correct values):

- **addressSize:** This indicates the size (in bits) of the I2C device address transmitted on the bus during interactions; per the earlier discussion, that usually should be 7; you can use the constant `I2CConstants.AddressSize.SIZE_7` (the default).

- **byteOrder:** This indicates the ordering of bytes in a multi-byte value on the bus; this is controlled by the specific I2C device; you can use one of the two values in `java.nio.ByteOrder` (the default `ByteOrder.BIG_ENDIAN` is correct for most devices).

Fortunately, the default values are the correct values for the majority of I2C devices. That means most of the time, you can use the simplest constructor that requires only the `controller` and `address` parameters.

`I2CDevice` also provides a nested `Builder` class that allows you to change only the parameters that differ from the default values.

Read and Write Methods

`I2CDevice` exposes many methods for reading bytes from and writing bytes to a device. To understand them, I must explain a bit about using I2C devices. I2C devices have the concept of *registers*. You *write* to *configuration and control* registers to get the device to perform its function in the way you want it done. You *read* from *data and status* registers to get the results of the device performing its function. In most I2C devices, a register has an address; thus, in an I2C operation, you'd find the device I2C address *and* a register address. The I2C devices in this book all use register addresses. Some I2C devices have so few registers or have such a simple function, they *don't* use register addresses for an I2C operation (e.g., see https://datasheets.maximintegrated.com/en/ds/MAX11041.pdf, a device with one control register and the logical equivalent of four data registers that are always read as a block).

You will find that I2C devices may or may not support *auto-increment* for block reads and block writes. With auto-increment, you can provide the starting register number and then perform read/write cycles to read/write a specific number of consecutive registers. Very convenient! Generally, the device datasheet contains a section describing the I2C capabilities, including any auto-increment capability.

I2CDevice provides methods to support I2C devices of both types. In addition, it provides several convenience methods that can simplify data manipulation. The *fundamental* read/write methods that use register addresses are

- readByteData reads a single byte from the register identified via the address parameter; it returns the byte read.

- readI2CBlockData reads a contiguous block of bytes starting at the register identified by the address parameter and attempts to fill the byte array parameter (up to a maximum of 32 bytes); it returns the number of bytes read.

- writeByteData writes a single byte to the register identified by the address parameter.

- writeI2CBlockData writes a contiguous block of bytes from the byte array parameter (a Java vararg) starting at the register identified by the address parameter (up to a maximum of 32 bytes).

The convenience methods that wrap these fundamental methods support reading a bit (boolean), int, short, unsigned byte (short), unsigned int (long), unsigned short (int), and java.nio.ByteBuffer. They also support writing a bit and a short.

For completeness, the fundamental read/write methods that *don't use* register addresses are readByte, readBytes, writeByte, and writeBytes.

Chapters 9 and 11 use I2CDevice.

Note   If you must read or write more than 32 bytes in a single interaction, you can do so using the readWrite method, though it is a bit difficult.

---

diozero SpiDevice

This section provides a brief introduction to the diozero base I/O API for SPI capability via the SpiDevice class. It supports communication with *SPI devices* that can be connected to the Raspberry Pi via the relevant pins on the GPIO header. You can find more documentation at www.javadoc.io/doc/com.diozero/diozero-core/latest/com/diozero/api/SpiDevice.html.

Background on Raspberry Pi SPI

Before digging into SpiDevice, I'll offer some useful background on SPI in the context of the Raspberry Pi. Like I2C, SPI is a bus. The SPI specification supports a *single* master and *multiple* slaves. The Raspberry Pi can only act as an SPI master (see www.raspberrypi.org/forums/viewtopic.php?t=230392). SpiDevice works as an SPI master.

The Raspberry Pi 3 Model B+ and the Zero W have two *SPI buses* (see
`www.raspberrypi.org/documentation/hardware/raspberrypi/spi/`
`README.md`). An SPI device can be connected to only one bus. SPI devices
have a *chip select* or *chip enable* pin that indicates traffic on the bus is
directed at that device. Pi SPI bus 0 has two chip enable pins (named CE0
and CE1), limiting you to two SPI devices on that bus; Pi SPI bus 1 has
three chip enable pins (named CE0, CE1, and C2), limiting you to three
SPI devices on that bus. If you need more devices on a single bus, you can
create multiplexing schemes.[5]

An SPI bus can run much faster than an I2C bus (see earlier
discussion), in part because it can use a faster clock and in part because
it can run *full duplex*. This makes SPI highly desirable for some devices.
Like an I2C device, an SPI device generally appears as a set of memory
locations or registers, each with an address, and you write and read control
or configuration registers and read data and status registers.

As with I2C, the viable speeds of an SPI bus on the Pi seem a bit hard to
confirm. The answer appears to be family dependent as well as operating
system version dependent. That said, the earlier reference suggests that
"anything over 50MHz is unlikely to work." Specific devices may limit the
speed even further.

Another advantage of SPI over I2C is that a device only looks at the bus
when selected. That means that the SPI bus speed can be set *per device*.
Thus, slow speed devices do not impact the performance of high-speed
devices as can happen with I2C.

Constructors

`SpiDevice` has three constructors. All constructors require a `chipSelect`
parameter. `SpiDevice` has CE0, CE1, CE2, and CE3 constants defined for the
parameter (remember diozero supports multiple SBCs).

---

[5] One hardware example is `www.farnell.com/datasheets/312519.pdf`.

The simplest constructor requires only the chipSelect parameter; the constructor uses default values for additional configurable characteristics. Additional constructors offer you the ability to tailor the following characteristics of an SpiDevice instance:

- The SPI bus or controller number: The class provides a constant for the default, DEFAULT_SPI_CONTROLLER.

- The SPI bus clock *frequency* and *mode*: The class provides a constant for the default frequency, DEFAULT_SPI_CLOCK_ FREQUENCY (2 MHz); an associated class SpiClockMode provides valid values, with the default of MODE_0.

- The order in which bits are transferred: The class provides a constant for the default, DEFAULT_LSB_FIRST (false).

SpiDevice also provides a Builder class. Builder allows you to change only the necessary characteristics from the default values.

Read and Write Methods

SpiDevice exposes three methods for writing bytes to and reading bytes from a device. It is important to realize that *all* the methods assume *block* operations. The methods are

- write writes a block of bytes to the device; the block contains both register address(es) and the data to write; the details depend on the device; there are two forms of write:

  - One parameter, a byte array (Java vararg), writes all bytes to the device

  - Three parameters, a byte array, a starting index, and a length, writes bytes to the device, starting at index and ending when length bytes are written

- `writeAndRead` writes a block of bytes to the device, generally to provide the address(es) from which to read, and reads a block of bytes from the device of the same length as that written (full duplex); as with `write`, the details of what you must write to be able to read the desired block depend on the device.

You will find that SPI devices may or may not support *auto-increment* for reads and writes. Generally, the device datasheet contains a section describing the SPI auto-increment capabilities.

You will also find that using SPI is a bit more complex than using I2C due to the full duplex nature of SPI. I'll compare `SpiDevice` and `I2CDevice` in Chapter 11. Chapter 12 also uses `SpiDevice`.

GPIO

This section provides a brief introduction to diozero support for what might be called "the rest of the digital I/O" capabilities of the Raspberry Pi, that is, whatever is not covered earlier regarding "specialized digital I/O" (serial, I2C, SPI). This includes general-purpose capabilities like "simple" digital input and "simple" digital output and PWM output. I'll describe the "basic" classes in the later subsections.

diozero includes a utility `GpioReadAll` that can help diagnose GPIO problems. It reads the state of the GPIO pins and produces a report that, to the extent possible, includes the mode (input or output) and state (0 [for 0V] or 1 [for 3.3V]) of the GPIO pins. Figure 7-3 shows a report captured immediately after booting.

```
Header: J8
+ GP# +        Name + Mode + V + gpiod + Physical + gpiod  + V + Mode + Name      + GP# +
|      |         3v3 |      |   |       |  1 || 2  |        |   |      | 5v        |     |
|   2  |        SDA1 | Unkn | 1 |  0:2  |  3 || 4  |        |   |      | 5v        |     |
|   3  |        SCL1 | Unkn | 1 |  0:3  |  5 || 6  |        |   |      | GND       |     |
|   4  |   GPIO_GCLK |   In | 1 |  0:4  |  7 || 8  |  0:14  | 1 | Unkn | TXD1      |  14 |
|      |         GND |      |   |       |  9 || 10 |  0:15  | 1 | Unkn | RXD1      |  15 |
|  17  |      GPIO17 |   In | 0 |  0:17 | 11 || 12 |  0:18  | 0 |   In | GPIO18    |  18 |
|  27  |      GPIO27 |   In | 0 |  0:27 | 13 || 14 |        |   |      | GND       |     |
|  22  |      GPIO22 |   In | 0 |  0:22 | 15 || 16 |  0:23  | 0 |   In | GPIO23    |  23 |
|      |         3v3 |      |   |       | 17 || 18 |  0:24  | 0 |   In | GPIO24    |  24 |
|  10  |    SPI_MOSI | Unkn | 0 |  0:10 | 19 || 20 |        |   |      | GND       |     |
|   9  |    SPI_MISO | Unkn | 0 |  0:9  | 21 || 22 |  0:25  | 0 |   In | GPIO25    |  25 |
|  11  |    SPI_SCLK | Unkn | 0 |  0:11 | 23 || 24 |  0:8   | 1 |  Out | SPI_CE0_N |  8  |
|      |         GND |      |   |       | 25 || 26 |  0:7   | 1 |  Out | SPI_CE1_N |  7  |
|   0  |      ID_SDA |   In | 1 |  0:0  | 27 || 28 |  0:1   | 1 |   In | ID_SCL    |  1  |
|   5  |       GPIO5 |   In | 1 |  0:5  | 29 || 30 |        |   |      | GND       |     |
|   6  |       GPIO6 |   In | 1 |  0:6  | 31 || 32 |  0:12  | 0 |   In | GPIO12    |  12 |
|  13  |      GPIO13 |   In | 0 |  0:13 | 33 || 34 |        |   |      | GND       |     |
|  19  |      GPIO19 |   In | 0 |  0:19 | 35 || 36 |  0:16  | 0 |   In | GPIO16    |  16 |
|  26  |      GPIO26 |   In | 0 |  0:26 | 37 || 38 |  0:20  | 1 |   In | GPIO20    |  20 |
|      |         GND |      |   |       | 39 || 40 |  0:21  | 1 |   In | GPIO21    |  21 |
+------+-------------+------+---+-------+---------+--------+---+------+-----------+-----+
Header: P5
+ GP# +        Name + Mode + V + gpiod + Physical + gpiod  + V + Mode + Name        + GP# +
|  54  |       BT_ON |   In |   |  1:0  |  0 || 1  |  1:1   |   |   In | WL_ON        |  55 |
|  56  | PWR_LED_OFF |   In |   |  1:2  |  2 || 3  |  1:3   |   |   In | GLOBAL_RESET |  57 |
|  58  | VDD_SD_IO_SEL |  In |   | 1:4  |  4 || 5  |  1:5   |   |   In | CAM_GPIO     |  59 |
|  60  |   SD_PWR_ON |   In |   |  1:6  |  6 || 7  |  1:7   |   |   In | SD_OC_N      |  61 |
+------+-------------+------+---+-------+---------+--------+---+------+--------------+-----+
```

Figure 7-3. *Report from GpioReadAll*

Background on Raspberry Pi GPIO

Before digging into GPIO, I'll offer some additional background on GPIO in the context of the Raspberry Pi. In addition to the highlights mentioned at the beginning of this chapter, www.raspberrypi.org/documentation/usage/gpio/ and www.raspberrypi.org/documentation/hardware/raspberrypi/gpio/README.md provide additional useful information for GPIO usage.

Pin Numbering

Note that a GPIO pin number *does not* correspond to the physical connector pin number. The former is often called the *BCM number*, and the latter is often called the *board number*. BCM is the officially supported pin numbering scheme from the Raspberry Pi Foundation. diozero uses the *BCM* numbers.

Pull-up and Pull-down

When you configure a GPIO pin as an input, you can configure one of the following states:

- *Pull-up*: The pin is attached to 3.3V via a 50–65 kΩ resistor; thus, the pin will read "high" or "on" unless the attached device does something to pull the pin to ground.

- *Pull-down*: The pin is attached to ground (0V) via a 50–65 kΩ resistor; thus, the pin will read "low" or "off" unless the attached device does something to pull the pin to 3.3V.

- *Float*: The pin floats; thus, the pin reads "high" or "low" depending on what the attached device does; generally, the assumption is that external pull-up or pull-down resistors are used.

There are two exceptions to these states. GPIO 2 and 3 (connector pins 3 and 5) are used for I2C. As a result, they are always pulled up to 3.3V using 1.8 kΩ resistors.

Tip   Your devices may force you to understand the initial state of the GPIO pins. Unfortunately, the subject is complex. At power on, all pins are inputs and GPIO 0–8 are pulled up and the rest are pulled down. However, this can change; see www.raspberrypi.org/documentation/configuration/pin-configuration.md for more information. The GpioReadAll utility mentioned earlier can help you understand the state of your GPIO at any time.

Current Limits

While voltage limits for the GPIO pins are easy to understand (0V minimum and 3.3V maximum), the current limits are not. In addition to the links at the beginning of this section, `www.mosaic-industries.com/embedded-systems/microcontroller-projects/raspberry-pi/gpio-pin-electrical-specifications` and `www.raspberrypi.org/documentation/hardware/raspberrypi/gpio/gpio_pads_control.md` provide some gory detail and recommendations. Some highlights:

- Never sink nor source more than 16 mA from a single output pin.

- Never sink nor source more than 0.5 mA from a single input pin.

- The maximum current that can be sourced from output pins at any instant is 50 mA.

- There is no limit specified on the total current sunk by GPIO pins.

- The source/sink current *drive strength* for *all* pins can be programmed from 2 mA to 16 mA. To be safe, the programmed limit should not be exceeded.

The last highlight deserves elaboration. You program the drive strength by writing to specific registers on the Raspberry Pi SoC (system on chip). I've looked at a few APIs for GPIO in Python, C, and Java. I've not seen any that allow programming the drive strength. The drive strength is set to 8 mA at power up by the Raspberry Pi hardware, but it can be changed by the OS kernel.

The moral of this story is ... *be careful*!

diozero GPIO Classes

In some ways, the GPIO capabilities offered by diozero are more interesting and more complex than the serial, I2C, and SPI capabilities discussed earlier. I'll describe the "basic" classes in the following subsections. You can read the Javadoc for information on the additional classes in the API.

There are two related concepts that are important to the GPIO capabilities. The *value* relates to the *physical* aspect of a GPIO pin; it can be *high* (3.3V) or *low* (0V). The *state* relates to the *logical* aspect of a GPIO pin; it can be *active* or *inactive*. You get to map logical to physical during construction.

DigitalInputDevice

As the name implies, DigitalInputDevice (www.javadoc.io/doc/com. diozero/diozero-core/latest/com/diozero/api/DigitalInputDevice. html) allows you to monitor the value and state of an attached device. You can read the value and state, wait for a particular value or state, get an event when a particular state is detected, or get an event on a level transition. The behavior of DigitalInputDevice is controlled by the following characteristics:

- *GPIO pin*: Pin (BCM number) to use for input (or its PinInfo equivalent)

- *Active state*: true = high (3.3V) or false = low (0V)

- *Pull-up resistor type*: Up, down, or none (float)

- *Event trigger type*: Rising edge, falling edge, both, or none

Active state allows you to map the logical active state to a physical state. For example, many devices produce a signal that is high when active and low when inactive. On the other hand, some devices produce a signal that is low when active and high when inactive. Since `DigitalInputDevice` works mostly in terms of active and inactive rather than high and low, it is important that you define the proper logical mapping for your physical device.

Constructors

`DigitalInputDevice` has several constructors, all but one of which use built-in defaults (see the Javadoc) for some or all of the above characteristics. It also has a `Builder` nested class.[6] Note that diozero defines constants for the pull-up resistor type and the event trigger type for use in a constructor or with `Builder`.

Methods

`DigitalInputDevice` has several key methods (among others) for understanding the state of the attached device. To read the value or state, you can use

- `getValue`: Returns the current *value* of the GPIO pin; true means high (3.3V) and false means low (0V).

- `isActive`: Returns whether the pin is *active*; per the earlier discussion, *active* is a logical state and can mean high or low.

To wait for a particular value or state (timeout possible):

- `waitForActive`: Wait for the pin to become active.

- `waitForInactive`: Wait for the pin to become inactive.

---

[6] I find the defaults, especially active state, sometimes don't match my needs, so I recommend using `Builder` to set all characteristics except the GPIO pin so you get the desired behavior from `DigitalInputDevice`.

- `waitForValue`: Wait for the pin to reach the desired value.

Chapter 14 shows an example of `waitForActive`.

To get an event when a particular state is detected, you can use the following methods:

- `whenActivated`: Calls an "event handler" when the device is active.

- `whenDectivated`: Calls an "event handler" when the device is inactive.

Those two methods enable what amounts to an "interrupt" capability. You must provide the "event handler" (the method to call) as a parameter on the methods. The class or method given as a parameter is of type `LongConsumer`. The class is a functional interface whose functional method is `accept(long event)`. In diozero, the `long` passed to the method is the *Linux® CLOCK_MONOTONIC timestamp* in nanoseconds. It represents the amount of time since an unspecified point in the past (e.g., system startup time). I find this "timestamped interrupt" capability to be really fantastic. I'll show you examples in Chapters 9 and 14.

To get an "interrupt" on a level transition, you must use the method `addListener` to identify the "event handler." The parameter class is another functional interface whose functional method is `accept(DigitalInputEvent event)`. The event trigger characteristic controls which edges (level transitions) generate events. `DigitalInputEvent` has two timestamps: Linux® CLOCK_MONOTONIC and *UNIX® epoch time*. Chapter 14 shows an example.

DigitalOutputDevice

As the name implies, DigitalOutputDevice (www.javadoc.io/ doc/com.diozero/diozero-core/latest/com/diozero/api/ DigitalOutputDevice.html) allows you to control an attached device. The class also distinguishes between state and level and allows you to set the mapping. You can simply set the output active or inactive, or high or low, or you can generate interesting waveforms. The behavior of DigitalOutputDevice is controlled by the following characteristics:

- *GPIO pin*: Pin (BCM number) to use for output (or its PinInfo equivalent)

- *Active state*: true = high (3.3V) or false = low (0V)

- *Initial value*: true = high (3.3V) or false = low (0V)

Constructors

DigitalOutputDevice has several constructors, one of which uses built-in defaults. The most useful constructor allows you to set all the characteristics mentioned earlier. DigitalOutputDevice has a Builder as well.

Methods

DigitalOutputDevice has the following key methods (among others):

- off: Sets the GPIO pin *inactive*; that could be 0V or 3.3V depending on the active state.

- on: Sets the pin *active*; that could be 0V or 3.3V depending on the active state.

- setOn: Sets the pin *active* (true) or *inactive* (false).

- setValue: Sets the pin high (true) or low (false).

- `toggle`: Toggles the device state/level.

- `onOffLoop`: Automatically toggles the output for a
  number of cycles; can generate an event when finished.

Chapter 13 uses `DigitalOutputDevice`.

PwmOutputDevice

As the name implies, `PwmOutputDevice` (www.javadoc.io/doc/com.
diozero/diozero-core/latest/com/diozero/api/PwmOutputDevice.
html) represents a device driven by a *PWM* (pulse width modulated)
signal. You can generate a PWM signal in various ways. The behavior of
`PwmOutputDevice` is controlled by the following characteristics:

- *GPIO pin*: Pin (BCM number) to use for output

- *Frequency*: Frequency of the PWM signal in Hz

- *Value*: The pulse width relative to the signal
  period (0..1)

Constructors

The most useful `PwmOutputDevice` constructor allows you to set all the
characteristics mentioned earlier. `PwmOutputDevice` has a `Builder` as well.

Note that a constructor starts a PWM signal at the frequency and value
defined by the parameters. The signal continues at that frequency and
value until changed.

Methods

`PwmOutputDevice` has the following "key" methods (among others):

- `setValue`: Sets the output pulse width relative to the
  signal period (0..1); the frequency stays the same.

- `setPwmFrequency`: Sets a *new* frequency of the signal; the value stays the same.

This book does not use `PwmOutputDevice`, but you can find examples in the diozero documentation and among the diozero prebuilt devices.

If you read the reference material cited earlier in this chapter, you know the Raspberry Pi supports hardware PWM on certain GPIO pins; doing so, however, requires running as root. To avoid that, the diozero built-in provider used in this book implements software PWM (using a background thread). If you feel motivated to use the hardware PWM, you can use the diozero pigpio provider, but you must run your application as root.

Tip   As mentioned in Chapter 6, diozero provides some devices (a.k.a. device libraries) built on the base I/O API classes. See `www.javadoc.io/doc/com.diozero/diozero-core/latest/com/diozero/devices/package-summary.html`. The devices supply additional examples of using the diozero base I/O classes.

Device Library and Application Structure

This section discusses some important guidelines for designing and developing

- Device library *classes* that use the diozero base I/O API device classes

- *Applications* that use either diozero base I/O API device classes or device library classes based on them

RuntimeIOException

diozero has a simple rule: *all device actions* in the base I/O API may throw the *unchecked* `RuntimeIOException`. The rule applies to constructors and to methods that read from the device or write to the device.

Unchecked exceptions are a bit controversial among Java developers because catching them is optional, and thus, in effect, they can be ignored "because you can't do anything about them." See `https://docs.oracle.com/javase/tutorial/essential/exceptions/runtime.html` for more information.

The ability to ignore unchecked exceptions can allow faster coding and can result in cleaner code, in particular when using Java lambda expressions. However, if not caught, an unchecked exception propagates down the call stack to the `main` method, and your program terminates. Thus, you might reasonably be concerned about "unpleasant" consequences from ignoring a `RuntimeIOException`. Consider the following scenario:

> Your program creates an instance of a motor controller class, `Motors`, to drive the motors for a mobile robot. `Motors` uses a `SerialDevice` to interact with the motor controller. You call `Motors.forward` to turn on the motors (they stay on until you call `Motors.stop`).

> You call a method for another device (with the motors running), and it throws a `RuntimeIOException`. If not caught, your program terminates, *with the motors running*. The robot likely crashes! Unpleasant indeed.

Safety Nets

How can you prevent these unpleasant consequences? Java and diozero offer some "safety nets" to address this and other issues.

try-with-resources Safety Net

Java provides a safety net that can prevent a crash in the Motors scenario with the java.lang.AutoCloseable interface and *try-with-resources* statement (https://docs.oracle.com/javase/tutorial/essential/exceptions/tryResourceClose.html). Any class that implements AutoCloseable *must* have a close method and can be considered a *resource* in a try-with-resources statement. The try-with-resources statement instantiates resources identified in the statement and ensures that the close method of each resource gets called before a program terminates.

You enable the try-with-resources safety net as follows:

1. In any device library class you create that uses diozero base I/O API classes to interact with physical devices, you implement java.lang. AutoCloseable.

2. In the mandatory close method in your device library class, you

    a. Terminate ongoing activities, especially those that have unpleasant consequences if not terminated

    b. Close the diozero base I/O API classes used in your class

3. In any application/program that uses *your* device library class or any class in the diozero base I/O API, you implement a try-with-resources statement, with *all* such classes in the list of resources.

Let's examine the `Motors` scenario with the try-with-resources safety net in place:

> `Motors` implements `java.lang.AutoCloseable` and uses a `SerialDevice` to interact with the motor controller. `Motors.close` stops any ongoing motor activity and then calls `close` on the `SerialDevice` instance.

> Your program encapsulates its task implementation in a try-with-resources statement with `Motors` in the resource list; the statement creates an instance of `Motors`. Inside the try-with-resources, you call `Motors.forward` to turn on the motors (they stay on until you call `Motors.stop`).

> You call a method for another device (with the motors running), and it generates a `RuntimeIOException`. Prior to program termination, `Motors.close` gets called and stops the motors, etc. The program terminates with the robot stopped. No crash!

The try-with-resources safety net handles situations where you interpret the `RuntimeIOException` to mean "you can't do anything" and want a graceful termination. I believe there are situations where you must think of the exception in terms of "what I wanted to happen didn't happen," and it is reasonable to catch the unchecked exception. You might retry the operation that caused the exception, return some indicator of failure, or even throw a checked exception. Only you can make such design decisions. The key point is that you should analyze each situation before deciding whether to catch it or not.

Tip   diozero includes a set of utility classes (see `www.javadoc.io/doc/com.diozero/diozero-core/latest/com/diozero/util/package-summary.html`) that can be used with the base I/O API to develop device libraries or to create extensions to diozero. One of the most useful classes, `SleepUtil`, wraps `Thread.sleep`, catches the `InterruptedException` (so you don't have to catch or throw it), and throws a subclass of `RuntimeIOException`. Thus, when you need to sleep, you can use `SleepUtil` and leverage your own approach to handling `RuntimeIOException`.

diozero Shutdown Safety Net

But wait, there's more! While reading about the GPIO devices, you may have wondered if diozero spawns threads "under the covers." The answer is yes (more work you don't have to do). But diozero ensures such threads get terminated under normal and abnormal circumstances so your application can exit properly, *except* when using a remote provider.

To address potential threading issues, diozero provides a utility class `com.diozero.util.Diozero`. It offers the static `shutdown` method that forces termination of all diozero-created threads, including those for the pigpio remote provider. To enable the safety net, you place the method call in a `finally` block associated with the try-with-resources statement mentioned in the previous subsection.

Java Shutdown Safety Net

But wait, there's even more! Java and diozero together offer you an additional safety net. Java provides a *shutdown mechanism* (see `www.baeldung.com/jvm-shutdown-hooks` and `www.geeksforgeeks.org/jvm-shutdown-hook-java/`) that allows you to release resources and handle potentially unpleasant situations prior to JVM termination (e.g., when a Ctrl-C bypasses a try-with-resources). On application startup, diozero registers its own *shutdown hook* (the `Diozero` utility class) that performs *internal* cleanup operations such as stopping any threads that it created. The shutdown hook has a method that allows applications to register additional class instances (e.g., devices) for inclusion in the diozero shutdown activities. You can register an instance of any class that implements `AutoCloseable` using the static method `Diozero.registerForShutdown`. When called during JVM shutdown, the diozero shutdown hook first calls `close` on all class instances registered with it and then performs internal cleanup operations. Thus, the registered `close` methods get called prior to JVM termination and can prevent unpleasantness.

There are two ways to enable the Java shutdown safety net. You can register your

- *Device* class instances inside the try-with-resources statement in your application

- *Application* class instance after creating the instance in the `main` method

Your device classes should be `AutoCloseable` already, so the first way is easy. To use the second way, you must make your application class `AutoCloseable` and implement a `close` method that then closes the relevant devices used in the application. You can choose the way you prefer.

It is especially important that you enable the Java shutdown safety net if your program runs in an infinite loop and requires a Ctrl-c or some other interrupt to terminate. Conversely, there is no harm in *always* engaging the Java shutdown safety net.

Caution   Do not register your own Java shutdown handler. The JVM does not guarantee the order in which shutdown handlers execute, so the diozero shutdown handler might run first, preventing your shutdown handler from communicating with any of its devices.

Automatic Safety Net

But wait, there's still more! diozero implements another safety net "under the covers." All devices in the diozero base I/O API (e.g., `SerialDevice`, `I2CDevice`, and `DigitalInputDevice`) implement `AutoCloseable`, and diozero automatically registers instances for the Java shutdown safety net. This ensures the `close` methods for all open diozero base I/O device instances get called prior to program termination. That said, explicit device closing is preferred (as in the `Motors` scenario discussed earlier); this "automatic" safety net should be considered a backup.

Safety Net Guidelines

There are some important implications of the safety net discussion for device libraries and applications in the context of diozero:

- The automatic safety net (based on Java shutdown) is always enabled, but you *should not* depend on it; you should explicitly close diozero API classes in your device libraries. Recognize that the automatic safety net *cannot* close *your* devices.

- You *should* enable the try-with-resources safety net in any application you write, treating your device classes and any diozero device classes (base I/O or otherwise) as resources.

- You *should* enable the diozero shutdown safety net (via `Diozero.shutdown` in a `finally` block), even for the default built-in provider primarily used in this book. You *must* enable the diozero shutdown safety net when using one of the remote providers to terminate threads that handle remote communication.

- You *may* enable the Java shutdown safety net (via `Diozero.registerForShutdown`), especially if you are concerned about unpleasant consequences. If so, under a normal program termination, a device's `close` method will be called *twice*, once at the end of the try-with-resources and again at shutdown. You must ensure that your `close` method is designed to handle multiple calls.

As you should expect, Chapters 8 through 14 all leverage the try-with-resources and the diozero safety nets. Chapters 8 and 14 leverage the Java shutdown safety net.

Caution   Bad news: there are situations in which none of the safety nets get engaged even when enabled (see the shutdown hook references). Good news: you've done the best you can.

Summary

In this chapter, you've learned about

- The base I/O capabilities of the Raspberry Pi

- The most important aspects of the diozero base I/O API and some useful diozero utilities

- Guidelines for developing device libraries and applications that leverage the diozero base I/O API

Now it is time to use the diozero base I/O API to create device libraries!

CHAPTER 8

A DC Motor Controller

In this chapter, we'll develop a diozero-based device library based on what you learned in earlier chapters. I've chosen a device commonly used in robotics, a DC motor controller, and, more narrowly, one accessed via serial I/O. That said, the chapter covers topics applicable to the development of a device library for *any* type of device using *any* form of base I/O and thus establishes significant context for later chapters. So, you should at least browse this chapter, even if your project doesn't target robotics, doesn't use the motor controller examined in this chapter, doesn't use a motor controller, or doesn't use a serial device.

Specifically, in this chapter, you'll learn

- How to choose which device library to port when multiple candidates exist

- Some general guidelines for porting an existing device library

- How to port a device library incrementally, using a *depth-first* approach

- How to use diozero serial I/O support

- Other activities to help you understand the device and port a library

© Greg Flurry 2021

G. Flurry, *Java on the Raspberry Pi*, https://doi.org/10.1007/978-1-4842-7264-0_8

Choose the Device

Let's say your project requires a DC motor controller. You can find a wide spectrum of controllers ranging from simple H-bridges to high-end devices that implement sophisticated PID motor control algorithms. As always, the best choice for your project is the one that meets the functional and cost needs of your project. In this chapter, we'll look at a DC motor controller I used to build an autonomous rover.[1] I chose a controller on the high end of the spectrum, the RoboClaw 2x15A Motor Controller from Basicmicro (`www.basicmicro.com/RoboClaw-2x15A-Motor-Controller_p_10.html`). There are several reasons for using it in this chapter:

- Its capabilities off-load work from the Raspberry Pi, leaving more CPU cycles for computational tasks and task coordination.

- I found it to be an excellent motor controller.

- The technical support from Basicmicro was stunningly good.

- It supports a USB interface so you can get experience with diozero serial I/O support.

- A device library for this specific controller should work for the family of RoboClaw controllers.

- It is a counterexample to the scarcity of device libraries I suggested in Chapter 1.

- It is a complex device that mandates a multi-pronged approach to porting a device library.

---

[1] If you wish to learn more about the autonomous rover, see `www.instructables.com/An-Autonomous-Rover/`.

One thing I won't do in this book is describe much about the RoboClaw or how to use it beyond the minimum needed to help design, implement, and test the device library.

Understand the Device

I've emphasized that you must understand your device. You of course had to understand the device capabilities at some level when you choose it for your project. You may have browsed a datasheet or even a user manual to help make the choice, but likely focused more on device capabilities than on how to use those capabilities. However, even if you don't have to port or create the library for it, you still have to understand the device *well* to use it *properly*. I recommend that before looking for existing device libraries, and especially before writing a device library from scratch, you read and absorb every datasheet, user manual, application note, etc., you can find. This is especially important in the case of a complex device, where you might skip "boring" but key details, because, as some wise person said, "the devil is in the details."

The RoboClaw is a good example of this aphorism. I've claimed the RoboClaw is a complex device. Here is some evidence:

- The **datasheet** is 16 pages long. See the *Downloads* tab on the product web page (mentioned earlier).

- The **User Manual** is 101 pages long and describes over 130 commands. See the *Downloads* tab on the product web page.

A few sections in the **User Manual** help you identify some "devilish details" important in understanding the device:

- *USB Control* section: You must run the device in "packet serial" mode. You don't need to worry about finding a low-level device driver for Raspberry Pi OS. You don't need to set a baud rate; the USB connection will run as fast as possible.

- *Packet Serial* section: "The basic command structures consist of an address byte, command byte, data bytes, and a CRC16 16-bit checksum." With a USB connection, the address byte can be 0x80–0x87, because the USB connection is unique (this eliminates the so-called *Multi-Unit Packet Serial* mode). The section has additional information about packet timeout, packet acknowledgment for write-only commands, CRC calculation,[2] and dealing with data type lengths. It also contains information on the most basic commands.

- *Advanced Packet Serial, Encoders, Advanced Motor Control* sections: These contain the detailed data requirements of the commands. You should browse these sections primarily to understand some of the existing library code complexity, especially around multiple data types in a single command.

- *Advanced Motor Control*: Relevant command descriptions explain how command buffering, an important but underappreciated feature of the RoboClaw, operates.

---

[2] CRC (cyclic redundancy check) is a simple way of detecting errors in a transmitted data stream. You don't need to understand the principles, but you do have to deal with CRC calculation in the context of the RoboClaw.

Having a good grasp of the device capabilities and its I/O requirements will help you understand device libraries you might use or port, help you develop your own library if necessary, and help you determine the proper device library interface in any case.

Find a Device Library

To find a device library to use or port, I'll follow the procedure outlined in Chapter 6.

Search for Java Libraries

First, look at the diozero device libraries. At the time of writing, the diozero documentation and Javadoc described some interfaces and concrete implementations that supported PWM-driven DC motors and servos. Nothing close to the RoboClaw.

Next, search for other Raspberry Pi serial I/O Java libraries in combination with RoboClaw. At the time of writing, I found nothing.

Next, search for RoboClaw and Java. That search produced a few hits worthy of consideration:

- snackbot (https://github.com/jarney/snackbot/ blob/master/src/main/java/org/ensor/robots/ roboclawdriver/RoboClaw.java): The device library appeared to be only partially complete and was at least six years old. It is embedded in a larger framework, though it could likely be extracted with a fair amount of work. It includes *lots* of classes; for example, there is a class for each command implemented (not all are). A possibility, but certainly not ideal.

- myrobotlab (https://github.com/MyRobotLab/
  myrobotlab/blob/develop/src/main/java/org/
  myrobotlab/service/RoboClaw.java): The device
  library appeared to be both complete and up to date.
  It too is embedded in a larger framework; it might be
  counterproductive to try to extract it. For the most part,
  it seems well structured. A much better starting point
  than snackbot, I think.

- project-capo (https://github.com/project-capo/
  amber-java-clients/blob/master/amber-java-
  roboclaw/src/main/java/pl/edu/agh/amber/
  roboclaw/RoboclawProxy.java): The device library
  appeared to be incomplete; there are classes I could not
  find. It was at least five years old. Probably not a good
  starting point.

Of the three hits, only myrobotlab seems worth considering. The only
significant disadvantage is dragging along the entire framework, which no
doubt includes unneeded function. I personally am not disposed to drag in
a lot of extras that would almost certainly go unused. Thus, I would at least
defer a decision until after examining the non-Java libraries.

Search for Non-Java Libraries

When you look at the **Downloads** tab on the RoboClaw product page (the
link is at the top of the chapter), you find *five* device libraries (or drivers) in
different programming languages:

- *Python* for the Raspberry Pi OS and other platforms

- *Python* for the Robot Operating System (ROS)

- *C#* for Windows

- *C++* for the Arduino

- *"G"* for LabVIEW

How do you choose the one (or more) to seed your porting effort? If you know one language much better than the other languages, that is usually the best choice. If that is not the case, you'll have to assess all the libraries to choose. So that is what I'll do. While doing so, I'll raise some specific issues that you can generalize to other languages and other devices.

I'll start with the easy ones. As far as I can tell, the "G" LabVIEW driver download contains only executables and no source; that renders it useless for porting. The Python library for ROS appears to be written by someone unaffiliated with Basicmicro; it had not been updated in at least four years; a brief look at it indicates it is not too much different than the Python library for Raspberry Pi OS, which is from Basicmicro and supported. Thus, the ROS Python library is not a good candidate.

A Look at the C# Library

I admit with some chagrin I have never used C#. A quick glance at the source code I downloaded (see the file `Roboclaw.cs`) suggests that C# demonstrates a C lineage but has some of the characteristics of Java. It understandably has some "Windows-isms" I don't fully understand, but I think can be safely ignored, though they do make the code more difficult to understand.

The file includes a `Commands` class that defines constants for commands; it appears to be easily copied into a Java class; nice, except it includes commands apparently for other Basicmicro devices, so be cautious. The file includes a `SerialPort` class that defines some *low-level* methods to read and write bytes. The low-level methods appear to be similar to those of the diozero `SerialDevice` described in Chapter 7.

197

The `Roboclaw.cs` file of course includes the `Roboclaw` class, which extends `SerialPort`. Now things get interesting. The class defines three *mid-level* methods, `ReadLenCmd`, `ReadCmd`, and `Write_CRC`, that deal with the multiple data types in the commands, do CRC generation and verification, and interact with the device using the low-level methods. Finally, `Roboclaw` defines *interface-level* methods that correspond to the device commands; the application using the device library calls the interface-level methods. The vast majority of the interface-level methods use the mid-level methods; one uses the low-level methods (that interface-level method gets the RoboClaw firmware version, something unlikely to be of interest to a robotics program).

By searching for the mid-level commands in the `Roboclaw` source code, you can determine that only four interface-level methods call `ReadLenCmd`, and none of them exist in the RoboClaw **User Manual**! This is because the `Roboclaw` class supports a wide range of Basicmicro devices. Fundamentally, that means you only have to worry about porting `ReadCmd` and `Write_CRC` to support the RoboClaw 2x15A.

In summary, the C# `Roboclaw` class exhibits *three layers*:

- The *low-level* methods for basic serial communication; this is where you'd insert diozero `SerialDevice` equivalents.

- The *mid-level* methods `ReadCmd` and `Write_CRC` that deal with translating between a byte array and multi-byte data types; both require porting.

- The *interface-level* methods implementing RoboClaw commands; you can implement as many as you need for your project and add more later.

So, the C# library looks like a good candidate for porting. However, once again, devilish details arise. The signature of `ReadCmd` method contains a C# `ref`. When a method like `GetM1Encoder` calls `ReadCmd`, the former must convert parameters from primitive form (e.g., Java `int`) to an object (e.g., Java `Integer`, or perhaps more analogous, `Object`) and add them to an `ArrayList`. ReadCmd checks the type of each parameter in the list to determine the length in bytes. While an elegant design and reasonably simple to implement, this seems like a lot of overhead, with a potentially noticeable impact on performance. This is probably a reasonable trade-off for a Windows machine which likely has many times the performance of a Raspberry Pi.

Note   I could find no usage examples in the C# device library download. You may be able to find some with a broader search.

A Look at the C++ Library

The C++ library (file `RoboClaw.cpp`) of course contains some Arduino-isms. As with the C# library, there are *three layers*. There are low-level methods analogous to what diozero `SerialDevice` provides. There are mid-level methods (`write_n`, `read_n`) that handle CRC generation and verification and send or receive byte arrays to or from the device using the low-level methods. There are additional mid-level methods that handle specific data exchange patterns (`Read1`, `Read2`, `Read4`, `Read4_1`). Interface-level methods corresponding to RoboClaw commands use the mid-level methods. The mid-level methods `write_n` and `read_n` are used many times. `Read1` is used 1 time, `Read2` 8 times, `Read4` 12 times, and `Read4_1` 6 times.

The C++ architecture is fundamentally the same as the C# architecture, but the implementation is different. The mid-level shows more specialization and thus more methods. But the C++ mid-level pushes some data type work to the interface level; the interface-level methods can be responsible for converting data types, for example, a 32-bit integer to a list of four bytes.

In summary, the C++ RoboClaw class also exhibits *three layers*:

- The *low-level* methods for basic serial communication, where you'd insert diozero SerialDevice equivalents.

- The *mid-level* methods write_n, read_n, Read1, Read2, Read4, and Read4_1, for writing or reading a byte array and for dealing with specific data exchange patterns; all require porting with the possible exception of Read1.

- The *interface-level* methods implementing RoboClaw commands; you can implement as many as you need for your project and add more later.

So, the C++ library also looks like a good candidate for porting. The overall design is not as elegant as that for C#. You'll likely have to write more code than for C#. I think, however, the performance would be better, and the memory requirements would be lower (there will not be a bunch of parameter objects around). That said, the reasonably slow performance of serial communication may make the difference negligible.

Note The C++ download includes several examples that will help you understand and even experiment with the RoboClaw. You would of course have to connect the RoboClaw to an Arduino to use the examples.

A Look at the Python Library

The download for Python for the Raspberry Pi contains code for both Python2 and Python3. I'll discuss only the latter.

The Python library (file roboclaw_3.py) is architecturally similar to the C# and C++ libraries in that there are *three layers*, low level, mid-level, and interface level. The implementation of the interface level is similar to that of the other two libraries in that the interface-level methods use the mid-level methods. But the similarity for the other two levels is tenuous at best; for reasons that must have to do with Python's data handling, the implementation of the lower two layers seems dominated by signed vs. unsigned data. There are roughly nine low-level methods for dealing with the byte length and sign of data. The mid-level implements over 30 methods for handling different patterns of data and whether the data is signed or unsigned.

Given the additional complexity for a concern that does not seem to apply to a language with a C heritage, the Python library does not seem to be a good candidate for porting.

Note   The Python download includes several examples that will help you understand and even experiment with the RoboClaw. Even though not recommended for porting, you could load the library and run examples anyway since you'll already need to have the RoboClaw connected to your Raspberry Pi.

And the Answer Is …

In my opinion

- The Java library from myrobotlab is an *acceptable* porting candidate.

- The C# library is a *good* porting candidate.

- The C++ library is a *good* porting candidate.

- The Python3 library is a *bad* porting candidate.

The Java library drags along a lot of framework. In addition to little value add (from my perspective), I fear the additional complexity introduced by the framework would result in performance problems.

The C# and C++ libraries exhibit the same architecture. I think the C# implementation is more elegant and simpler to implement. I think the C++ implementation offers higher performance and lower memory consumption, though it likely requires more coding.

While you might arrive at a different conclusion, based on performance and better familiarity with C++, I chose the C++ library as the *primary* library to seed the development of a Java device library for the RoboClaw. Of course, you are not restricted to leveraging just one library, and in fact, I'll also use some aspects of the C# library.

The rest of this chapter describes the porting process using diozero `SerialDevice` as the low level. Before continuing, you should review, if necessary, the material in Chapter 7 covering the Raspberry Pi serial I/O capability and the extensive diozero serial device support.

Porting Issues

With a device library to port identified, you should now give some thought to some general issues that arise when porting from any language and some that arise when porting from C/C++.

Device Library Interface

A very important issue is the interface *your* Java device library exposes. There are three interrelated aspects to consider:

- *Source* refers to what interface model guides your interface.

- *Scope* refers to how much of the device capabilities your interface exposes. A device can do more than your project requires.

- *Granularity* refers to how much of a capability or task is accomplished in a single call to the interface.

There are likely many sources to guide your interface definition, but the most important I think are

- The device itself

- An existing device library

- Your requirements

My experience suggests the first and second sources generally align. In other words, a device library interface exposes the same interface the device itself exposes, at least to a large degree. Thus, they have the same scope (often everything) and the same granularity. This makes sense because the developer of an existing device library is highly motivated to do as little work as possible to expose as much function as possible with as much flexibility as possible, and of course, that developer cannot know *your* requirements.

There are sometimes exceptions to the broad generalization about the first and second sources. Sometimes the device interface is overly granular, for example, you have to write to multiple registers to accomplish a single task. In such cases, a device library might hide some details of the device itself and expose a larger-grained interface, reducing "busy work" on the part of the library user. Sometimes the developer of an existing device library gets "lazy" and exposes a subset of the device capabilities.

The third source makes the reasonable assumption that you have some sort of interface in mind that represents the capabilities you need independent of a specific device that offers those capabilities. I assert that in most cases, your *ideal* interface will be larger grained than that of the device or an existing device library. In some, maybe even most cases, your interface will be smaller in scope.

So, how do you proceed? In my opinion, if you find an existing device library to port, it should be the major guide for your library interface. Clearly you might have to subset it if you only need a subset of the device capabilities (guided by your requirements). You can make reasonably minor tweaks to reduce granularity. You may have to extend the interface where you find a needed capability missing. But in general, mimicking an existing interface with an implementation behind it will lead to less development time and a more flexible result. If you need a larger-grained interface, you can create a wrapper on top of the ported interface based on your requirements.

If you don't find an existing library worth porting, the proper guidance is less clear. If you expect to use the device in only one project, the best source is probably your requirements. If you expect to use the device in many projects, flexibility might be beneficial, and the device itself is likely the best source. Your mileage may vary!

For the RoboClaw, reasonable device libraries exist, so it makes sense to use them as a model. With 130+ commands, it seems likely that only a subset of the device capability is needed, so the new library will implement only a subset of the existing libraries. Since the RoboClaw is so sophisticated, the granularity of the new interface will be identical to the existing libraries.

A related question is whether to separate the library interface from the implementation of the interface. The primary motivation for separation is whether or not you plan to have several "providers" of the interface. Usually the answer is "no," but your project may be different.

Device Instances

Should your device library support only one instance of the device or multiple instances? Will an instance be used only by a single thread or shared among multiple threads? As mentioned in Chapter 7, this question forces consideration of Java concurrency, a subject beyond the scope of this book.

In the context of the RoboClaw, a four-wheel drive robot would clearly require *two* devices, and a six-wheel drive robot would require *three* devices. Thus, multiple instances of the device can exist in a project. If you use multi-unit mode, it is possible to send commands to multiple devices via a single serial connection (see section *Multi-Unit Packet Serial Wiring* in the **User Manual**); this accounts for the address parameter in the interface-level methods of the C++ library. Conversely, the C# library does not allow an address parameter in the interface-level methods, so it cannot support multi-unit mode. In any case, the expectation is to use the RoboClaw USB connection, which eliminates multi-unit mode, leading to a library (class) instance per device. The Raspberry Pi OS prevents multiple *processes* from sharing a device. I cannot find a rational reason to allow more than one thread to use a library instance, so concurrency should be moot.

Chapter 7 discusses an interesting conundrum regarding multiple instances of the same USB device. Using only the *USB device identity*, it is impossible to distinguish between multiple instances of a RoboClaw; you must be able to distinguish, for example, the controller for the front wheels from the controller for the back wheels. So how can you distinguish two different RoboClaws? The **User Manual** states that when connected via USB, a RoboClaw can respond to an address 0x80–0x87. The address to which a RoboClaw responds gets set using the Basicmicro *Motion Studio* configuration tool (see the **User Manual**). I determined via testing, and confirmed with Basicmicro technical support, that when you send a command over USB to the wrong address, the RoboClaw simply *does not respond*. Thus, you must be careful about attempting to read any expected response since the diozero `SerialDevice` only implements blocking reads with no timeout. This is important because the device library should offer a way to verify the *device instance ID* of the RoboClaw attached to a particular USB port, implementing the second phase of identity verification mentioned in Chapter 7.

Verbatim vs. Cleansing Port

An interesting issue is what and how much *voluntary* change you make to the code you port. There are a few aspects of this issue.

Think about naming. Do you use, to the extent possible, constant names, variable names, method names, etc., as defined in the existing library, or "cleanse" them? Cleansing could be as simple as following Java naming conventions. Or it could be changing names to be friendlier to you or other users of your device library.

Think about design changes. Do you maintain, to the extent possible, the existing design or enhance it where possible, perhaps to improve performance, or be more Java-like?

In the context of the RoboClaw, due to the need to generate a CRC, some mid-level methods in `RoboClaw.cpp` add a byte to the CRC, then write the byte, and then repeat for additional bytes. There is obviously avoidable overhead in that design. For situations of this sort, I try to follow advice given to me a long time ago: "First make it work, then make it work fast."

There are other examples. Note that neither `Roboclaw.cs` nor `RoboClaw.cpp` introduced "data classes" for dealing with parameters or returned data, a practice that is common in Java. I believe the reason is that both C# and C++ allow pointers or references to primitive types, something that is not possible in Java. For example, when a method in `RoboClaw.cpp` needs to return multiple variables that are primitive types, it can do so using pointers to those variables. If the variables to return are all the same type, in Java you could use an array; if they are not all the same type, in Java you have two choices: you can use multiple arrays, or you can define a new class.

Most of the interface-level methods in RoboClaw.cpp and all of them in Roboclaw.cs return a boolean indicating the success or failure of device read and write operations. This of course eliminates the ability to return data other than via parameters. In a typical Java library, exceptions would be used in place of a status return, making it possible to return data (though only a primitive type, an array, or a data class).

For this issue, it is obvious that anything you do beyond the basic necessities adds to the work and time needed to complete the port to Java. But, as I hinted earlier, sometimes it can be beneficial to "cleanse" or "enhance" the existing library, especially if you can verify performance benefits, expect others to use the library, or if you expect to use the library in multiple projects over a long time period. Only you can decide what is right for your project.

Porting Approach

I want to discuss some development philosophy for device libraries (and other development activities). I think there are two fundamental approaches: *breadth first* and *depth first*. Breadth first means that once you've done the interface analysis, you "just get going." Applied to the RoboClaw libraries described earlier, you first implement the constructor(s). Then you implement the low-level methods (enhancing as necessary when there is no match with diozero capabilities). Then you implement the mid-level methods. Then you implement the necessary interface-level methods. Then you start debugging the whole thing.

Depth first means you do a bit more analysis of the interface to identify one or two "easy" interface-level methods and the mid-level and low-level methods they need. Then you implement what I call the *core*, which refers to the minimal code that supports meaningful testing with a depth-first approach. That means a constructor and the "call stacks" for the chosen interface-level methods. Then you start debugging. Once the core works, you can pick more interface-level methods and repeat.

Breadth first has the advantage of being able to be more holistic at any level; thus, you likely end up making fewer design tweaks. On the other hand, if you do make a mistake, you may not find it till you've written a lot of code. Depth first has the advantage of narrowing the scope of the initial coding and getting to working code more quickly. On the other hand, you might find that when you tackle the next "call stack," you have to do more tweaking than with breadth first.

I generally prefer depth first, but especially prefer depth first when porting. The incremental nature of the approach makes it much easier to achieve early success (a big psychological boost), test techniques for dealing with language differences, and verify design decisions. After initial success, I sometimes keep going depth first and sometimes switch to breadth first.

Of course, you don't have to strictly follow either of the two approaches. Variations are feasible and possibly better.

Play with the Device

I need to mention an activity that applies whether porting an existing device library or developing a device library from scratch – *playing* with the device. By playing, I mean ignoring formal development steps and just interacting with the device to give you the confidence to proceed with formal development. Playing is especially useful when using an unfamiliar form of base I/O.

To play, the device must offer some very simple functions, for example, reading a known value, without a lot of configuration, etc., to enable it. You don't need to define formal constants for artifacts like commands, registers, etc. You don't necessarily worry about good names for classes, variables, etc. You probably write just a few lines of code in a main class.

You can play any time after you understand the device sufficiently to do so. That generally means after you've read some or all of the relevant documentation. So, you can play before you look for existing device libraries, before you do interface analysis, or before you start library development. In some cases, you might play even after you've started library development, though this would usually be to play with something complex rather than something simple.

If you look at the material for the RoboClaw, you probably realize it *does not* lend itself to play. The presence of a CRC eliminates any very simple interactions. So, sadly, we'll have to start formal development. However, we will be able to play with devices used in later chapters.

Device Library Development

How to start building the new device library? I recommend first choosing the interface-level commands. Study the **User Manual** to determine what commands you need to meet the requirements of your project.

Table 8-1 shows the names and codes of the commands (both from the **User Manual**) I will implement, as well as the corresponding method names used in RoboClaw.cpp. The commands listed are those I used in my autonomous rover; as you can see, I used only 12 of the 130+ commands!

Table 8-1. *RoboClaw commands used*

Command name	Code	Method name
Set Velocity PID Constants M1	28	SetM1VelocityPID
Set Velocity PID Constants M2	29	SetM2VelocityPID
Read Motor 1 Velocity PID and QPPS Settings	55	ReadM1VelocityPID
Read Motor 2 Velocity PID and QPPS Settings	56	ReadM2VelocityPID
Buffered Drive M1 / M2 With Signed Speed, Accel And Distance	46	SpeedAccelDistanceM1M2
Drive M1 / M2 With Signed Speed	37	SpeedM1M2
Drive M1 / M2 With Signed Speed And Acceleration	40	SpeedAccelM1M2
Buffered Drive M1 / M2 With Signed Speed And Distance	43	SpeedDistanceM1M2
Read Encoder Count/Value M1	16	ReadEncM1
Read Encoder Counters	78	ReadEncoders
Reset Quadrature Encoder Counters	20	ResetEncoders
Read Main Battery Voltage Level	24	ReadMainBatteryVoltage

Next, you should determine the mid-level (and low-level, if applicable) methods called by the interface-level methods. Table 8-2 shows the mid-level methods for the commands listed in Table 8-1. The results in Table 8-2 are quite interesting. The 12 commands require only 4 mid-level methods! Accepting a small performance degradation allows you to eliminate the use of Read4_1 by using ReadEncoders instead of ReadEncM1. If you are willing to forgo knowing the main battery voltage, you can eliminate the use of Read_2 as well.

Table 8-2. *RoboClaw.cpp mid-level methods called by interface-level methods (commands)*

Mid-level method	Interface-level method
write_n	SetM1VelocityPID, SetM2VelocityPID, SpeedAccelDistanceM1M2, SpeedM1M2, SpeedAccelM1M2, SpeedDistanceM1M2, ResetEncoders
read_n	ReadM1VelocityPID, ReadM2VelocityPID, ReadEncoders
Read4_1	ReadEncM1
Read_2	ReadMainBatteryVoltage

In my opinion, dropping ReadEncM1 is acceptable. If performance issues arise, you can implement it later. There is a subtle trade-off, however. The encoder counts are 32-bit *unsigned* values. ReadEncM1 returns a status byte in addition to the count; status indicates the sign of the count. ReadEncoders does not return any status, so the caller must have the knowledge of motor direction (forward/backward) to interpret the counts correctly.

Dropping ReadMainBatteryVoltage is a very different story. I've killed a few LiPo batteries due to over-draining them, so I think frequent checking of the main battery voltage is prudent, and supporting the command is worth the extra work.

Next, you should choose one or two simple interface-level methods (in this case, commands) for the core, as mandated by a depth-first approach. It is of course best to choose from those methods/commands you expect to use in your project. One reasonable exception to that guideline is if none of the methods you need are simple; then it can be a good idea to choose something simple to start, even if you don't plan on using it later.

Table 8-2 can help you make choices for the RoboClaw. The table shows that implementation of write_n and read_n provides a lot of value. Four methods using write_n drive the motors; they are not good candidates for the core. Two methods write the velocity PID values, so these are candidates but require a lot of data. ResetEncoders looks like the best candidate; however, since the motors won't be running, testing it is problematic.

Table 8-2 shows two methods using read_n read the velocity PID values; these are candidates but require a lot of data. ReadEncoders looks like the best candidate; however, as with ResetEncoders, testing it is problematic. Reading the main voltage battery is very simple, so it is a candidate, but does not provide the value of implementing a method using read_n.

Looking at the **User Manual** and RoboClaw.cpp, you can find there are commands to set the value of the individual encoders, and they use write_n! So, a very nice pair of commands to test both reading and writing data would be command 78 in Table 8-1, which uses read_n, and command 22 ("Set Quadrature Encoder 1 Value," SetEncM1) which uses write_n.

RoboClaw Class

Now you can begin the coding of the core. As with any new diozero-based project, you must create a new NetBeans project, package, and class; then configure the project for remote development on your Raspberry Pi; and then configure the project to use diozero. See Chapter 7 for a summary of the steps and Chapters 5 and 6 for details. I'll call my project **RoboClaw**, my package org.gaf.roboclaw, and my class RoboClaw.

After you've created RoboClaw, you should ensure that it implements AutoCloseable to follow the safety net guidelines in Chapter 7. Since the RoboClaw drives motors autonomously, it is prone to the sort of unpleasant situations described in that chapter; thus, you should enable the Java shutdown safety net in any application using RoboClaw.

Next, you should deal with the RoboClaw command codes. RoboClaw.h (C++ download) has an enum defining command codes. Roboclaw.cs (C# download) has an inner class defining command codes. I think both follow a best practice of consolidating command type codes in one place rather than scattering the codes in the interface-level methods. The inner class (Commands) is more Java friendly, and the code names are identical to those in RoboClaw.cpp. Thus, it is quite convenient to simply copy the inner class. I shall only copy the command codes for the 13 commands mentioned earlier, just to keep code listings short; you should simply comment out those you don't need in case you need them later (as I've done for code 16). Recognize that I used a verbatim approach; I left Commands a normal class rather than using a Java enum, and I used the existing command code names, even though they don't adhere to generally accepted naming conventions used in Java. After you copy the inner class from Roboclaw.cs, you must change "public const" found in Roboclaw. cs to "static final", but that is really easy in NetBeans.

Note   Not all the commands described in the **User Manual** have codes defined in RoboClaw.h or Roboclaw.cs. I learned from Basicmicro technical support that most of the missing commands are intended for use only by their Motion Studio application. It is extremely unlikely you will need any of the missing commands.

Listing 8-1 shows the initial code for RoboClaw, including the Commands inner class.

Listing 8-1. RoboClaw class

```
package org.gaf.roboclaw;

public class RoboClaw implements AutoCloseable {

    private class Commands {
//        static final int GETM1ENC = 16;
        static final int RESETENC = 20;
        static final int SETM1ENCCOUNT = 22;
        static final int GETMBATT = 24;
        static final int SETM1PID = 28;
        static final int SETM2PID = 29;
        static final int MIXEDSPEED = 37;
        static final int MIXEDSPEEDACCEL = 40;
        static final int MIXEDSPEEDDIST = 43;
        static final int MIXEDSPEEDACCELDIST = 46;
        static final int READM1PID = 55;
        static final int READM2PID = 56;
        static final int GETENCODERS = 78;
    }
```

Note   The source code listings *do not* include Javadoc or comments
(for the most part). The source code in the book's code repository
includes both. *You should* include both when you port or write code!

Constructor Analysis and Implementation

There are generally a lot of considerations relevant to the implementation
of a device library constructor. This subsection discusses some relevant to
the RoboClaw as a USB serial device.

Identity

As discussed earlier, it is possible that multiple instances of a RoboClaw exist in a project. Further, each RoboClaw should be assigned a unique *device address* (0x80–0x87); the device address in effect is the device instance ID mentioned in Chapter 7. This means the constructor should have a device address parameter. Setting the device address on the constructor has an important side effect: the interface-level commands *do not need an address parameter*!

Per the discussion earlier, the device library should support verification of the device instance ID. Should identity verification be done in the constructor or externally? I personally think the best choice is externally. I'll show you how to do it later in this chapter.

Caution   Remember that a USB connection *does not* support the RoboClaw's multi-unit mode. This allows a design with a class instance per unit and no address on interface-level methods. For multi-unit mode, the proper design requires a single class instance supporting all units and a unit address on each interface-level method.

Serial Characteristics

In general, for a serial device, it is worth considering several characteristics of a serial connection that may require tailoring, at least if you can control both sides of the connection. Examples include baud rate, parity bits, and stop bits.

According to the RoboClaw **User Manual**, with a USB connection there is no need to include a baud rate on the constructor, as the device runs as fast as possible. Further, the other serial characteristics don't change, so there is no need for them in the constructor. In fact, the serial characteristics match the defaults for SerialDevice, so the simplest form can be used.

Both RoboClaw.cpp and Roboclaw.cs make provisions for a read timeout. Since SerialDevice does not support timeout, there is no need for the constructor to have a timeout parameter.

Additional Considerations

Listing 8-2 shows the RoboClaw constructor and the close method mandated by AutoCloseable. Since the constructor must create an instance of SerialDevice, you must supply a device file to the RoboClaw constructor. Since we want to support multiple devices, you must supply an address parameter as well. Note that RoboClaw.h defines a variable for the serial port used to communicate with the RoboClaw. Similarly, you need a class variable to refer to the instance of SerialDevice you create in the constructor.

SerialDevice constructors throw the unchecked RuntimeIOException. I've decided to catch it and then throw the checked IOException to ensure explicit knowledge of failure. You may decide to do something different.

Listing 8-2. RoboClaw constructor and close method

```
import com.diozero.api.SerialDevice;
import com.diozero.util.RuntimeIOException;
import java.io.IOException;

private final SerialDevice device;
private final int address;
```

```java
public RoboClaw(String deviceFile,
        int deviceAddress)
    throws IOException {
    try {
        this.device = new
            SerialDevice(deviceFile);
        this.address = deviceAddress;
    } catch (RuntimeIOException ex) {
        throw new IOException(ex.getMessage());
    }
}

@Override
public void close() {
    if (this.device != null) {
        // stop the motors, just in case
        speedM1M2(0, 0);
        // close SerialDevice
        this.device.close();
        this.device = null;
    }
}
```

The RoboClaw, as an autonomous motor controller, offers a good example of the potential for "unpleasant consequences," discussed in Chapter 7, related to the unchecked RuntimeIOException or other conditions. The motors could be running when a condition occurs. Thus, RoboClaw.close must ensure the motors get stopped. The simplest RoboClaw command to do that is "SpeedM1M2" mentioned in Table 8-1, so the close method uses the Java implementation of the method, speedM1M2. Of course, that method is not yet implemented, so you will need to comment the statement until you implement the method. Per Chapter 7, close also calls SerialDevice.close and guards against being called multiple times.

Mid-level Methods Analysis

Now you must look at the implementation of write_n and read_n to determine what low-level methods they call. The write_n implementation is quite straightforward. It writes what amounts to an array of bytes representing the address, command code, and command parameters, calculates the CRC while doing so, then writes the CRC, and then reads the return status to verify the transmission. The implementation requires the CRC-related methods, a "write byte" method and a "read byte with timeout" method.

The read_n implementation writes the address and command bytes, updating the CRC. It then reads a given number of four-byte integers one byte at a time, while updating the CRC for each byte. It finally reads the two-byte CRC and checks it. The implementation requires the CRC-related methods, a "write byte" method and a "read byte with timeout" method. Note that read_n also uses a flush method; that capability seems to be unique to the Arduino. The diozero SerialDevice does not support it, nor does any other available Java library; I shall ignore it.

There is a fortuitous equality in the low-level requirements for the two mid-level methods. Both require the CRC-related methods (clear, update, get), a "write byte" method and a "read byte with timeout" method.

CRC-Related Methods

I'll tackle the CRC-related methods first. All work on a class variable (crc in RoboClaw.h and in RoboClaw.java). You can copy the CRC-related methods and then make the appropriate changes for Java, for example, for data types; I've also decided to do a bit of cleansing and use method and variable names that adhere to Java naming conventions. The methods should be private. Listing 8-3 shows the code supporting CRC usage.

Listing 8-3. RoboClaw CRC-related methods

```java
private int crc = 0;

private void crcClear() {
    this.crc = 0;
}

private void crcUpdate(byte data) {
    this.crc = this.crc ^ (data << 8);
    for (int i = 0; i < 8; i++) {
        if ((this.crc & 0x8000) == 0x8000) {
            this.crc = (this.crc << 1) ^ 0x1021;
        } else {
            this.crc <<= 1;
        }
    }
}

private int crcGet() {
    return this.crc;
}
```

There are a few things worth noting in the implementation of the CRC
methods. The CRC is only 16 bits (2 bytes). Java does not have a 16-bit
unsigned data type; it is easiest to use a Java `int` to hold the CRC. You
must remain cognizant of that difference throughout the implementation
of the library. A good example of that difference is in the `if` statement in
`crcUpdate`, which must use a slightly different test than `crc_update`.

Low-Level Methods Analysis

The "write byte" method (`write()` in `RoboClaw.cpp`) writes a single byte and returns the number of bytes written. In the Arduino environment, there appears to be no expectation of failure, and so there is no mechanism for reporting a failure. Thus, the mid-level methods simply expect it to work. The diozero `SerialDevice.writeByte` method returns nothing; it can, however, throw the *unchecked* `RuntimeIOException` if an error occurs, as do the read methods mentioned in the following.

The "read byte with timeout" method (`read(uint32_t timeout)` in `RoboClaw.cpp`) requires some thought. Given that `SerialDevice` does not support timeout, the question becomes whether to implement a timeout capability or ignore the absence. It is certainly possible to implement something similar to what `RoboClaw.cpp` does, but it consumes a lot of CPU cycles. In any case, I suggest ignoring the absence unless doing so proves to be problematic.

Note also that `read(uint32_t timeout)` returns an `int` rather than a `byte` (the byte read is in the least significant byte of the `int`). Further, the method returns -1 if the read fails for any reason. The diozero `SerialDevice.read` method behaves identically.

Mid-level Methods Implementation

Before implementing the equivalent of `write_n` and `read_n`, you must examine a couple of other topics. Both methods allow for a *retry* in the event of failure of the "read with timeout" method. Thus, you need a class constant that sets the number of retries. The value is set to 2 in `RoboClaw.cpp`, so I'll use that. The previous subsection showed that the low-level methods propagate the unchecked `RuntimeIOException` to indicate write or read errors. So, exception handling should be involved in the retry mechanism.

write_n

write_n uses the C++ *variable argument list*. The list type for write_n
is byte. However, examining the interface-level commands shows that
macros get used to produce a comma separated string of bytes during
preprocessing. Java does not have a standard preprocessor. The simplest
thing I believe works well enough is to use the Java *varargs* capability and
list individual bytes, or create an array, as appropriate, in the interface-
level methods.

Listing 8-4 shows the Java equivalent of write_n. The writeN method
uses varargs (a byte array) as the parameter, as suggested earlier. It catches
the unchecked exception and causes a retry of the entire operation if it
occurs. MAX_RETRIES is the constant discussed earlier.

Listing 8-4. RoboClaw writeN method

```
private final int MAX_RETRIES = 2;

private boolean writeN(byte... data) {

    int trys = MAX_RETRIES;

    do { // retry per desired number
        crcClear();
        try {
            for (byte b : data) {
                crcUpdate(b);
                device.writeByte(b);
            }
            int crcLocal = crcGet();
            device.writeByte(
                (byte) (crcLocal >> 8));
            device.writeByte((byte) crcLocal);
```

```
            if (device.readByte() ==
                ((byte) 0xFF)) return true;
        } catch (RuntimeIOException ex) {
            // do nothing but retry
        }
    } while (trys-- != 0);
    return false;
}
```

The writeN method uses the SerialDevice blocking read with no "timeout protection." This could be considered risky. I find, however, that frequently it is better to assume success and adapt to failure. In this context, start with the assumption that the device always responds, and if it does not occasionally, then implement a "blocking read with timeout."

Note the inner loop in Listing 8-4 that updates the CRC with a byte and then writes that byte. A potential performance improvement would have a loop to update the CRC and then write the entire byte array. Per the earlier guidelines, that should be a secondary activity.

read_n

read_n also uses the C++ *variable argument list*. The variable argument list type for read_n is the *address* of a uint32_t. Java does not support addresses nor unsigned 32-bit integers. The approach I recommend is to use an array of int and deal with the signed vs. unsigned issue per the requirements of the calling interface-level method.

Listing 8-5 shows the Java equivalent of read_n. The readN method uses an int array as the parameter in which to return results. It catches the unchecked exception and causes a retry of the entire operation if it occurs.

Listing 8-5. RoboClaw readN method

```java
private boolean readN(int commandCode,
    int[] response) {

    int trys = MAX_RETRIES;

    do { // retry per desired number
        crcClear();
        try {
            device.writeByte((byte) address);
            crcUpdate((byte) address);
            device.writeByte((byte) commandCode);
            crcUpdate((byte) commandCode);
            for (int i = 0; i < response.length;
                i++) {
                byte data = device.readByte();
                crcUpdate(data);
                int value =
                    Byte.toUnsignedInt(data) << 24;
                data = device.readByte();
                crcUpdate(data);
                value |=
                    Byte.toUnsignedInt(data) << 16;
                data = device.readByte();
                crcUpdate(data);
                value |=
                    Byte.toUnsignedInt(data) << 8;
                data = device.readByte();
                crcUpdate(data);
                value |= Byte.toUnsignedInt(data);
                response[i] = value;
            }
```

```
                dataI = device.read();
                int crcDevice = dataI << 8;
                dataI = device.read();
                crcDevice |= dataI;
                return ((crcGet() & 0x0000ffff) ==
                    (crcDevice & 0x0000ffff));
            } catch (RuntimeIOException ex) {
                // do nothing but retry
            }
        } while (trys-- != 0);
        return false;
}
```

The inner loop in Listing 8-5 offers another candidate for performance improvement. It too shall be deferred.

Finish the Core

Now it is possible to finish the core. Earlier I concluded that the best test would be command 22 ("Set Quadrature Encoder 1 Value," SetEncM1) to write a value to the motor 1 encoder and command 78 ("Read Encoder Counters," ReadEncoders) to read the value of both motor encoders.

First, we'll work on the Java equivalent of SetEncM1. The **User Manual** says, "quadrature encoders have a range of 0 to 4,294,967,295" (see the description of command 16). Since an encoder count is represented by a 32-bit value, it has to be treated as unsigned. In Java, that means using a long type rather than an int.

Since writeN accepts byte varargs, the parameters and the command code must be inserted into an array. That is easy for the address parameter and the command code. The four-byte encoder count parameter has to be inserted into the array one byte at a time. I decided to create a private helper method to do that so it can be used in other methods.

Listing 8-6 shows the setEncoderM1 method, the equivalent of SetEncM1 with a Java-friendly name. The listing includes the helper method as well.

Listing 8-6. RoboClaw setEncoderM1

```java
public boolean setEncoderM1(long count){
    byte[] buffer = new byte[6];
    buffer[0] = (byte) address;
    buffer[1] = (byte) Commands.SETM1ENCCOUNT;
    insertIntInBuffer((int) count, buffer, 2);
    return writeN(buffer);
}

private void insertIntInBuffer(int value,
    byte[] buffer, int start) {
    buffer[start] = (byte) (value >>> 24);
    buffer[start + 1] = (byte) (value >>> 16);
    buffer[start + 2] = (byte) (value >>> 8);
    buffer[start + 3] = (byte) (value);
}
```

Now we'll work on the Java equivalent of ReadEncoders. In ReadEncoders, the two count parameters are *addresses*. Since Java doesn't do addresses, I'll use a two-element array. Remember that encoder counts have to be of type long.

Listing 8-7 shows the getEncoders method, the equivalent of ReadEncoders with a Java-friendly name. Note the long array must be created by the caller rather than the method.

Listing 8-7. RoboClaw getEncoders

```
public boolean getEncoders(long[] encoderCount) {
    int[] response = new int[2];
    boolean valid = readN(address,
            Commands.GETENCODERS, response);
    if (valid) {
        encoderCount[0] = Integer.toUnsignedLong(
                response[0]);
        encoderCount[1] = Integer.toUnsignedLong(
                response[1]);
    }
    return valid;
}
```

Test the Core

Now it is time to test the core! Testing requires a main method. Where should it be located? There are some options:

1. In RoboClaw itself: This means at runtime, the test implementation gets loaded when RoboClaw gets loaded.

2. In a class in the same package as RoboClaw: This means the test class gets included in the jar file for the device library.

3. In a class in a different *source* package in the **RoboClaw** project: This produces the same results as 2.

4. In a class in a *test* package in the **RoboClaw** project:
    As mentioned in Chapter 5, classes in a test package
    do not get included in the jar file, and that means
    they don't get downloaded to the Raspberry Pi and
    thus *cannot* support remote development.

5. In a class in a different NetBeans project: This
    means the test class gets placed in a different jar
    file than the device library; this provides a clean
    separation of the library and test class.

Option 5 is the best option. Option 4 does not work.[3] Option 1 is the
least desirable of the options that work. I feel option 2 is "polluting" and
error prone as it puts unnecessary classes in the same package and may
not catch access errors. Option 3 is the second-best option. I recommend
that you use option 5 in a real project. I will use option 3 because I am lazy;
I can also assert that sometimes it is useful to have a test class downloaded
with the library.

Following the instructions in Chapter 5, create a new source package in
RoboClaw for the new main class and then create a new main class within
that package. I'll name the package org.gaf.roboclaw.test and name the
class TestRoboClawCore.

What should TestRoboClawCore do? Clearly it must instantiate
a RoboClaw. It should exercise the two methods, setEncoderM1 and
getEncoders. TestRoboClawCore should also deal with identity verification
discussed in Chapter 7.

Identity Verification

Phase one of identity verification is provided by the method
SerialUtil.findDeviceFiles discussed in Chapter 7. That means you

---

[3] Using a diozero remote provider for testing and then switching to the desired
provider for production could make this a reasonable option.

must add the **Utilities** project as a library in the **RoboClaw** project. See Chapter 5 for instructions on how to add the library.

How can you do phase two for the RoboClaw? As stated in the **User Manual** and discussed earlier, all commands to the RoboClaw require writing the command and reading the response. Further, every command contains an address (think of it as the device instance ID). If the command address matches the address configured into the RoboClaw, the RoboClaw responds. If there is no match, there is no response, and an attempt to read the response will fail.

A simple approach to phase two is to issue an "innocuous" command and wait for the response. Unfortunately, the fact that there may be no response requires a blocking read with timeout, which SerialDevice does not support. In addition, all the commands implement a retry mechanism, and there is no reason to retry an operation known to fail again if it fails the first time.

There are several ways to design a solution. I chose one that minimizes code duplication. First, I looked at the commands in Table 8-1. The absolute simplest, in terms of the number of bytes written and read, is the "Reset Quadrature Encoder Counters" command, which requires the mid-level method writeN present in the core (see Table 8-2). Such good fortune! Second, you can redesign writeN to eliminate both the blocking read and retries when necessary. Third, you can implement a blocking read with timeout. Finally, you can create a method that implements the totality of phase two.

Listing 8-8 shows the resulting changes to RoboClaw. The first writeN reflects the changes to the original writeN in Listing 8-4 to allow eliminating retries and the blocking read. The second writeN retains the signature of the original writeN so that interface-level methods don't need to use the more complex signature.

Listing 8-8. Changes to RoboClaw to support identity verification

```java
import com.diozero.util.SleepUtil;

private boolean writeN(int retries,
        boolean readResponse, byte ... data) {

    do { // retry per desired number
        crcClear();
        try {
            for (byte b : data) {
                crcUpdate(b);
                device.writeByte(b);
            }
            int crcLocal = crcGet();
            device.writeByte((byte)
                (crcLocal >> 8));
            device.writeByte((byte) crcLocal);
            if (readResponse) {
                if (device.readByte() ==
                        ((byte) 0xFF)) return true;
            }
        } catch (RuntimeIOException ex) {
            // do nothing but retry
        }
    } while (retries-- != 0);
    return false;
}

private boolean writeN(byte ... data) {
    return writeN(MAX_RETRIES, true, data);
}
```

```java
private int readWithTimeout(int timeout)
        throws RuntimeIOException {
    int count = 0;
    while(device.bytesAvailable() < 1) {
        SleepUtil.sleepMillis(1);
        if (++count >= timeout) break;
    }
    if (count >= timeout) return -1;
    else return device.read();
}

public boolean verifyIdentity() throws IOException {
    try {
        writeN(0, false, (byte) address,
                (byte) Commands.RESETENC);
        return readWithTimeout(20) >= 0;
    } catch (RuntimeIOException ex) {
        throw new IOException(ex.getMessage());
    }
}
```

The readWithTimeout method in Listing 8-8 implements a crude "read with timeout." There are two aspects worth noting: first, it uses the diozero SleepUtil class to avoid dealing with the InterruptedException (see Chapter 7); second, in the event of finding the expected single byte available, the method reads the byte to keep serial communication synchronized.

The verifyIdentity method in Listing 8-8 first issues the "Reset Quadrature Encoder Counters" command to the device address from the RoboClaw constructor using the new writeN method. It then calls readWithTimeout to get any response. It makes a reasonable assumption that any response validates identity.

To formalize the two-phased identity verification for the RoboClaw, I decided to create a new utility method to implement identity verification. Listing 8-9 shows the class RoboClawUtil that contains the static method findDeviceFile. For phase one, the method leverages SerialUtil.findDeviceFiles to produce a list of device files that match the USB device identity. The method loops through the list of device files performing phase two of identity verification, checking the device instance ID for a USB device using RoboClaw.verifyIdentity. Note that the method closes the device whether successfully verified or not. It returns the device file when successful. This enables use of try-with-resources when creating the RoboClaw instance that actually gets used.

Listing 8-9. RoboClawUtil

```
package org.gaf.roboclaw;

import java.io.IOException;
import java.util.List;
import org.gaf.util.SerialUtil;

public class RoboClawUtil {

    public static String findDeviceFile(
            String usbVendorId, String usbProductId,
            int instanceId) throws IOException {
        // identity verification - phase 1
        List<String> deviceFles =
                SerialUtil.findDeviceFiles(
                        usbVendorId, usbProductId);
        // identity verification - phase 2
        if (!deviceFles.isEmpty()) {
            for (String deviceFile : deviceFles) {
                System.out.println(deviceFile);
```

```
                    RoboClaw claw =
                         new RoboClaw(
                             deviceFile,
                                 instanceId);
                    boolean verified =
                         claw.verifyIdentity();
                    claw.close();
                    if (verified) return deviceFile;
                }
            }
        return null;
    }
}
```

Note   Using parameters for the USB device identity in findDeviceFile is probably overkill. The USB device identity could be hard coded in the method.

TestRoboClawCore Implementation

Listing 8-10 shows TestRoboClawCore. The class must

- Perform USB device identity verification using RoboClawUtil.findDeviceFile

- Per Chapter 7, enable the try-with-resources and diozero shutdown safety nets

- Per Chapter 7, register the RoboClaw instance for shutdown, to enable the Java shutdown safety net

- Set the value of encoder M1 using setEncoderM1

- Read the values of both encoders using getEncoders

The RoboClaw USB device identity comes from Table 7-1 where {usbVendorId, usbProductId} = {03eb, 2404}. The device address (or device instance ID) comes from the value I used when I configured my RoboClaw (0x80).

Listing 8-10. TestRoboClawCore

```
package org.gaf.roboclaw.test;

import com.diozero.util.Diozero;
import java.io.IOException;
import org.gaf.roboclaw.RoboClaw;
import org.gaf.roboclaw.RoboClawUtil;

public class TestRoboClawCore {

    private final static int ADDRESS = 0x80;

    public static void main(String[] args)
        throws IOException {
        // identity verification
        String clawFile =
                RoboClawUtil.findDeviceFile(
                    "03eb", "2404", ADDRESS);
        if (clawFile == null) {
            throw new IOException(
                "No matching device!");
        }

        try (RoboClaw claw = new RoboClaw(clawFile,
            ADDRESS)) {

            Diozero.
                registerForShutdown(claw);
```

233

```
        long[] encoders = new long[2];
        boolean ok = claw.setEncoderM1(1234561);
        if (!ok) {
            System.out.println("writeN failed!");
        }

        ok = claw.getEncoders(encoders);
        if (!ok) {
            System.out.println("readN failed");
        } else {
            System.out.println("Encoder M1:" +
                    encoders[0]);
        }
    } finally {
        Diozero.shutdown();
    }
  }
}
```

Prior to running `TestRoboClawCore`, you must follow the **User Manual** to:

- Connect a main battery to the RoboClaw.

- Connect encoded motors to the RoboClaw (though this could be done later).

- Use the Basicmicro *Motion Studio* application to:

  - Update the RoboClaw firmware (on the Device Status screen).

  - Ensure the device is running in *packet serial mode* (on the General Settings screen).

  - Assign the desired address (0x80–0x87, on the General Settings screen); I used 0x80.

- Connect your Raspberry Pi to the RoboClaw via a USB cable.

Note   At the time of writing, Motion Studio only ran on Windows – problematic for non-Windows users. I use macOS. Fortunately, I had Parallels (`www.parallels.com`) hosting Windows 8.2, so I was able to run Motion Studio. You can create similar environments for your workstation, or use a cheap Windows machine.

You don't need the motors connected at this time, but it harms nothing if they are connected. Run `TestRoboClawCore` remotely using NetBeans as described in Chapter 5. You should see results that look something like Listing 8-11 (your device file might differ). The core works!

Listing 8-11. Results of successful execution of TestRoboClawCore

```
/dev/ttyACM1
Encoder M1:123456
```

Now for some "fun." In `TestRoboClawCore`, change the `ADDRESS` field to `0x81`. Clearly, phase two of identity verification should fail. Run `TestRoboClawCore` again. You should see the following:

```
java.io.IOException: No matching device!
```

If so, that is good! It means that verification of the device instance ID works both when the device instance ID matches and when it does not.

Complete the Implementation

Success is great, but there is more work to do. You need to implement the mid-level method `Read2` and the interface-level method that uses it, plus the rest of the interface-level methods in Table 8-2 that use either `write_n` or `read_n`.

First, let's analyze and implement Read2. It is similar to read_n in that it provides both data read from the device and a status indicating success or failure of the operation. However, Read2 returns a two-byte unsigned integer that contains the data rather than status and provides the status in a parameter rather than the data.

Look at the interface-level methods that use Read2 and you'll find more inconsistencies. Some, like the desired method ReadMainBatteryVoltage, return an integer and provide the status in a parameter, and some return the status and provide the integer or the two bytes as parameters. To satisfy my curiosity, I looked at Roboclaw.cs and found that it consistently returns the status and provides any data using one or more parameters.

I feel highly motivated to introduce consistency, but it creates some problems. Java does not allow references other than to objects. There are a few ways to deal with this issue:

- Use exceptions to indicate status and return the value(s). That may be too much Java-ism and, for consistency, would impact the work already done.

- Use subclasses to return both status and value(s). This introduces some Java-ism but does not impact work already done.

- Use arrays, even when unnecessary, for parameters. This introduces some Java-ism but does not impact work already done.

I think arrays are the easiest approach. Thus, the interface-level methods will directly return status and assume parameters for returning data.

To make the Java implementation of Read2 consistent with other mid-level methods, it too should return status. Since the Read2 callers have to consider the "two-byte-ness" anyway, I suggest returning a byte array via parameter. This produces a design very similar to read_n (or readN) for the read2 method shown in Listing 8-12.

Listing 8-12. RoboClaw read2

```java
private boolean read2(int commandCode,
    byte[] response) {

    int trys = MAX_RETRIES;

    do { // retry per desired number
        crcClear();
        try {
            device.writeByte((byte) address);
            crcUpdate((byte) address);
            device.writeByte((byte) commandCode);
            crcUpdate((byte) commandCode);

            byte data = device.readByte();
            crcUpdate(data);
            response[0] = data;
            data = device.readByte();
            crcUpdate(data);
            response[1] = data

            // check the CRC
            int crcDevice;
            int dataI;
            dataI = device.read();
            crcDevice = dataI << 8;
            dataI = device.read();
            crcDevice |= dataI;
            return ((crcGet() & 0x0000ffff) ==
                (crcDevice & 0x0000ffff));
        } catch (RuntimeIOException ex) {
            // do nothing but retry
        }
```

```
    } while (trys-- != 0);
    return false;
}
```

Table 8-2 indicates that `ReadMainBatteryVoltage` is the only method that uses `read2`, so we will implement that interface-level method next. Listing 8-13 shows the implementation with the Java-friendly name of `getMainBatteryVoltage`.

Listing 8-13. RoboClaw getMainBatteryVoltage

```java
public boolean getMainBatteryVoltage(int[] voltage) {
    byte[] response = new byte[2];
    boolean ok = read2(Commands.GETMBATT, response);

    if (ok) {
        int value =
            Byte.toUnsignedInt(response[0]) << 8;
        value |= Byte.toUnsignedInt(response[1]);
        voltage[0] = value;
    }
    return ok;
}
```

To test both `read2` and `getMainBatteryVoltage`, add the code shown in Listings 8-12 and 8-13 to RoboClaw. Add the code in Listing 8-14 to `TestRoboClawCore`; I put it just before the end of the try-with-resources.

Listing 8-14. Testing getMainBatteryVoltage and read2

```java
int[] voltage = new int[1];
ok = claw.getMainBatteryVoltage(voltage);
if (!ok) {
    System.out.println("read2 failed");
```

```
} else {
    System.out.println("Main battery voltage: " +
        voltage[0]);
}
```

When you run `TestRoboClawCore`, you should see results in Listing 8-10 plus something similar to the following:

```
Main battery voltage: 120
```

Since the reported value is in tenths of volts, the voltage is 12.0V, which is reasonable for my 3-cell LiPo main battery. You will almost certainly see a different value for the voltage, depending on the voltage rating and charge level of your battery.

The remaining interface-level command methods use either `writeN` or `readN` which have already been tested. Listing 8-15 shows the implementation of the `getM1VelocityPID` method for getting the velocity PID for motor 1. It must provide three floating-point values and one integer. Consistency demands returning a `boolean` for status and using parameters for the four "interesting" values. The only two choices are

- A three-`float` array and a one-`int` array

- An inner class with three `float` fields and an `int` field

Both choices are a bit unpleasant. The latter however demonstrates something new and is definitely more Java friendly, so I'll use a nested class.

The implementation of `getM1VelocityPID` in Listing 8-15 reflects

- There is an otherwise identical method for getting the PID for motor 2.

- The method is not performance critical.

As a result, I've put the common part of the implementation in its own method. This makes it very easy to implement the same command for motor 2, as well as reducing coding and testing.

Listing 8-15. RoboClaw getM1VelocityPID and VelocityPID inner class

```java
public boolean getM1VelocityPID(
    VelocityPID velocityPID) {
    return getVelocityPID(Commands.READM1PID,
        velocityPID);
}

private boolean getVelocityPID(int commandCode,
    VelocityPID velocityPID) {

    int[] response = new int[4];
    boolean valid = readN(commandCode, response);
    if (valid) {
        velocityPID.kP =
            ((float) response[0]) / 65536f;
        velocityPID.kI =
            ((float) response[1]) / 65536f;
        velocityPID.kD =
            ((float) response[2]) / 65536f;
        velocityPID.qPPS = response[3];
    }
    return valid;
}

public static class VelocityPID {
    public float kP;
    public float kI;
    public float kD;
    public int qPPS;
```

```
public VelocityPID() {
}

public VelocityPID(float kP, float kI,
        float kD, int qPPS) {
    this.kP = kP;
    this.kI = kI;
    this.kD = kD;
    this.qPPS = qPPS;
}

@Override
public String toString() {
    return "Velocity PID kP: " + kP +
    "  kI: " + kI + "  kD: " + kD +
    "  qpps: " + qPPS;
}
}
```

Listing 8-16 shows the implementation of the setM1VelocityPID method for setting the velocity PID for motor 1. While it would be possible to use individual parameters for the three float values and single int value, since the VelocityPID class already exists, setM1VelocityPID will use it.

As with getting the PID, you can factor out the common function into a different method. Again, this reduces coding and testing.

Listing 8-16. RoboClaw setM1VelocityPID

```
public boolean setM1VelocityPID(
        VelocityPID velocityPID) {
    return setVelocityPID(Commands.SETM1PID,
            velocityPID);
}
```

```java
private boolean setVelocityPID(int commandCode,
        VelocityPID velocityPID) {
    byte[] buffer = new byte[18];

    // calculate the integer values for device
    int kPi = (int) (velocityPID.kP * 65536);
    int kIi = (int) (velocityPID.kI * 65536);
    int kDi = (int) (velocityPID.kD * 65536);

    // insert parameters into buffer
    buffer[0] = (byte) address;
    buffer[1] = (byte) commandCode;
    insertIntInBuffer(kDi, buffer, 2);
    insertIntInBuffer(kPi, buffer, 6);
    insertIntInBuffer(kIi, buffer, 10);
    insertIntInBuffer(velocityPID.qPPS, buffer, 14);
    return writeN(buffer);
}
```

It is time to test the new methods. Add the code in Listing 8-16 to
RoboClaw. Add the code in Listing 8-17 to TestRoboClawCore before the
end of the try-with-resources statement.

Listing 8-17. More in TestRoboClawCore

```java
RoboClaw.VelocityPID m1PID =
    new RoboClaw.VelocityPID();
ok = claw.getM1VelocityPID(m1PID);
if (!ok) {
    System.out.println("readN failed");
} else {
    System.out.println("M1:" + m1PID);
}
```

```
m1PID = new RoboClaw.VelocityPID(8, 7, 6, 2000);
ok = claw.setM1VelocityPID(m1PID);
if (!ok) {
    System.out.println("writeN failed");
}

ok = claw.getM1VelocityPID(m1PID);
if (!ok) {
    System.out.println("readN failed");
} else {
    System.out.println("M1:" + m1PID);
}
```

Run `TestRoboClawCore` and you should see something like the output in Listing 8-18. Your M1 velocity PID values will likely differ. Again, your voltage will likely differ.

Listing 8-18. Output

```
/dev/ttyACM1
Encoder M1:123456
Main battery voltage:120
M1:Velocity PID kP: 10.167343  kI: 1.7274933  kD: 0.0  qpps: 2250
M1:Velocity PID kP: 8.0  kI: 7.0  kD: 6.0  qpps: 2000
```

After running the test successfully, disconnect the main battery from the RoboClaw and then reconnect (I have my battery connected via a switch per the **User Manual**). This restores the original PID values.

Now for some scary work. We'll implement a command that drives the motors! Listing 8-19 shows the implementation of `speedAccelDistanceM1M2`. The only interesting aspect is the use of `long` for some parameters; as you can guess, this is because Java does not support an unsigned 32-bit integer.

243

Listing 8-19. RoboClaw speedAccelDistanceM1M2

```
public boolean speedAccelDistanceM1M2(
    long acceleration, int speedM1, long distanceM1,
    int speedM2, long distanceM2, boolean buffer) {
    byte[] buf = new byte[23];

    buf[0] = (byte) address;
    buf[1] = (byte) Commands.MIXEDSPEEDACCELDIST;
    insertIntInBuffer((int) acceleration, buf, 2);
    insertIntInBuffer(speedM1, buf, 6);
    insertIntInBuffer((int) distanceM1, buf, 10);
    insertIntInBuffer(speedM2, buf, 14);
    insertIntInBuffer((int) distanceM2, buf, 18);
    buf[22] = (buffer) ? (byte) 0 : 1;
    return writeN(buf);
}
```

To simplify testing, I'll create a new main class TestClawMotor shown
in Listing 8-20. It has some obvious similarities to TestRoboClawCore,
but it only calls speedAccelDistanceM1M2. Of course, to run this test, you
must have the battery connected to the RoboClaw and have encoded
motors connected to the RoboClaw. Note there are two invocations of the
command. Both commands get buffered. The first executes and causes the
RoboClaw to accelerate at 400 encoder PPS^2 to reach 400 PPS and travel for
a total distance of 2400 pulses. Then the second executes and causes the
RoboClaw to decelerate at 400 PPS^2 to reach 0 PPS.

You might be curious about the sleep statement. The
speedAccelDistanceM1M2 method simply sends the command to
the RoboClaw and returns; thus, the method returns long before the
movement initiated by the command completes. The sleep simply gives
the buffered commands time to complete before the device gets closed.
Read the **User Manual** for more detail on buffering.

Listing 8-20. TestClawMotor

```java
package org.gaf.roboclaw.test;

import com.diozero.util.Diozero;
import java.io.IOException;
import org.gaf.roboclaw.RoboClaw;
import org.gaf.roboclaw.RoboClawUtil;

public class TestClawMotor {
    private final static int ADDRESS = 0x80;

    public static void main(String[] args)
        throws IOException {
        // identity verification
        String clawFile =
            RoboClawUtil.findDeviceFile(
                "03eb", "2404", ADDRESS);
        if (clawFile == null) {
            throw new IOException(
                "No matching device!");
        }

        try (RoboClaw claw = new RoboClaw(clawFile,
            ADDRESS)) {

            Diozero.
                registerForShutdown(claw);

            boolean ok =
                claw.speedAccelDistanceM1M2(
                    400, 400, 2400, 400, 2400,
                    true);
            ok = claw.speedAccelDistanceM1M2(
                400, 0, 0, 0, 0, true);
```

```
        // wait for buffered commands to finish
        Thread.sleep(10000);
    } finally {
        Diozero.shutdown();
    }
  }
}
```

When you run `TestClawMotor`, you should see the motors accelerate to nominal speed, run at nominal speed, and then decelerate to zero (stop), all in a total time of approximately seven seconds. If this does not happen, you may have something wired incorrectly.

Congratulations! You've done all the hard work on porting a C++ library to Java! I've not covered all the commands in Table 8-2, but those not implemented are simple variations of those already implemented. The complete implementation is included in the book's code repository.

Caution   Don't forget that `speedM1M2` is required for `RoboClaw. close` to work properly.

Summary

In this chapter, you've learned how to

- Evaluate an existing device library for porting to Java

- Choose among multiple libraries if you have that luxury

- Identify and assess porting issues and make trade-offs in how to port an existing library and also how much of it to port

- Address the gory details of porting a C++ library to Java

- Evolve a design as new requirements surface with a depth-first development approach

- Create a fully functioning Java library for a complex serial device

Well done!

CHAPTER 9

An Inertial Measurement Unit

In this chapter, we'll examine another device I used in my autonomous rover – an inertial measurement unit (IMU). An IMU is present in many mobile robotics projects, as it helps determine the robot's orientation as it travels from one point to another. The device is the *Adafruit Precision NXP 9-DOF Breakout Board - FXOS8700 + FXAS21002* (see `www.adafruit.com/product/3463`). That name is way too long, so I'll use the term *PIMU* in this chapter.

Logically, you can consider an IMU as *three* devices, as it includes an *accelerometer*, which measures *linear acceleration* in three dimensions (three degrees of freedom); a *gyroscope*, which measures *angular velocity*, in three dimensions (three DOF); and a *magnetometer*, which measures *magnetic field strength* in three dimensions (three DOF). Sum up all the degrees of freedom measured, and you get the nine DOF in the real name of the PIMU. Physically, the PIMU has two devices, the FXOS8700CQ and the FXAS21002C.

In this chapter, I'll cover

- A device that is actually *two* devices, or *three* devices, depending on your point of view!

- Implementation of a device library for an I2C device, using diozero

- Implementing only a subset of device functions

- Porting using a C++ library and a Java library in tandem

- Identifying and resolving various design issues using "data analysis"

- Leveraging diozero to handle device interrupts

Understand the Device

On the PIMU breakout board, the FXOS8700CQ (`www.nxp.com/docs/en/data-sheet/FXOS8700CQ.pdf`) supplies the accelerometer and the magnetometer; the FXAS21002C (`www.nxp.com/docs/en/data-sheet/FXAS21002.pdf`) supplies the gyroscope. This means you have to deal with *two* datasheets! It also makes some design decisions a bit more difficult.

Examining the FXOS8700CQ datasheet shows it to be a rather complex device. Some of the interesting highlights of the datasheet:

- The datasheet is 116 pages, references a few design notes, and includes some sample code.

- It supports I2C and SPI (point to point). The PIMU breakout board only exposes I2C.

- You can turn on the accelerometer, the magnetometer, or both.

- The accelerometer full-scale range is configurable.

- The output data rate is configurable up to 800 Hz (400 Hz when running both sensors).

- The resolution of the accelerometer is 14 bits; for the magnetometer, it is 16 bits.

- It supports a 32-sample FIFO for the accelerometer.

- It can be configured to recognize several types of acceleration and magnetic "events" that can generate interrupts. You have to read closely to determine that there is also a more general "data ready" interrupt.

  - It has almost 120 registers, most of which are for configuration of various functions and events.

  - It supplies an eight-bit temperature sensor.

Examining the FXAS21002C datasheet shows it too is a rather complex device. Some of the interesting highlights of the datasheet:

  - The datasheet is 58 pages, and it mentions "a variety of reference manuals, user guides, and application notes."

  - The gyroscope full-scale range is configurable.

  - The output data rate is configurable up to 800 Hz.

  - The resolution of the gyroscope is 16 bits.

  - It supports I2C and SPI. Again, the PIMU breakout board only exposes I2C.

  - It supports a 32-sample FIFO.

  - It can generate interrupts in the "event" the angular acceleration exceeds the configured threshold. Once again, reading closely exposes that it can generate a "data-ready" interrupt.

  - It supplies an eight-bit temperature sensor.

Both the FXOS8700CQ and FXAS21002C support I2C bus speeds of 100 kHz or 400 kHz. Neither supports I2C clock stretching (used to slow down the clock as needed). Both also auto-increment register addresses for block reads and block writes.

Looking at the datasheet and thinking about your requirements allows you to understand how you need to configure the PIMU to meet your requirements. That means it is necessary to be clear about the functional expectations for the PIMU. For the purposes of this book, I'll assume the accelerometer/magnetometer must support determining the *compass or absolute heading* for the rover mentioned earlier, and the gyroscope must support determining the magnitude of rotation, or *relative heading*, for the rover. Given those requirements, it is clear from the datasheets that there is no need for the "events" from either device, except perhaps "data ready."

Find a Device Library

To find a device library to use or port, I'll follow the procedure outlined in Chapter 6.

A Search for Java Libraries

At the time of writing, the diozero documentation did not include anything relevant to an IMU, nor did the distribution ZIP file contain any relevant classes. However, there was a com.diozero.devices.imu package in the diozero GitHub code repository (https://github.com/mattjlewis/diozero/tree/main/diozero-imu-devices/src/main/java/com/diozero/devices/imu) that contained several classes relevant to an IMU. The package had two IMU implementations: the MPU9150 with an accelerometer, a gyroscope, and a magnetometer and the ADXL345 with only an accelerometer. That said, there was nothing directly relevant to the PIMU.

The interfaces and abstract classes in com.diozero.devices.imu are interesting, especially the high-level ImuInterface and ImuData since they abstract the data acquisition for IMUs. They are at such a high level that I think you should consider using them only after the initial PIMU library implementation.

The implementation of the MPU9150 library (classes `MPU9150Device`, `MPU9150Driver`, and `AK8975Driver`) shows it to be a rather complex device and more different than the PIMU than I expected.[1] There are a lot of good interface design ideas in terms of configuration flexibility, though not all are applicable to the PIMU, and might be overkill based on PIMU requirements for my rover. Unfortunately, the differences between the MPU9150 and the PIMU suggest searching for PIMU-specific libraries before trying to use the MPU9150 library.

A search for other Java libraries for the FXOS8700CQ and FXAS21002C resulted in only one hit for each. Both libraries came from the same Android-based project (see `https://github.com/ekalyvio/CowBit/tree/master/SensorApp/src/main/java/com/kaliviotis/efthymios/cowsensor/sensorapp`).

An examination suggests they are at least reasonable candidates, with a few minor concerns, such as possibly being incomplete, having Android dependencies, having framework dependencies, exhibiting violations of Java naming standards, and unneeded support for configuration of capabilities like the FIFO and "events."

In contrast to the device libraries for the RoboClaw (Chapter 8), there are basically only two levels of device access:

- Low-level methods that wrap Android I2C access methods; diozero methods would be substituted.

- Interface-level methods that invoke the low-level methods.

The libraries take a *maximalist* approach to configuration and allow you to configure *almost* anything configurable. The libraries include the ability to change the power state of the device and to reset the device. These abilities may or may not be useful in your project.

---

[1] One interesting surprise: it appears that the MPU9150, like the PIMU, is actually two devices. The magnetometer is actually the AKM AK8975.

The one additional disappointment from the FXOS8700CQ library is that it works only in hybrid mode, that is, that it reads both the accelerometer and magnetometer; allowing all three modes would introduce some configuration dependencies. I could find no additional disappointments in the FXAS21002C library.

A Search for Non-Java Libraries

Normally, with a Java library found, you'd move on, but I thought it would be good to see what other libraries exist. Adafruit supplies Arduino C++ libraries for both devices. To support the growth of CircuitPython, Adafruit also supplies CircuitPython libraries. Finally, the manufacturer of the individual devices, NXP, provides Android C libraries.

Since Java libraries exist, I see no reason to examine the CircuitPython libraries. On the other hand, I think it is instructive to at least peek at the other libraries.

A Look at the C++ Libraries

You can find the C++ libraries at https://github.com/adafruit/ Adafruit_FXOS8700 and https://github.com/adafruit/Adafruit_ FXAS21002C. An examination suggests they are at least reasonable candidates, with a few minor concerns, such as a dependence on an Adafruit sensor framework and use of single-byte reads.

Like the Java libraries, there are basically only two levels of device access. Unlike the Java libraries, the C++ libraries take a *minimalist* approach to overall function, for example, they

- Define only some of the configuration registers.

- Allow configuration of only the full-scale range of the accelerometer (FXOS8700CQ) or gyroscope (FXAS21002C); all other configuration is defaulted in some manner.

- Always read both sensors (FXOS8700CQ, though the interface allows returning the sensor readings for the accelerometer, the magnetometer, or both).

- Do not support the "events" the device can produce.

- Do not support the use of the FIFO.

- Do not offer methods for retrieving status.

A Look at the C Libraries

Unfortunately you must download the C libraries to view them; you can do so from www.nxp.com/webapp/sps/download/license.jsp?colCode=FXAS2100X-DRVR&location=null and www.nxp.com/webapp/sps/download/license.jsp?colCode=FXOS8700-DRVR&location=null. An examination shows the libraries are possible candidates but have "Linux for Android" aspects that I don't understand and show evidence of a larger framework (I don't understand the details).

Like the Java and C++ libraries, there are basically only two levels of device access. The libraries take the minimalist approach for configuration like the C++ libraries, but also appear to support "events" like the Java libraries. The FXOS8700CQ library has one interesting quirk; it returns data for the accelerometer and magnetometer independently, resulting in two block read operations when one would suffice.

And the Answer Is …

I think it is fair to characterize the device libraries examined earlier as *minimalist* (C++), *maximalist* (Java), or *in between* (C). In truth, I think the "Linux for Android" aspects of the C library obfuscate so much of what is necessary to port that I'd eliminate it from consideration. The choice then is between the *minimalist* (C++) and the *maximalist* (Java).

Given the differences between those device libraries, it is more important than normal to determine how you are going to use the devices in your project. A brief usage description earlier indicated there is no need for most events. That leans toward minimalist. On the other hand, the ability to configure everything sounds quite attractive. That said (and this may be considered cheating), experience with two different IMUs and other complex devices suggests you generally start with a configuration that seems good for your situation, experiment a bit, and eventually settle on a configuration and never change it again. So, the ability to configure everything programmatically sounds great, but is unnecessary in practice. That is definitely a minimalist bias.

Thus, as absurd as it sounds, given the minimalist needs of *my* project, I'll use the C++ libraries as the *primary* libraries to start the port and heavily leverage aspects of the Java libraries.

The rest of this chapter describes the porting process using diozero I2CDevice at the low level. Before continuing, you should review, if necessary, the material in Chapter 7 covering the Raspberry Pi I2C I/O capability and diozero I2C device support.

Device Library Port

Chapter 8 identified some aspects of the Java device library that must be considered before starting to develop code. This section addresses the aspects relevant to the PIMU.

The PIMU presents an interesting challenge in designing the interface. Is the PIMU one device: (accelerometer, gyroscope, magnetometer)? Is it two devices: (accelerometer, magnetometer), gyroscope? Is it three devices: accelerometer, gyroscope, magnetometer?

Clearly, all the existing libraries examined treat the PIMU breakout board as two devices, aligned with the two real devices on the board, the FXOS8700CQ and the FXAS21002C. I'll go with that design point.

If you need to treat the PIMU as a single device, you can create a class that encapsulates the two real devices (somewhat along the lines of MPU9150Device mentioned earlier).

Based on earlier discussions, a Java device library interface should focus on methods to retrieve sensor readings. It should possibly include methods to support some configuration and to read status.

Each of the sensors measures three DOF. Three dimensions are required for aerial vehicles. However, the rover, constrained to travel on a flat surface, requires only one dimension from the gyroscope (the Z axis) and two dimensions from the accelerometer/magnetometer (the X and Y axes). Thus, it makes sense to support an additional set of methods to get only the information needed.

I think it *very* unlikely a single robot would require multiple PIMUs. Thus, there is no need for multiple instances of a library. You could create a singleton class (see www.benchresources.net/singleton-design-pattern-restricting-all-4-ways-of-object-creation-in-java/), or you could make all the methods static, or you could assume that no user would try to create more than one instance. Since I'm lazy, I'll make that assumption, as apparently did the designers of the existing libraries.

Since I'm porting mostly from C++, I'll likely do a fair amount of cleansing. I'll follow, at least mostly, a depth-first development porting approach. Finally, since the FXAS21002C is a bit simpler than the FXOS8700CQ, I'll start with the former.

Play with the Device (FXAS21002C)

Per the suggestion in Chapter 8, we'll first try to play with the device. Fortunately, the FXAS21002C does support a simple interaction that should verify success, namely, reading the "who am I" register. So, we shall play!

Obviously, before you can run any code, you must hook up the PIMU to your Raspberry Pi; see https://learn.adafruit.com/assets/59489 for the proper I2C connections. You should power down your Pi; connect SDA, SCL, ground, and 3.3V; check the connections; check again; and then power on your Pi. You can also then determine if all is well using the command "i2cdetect -y 1" in a terminal ssh'ed to your Pi; in the report, you should see two I2C device addresses, 0x1f and 0x21 (see www.raspberrypi-spy.co.uk/2014/11/enabling-the-i2c-interface-on-the-raspberry-pi/).

To play, you must first take the same steps needed to build a library. You must create a new NetBeans project, package, and class; configure the project for remote development on your Raspberry Pi; and configure the project to use diozero. See Chapter 7 for a summary of the steps. I called my project **PIMU**, my package org.gaf.pimu, and my class FXAS21002C. But, since we are going to do some testing, you then want to create a new package; I'll call mine org.gaf.pimu.test. In that package, create a new *main* class; I'll name my class PlayFXAS.

Listing 9-1 shows the implementation for reading the "who am I" register. As you can see, it is very simple:

- The import allows us to use the diozero I2CDevice to interact with the FXAS21002C.

- Since we can use all the defaults for I2C communication, we use the I2CDevice.Builder to construct an instance using only the address of the FXAS21002C, 0x21.

- We read a single byte from the "who am I" register, 0x0C, and print it.

- We close the instance.

Listing 9-1. PlayFXAS

```
package org.gaf.pimu.test;

import com.diozero.api.I2CDevice;

public class PlayFXAS {

    public static void main(String[] args) {
        I2CDevice device =
                I2CDevice.builder(0x21).build();
        byte whoID = device.readByteData(0x0C);
        System.out.format("who am I: %2x%n", whoID);
        device.close();
    }
}
```

Run PlayFXAS on the Pi, and you should see the following:

```
who am I: 0xd7
```

If so, success! Then we can proceed to library development. If not, …
hmm; check everything, connections and code, and try again.

Device Library Development (FXAS21002C)

We've already done the initial tasks for library development, so we can
start building the core. But what is in the core? Based on the guidelines in
Chapter 8, we should try to read some data. To do so, we need

- A constructor

- Definitions for register addresses and other constants

- A configuration that enables reading something
  meaningful

- A method to read data

259

Constructor Analysis and Implementation

The existing Java device library constructor requires an operational I2C device; it sets up the default device configuration (13 parts) but does not write to the device; that is done later in the library's begin method. The existing C++ device library constructor requires some sort of ID for the larger framework; all the "real work" gets done in the library's begin method, including checking the "who am I" register. So, in effect, both constructors do nothing, not even create an I2C device nor check the "who am I" register. I personally think that makes no sense, so I'll do more work in the FXAS21002C constructor.

Listing 9-2 shows the FXAS21002C constructor. The constructor creates an I2C device and checks the "who am I" register. Once again, I've chosen to throw a checked exception in the case of failure, but you can do something else.

Note that FXAS21002C implements AutoCloseable, as recommended in Chapter 7. Thus, there must be a close method. I can't think of anything unpleasant that can happen with the PIMU, but it is a best practice to make sure any resources get closed.

Note   Again, I'm not including Javadoc or comments (for the most part), but *you should.*

Listing 9-2. FXAS21002C constructor and constants

```
package org.gaf.pimu;

import com.diozero.api.I2CDevice;
import com.diozero.api.RuntimeIOException;
import com.diozero.util.SleepUtil;
import java.io.IOException;
```

```java
public class FXAS21002C implements AutoCloseable {

    private static final int FXAS21002C_ADDRESS =
            0x21;
    private static final byte FXAS21002C_ID =
            (byte) 0xD7;

    private I2CDevice device = null;

    public FXAS21002C() throws IOException {
        try {
            device =
                I2CDevice.builder(
                    FXAS21002C_ADDRESS).build();

            byte whoID = device.readByteData(
                Registers.WHO_AM_I.register);
            if (whoID != FXAS21002C_ID) {
                throw new IOException(
                    "FXAS21002C not found
                    at address " +
                    FXAS21002C_ADDRESS);
            }
        } catch (RuntimeIOException ex) {
            throw new IOException(ex.getMessage());
        }
    }

    @Override
    public void close() {
        if (device != null) device.close();
    }
```

```
    private enum Registers {
        STATUS(0x00),
        OUT_X_MSB(0x01),
        OUT_X_LSB(0x02),
        OUT_Y_MSB(0x03),
        OUT_Y_LSB(0x04),
        OUT_Z_MSB(0x05),
        OUT_Z_LSB(0x06),
        DR_STATUS(0x07),
        F_STATUS(0x08),
        F_SETUP(0x09),
        F_EVENT(0x0A),
        INT_SOURCE_FLAG(0x0B),
        WHO_AM_I(0x0C),
        CTRL_REG0(0x0D),
        CTRL_REG1(0x13),
        CTRL_REG2(0x14),
        CTRL_REG3(0x15);

        public final int register;

        Registers(int register) {
            this.register = register;
        }
    }

    public enum Range {
        DPS250(250, 3, 0.0078125F),
        DPS500(500, 2, 0.015625F),
        DPS1000(1000, 1, 0.03125F),
        DPS2000(2000, 0, 0.0625F);
```

```java
    public final int range;
    public final int rangeCode;
    public final float sensitivity;

    Range(int range, int rangeCode,
            float sensitivity) {
        this.range = range;
        this.rangeCode = rangeCode;
        this.sensitivity = sensitivity;
    }
}

public enum ODR {
    ODR_800(800f, 0 << 2),
    ODR_400(400f, 1  << 2),
    ODR_200(200f, 2 << 2),
    ODR_100(100f, 3 << 2),
    ODR_50(50f, 4 << 2),
    ODR_25(25f, 5 << 2),
    ODR_12_5(12.5f, 6 << 2);

    public final float odr;
    public final int odrCode;

    ODR(float odr, int odrCode) {
        this.odr = odr;
        this.odrCode = odrCode;
    }
}
```

```java
public enum LpfCutoff {
    Highest(0 << 6),
    Medium(1 << 6),
    Lowest(2 << 6);

    public final int level;

    LpfCutoff(int level) {
        this.level = level;
    }
}

public enum PowerState {
    StandBy(0),
    Ready(1),
    Active(2),
    Reset(0x40);

    public  final int state;

    PowerState(int state) {
        this.state = state;
    }
}
}
```

Listing 9-2 also shows the definition of constants for the class. The existing Java class has some nice code that exhibits some "best practices" to use as a model. But you can see that I've done a bit of cleansing; I

- Changed the names as I feel there is no need for "enum" in a name

- Changed access from public to private, where I see no need for access outside the class

- Enhanced some of the enums to make them more useful

  - Added information to Range

  - Modified ODR so that the value can be used to help define the content of a control register

  - Added a value to PowerState to support reset

- Added LpfCutoff to increase consistency in the use of constants

- Removed FifoModeEnum since I don't plan to use the FIFO

Configuration

The existing libraries support various levels of configuration in the interface, with the maximalist Java library allowing nearly everything and the minimalist C++ library allowing only the full-scale range. While the general idea is to create a minimalist library, it is a good idea to determine what is possible and, of course, what is needed. Given the assumption of no FIFO and no events, the configuration registers that matter are

- *CTRL_REG0*, which controls

  - Low-pass filter bandwidth cutoff

  - High-pass filter enabling and bandwidth cutoff

  - Full-scale range

- *CTRL_REG1*, which controls

  - Output data rate

  - Power mode

- *CTRL_REG3*, which controls

  - Full-scale range doubling

What you might need likely differs from what the designers of the existing libraries decided was needed and from what I eventually decided I needed. The rover goals included traveling in a straight line and rotating in increments of 90°. So, any angular changes would be very small or take place over a few seconds. That means angular changes occur "slowly" based on the device's capability, indicating the device should always be configured at its most sensitive, with no need for configuring the full-scale range (or doubling it). Further, since any *real* angular change occurs "slowly," I decided the low-pass filter should be engaged and the high-pass figure always disabled to eliminate "noise" from the mechanical nature of the rover. That leaves only the power mode, which could be used to place the device in ready rather than active to save power; I felt that was unnecessary, and so the only configuration required is for

- Low-pass filter bandwidth cutoff (in *CTRL_REG0*)

- Output data rate (in *CTRL_REG1*)

Quite frankly, even those two configuration options were required only to make it easier to find the optimal configuration for the rover. Once I found what I felt was optimal, I never changed them again. The moral of the story is to think hard about what you need to change and how often you need to change it before you spend a lot of effort allowing change.

Tip   Based on my experience with the PIMU, you will likely have to try different configurations of full-scale range and filtering to find one or more that produce the best results for your project. Conversely, the needs of your project determine the output data rate without much experimentation.

Listing 9-3 shows the FXAS21002C.begin method that configures and activates the device. The method first resets the device and then, per the datasheet, puts the device in standby mode so the proper configuration can be established. The method sleeps after the configuration gets established, per the datasheet (and existing libraries).

Listing 9-3. FXAS21002C begin method

```
public void begin(LpfCutoff lpfCutoff, ODR odr)
        throws RuntimeIOException {
    // reset
    device.writeByteData(
            Registers.CTRL_REG1.register,
            PowerState.StandBy.state);
    try {
        device.writeByteData(
                Registers.CTRL_REG1.register,
                PowerState.Reset.state);
    } catch (RuntimeIOException ex) {
        // expected so do nothing
    }

    // go to standby state
    device.writeByteData(
            Registers.CTRL_REG1.register,
            PowerState.StandBy.state);

    // set the lpf value
    int cntl_reg0 = lpfCutoff.level;
    // set the default full scale range
    cntl_reg0 |= DEFAULT_FSR_250DPS;
    // write the FSR and LPF cutoff
    device.writeByteData(
            Registers.CTRL_REG0.register,
            (byte) cntl_reg0);
```

```
// set the odr value
int cntl_reg1 = odr.odr;
// write ODR as requested and active state
cntl_reg1 |= PowerState.Active.state;
device.writeByteData(
          Registers.CTRL_REG1.register,
          (byte) cntl_reg1);
SleepUtil.sleepMillis(100);
}
```

One subtlety in begin deserves elaboration. When the device gets reset, you'll notice that the method catches an *expected* RuntimeIOException and does nothing, while the C++ constructor does not have to do so. This is because of a difference in Raspberry Pi and Arduino I2C operation. Due to the device resetting during the I2C interaction, the device does not send the expected acknowledgment. The missing "ACK" does not bother the Arduino but causes the Pi lots of trouble, resulting in an exception in Java. Fortunately, the exception can safely be ignored.

Note that in keeping with the guidelines from Chapter 7, any *unexpected* RuntimeIOException gets propagated, including that from SleepUtil. The same is true for other methods in FXAS21002C.

Read a Sample

Now it is time to do the main work of the library, that is, read the gyroscope. However, first, there are a few issues I'll address, some trivial, some quite important.

Naming

The existing libraries call their data reading methods getEvent, which I find inappropriate, given that reading the data is not necessarily a reaction to an event according to the datasheet. In another bit of cleansing, I'll use a different name (readRaw) that I deem more appropriate.

Status

The FXAS21002C DR_STATUS register indicates when new data is available and when old data is overwritten; the STATUS register mirrors the DR_STATUS register with the configuration established in the begin method in Listing 9-2.

The existing Java library *does not* read STATUS when reading data; it *does* include a method to read DR_STATUS and several methods to assess its content. The C++ library *does* read STATUS when reading data but does nothing with it; the library *does not* include a method to read status.

I think the existing Java library approach is the proper one. That said, reading status does not necessarily belong in the core. I'll defer it till later.

Units

The *units* in which data is returned is by far the most interesting of the issues. The device provides **raw** data in units of least significant bits (LSB). To be useful, the raw data must be converted to degrees per second (dps). The datasheet indicates the configured full-scale range of 250 dps produces a sensitivity of 7.8125 mdps/LSB. Both existing libraries multiply the **raw** data read from the device (units = LSB) by the sensitivity to produce **converted** data (units = dps).

This sounds like a good idea since dps units are more meaningful than LSB. I *don't* think it is a good idea. An unfortunate reality of dealing with real-world devices is imperfection. Consider Table 5 in the datasheet. The raw data is subject to "noise" related to temperature,[2] what is happening on the other axes, nonlinearities, noise density, and *zero-rate offset*. In the perfect world, if the device is stationary, and you take a series of raw

---

[2] I think this is the reason the device measures temperature.

readings for the Z axis, you'd expect the series 0, 0, ..., 0. Due to the zero-rate offset, you'd get, for example, 20, 20, ..., 20. Unfortunately, you don't really know what the zero-rate offset is until you work with the device to calculate it. But the various other sources of "noise" come into play as well, so you really get a series of seemingly random numbers!

Because of this reality, we'll produce only raw data for now. We'll look at raw data later to solidify the discussion in this subsection.

Implementation

Listing 9-4 shows the implementation of FXAS21002C.readRaw that reads data from the device. Following the discussion earlier, the method does not read status and returns raw data. The implementation is quite straightforward. It does a block read to get the values for all three axes (a total of six bytes) and then creates integers to return to the caller.

Listing 9-4. Method to read raw data from the FXAS21002C

```
public int[] readRaw() throws RuntimeIOException {
    // read the data from the device
    byte[] buffer = new byte[6];
    device.readI2CBlockData(
            Registers.OUT_X_MSB.register, buffer);

    // construct the response as an int[]
    int[] res = new int[3];
    res[0] = (int) (buffer[0] << 8);
    res[0] = res[0] | Byte.toUnsignedInt(buffer[1]);
    res[1] = (int) (buffer[2] << 8);
    res[1] = res[1] | Byte.toUnsignedInt(buffer[3]);
    res[2] = (int) (buffer[4] << 8);
    res[2] = res[2] | Byte.toUnsignedInt(buffer[5]);
    return res;
}
```

Test the Core

You can now test the FXAS21002C core implementation. Based on the discussion in Chapter 8, you should create a main class in a different package. Because we played earlier, package org.gaf.pimu.test already exists. I'll name the main class TestFXASCore.

What should TestFXASCore do? Clearly it must create a FXAS21002C (see Listing 9-2). It must configure the device using the begin method (see Listing 9-3). Finally, it must invoke readRaw (see Listing 9-4) to read data.

Listing 9-5 shows TestFXASCore. It configures the low-pass filter cutoff at the lowest frequency and the output data rate at 50 Hz. It defines the private method readXYZ that reads all three axes a number of times and prints the value of one axis. TestFXASCore invokes readXYZ twice, immediately after activation and after a delay. The variable axis determines whether readXYZ prints the X, Y, or Z axis (axis = 0, 1, or 2, respectively).

Note that TestFXASCore enables the try-with-resources and diozero safety nets per the guidelines in Chapter 7, as do all other devices and applications in this chapter. Since the PIMU cannot cause harm, there is no need for the Java shutdown safety net.

Listing 9-5. TestFXASCore

```
package org.gaf.pimu.test;

import com.diozero.api.RuntimeIOException;
import com.diozero.util.Diozero;
import com.diozero.util.SleepUtil;
import java.io.IOException;
import org.gaf.pimu.FXAS21002C;
```

```java
public class TestFXASCore {

    public static void main(String[] args) throws
            IOException, InterruptedException {
        try (FXAS21002C device = new FXAS21002C()) {
            device.begin(
                FXAS21002C.LpfCutoff.Lowest,
                FXAS21002C.ODR.ODR_50);

            int num = Integer.valueOf(args[0]);

            int axis = 2;

            readXYZ(device, num, axis);

            System.out.println("\n ... MORE ... \n");
            Thread.sleep(2000);

            readXYZ(device, num, axis);
        } finally {
            Diozero.shutdown();
        }
    }

    private static void readXYZ(FXAS21002C device,
            int num, int axis)
            throws RuntimeIOException {
        int[] xyz;
        for (int i = 0; i < num; i++) {
            xyz = device.readRaw();
            System.out.println(xyz[axis]);
            SleepUtil.sleepMillis.sleep(20);
        }
    }
}
```

I ran `TestFXASCore` with an argument = 200 (use the *Run* property of project **PIMU** to set the argument) and with ODR = 50 Hz and the PIMU *completely stationary*. Listing 9-6 shows the output.

Listing 9-6. Output from TestFXASCore execution

```
-256
-188
-125
-76
-47
...
 ... MORE ...
...
-33
-28
-25
-22
-21
```

I ran `TestFXASCore` again. Figure 9-1 shows a plot of the output (200 values or 4 seconds) starting *immediately after activation*, with the same conditions. Note two important characteristics:

- There is a time period from 0 seconds to roughly 0.1 seconds where the device appears to "warm up" before it produces values around the zero-rate offset value.

- Even after "warm up" has ended, there is still significant randomness in the actual value.

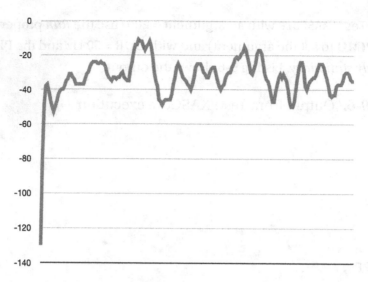

Figure 9-1. *Plot of Z-axis raw values immediately after activation*

Figure 9-2 shows the 200 samples after the data shown in Figure 9-1, for the same period and configuration. There is no "warmup," but it too shows randomness in the values. The mean = -32.3 and is shown by the thick horizontal line; the mean estimates the *zero-rate offset* (for the sake of brevity, I'll use "zero offset" henceforth) for the time period. The standard deviation = 7.9. The diagonal line plotted in Figure 9-2 shows the trend line for the values; it suggests that the zero offset changes over time, even over the four-second period. Not good news.

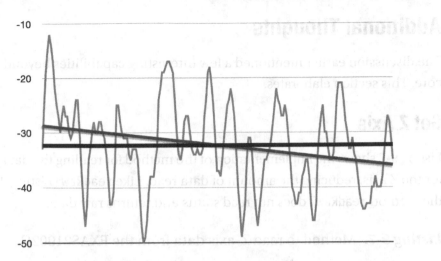

Figure 9-2. *Plot of Z-axis raw value long after "warm up"*

The results in Listing 9-6 and Figures 9-1 and 9-2 show clearly you cannot treat the Z raw value, or its converted counterpart, as "real." You have to do a fair amount of work on any such data prior to believing it is "real." I'll discuss that work later in this chapter.

As you should expect, the X and Y axes behave the same as the Z axis regarding the zero offset and noise. So, you'll have to deal with zero offset and noise for all three axes if you use them all.

All that said, you have data that proves you have a working gyroscope! You just have more work to do.

Tip   I created Figures 9-1, 9-2, and others later in this chapter using a spreadsheet application. I've found it to be a valuable tool when working with sensors to help visualize sensor data.

Additional Thoughts

The discussion earlier mentioned a few interesting capabilities beyond the core. This section elaborates.

Get Z Axis

Listing 9-7 shows the implementation of the method for reading the data just for the Z axis, reducing the amount of data read. Like readRaw (Listing 9-4), the method readRawZ does not read status and returns raw data.

Listing 9-7. Method to read Z-axis data from the FXAS21002C

```
public int readRawZ() throws RuntimeIOException {
    // read only the Z axis
    byte[] buffer = new byte[2];
    device.readI2CBlockData(
            Registers.OUT_Z_MSB.register,
            buffer);

    // construct the int data
    int value = buffer[0] << 8;
    value = value |
            Byte.toUnsignedInt(buffer[1]);
    return value;
}
```

Status

To achieve synchronization between data ready and reading the data, it is mandatory to access the device status. Since it is possible to need information about all three axes or just the Z axis, I'll create separate methods. Listing 9-8 shows the status methods. The private method isDataReady reads the DR_STATUS register and checks the appropriate status bit; a wait parameter indicates whether to wait for data to become ready. The public methods isXYZReady and isZReady call isDataReady using the appropriate status bit for all three axes or just the Z axis, respectively.

Listing 9-8. FXAS21002C data-ready status methods

```
public boolean isXYZReady(boolean wait)
        throws  RuntimeIOException {
    return isDataReady(0x08, wait);
}

public boolean isZReady(boolean wait)
        throws RuntimeIOException {
    return isDataReady(0x04, wait);
}

private boolean isDataReady(int type, boolean wait)
        throws RuntimeIOException {
    do {
        byte status =
                device.readByteData(
                Registers.DR_STATUS.register);
        if ((status & type) > 0) {
            return true;
        }
    } while (wait);
    return false;
}
```

Caution   The wait loop in isDataReady is *not* system friendly. Initially, I coded a 250-microsecond sleep between register reads. However, on my Pi3B+, apparently Java sleeps for a minimum of one millisecond. I felt that was too long and abandoned sleeping. You may wish to sleep. Later in the chapter, I'll show you how to eliminate the need to use isDataReady.

Listing 9-9 shows TestFXASCore_S, a main class for testing status. It is based on TestFXASCore but does only a single set of readings. In addition, the private method readZ uses the appropriate status method to gate reading the Z-axis data, plus calculates the time period between samples.

The FXAS21002C datasheet states that the status bits get cleared after reading the appropriate data. To ensure that the loop in readZ does not immediately see a ready status, the method does an initial read before entering the loop.

Listing 9-9. TestFXASCore_S

```java
package org.gaf.pimu.test;

import com.diozero.api.RuntimeIOException;
import com.diozero.util.Diozero;
import com.diozero.util.SleepUtil;
import java.io.IOException;
import org.gaf.pimu.FXAS21002C;

public class TestFXASCore_S {

    private static FXAS21002C device;

    public static void main(String[] args) throws
            IOException, InterruptedException {
```

```
    try (FXAS21002C device = new FXAS21002C()) {

        device.begin(
            FXAS21002C.LpfCutoff.Lowest,
            FXAS21002C.ODR.ODR_50);

        int num = Integer.valueOf(args[0]);

        readZ(device, num);
    } finally {
        Diozero.shutdown();
    }
}

private static void readZ(FXAS21002C device,
        int num)
        throws RuntimeIOException {
    long tCurrent, tLast, tDelta;
    tLast = System.nanoTime();
    device.readRawZ();
    for (int i = 0; i < num; i++) {
        device.isZReady(true);
        tCurrent = System.nanoTime();
        tDelta = (tCurrent - tLast) / 100000;
        tLast = tCurrent;
        int z = device.readRaw();
        System.out.println(z +
                ", " + tDelta);

        SleepUtil.sleepMillis(15);
    }
}
}
```

There is another *very important* difference in the "read" methods in TestFXASCore and TestFXASCore_S. Between reads, the former sleeps for the sample period of 20 milliseconds (ms), while the latter sleeps for 15 ms and then waits for a ready status. Why sleep for a (relatively) long period? You don't want to waste CPU cycles reading status during a period when the data cannot possibly be ready. Fundamentally, the readZ method sleeps for 15 ms, freeing up the CPU during that period, and then spends around 5 ms reading status waiting for data ready and then reads the data.

How did I arrive at 15 ms? I cheated. I fired up my oscilloscope and monitored the I2C clock signal sent to the PIMU breakout while running TestFXASCore_S. Figure 9-3 shows the results. In the figure, the top signal is the I2C clock (running at 100 kHz). The time span shown (24 ms) includes a bit more than one complete cycle. On the left side, you can see the clock running while reading status and then reading data. Then, you can see the roughly 15 ms delay and then the first part of another period of reading status. So, 15 ms seemed to guarantee that status reading starts before data is ready, meaning a consistent 20 ms between data reads.

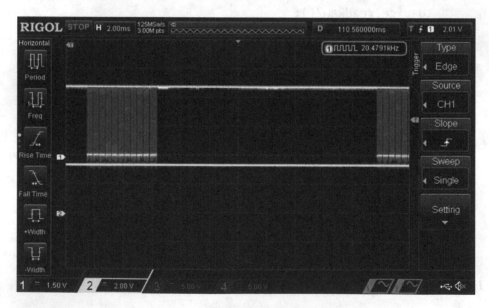

Figure 9-3. *I2C clock signal during TestFXASCore_S*

However, I initially used an 18 ms sleep in TestFXASCore_S. I discovered that on occasion, the vagaries of timing in the multitasking Raspberry Pi OS caused "misses" so that sometimes data was read too late and had been overwritten. While I did not experiment extensively, 15 ms seemed adequate to avoid misses.

In any case, Listing 9-10 shows the first few results of running TestFXASCore_S with the PIMU stationary. The first number in a row is the Z-axis value, and the second is the time period between readings in tenths of a millisecond.

Listing 9-10. TestFXASCore_S results

```
-185, 62
-37, 911
-37, 166
-37, 166
-37, 166
-38, 191
-40, 200
-43, 200
-43, 200
-40, 200
```

You can see that there is something odd going on immediately after configuration for several readings, both in terms of the Z value and the time between readings. This phenomenon was partially observed in Figure 9-1. I am not 100% sure of the cause; I'll address potential causes in the next subsection. In any case, it does suggest either a delay after configuration, additional delay in begin itself, or throwing away several readings before using the device in earnest.

Events After All …

The discussion of status and the results shown in Figure 9-3 caused me to wonder about the "data-ready" event and interrupt produced by the FXAS21002C. Getting an interrupt when data is ready rather than polling should save lots of CPU cycles.

The datasheet shows it is really easy to configure a "data-ready" interrupt (see CTRL_REG2 description). It is easy to clear the interrupt (see INT_SOURCE_FLAG description), though you must read *all three axes* to do so. The interrupt pins from the FXAS21002C are available on the breakout board (see `https://learn.adafruit.com/nxp-precision-9dof-breakout/downloads`).

The hardware is capable of producing a "data-ready" signal that can be sent to a Raspberry Pi GPIO pin. Can the software treat it as an interrupt and invoke an "interrupt handler"? The diozero `DigitalInputDevice` discussed briefly in Chapter 7 supports "interrupts" and "interrupt handlers" (I'm using these terms somewhat loosely)! This subsection shows how to use interrupts in the context of the FXAS21002C.

The proper place to enable interrupts is in the `begin` method. Obviously, you want to enable a "data-ready" interrupt. I decided to use gyroscope interrupt pin 1 (pin GI1 on the breakout board), make the interrupt signal active high, and use the push-pull output driver (avoiding the need for external pull-up or pull-down resistors). That means writing 0x0E to CTRL_REG2. To do this, I added the following constant to `FXAS21002C`:

```
private static final byte DATA_READY_INTERRUPT = 0x0e;
```

To actually write the value, I added the following statement to the begin method between the writes to CTRL_REG0 and CTRL_REG1:

```
device.writeByteData(
        Registers.CTRL_REG2.register,
        DATA_READY_INTERRUPT);
```

Once the FXAS21002C generates interrupts, we need to use a DigitalInputDevice to catch them and call an interrupt handler. I believe that suggests a *composite* device that uses an FXAS21002C and a DigitalInputDevice. I'll call the new class Gyro and put it in package org. gaf.pimu.

To design an interrupt handler, we must consider how the data from the FXAS21002C will be used and how DigitalInputDevice works. For my rover, I want to wait for a sample of the Z axis and get a relative *heading* derived from that sample. DigitalInputDevice introduces concurrency since an interrupt handler runs in a separate thread. Thus, we need to share data between the interrupt handler thread and the application thread. Further, it is conceivable that the application could sometimes fail to consume headings as fast as they get produced, so a shared FIFO queue would be nice. A very convenient way to do this is with a class that implements java.util. concurrent.BlockingQueue. The interrupt handler can queue the heading and the application can wait on a heading from the queue.

Unfortunately, we don't have everything in place to calculate a heading, so initially, the interrupt handler will simply queue the Z-axis raw value of the sample.

Listing 9-11 shows the initial Gyro class. The constructor requires a parameter to indicate the GPIO pin to be used to detect interrupts and a parameter identifying an object that implements BlockingQueue. The constructor creates a FXAS21002C and a DigitalInputDevice configured appropriately for the interrupt signal (no pull-up or pull-down, trigger on rising edge). You can also see the obligatory close method after the constructor.

Listing 9-11. Gyro

```
package org.gaf.pimu;

import com.diozero.api.DigitalInputDevice;
import com.diozero.api.GpioEventTrigger;
import com.diozero.api.GpioPullUpDown;
import com.diozero.api.RuntimeIOException;
import com.diozero.util.SleepUtil;
import java.io.IOException;
import java.util.concurrent.BlockingQueue;

public class Gyro implements AutoCloseable {
    private final BlockingQueue queue;
    private FXAS21002C fxas = null;
    private DigitalInputDevice catcher = null;
    private FXAS21002C.ODR odr;

    private long tsLast;
    private boolean active = false;

    public Gyro(int interruptPin,
            BlockingQueue queue) throws IOException {
        this.queue = queue;
        this.fxas = new FXAS21002C();
        try {
            catcher = new DigitalInputDevice(
                    interruptPin,
                    GpioPullUpDown.NONE,
                    GpioEventTrigger.RISING);
        } catch (RuntimeIOException ex) {
            throw new IOException(ex.getMessage());
        }
    }
```

```java
@Override
public void close() {
    System.out.println("Gyro close");
    if (fxas != null) {
        fxas.close();
        fxas = null;
    }
    if (catcher != null) {
        catcher.close();
        catcher = null;
    }
}

public void begin(
        FXAS21002C.LpfCutoff lpfCutoff,
        FXAS21002C.ODR odr)
        throws RuntimeIOException {
    this.odr = odr;
    fxas.begin(lpfCutoff, odr);
}

public void activateIH()
        throws RuntimeIOException {
    fxas.readRaw();
    queue.clear();
    tsLast = 0;
    this.active = true;
}

public void activateRaw()
        throws RuntimeIOException {
    catcher.whenActivated(this::queueRaw);
    activateIH();
}
```

```java
    public void deactivate() {
        this.active = false;
    }

    private void queueRaw(long timestamp)
            throws RuntimeIOException {
        if (active) {
            int[] xyz = fxas.readRaw();
            long tsDelta = timestamp - tsLast;
            tsLast = timestamp;
            long[] sample = {xyz[2], tsDelta};

            // queue it if queue not full
            if (!queue.offer(sample))
                System.err.println("Queue Full!");
        }
    }
}
```

Gyro.begin is analogous to the FXAS21002C.begin method. In fact, the former uses the latter and simply passes through the configuration parameters.

The activateRaw, activateIH, and deactivate methods deserve a bit of elaboration. There is no reason to continuously read data from the FXAS21002C; it is only necessary when the rover is moving. The methods allow data gathering to be turned on and off. The activateRaw method enables simple data gathering and deactivate disables it. activateRaw registers the simple interrupt handler (method queueRaw) and calls activateIH which reads raw data to clear any interrupt, empties the queue, clears the time of the last interrupt, and sets the interrupt handler status active.

The queueRaw method *is* an interrupt handler. In this simple implementation, it reads a raw sample, finds the time period between this sample and the last, creates an array from those pieces of data, and queues the array. I must admit that I've been a little lazy with the reaction to a full queue; a more appropriate action might be throwing a RuntimeIOException, but I thought that a bit drastic; you should analyze your project to determine an appropriate reaction.

You could reasonably ask at this point "why not print the data in queueGyro, as TestFXASCore_S does?" I'm glad you asked. Initially, I did print, but the anomalies identified in the discussion of the results (Listing 9-10) from running TestFXASCore_S appeared in the results of executing queueRaw. After extensive investigation, I found that printing was responsible for *some* of the anomalous behavior! Thus, I decided to simply queue the data as collected (as would be done in production) and print it later.

Listing 9-12 shows the main class TestGyro used to test Gyro. It first creates a queue; obviously, I chose ArrayBlockingQueue, but there are other candidates that order elements in a FIFO manner. TestGyro then creates a new Gyro, configures it, activates the interrupt handler, and collects and prints 100 data samples.

Prior to running TestGyro, you must connect the PIMU GI1 interrupt pin to the Raspberry Pi GPIO pin you use to monitor it with a DigitalInputDevice. I used GPIO 18. Again, I recommend powering down the Pi prior to making the connection.

Listing 9-12. TestGyro

```
package org.gaf.pimu.test;

import com.diozero.util.Diozero;
import java.io.IOException;
import java.util.concurrent.ArrayBlockingQueue;
import org.gaf.pimu.FXAS21002C;
import org.gaf.pimu.Gyro;
```

287

```java
public class TestGyro {

    public static void main(String[] args)
            throws IOException,
            InterruptedException {
        ArrayBlockingQueue queue =
            new ArrayBlockingQueue(10);

        try (Gyro gyro = new Gyro(18, queue)) {

            gyro.begin(FXAS21002C.LpfCutoff.Lowest,
                FXAS21002C.ODR.ODR_50);

            gyro.activateRaw();

            for (int cnt = 0; cnt < 100; cnt++) {
                long[] sample = (long[])
                    queue.take();
                System.out.println(sample[0] + ", " +
                    sample[1]/100000);
            }

            gyro.deactivate();
        } finally {
            Diozero.shutdown();
        }
    }
}
```

Listing 9-13 shows a snippet of the output from running TestGyro with the PIMU stationary. You can see the first few data values (3 to 4) after device activation are bogus; this is consistent with previously observed behavior. The timing also shows some anomalous behavior. The first time is really just the timestamp as the first reading has no time reference. The second and third readings are off; I believe this is because of the vagaries of when the device has stabilized and when all of the diozero classes are loaded. Subsequent time values look as expected. Additional testing confirmed that the data value anomalies occur only immediately after device activation. The net of this is that the data values and timing in the first few readings after activation *must be ignored*.

Listing 9-13. Output from TestGyro

```
-122, 16167848657463
-122, 510
-75, 800
-47, 200
-37, 200
-37, 200
-34, 200
-31, 200
-28, 200
-25, 200
-25, 200
-28, 200
-33, 200
-35, 200
-38, 200
```

Another important point evident in Listing 9-13 is the regularity at which readings take place, after the anomalous period. The average time between readings is at least as good as when sleeping and reading status to wait for data ready.

Figure 9-4 shows an oscilloscope image captured when running TestGyro. The top signal is the I2C clock. The bottom signal is the interrupt signal from the device. Note that the interrupt occurs at (within the ability to measure) 20 ms intervals, as expected (my oscilloscope measured

49.985 Hz). Further, the burst of I2C clock pulses shows that reading data takes place only after the interrupt handler gets called to read the data for the three axes.

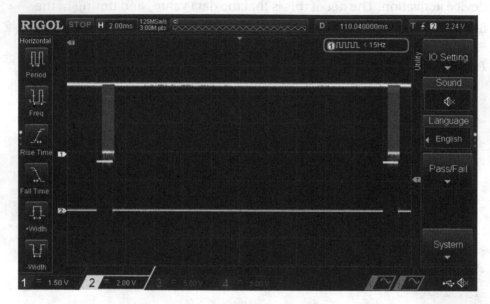

Figure 9-4. *Interrupt signal and I2C clock signal when running TestGyro*

One final subject relevant to interrupt handling is shown in Figure 9-5. The time interval beween the interrupt signal and when the interrupt handler readPrintGyroRaw began reading data was a bit less than 400 microseconds. Not bad! In addition, you can see that it took a bit over 800 microseconds to read the data. Again, not bad!

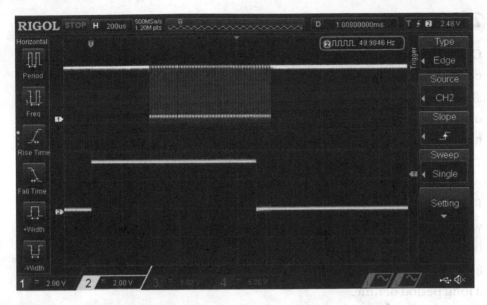

Figure 9-5. *Interrupt latency and data read time*

Note   After completing this chapter, I decided to try to change the I2C clock frequency from the default 100 kHz to 400 kHz per the instructions in Chapter 7. It worked on my Raspberry Pi 3 B+. As expected, afterward, it took a bit over 200 microseconds to read the data vs. the 800 microseconds in Figure 9-5.

Address Zero Offset and Noise

I suggested earlier in this chapter that the raw data is unreliable because of the zero offset and noise. In this subsection, I'll discuss some steps to deal with both.

Zero Offset

Compensation for zero offset would seem pretty simple under ideal conditions. You sample many times and calculate an average, as was shown in Figure 9-2. Then when you get a reading, you subtract the zero offset. In fact, one article I found on the subject (see https://sensing. honeywell.com/auto-zero-calibration-technique-pressure-sensors-technical-note.pdf) does exactly that.

However, Figure 9-2 showed that the actual conditions are not ideal. First, there is high-frequency noise, indicated by the widely differing values around the average. Second, there is low-frequency noise, indicated by the trend line. Despite quite a bit of searching, I could find nothing that accounted for the real-world conditions, other than taking an average over a long period of time.

Figure 9-6 shows a plot of the Z-axis raw data read over a period of 20 seconds. The thick horizontal line represents the average over the 20 seconds (-33.3, with a standard deviation of 6.2). The thick "signal" that meanders between roughly -30 and -37 represents the running average for a period of 2 seconds (100 readings).

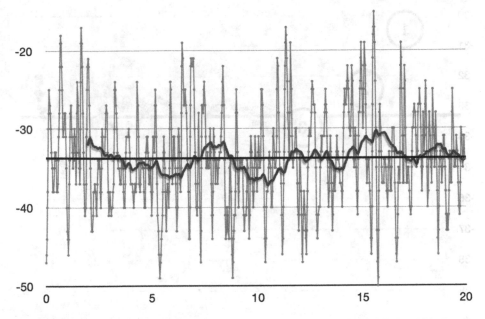

Figure 9-6. *Z-axis raw data*

I wondered how many readings are required to get a good estimate of the zero offset. Figure 9-7 shows the plot of the running average for various time periods. Number 1 shows a period of two seconds, the same as in Figure 9-6. Number 2 shows four seconds. Number 3 shows eight seconds. As in Figure 9-7, the thick horizontal line shows the 20-second average.

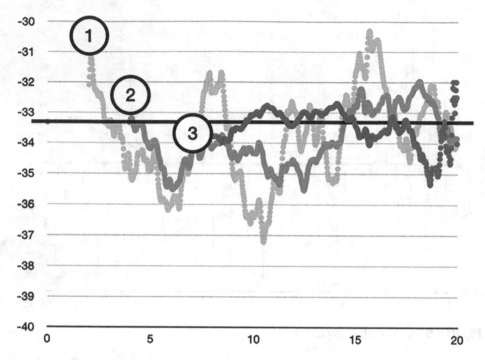

Figure 9-7. *Various average zero offset for Z axis*

The results in Figure 9-7 suggest there is no perfect time period for determining the zero offset. Even an averaging period of 8 seconds produces values that can differ from the longer-term average by quite a bit. And of course, the 20-second average could change in the next 20 seconds. Thus, I claim there are two ways to go about finding the zero offset:

- When bringing up the FXAS21002C, read for a "long" period of time, and use the average zero offset for *all* instances of device use during a trial, which could last hours. It is not clear how long is "long."

- Prior to each instance of device use during a trial, read for a "reasonable" period of time, and use the average zero offset for only that *one* instance of device use during a trial. It is not clear how long "reasonable" might be.

I have to admit that I'm not certain of the best way. That said, for my rover, I used the second.

Listing 9-14 shows the changes to Gyro to address zero offset. You can see some new variables: the accumulation of a number of raw readings, the total of readings, and finally the calculated zero offsets. Note in particular the constant BAD_DATA; it is used to skip the potentially anomalous readings when calculating the zero offset.

The interrupt handler accumulateRaw does the accumulation of a number of raw data samples; it skips the "bad data" while accumulating. The method calcZeroOffset initializes the required variables and then activates the interrupt handler; it waits[3] for raw data accumulation for a designated period of time and then calculates the zero offsets for later use. Note that I left two debug prints in calcZeroOffset to help understand the results.

Listing 9-14. Gyro changes for zero offset

```
private static final int BAD_DATA = 5;
private final long[] acc = new long[3];
private int total;
private final float[] zeroOffset = new float[3];

private void accumulateRaw()
        throws RuntimeIOException {
    if (active) {
        int[] xyz = device.readRaw();

        if (total >= BAD_DATA) {
            acc[0] += xyz[0];
```

---

[3] The sleep is not very friendly as it hangs the caller. To improve the behavior, we'd have to dig further into concurrency.

```java
        acc[1] += xyz[1];
        acc[2] += xyz[2];
    }
    total++;
  }
}

public void calcZeroOffset(int period)
      throws RuntimeIOException {

  acc[0] = 0;
  acc[1] = 0;
  acc[2] = 0;
  total = 0;

  catcher.whenActivated(this::accumulateRaw);
  activateIH();

  // sleep to gather raw data
  SleepUtil.sleepMillis(period);
  deactivate();

  // calculate the zero offsets
  float denom = (float) (total - BAD_DATA);
  zeroOffset[0] = (float) acc[0] / denom;
  zeroOffset [1] = (float) acc[1] / denom;
  zeroOffset [2] = (float) acc[2] / denom;
  System.out.println("Total = " + denom);
  System.out.format("Zero offsets: z=%f ",
      zeroOffset[2]);
}
```

```java
public void activateZO() throws RuntimeIOException {
        catcher.whenActivated(this::queueO);
        activateIH();
}

public void queueO(long timestamp)
        throws RuntimeIOException {
    if (active) {
        int[] xyz = fxas.readRaw();

        long tsDelta = timestamp - tsLast;
        tsLast = timestamp;

        long z =  xyz[2] - (long) zeroOffset[2];
        long[] sample = {z, tsDelta};

        // queue it if queue not full
        if (!queue.offer(sample))
            System.err.println("Queue Full!");
    }
}
```

The method activateZO activates an interrupt handler that applies zero offsets. The interrupt handler queueO applies the zero offsets to the raw readings; it queues the adjusted Z-axis value.

Listing 9-15 shows the main class TestGyro_ZO that tests the changes to Gyro. Since it derives from TestGyro, I'm leaving out the identical package and import statements. TestGyro_ZO operates much like TestGyro, except

- Prior to processing raw data, it spends four seconds accumulating raw data to calculate the zero offset.

- It activates queueO which applies the zero offset before queuing the sample.

Listing 9-15. TestGyro_ZO

```java
public class TestGyro_ZO {

    public static void main(String[] args)
            throws IOException, InterruptedException {
        // set up queue
        ArrayBlockingQueue queue =
            new ArrayBlockingQueue(10);

        try ( Gyro gyro = new Gyro(18, queue)) {

            gyro.begin(FXAS21002C.LpfCutoff.Lowest,
                FXAS21002C.ODR.ODR_50);

            System.out.println(
                "\n... Calculating offset ...\n");
            gyro.calcZeroOffset(4000);

            gyro.activateZO();

            for (int cnt = 0; cnt < 100; cnt++) {
                long[] sample =
                    (long[]) queue.take();
                System.out.println(sample[0] + ", " +
                    sample[1] / 100000);
            }

            gyro.deactivate();
        } finally {
            Diozero.shutdown();
        }
    }
}
```

Figure 9-8 shows the results of graphing the zero-offset corrected data for a period of four seconds with the PIMU stationary. The zero-offset calculated for the Z axis immediately prior to this four-second plot was -33.4. You can see that while the plotted data is centered around 0, there is a significant variability in the individual readings, in effect *noise*. The next subsection addresses noise.

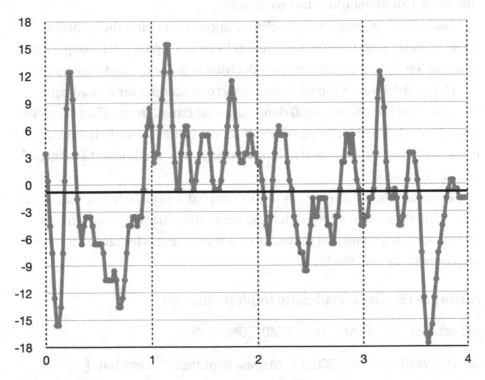

Figure 9-8. *Zero-offset corrected Z-axis data*

Noise

As stated earlier, the data from the FXAS21002C represents the rate of angular change in °/second. In Figure 9-8, the thick horizontal line shows the average for the data = -0.85 (the standard deviation = 6.6). Remember that the data was captured while the PIMU was stationary. But calculating the reported angle from the average by using the sensitivity factor (7.8125 mdps/LSB) and the time period (4 seconds) results in an ending angle of -0.026°, not 0°!

That might not sound like a large error, and for some projects, it is probably acceptable. With my rover, however, I needed to measure angles of a few tenths of a degree over a period of up to 25 seconds. You can see that noise would definitely be problematic.

I decided to implement a *dead-zone* approach to limit the impact of noise. Note that the maximum variation from 0 in Figure 9-8 is roughly ±16, or about 3 standard deviations. So, I decided to make the dead zone ±20.

Listing 9-16 shows the additions to Gyro to account for a dead zone. The interrupt handler queueOD determines whether a zero-offset corrected value is within the dead zone or not. If so, the value is assumed to be zero; if not, it is assumed to be real and passed as is. The method activateZODZ activates queueOD.

There are clearly limitations to this simplistic approach. For example, the earlier discussion showed that the zero offset changes over time. In addition, even a value that indicates true movement is impacted by noise. Welcome to the real world.

Listing 9-16. Gyro dead-zone implementation

```
private static final long DEAD_ZONE = 20;

public void activateZODZ() throws RuntimeIOException {
    catcher.whenActivated(this::queueOD);
    activateIH();
}

public void queueOD(long timestamp)
        throws RuntimeIOException {
    if (active) {
        int[] xyz = fxas.readRaw();
```

```
long tsDelta = timestamp - tsLast;
tsLast = timestamp;
long z =  xyz[2] - (long) zeroOffset[2];
if ((-DEAD_ZONE <= z) && (z <= DEAD_ZONE)) {
    z = 0;
}

long[] sample = {z, tsDelta};
// queue it if queue not full
if (!queue.offer(sample))
    System.err.println("Queue Full!");
    }
}
}
```

To test the dead-zone approach, in TestGyro_ZO, I simply substituted gyro.activateZODZ for gyro.activateZO. Running with the PIMU stationary resulted in a zero offset of -34.8 just prior to the four-second capture period. During the entire test, the corrected data shown was 0, as hoped.

Note   A likely superior approach to the dead zone is to not only calculate the zero offset, but from the same data set calculate the standard deviation and make the dead zone around ±3 standard deviations. I am too lazy to do that, but you might not be. You can also consider making the size of the dead zone a parameter on activateZODZ.

Get Real

All the previous work is great for understanding the FXAS21002C and "making it behave." The work does not, however, produce the *relative heading angle* that can be used to correct heading errors.

The shortcoming is easy to resolve using integration to calculate the current heading angle from the data produced by the device. The calculation involves the sensitivity of the device and the sampling period.

Listing 9-17 shows the additions to Gyro to support heading calculation. There are some new fields that support calculation. The interrupt handler queueHeading integrates to calculate the current heading angle and then puts the result in the queue. The method activateHeading activates queueHeading.

Listing 9-17. Gyro heading implementation

```
private float angle;
private float sensitivity;
private float period;

public void activateHeading(FXAS21002C.Range range)
        throws RuntimeIOException {
    // initialize
    angle = 0;
    sensitivity = range.sensitivity;
    period = 1 / odr.odr;
    System.out.println("sensitivity = " +
        sensitivity + " period = " + period);

    // identify interrupt handler
    catcher.whenActivated(this::queueHeading);

    activateIH();
}
```

```
public void queueHeading(long timestamp)
        throws RuntimeIOException {
    if (active) {
        int[] xyz = fxas.readRaw();
        float z =  (float) xyz[2] -
            zeroOffset[2];
        if ((-DEAD_ZONE <= z) && (z <= DEAD_ZONE)) {
            z = 0;
        }
        // integrate
        angle += (z * sensitivity) * period;

        // put the angle in queue if queue not full
        if (!queue.offer(angle))
            System.err.println("Queue Full!");
    }
}
```

To test heading calculation, I created TestGyro_Heading shown in Listing 9-18. Since it derives from TestGyro_ZO, I'm leaving out the identical package and import statements. TestGyro_Heading operates much like TestGyro_ZO, except

- It uses activateHeading instead of activateZODZ.
- It prints the relative heading rather than the corrected sample.

Listing 9-18. TestGyro_Heading

```
public class TestGyro_Heading {

    public static void main(String[] args)
            throws IOException, InterruptedException {
        ArrayBlockingQueue queue =
            new ArrayBlockingQueue(10);
```

```
    try ( Gyro gyro = new Gyro(18, queue)) {
        gyro.begin(FXAS21002C.LpfCutoff.Lowest,
            FXAS21002C.ODR.ODR_50);

        System.out.println(
            "\n... Calculating offset ...\n");
        gyro.calcZeroOffset(4000);

        gyro.activateHeading(
            FXAS21002C.Range.DPS250);

        for (int cnt = 0; cnt < 5000; cnt++) {
            float heading = (float) queue.take();
            System.out.println(heading);
        }

        gyro.deactivate();
    } finally {
        Diozero.shutdown();
    }
    }
}
```

To test heading calculation, I ran TestGyro_Heading with the PIMU
mounted on a breadboard so that I could manually rotate the assembly
approximately 90° counterclockwise, then approximately 180° clockwise,
and finally 90° counterclockwise (back to 0°). Figure 9-9 shows the results.
Of course, the plot starts at 0°; it reaches 90.8°; it goes through 0° and
reaches -89.4° and finally returns to 0.2°. Given the manual nature of the
rotation, not bad at all!

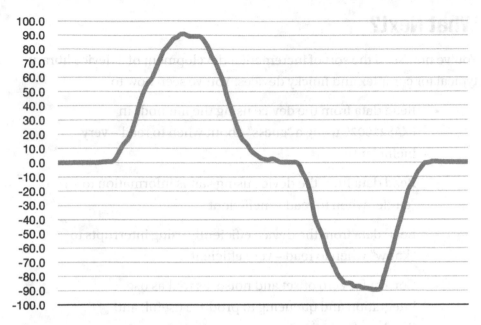

Figure 9-9. Heading angle during manual rotation

Caution   If you've been reading carefully, you probably spotted more lazy coding in Gyro.queueHeading. The method assumes the period between samples is the ideal (the inverse of the output data rate). You cannot really assume that; it is better to actually measure the time period between samples and use that in the integration. Good news: Listing 9-13 suggests that the measured time period is at least close to the ideal. But for the utmost precision, you should use the measured time period.

What Next?

You've now seen the sort of incremental development of a device library typical for complex and finicky devices. You've seen how to

- Read data from the device using the methods in FXAS21002C using a "guess" about when to read – very inefficient

- Read data from the device using status information to "guide" when to read – inefficient

- Read data from the device efficiently using interrupts to "know" when to read – very efficient

- Correct for zero offset and noise, as well as use integration and queueing to produce useful, and timely, information

All that said, you can correctly assert that the library is incomplete. The previous work mostly deals only with the Z axis. Most of the work must be considered in the category of "learning" or "debugging." The choices made for device configuration may not match what you need.

The next steps depend on how *you* want to use the device, and obviously, I can't know that. For now, we'll leave the FXAS21002C and look into the FXOS8700CQ.

Device Library Development (FXOS8700CQ)

For the FXOS8700CQ, I'll create a class FXOS8700CQ in the same project and package as FXAS21002C. We'll develop FXOS8700CQ the same way as FXAS21002C, with differences as needed.

We'll skip playing, as the devices are so similar, and start building the core. We'll first deal with the register addresses, constants, etc., since there are more than for FXAS21002C. See Listing 9-19. Again, the existing Java class has some nice code that exhibits some "best practices" to use as a model. As with FXAS21002C, I've done a bit of cleansing of the constant definitions. I've also eliminated many registers from the Registers enum to reflect the minimalist approach, per the discussion earlier in the chapter.

Listing 9-19. FXOS8700CQ

```
package org.gaf.pimu;

import com.diozero.api.I2CDevice;
import com.diozero.api.RuntimeIOException;
import com.diozero.util.SleepUtil;
import java.io.IOException;

public class FXOS8700CQ implements AutoCloseable {

    private enum Registers {
        STATUS(0x00),
        OUT_X_MSB(0x01),
        OUT_X_LSB(0x02),
        OUT_Y_MSB(0x03),
        OUT_Y_LSB(0x04),
        OUT_Z_MSB(0x05),
        OUT_Z_LSB(0x06),

        WHO_AM_I(0x0D),
        XYZ_DATA_CFG(0x0E),

        CTRL_REG1(0x2A),
        CTRL_REG2(0x2B),
        CTRL_REG3(0x2C),
        CTRL_REG4(0x2D),
        CTRL_REG5(0x2E),
```

```java
    OFF_X(0x2F),
    OFF_Y(0x30),
    OFF_Z(0x31),
    M_DR_STATUS(0x32),
    M_OUT_X_MSB(0x33),
    M_OUT_X_LSB(0x34),
    M_OUT_Y_MSB(0x35),
    M_OUT_Y_LSB(0x36),
    M_OUT_Z_MSB(0x37),
    M_OUT_Z_LSB(0x38),

    M_CTRL_REG1(0x5B),
    M_CTRL_REG2(0x5C),
    M_CTRL_REG3(0x5D);

    public final int register;

    Registers(int code) {
        this.register = code;
    }
}

public enum AccelRange
{
    RANGE_2G(0x00),
    RANGE_4G(0x01),
    RANGE_8G(0x02);

    public final int rangeCode;

    AccelRange(int rangeCode) {
        this.range = rangeCode;
    }
}
```

```java
public enum ODR {
    ODR_800(0),
    ODR_400(1),
    ODR_200(2),
    ODR_100(3),
    ODR_50(4),
    ODR_12_5(5),
    ODR_06_25(6),
    ODR_01_56(6);

    public final int odrCode;

    ODR(int odrCode) {
        this. odrCode  = odrCode;
    }
}

public enum ReadSpeed {
    Normal(0 << 1),
    Fast(1 << 1);

    public final int speedCode;

    private ReadSpeed(int speedCode) {
        this.speedCode = speedCode;
    }
}

public enum NoiseMode {
    Normal(0 << 2),
    Reduced(1 << 2);
```

```java
        public final int noiseCode;

        private NoiseMode(int noiseCode) {
            this.noiseCode = noiseCode;
        }
    }

    public enum AccelOSR {
        Normal(0),
        LowNoiseLowPower(1),
        HighResolution(2),
        LowPower(3);

        public final int osrCode;

        AccelOSR(int osrCode) {
            this. osrCode = osrCode;
        }
    }

    public enum PowerState {
        StandBy(0),
        Active(1);

        public final int stateCode;

        PowerState(int stateCode) {
            this.state = stateCode;
        }
    }

    public enum OperatingMode {
        OnlyAccelerometer(0),
        OnlyMagnetometer(1),
        HybridMode(3);
```

```java
    public final int mode;

    OperatingMode(int mode) { this.mode = mode; }
}

private static final int HYBRID_AUTO_INC = 0x20;
private static final int RESET = 0x40;

public enum MagOSR {
    R0(0 << 2),
    R1(1 << 2),
    R2(2 << 2),
    R3(3 << 2),
    R4(4 << 2),
    R5(5 << 2),
    R6(6 << 2),
    R7(7 << 2);

    public final int osrCode;

    MagOSR(int osrCode) {
        this.osrCode = osrCode;
    }
}
}
```

Constructor Analysis and Implementation

The analysis for the FXOS8700CQ constructor is identical to that for the FXAS21002C, and therefore, the result is quite similar. Listing 9-20 shows the FXOS8700CQ constructor and some additional constants used in the class. Since the class implements AutoCloseable, there is also a close method.

Listing 9-20. FXOS8700CQ constructor

```java
private static final int FXOS8700CQ_ADDRESS = 0x1F;
private static final byte FXOS8700CQ_ID = (byte) 0xC7;

private I2CDevice device = null;

public FXOS8700CQ() throws IOException {
    try {
        device = I2CDevice.builder(
            FXOS8700CQ_ADDRESS).build();
        byte whoID = device.readByteData(
                Registers.WHO_AM_I.register);
        if (whoID != FXOS8700CQ_ID) {
            throw new IOException(
                "FXOS8700CQ not found at address " +
                FXOS8700CQ_ADDRESS);
        }
    } catch (RuntimeIOException ex) {
        throw new IOException(ex.getMessage());
    }
}

@Override
public void close() {
    if (device != null) device.close();
}
```

Configuration

The FXOS8700CQ is a more complex device than the FXAS21002C. Thus, FXOS8700CQ configuration is more complex. Further, I must admit I have little practical experience with the FXOS8700CQ. I learned from previous robots that the abundant rebar in my floor plays havoc with any magnetometer (or analog compass), rendering it worthless in my environment. I experimented with the accelerometer, but the only dimension of interest (X) generated acceleration low enough it got lost in the noise. As a result, I have little to guide my recommendations for configuration other than the existing libraries and perhaps some synergy with FXAS21002C.

The maximalist Java library supports configuration of almost everything, and the minimalist C++ library supports only the accelerometer full-scale range. Again, the general idea is to create a minimalist library. Because of inexperience, I'll make *nothing* configurable. Of course, your requirements might be different. It is worth looking at the datasheet and making some assertions about a reasonable *default* configuration:

- Use 14-bit resolution for the accelerometer and 16-bit resolution for the magnetometer.

- Use oversampling to optimize resolution.

- Use hybrid mode (sample both accelerometer and magnetometer).

- Use reduced noise.

- Do not use any events, except data ready.

- Do enable data ready interrupts (eventually).

- Configure output data rate the same as the gyroscope.

- Use best accelerometer full-scale range.

Listing 9-21 shows the begin method for class FXOS8700CQ that configures and activates the FXOS8700CQ. The method first resets the device and then puts the device in standby mode so the proper configuration can be established.

Listing 9-21. FXOS8700CQ begin method

```
public void begin() throws RuntimeIOException {
    // reset
    device.writeByteData(
            Registers.CTRL_REG1.register,
            PowerState.StandBy.stateCode);
    try {
        device.writeByteData(
                Registers.CTRL_REG2.register, RESET);
    } catch (RuntimeIOException ex) {
            // expected so do nothing
    }
    SleepUtil.sleepMillis(10);

    // go to standby state
    device.writeByteData(
            Registers.CTRL_REG1.register,
            PowerState.StandBy.stateCode);

    // set up high res OSR for mag, and hybrid mode
    int m_ctrl_reg1 = MagOSR.R7.osrCode |
            OperatingMode.HybridMode.mode;
    device.writeByteData(
            Registers.M_CTRL_REG1.register,
            m_ctrl_reg1);
```

```
// set address increment to read ALL registers
device.writeByteData(
        Registers.M_CTRL_REG2.register,
        HYBRID_AUTO_INC);
// set accel sensitivity and no HPF
device.writeByteData(
        Registers.XYZ_DATA_CFG.register,
        AccelRange.RANGE_2G.rangeCode);

// set up high res OSR for accelerometer
device.writeByteData(
        Registers.CTRL_REG2.register,
        AccelOSR.HighResolution.osrCode);
// set ODR, normal read speed, and device ACTIVE
int cntl_reg1 = ODR.ODR_100.odrCode |
        NoiseMode.Reduced.noiseCode |
        ReadSpeed.Normal.speedCode |
        PowerState.Active.stateCode;
device.writeByteData(
        Registers.CTRL_REG1.register,
        cntl_reg1);
}
```

Notice the output data rate set near the end of the begin method. It is set to 100 Hz. Since the device is configured to operate in hybrid mode, the actual output data rate will be 50 Hz, just like the FXAS21002C.

Read Sample and Status

As indicated earlier, for the FXOS8700CQ, we'll create a method to read the *raw* data for both the accelerometer and magnetometer (hybrid mode). We'll also create a method to read the "data-ready" status.

The goal is to read both the accelerometer and the magnetometer in a single block. There are two ways. The first, used in the C++ library, starts with the accelerometer registers and segues into the magnetometer registers. The second, used in the existing Java library, starts with the magnetometer registers and continues into a copy of the accelerometer registers (see Section 14.14.3 of the datasheet). The first way works, but the datasheet does not specifically state the accelerometer and magnetometer results are time aligned. The datasheet states the results from the second way *are* time aligned, but there are some constraints on oversample rate configuration (see https://community.nxp.com/t5/ Sensors/FXOS8700CQ-Time-aligned-accelerometer-magnetometer- measurements/td-p/345298).

The configuration setup in the begin method in Listing 9-21 works for either way. The readRaw method in Listing 9-22 implements the second, time-aligned, way. It reads and returns raw data for all three magnetometer axes and all three accelerometer axes. Note the 18-bit shifting for the accelerometer data; it is needed to propagate the sign of the 14-bit data.

Listing 9-22. FXOS8700CQ methods readRaw and isDataReady

```
public int[] readRaw() throws RuntimeIOException {
    // read the data from the device
    byte[] buffer = new byte[12];
    device.readI2CBlockData(
            Registers.M_OUT_X_MSB.register,
            buffer);
```

```
    // construct the response as an int[]
    int[] res = new int[6];
    // magnetometer
    res[0] = (int) (buffer[0] << 8);
    res[0] = res[0] | Byte.toUnsignedInt(buffer[1]);
    res[1] = (int) (buffer[2] << 8);
    res[1] = res[1] | Byte.toUnsignedInt(buffer[3]);
    res[2] = (int) (buffer[4] << 8);
    res[2] = res[2] | Byte.toUnsignedInt(buffer[5]);
    // accelerometer
    res[3] = (int) (buffer[6] << 8);
    res[3] = ((res[3] |
            Byte.toUnsignedInt(buffer[7]))
            << 18) >> 18 ;
    res[4] = (int) (buffer[8] << 8);
    res[4] = ((res[4] |
            Byte.toUnsignedInt(buffer[9]))
            << 18) >> 18 ;
    res[5] = (int) (buffer[10] << 8);
    res[5] = ((res[5] |
            Byte.toUnsignedInt(buffer[11]))
            << 18) >> 18 ;
    return res;
}

public boolean isDataReady(boolean wait)
        throws RuntimeIOException {
    do {
        byte status = device.readByteData(
                Registers.M_DR_STATUS.register);
```

```
        if ((status & 0x08) > 0) {
            return true;
        }
    } while (wait);
    return false;
}
```

The isDataReady method must check the "data-ready" status of the magnetometer since it controls the timing.

Test the Core

We can now test the FXOS8700CQ core implementation. I'll create a new main class, TestFXOSCore, in package org.gaf.pimu.test.

What should TestFXOSCore do? Clearly it must instantiate a FXOS8700CQ (Listing 9-20). It must configure the device using the begin method (Listing 9-21). Finally, it must invoke readRaw and isDataReady (Listing 9-22).

Listing 9-23 shows TestFXOSCore. It defines a private method readAM to read all six axes a number of times and print a value. The variable axis determines whether readAM prints the X, Y, or Z axis for the magnetometer or accelerometer (axis = 0, 1, 2, 3, 4, or 5 respectively).

Listing 9-23. TestFXOSCore

```
package org.gaf.pimu.test;

import com.diozero.api.RuntimeIOException;
import com.diozero.util.Diozero;
import com.diozero.util.SleepUtil;
import java.io.IOException;
import org.gaf.pimu.FXOS8700CQ;
```

```java
public class TestFXOSCore {

    public static void main(String[] args)
            throws IOException, InterruptedException {

        try (FXOS8700CQ device = new FXOS8700CQ()) {

            device.begin();

            int num = Integer.valueOf(args[0]);

            int axis = 3;

            readAM(num, axis);
        } finally {
            Diozero.shutdown();

        }

    }

    private static void readAM(FXOS8700CQ device,
            int num, int axis)
            throws RuntimeIOException {
        int[] am;
        long tCurrent, tLast, tDelta;
        tLast = System.nanoTime();
        device.readRaw();
        for (int i = 0; i < num; i++) {
            device.isDataReady(true);
            tCurrent = System.nanoTime();
            tDelta = (tCurrent - tLast) / 100000;
            tLast = tCurrent;
            am = device.readRaw();
            System.out.println(am[axis] +
                    ", " + tDelta);
```

```
        SleepUtil.sleepMillis(15);
    }
  }
}
```

I ran TestFXOSCore with axis=3 (accelerometer X axis) and with the PIMU stationary. I got the output shown in Listing 9-24; the first number is the X-axis output, and the second number is the time delta in tenths of milliseconds.

Listing 9-24. Output from TestFXOSCore execution for accelerometer x axis

```
106, 204
94, 936
92, 172
102, 171
107, 171
110, 179
106, 200
98, 205
97, 205
95, 201
```

You can clearly see some anomalous timing behavior in the first few readings. This appears to be very similar to the behavior of the gyroscope. However, there does not appear to be any anomalies in the sample values. That said, you can see a zero offset and noise in the sample values.

I ran TestFXOSCore again for 200 samples while moving the device back and forth along the X axis. Figure 9-10 shows a plot of the results. The plot clearly shows a zero offset of roughly 100 LSB. You can easily see acceleration in both +X and -X directions.

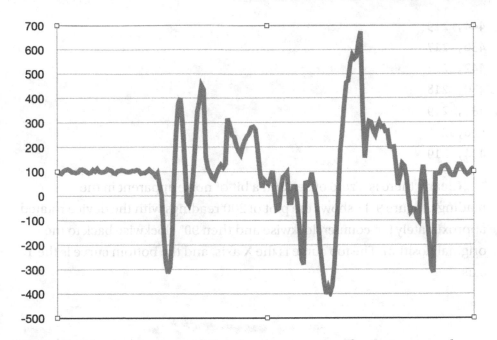

Figure 9-10. *Accelerometer X axis when moving device in +x and -x directions*

I also ran TestFXASCore showing the Y and Z axes. Both behaved in a manner similar to the X axis, exhibiting a zero offset (about -200 for Y and 4220 for Z), noise, and positive and negative acceleration.

To test the magnetometer, in TestFXOSCore I substituted the following line for the statement printing the axis indicated by the axis parameter:

```
System.out.println(am[0] + ", " + am[1]);
```

This statement prints the X and Y axes for the magnetometer. With the device stationary, I got the results shown in Listing 9-25.

Listing 9-25. Magnetometer X and Y axes; stationary

```
439, 211
435, 219
436, 221
```

```
444, 219
436, 217
442, 217
430, 218
433, 219
436, 211
434, 219
```

Clearly there is a zero offset, and a bit of noise apparent in the readings. Figure 9-11 shows the plot of 200 readings with the device rotated approximately 90° counterclockwise and then 90° clockwise back to the original position. The top curve is the X axis, and the bottom curve is the Y axis.

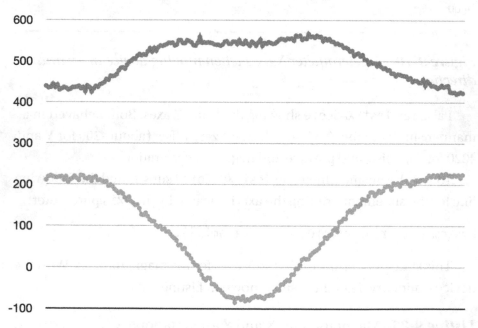

Figure 9-11. *Magnetometer X (top) and Y (bottom) axes; in motion*

Events Again

Given the success with interrupts for the FXAS21002C, it makes sense to use them with the FSOX8700CQ. The interrupt pins from the FSOX8700CQ are also available on the breakout board. It is easy to configure interrupts (though you must deal with three registers rather than one). It is easy to clear interrupts, again by simply reading the data.

Listing 9-26 shows the code added to FSOX8700CQ to configure data-ready interrupts, using accelerometer/magnetometer interrupt 1 (pin AI1 on the breakout board). The constants at the beginning of Listing 9-26 show the values put in the control registers. The statements at the end get added to the begin method just after the statement putting the device in standby state.

Listing 9-26. Configuring interrupts in FSOX8700CQ

```
/* Configure interrupt : CNTL_REG3
-- active high
-- push-pull output driver
*/
private static final byte INTERRUPT_HIGH_PP = 0x02;
/* Configure interrupt : CNTL_REG4
-- on data ready
*/
private static final byte INTERRUPT_DATA_READY = 0x01;
/* Configure interrupt : CNTL_REG5
-- to pin 1
*/
private static final byte INTERRUPT_PIN1 = 0x01;
```

```
// configure a data ready interrupt
device.writeByteData(
        Registers.CTRL_REG3.register,
        INTERRUPT_HIGH_PP);
device.writeByteData(
        Registers.CTRL_REG4.register,
        INTERRUPT_DATA_READY);
device.writeByteData(
        Registers.CTRL_REG5.register,
        INTERRUPT_PIN1);
```

Using the same argument as for the FXAS21002C, I suggest creating a composite device. I'll call my class AccelMag, shown in Listing 9-27. Its implementation is nearly identical to the initial implementation of Gyro in Listing 9-11. AccelMag exhibits the following differences from Gyro:

- It uses FXOS8700CQ.

- Since FXOS8700CQ.begin has no configuration parameters, neither does AccelMag.begin.

- It queues the accelerometer X axis.

Listing 9-27. AccelMag

```
package org.gaf.pimu;

import com.diozero.api.DigitalInputDevice;
import com.diozero.api.GpioEventTrigger;
import com.diozero.api.GpioPullUpDown;
import com.diozero.api.RuntimeIOException;
import java.io.IOException;
import java.util.concurrent.BlockingQueue;
```

```java
public class AccelMag implements AutoCloseable {

    private final BlockingQueue queue;
    private FXOS8700CQ fxos = null;
    private DigitalInputDevice catcher = null;

    private long tsLast;
    private boolean active = false;

    public AccelMag(int interruptPin,
            BlockingQueue queue) throws IOException {
        this.queue = queue;
        this.fxos = new FXOS8700CQ();
        try {
            catcher = new DigitalInputDevice(
                    interruptPin,
                    GpioPullUpDown.NONE,
                    GpioEventTrigger.RISING);
        } catch (RuntimeIOException ex) {
            throw new IOException(ex.getMessage());
        }
    }

    @Override
    public void close() {
        if (fxos != null) {
            fxos.close();
            fxos = null;
        }
        if (catcher != null) {
            catcher.close();
            catcher = null;
        }
    }
```

325

```java
    public void begin() throws RuntimeIOException {
        fxos.begin();
    }

    public void activateIH() throws
            RuntimeIOException {
        // read to clear interrupt status
        fxos.readRaw();

        // empty the queue
        queue.clear();

        // set active
        tsLast = 0;
        this.active = true;
    }

    public void activateRaw()
            throws RuntimeIOException {
        catcher.whenActivated(this::queueRaw);
        activateIH();
    }

    public void deactivate() {
        this.active = false;
    }

    private void queueRaw(long timestamp)
            throws RuntimeIOException {
        if (active) {
            int[] xyzxyz = fxos.readRaw();

            long tsDelta = timestamp - tsLast;
            tsLast = timestamp;
            long[] sample = {xyzxyz[3], tsDelta};
```

```
        // queue it if queue not full
        if (!queue.offer(sample))
            System.err.println("Queue Full!");
    }
  }
}
```

Listing 9-28 shows the main class TestAccelMag that tests AccelMag. Not surprisingly, its implementation is nearly identical to that of TestGyro in Listing 9-12.

Prior to running AccelMag, you must connect the PIMU AI1 interrupt pin to the Raspberry Pi GPIO pin you use to monitor it with DigitalInputDevice. I used GPIO 18. Again, I recommend powering down the Pi prior to making the connection.

Caution   I used the same GPIO pin in both TestGyro and TestAccelMag. If you use both Gyro and AccelMag at the same time, you must use two different pins.

Listing 9-28. TestAccelMag

```
package org.gaf.pimu.test;

import com.diozero.util.Diozero;
import java.io.IOException;
import java.util.concurrent.ArrayBlockingQueue;
import org.gaf.pimu.AccelMag;
```

```java
public class TestAccelMag {

    public static void main(String[] args)
            throws IOException, InterruptedException {
        ArrayBlockingQueue queue =
                new ArrayBlockingQueue(10);

        try (AccelMag am = new AccelMag(18, queue)) {

            am.begin();

            am.activateRaw();

            for (int cnt = 0; cnt < 100; cnt++) {
                long[] sample = (long[])
                        queue.take();
                System.out.println(sample[0] + ", " +
                    sample[1]/100000);
            }

            am.deactivate();
        } finally {
            Diozero.shutdown();
        }
    }
}
```

Listing 9-29 shows snippets of the output from running TestAccelMag with the PIMU stationary. You can see the first few time deltas are anomalous, but after that very consistent. All values of the readings appear within the expected bounds, given noise. Not much different than the FXAS21002C. Great news!

Listing 9-29. Output from TestAccelMag

```
92, 16168669712057
92, 52
104, 1131
94, 202
84, 202
88, 202
94, 202
104, 202
...
```

As with the FXAS21002C, I used an oscilloscope and measured the period of the interrupt. I was a bit disappointed to find that the frequency was about 49.3 Hz, not nearly as close to 50 Hz as the FXAS21002C. I measured interrupt latency, and it was the same (not surprising). I also measured the time to read the data for both the accelerometer and the magnetometer at about 1400 microseconds (with the I2C clock at 100 kHz). That is quite nice!

Caution   To use the accelerometer, you usually need to do integration. Note with the FXAS21002C, the *measured* time period between samples is obviously different than the *ideal* time period calculated from the output data rate! You must use the measured time period for integration.

What Next?

You've now developed a library that enables the basics of using the FXOS8700CQ. That said, the previous work shows that both the accelerometer and magnetometer present some of the tough issues

raised by the FXAS21002C gyroscope: zero offset and noise (though
the noise level appears much lower). The good news is that you can
duplicate the work done for the FXAS21002C to "harden" the data from the
FXOS8700CQ.

The bad news is that hardening the data is the easy part. There are
some questions you must address. What about aspects of both devices
left untouched, for example, configuration flexibility, other events,
and the FIFO? What about aspects of the FXOS8700CQ left untouched,
for example, calibration of the magnetometer? Any of these could be
important in *your* project.

A big question is the interface model: Do you expose

- Two low-level devices, FXAS21002C and FXOS8700CQ, or
  one low-level device, PIMU, which leverages FXAS21002C
  and FXOS8700CQ?

- Two composite devices, Gyro and AccelMag, or
  one composite device, the PIMU, which leverages
  FXAS21002C and FXOS8700CQ, or maybe Gyro and
  AccelMag?

No matter what you expose, do you use the diozero IMU-related
classes mentioned earlier?

Another big question is how do you do something useful with the
data? I showed you how to use the gyroscope Z axis to determine a relative
heading; it used some trivial mathematics. You can use the magnetometer
X and Y axes to create a crude compass to offer an absolute heading; that
requires some more complex mathematics as well as some calibration
work. You can use the accelerometer, magnetometer, and gyroscope to
create an AHRS (attitude and heading reference system); that requires
some very complex mathematics. The latter is complicated by the
discovery that the FXAS21002C and FXOS8700CQ don't sample at exactly
the same frequency.

Fundamentally, what's next is for you to determine your requirements for the PIMU and proceed accordingly.

Summary

In this chapter, we've covered a *lot* of ground. You've once again had to

- Evaluate existing device libraries for porting, some in Java!

- Choose among multiple libraries

- Identify and assess porting issues and make trade-offs

- Evolve a design as new requirements surface

You also learned how to

- Address the details of porting a C++ *and* a Java library to *your* Java library

- Identify, investigate, and mitigate device or device library anomalies or idiosyncrasies, a.k.a. the devil can hide in the details

- Leverage the ability of diozero to support device interrupts

- Leverage Java concurrency classes for simple concurrency situations

I think it is worth emphasizing an important "lesson learned" regarding the effort involved in developing the FXAS21002C and FXOS8700CQ libraries. A significant portion of the effort had *nothing* to do with the port from existing libraries to a Java library based on diozero. That portion resulted from understanding and "taming" the behavior of the devices so they could produce information useful for a project. Of course, I mean the need to address zero offset, noise, and integration. But I also mean the need to expose the data in a timely and efficient fashion, leading to the introduction of interrupts and concurrency. None of these aspects were addressed in the existing libraries. Keep the lesson in mind for the next complex device you tackle.

CHAPTER 10

A Lidar Unit

In this chapter, we'll examine another device I used in my autonomous rover – a *Lidar Unit* that supports localization and navigation. Appendix A2 describes the simple *custom-built* Lidar Unit built around a USB-connected Arduino. The Lidar Unit is a real-life example of off-loading tasks from the Raspberry Pi to an Arduino, in particular to leverage the microcontroller's "near-real-time" nature.

In this chapter, I'll cover

- Implementation of a device library for a USB serial device

- Design and implementation of a device library from scratch

- Identifying and resolving various design issues

- Iteration on a design

- Processing raw data to make it more useful

Before continuing, you should review, if necessary, the material in Chapter 7 covering the Raspberry Pi serial I/O capability and diozero serial device support.

Note Fun fact: The LIDAR sensor used in the Lidar Unit described in Appendix A2 was used in the Ingenuity helicopter, part of NASA's 2020 Mars mission. See www.sparkfun.com/news/3791.

Understand the Device

The Lidar Unit in this chapter is described by the *Lidar Unit "datasheet"* section in Appendix A2. Looking at the datasheet, you can find some interesting aspects of the interface exposed by the Lidar Unit:

- The device exposes *commands* for doing or initiating tasks.

- A *command* consists of a one-byte *type* and an optional two-byte integer *parameter*. The task implied by the command can *return* zero or more two-byte integers.

- Some of the tasks need to be used only during device identification, testing, or calibrating, not in "production."

- Some of the tasks complete immediately; some are *long running*.

- The range data produced can include codes indicating different errors; true ranges below 100 cm are nonlinear.

Find a Device Library

As a custom device, there is no possibility of finding an existing device library for the Lidar Unit, so there is no need to search for one. Thus, good news or bad news, you have a clean slate. How do you proceed? The next section addresses the question.

Device Library Design

In "clean slate" situations, I claim you should start by defining your library's interface methods. Then you can look for common methods that can be used to implement the interface-level methods. As with any device, there are also other considerations.

Interface

Per the discussion in Chapter 8, the best source of guidance for the new library interface is "my requirements." The next best is the device interface. Since I designed the Lidar Unit, these two are identical! Sort of cheating, but there it is.

A good starting point for the Lidar Unit library interface is a method for each command in the reasonably simple interface. For some devices, the interface can be much more complex and could need more abstraction. For example, sometimes it requires multiple interactions with a device to implement a reasonable abstraction in the device library interface. In addition, you will find it sometimes takes a few iterations to identify the proper device library interface and all of the private methods.

The datasheet indicates that some commands need not, and, indeed, perhaps should not, be used in production. You have two choices: ignore the difference in commands, leaving it up to the user to know the difference, or incorporate access restrictions, which complicates the design. I'll take the latter approach as I find it interesting. There are a few techniques to properly restrict access in Java; some that come to mind immediately:

1. A single device class with *public access* "production" methods and *default access* "other" methods. This approach restricts any "other" methods to main classes in the *same package* as the device class. Probably not the best solution because those classes get packaged in the library jar file.

2. A device class with *public access* "production" methods and *protected access* "other" methods. This approach requires that any main classes *outside the package* of the device class extend the device class to access "other" methods.

3. A device "production" class containing only the public access "production" methods and an "other" *subclass* that extends the "production" class and includes the public access "other" methods. This approach places no restrictions on the package method access, other than according to the class used. However, the "production" class requires a mixture of *public*, *default*, and *private access* methods.

There is not a huge difference between techniques 2 and 3. I think approach 2 is the most efficient technique, and I will use it in the implementation of the Lidar Unit device library.

A look at the datasheet suggests a "production" project that needs only the Lidar scans provided by the Lidar Unit requires only the following commands:

- Get Servo Parameters

- Scan

- Scan Retrieve

- Warmup

It is possible some projects might want the ability to do custom scans, or to do simple static ranging. If so, the "production" project would require in addition the following commands:

- Set Servo Position

- Get Ranges

Fortunately, with technique 2, it is very easy to switch by just changing the access level from protected to public. In either case, the remaining commands would be candidates for protected access.

Common Methods

What next? Think about what the interface-level methods do, in hope of finding some common functions that can be encapsulated as reusable private methods. Typically, you'll identify mid-level methods, like those in Chapter 8, that will use the low-level SerialDevice methods described in Chapter 7.

For the Lidar Unit, the relevant information is the nature of the command sent to the device and the nature of the returned information. There are basically two generic command forms:

- Type only (e.g., Get ID), which requires

  a. Write the command type (a byte)

  b. If needed, read the response (two bytes); create a short from the bytes

- Type and parameter (e.g., Echo Parameter, Warmup), which requires

  a. Create two bytes from the integer parameter

  b. Write the command type and parameter bytes

  c. If needed, read the response (two bytes); create a short from the bytes

Clearly, step b in the "type only" form and step c in the "type and parameter" form are the same. That suggests a "read response" method that implements those steps. For commands that return multiple two-byte integers, we can just loop to read them.

While there are a few ways to deal with the other actions needed in the two forms, I'll define a "write command type" method for the "type-only" form and a "write command type and parameter" method for the "type and parameter" form.

Other Considerations

Chapter 8 mentioned other considerations that apply when porting an existing device library or developing a device library from scratch. For example, should you separate the library interface from the implementation of the interface? Should the library instance be a singleton shared by many users, or should there be many instances with one for each user? These sorts of decisions you'll have to make on your own based on your project needs and your device(s).

For the Lidar Unit

- It seems impossible that there would be another Lidar Unit implementation with a similar interface, and thus little reason to separate interface from implementation.

- I think it *very* unlikely a single robot would require multiple Lidar Units. Thus, there is no need for multiple instances of the library. I'll again ignore the alternatives mentioned in Chapter 9 and assume that no user would try to create more than one instance.

Chapter 7 described the problem of USB device identity. In the preceding text, I assume a single Lidar Unit, so there is no need to distinguish one Lidar Unit from another. However, since the Lidar Unit is Arduino based, it is possible to find multiple Arduinos that have the same USB device identity (e.g., see Table 7-1). Thus, the Lidar Unit must provide some unique device instance ID. Fortunately, the Lidar Unit has a Get ID command that should suffice. I'll discuss an implementation of the two phases of identity verification later in this chapter.

Chapter 8 also mentioned the interesting question of whether a library instance is shared among multiple threads. The Lidar Unit has some commands (e.g., Scan) that take a very long time to complete. This means the overall project design should consider concurrency. Unfortunately, Java concurrency in general is a subject beyond the scope of this book. Thus, I'll assume a single device library instance and a single thread using the instance. You might wish to get more sophisticated.

Play with the Device

A quick look at the Lidar Unit datasheet shows it has two commands (Get ID and Echo Parameter) that meet the "simplicity" requirement for playing, so we'll play!

To play, you must first create a new NetBeans project, package, and class; configure the project for remote development on your Raspberry Pi; and configure the project to use diozero (see Chapter 7 for more detail). I called my project **Lidar**, my package org.gaf.lidar, and my device class Lidar. But, since we are going to do some playing, you need to create a new package; I'll call mine org.gaf.lidar.test. In that package, create a new *main* class; I'll name mine PlayLidar.

Listing 10-1 shows PlayLidar. We first need to create an instance of SerialDevice. The Lidar Unit runs at 115,200 baud. All the other serial parameters are the default values. After I connected the Lidar Unit to a Raspberry Pi and applied power to the Unit, its device file was /dev/ttyACM0 (see Chapter 7 for information on the USB device file). You can see this reflected in the first statement of the main method.

You can find two code blocks in the listing. The first attempts to get the ID following the design described earlier. We must first write the command byte (10). You might think we should then read the response.

However, when testing, I found that if the Lidar sensor has no power, the read never returns, and PlayLidar hangs! You must Ctrl-C to terminate the application. Thus, the next few statements check to see if a response got returned. If not, we throw an exception; if so, then we do a block read to get the two-byte response. Next, we must manipulate the two bytes to create a short. Finally, we can print the resulting value.

Listing 10-1. PlayLidar

```java
package org.gaf.lidar.test;

import static com.diozero.api.SerialConstants.*;
import com.diozero.api.SerialDevice;

public class PlayLidar {

    public static void main(String[] args)
            throws InterruptedException {
        SerialDevice device = new SerialDevice(
                "/dev/ttyACM0", BAUD_115200,
                DEFAULT_DATA_BITS,
                DEFAULT_STOP_BITS,
                DEFAULT_PARITY);

        // get the ID
        device.writeByte((byte) 10);
        byte[] res = new byte[2];

        // see if active
        Thread.sleep(100);
        if (!(device.bytesAvailable() > 1)) {
            System.out.println("Lidar not powered!");
            System.exit(-1);
        }
```

```
// read the response byte array
device.read(res);
// construct response as short
short value = (short)(res[0] << 8);
value = (short) (value |
    (short) Byte.toUnsignedInt(res[1]));
System.out.println("ID= " + value);

// echo a parameter
short parameter = 12345;
device.write((byte) 11,
    (byte) (parameter >> 8),
    (byte) parameter);
// read the response byte array
device.read(res);
// construct response as short
value = (short)(res[0] << 8);
value = (short) (value |
    (short) Byte.toUnsignedInt(res[1]));
System.out.println("Parameter= " + value);
    }
}
```

You can run PlayLidar *before* entering the second group of statements. You should see this: ID= 600.

The second code block tries to echo a parameter, again guided by the earlier design. First, we define a parameter. Then, we write the command byte (11) and the two bytes that comprise the parameter. We then do the block read (with no fear of failure) and manipulation for getting the response. Lastly, we print the result.

Run `PlayLidar` and you should see the following:

```
ID= 600
Parameter= 12345
```

Success! On we go to library development.

Tip   I think the experience with the Lidar Unit emphasizes the benefit of play; discovering the "hang" with no power to the sensor while playing makes it much less disruptive than discovering it during development. Further, the experience suggests testing various conditions (e.g., missing connections for signals or power) to understand and react to the impact.

Device Library Development

We've already created the necessary NetBeans project, package, and class, configured the project for remote development, and configured the project to use diozero. We can start developing `Lidar`.

Development Approach

In Chapter 8, I mentioned two fundamental device library development approaches: *breadth first* and *depth first*. The issue arises even when developing a "clean slate" device library. As with porting, I prefer to start depth first when developing from scratch. As suggested in Chapter 8, we'll first develop the "core."

Lidar Core

The Lidar core requires a constructor, some of the interface-level methods, and the mid-level methods used by them. A SerialDevice supplies the low-level methods.

Interface-Level and Mid-Level Methods

The earlier analysis derived the needed mid-level methods from commands similar to Get ID and Echo Parameter. Since we now have experience with those commands, implementing them in the core seems like a good idea.

The earlier analysis identified three mid-level methods: "write command type," "write command type and parameter," and "read response." To implement the Get ID and Echo Parameter commands, the core must include all three.

Constructor

There are generally a lot of considerations relevant to the implementation of a device library constructor. This subsection discusses some relevant to the Lidar Unit as a USB serial device.

Identity

As discussed earlier, the Lidar Unit presents a USB device identity challenge. As with the RoboClaw in Chapter 8, I think verification should be done externally. I'll show you how to do it later in this chapter.

Serial Characteristics

While technically it is possible to control both sides of the Lidar Unit connection, I will pretend that is not the case, that is, that the serial characteristics defined in the datasheet cannot be changed. Thus, I'll

343

assume that the Lidar Unit is fixed at 115,200 baud and that the other serial characteristics require no parameter on the constructor.

Implementation

Listing 10-2 shows the core implementation for `Lidar` based on the design discussed earlier. Again, I am leaving out most comments and all Javadoc. You should not!

Some important points about the implementation:

- The `import` statements reflect the requirements for various diozero classes.

- Note the `LIDAR_ID` constant which uniquely identifies the Lidar Unit (the device instance ID).

- The constructor uses `SerialDevice.Builder` to create a `SerialDevice` instance since all other serial characteristics match the diozero defaults.

- The class implements `AutoCloseable`, and you will find a `close` method in the `Lidar` implementation per the discussion in Chapter 7.

- The mid-level methods must have access to the `SerialDevice` instance used in a `Lidar` instance, so you must create an *instance variable*, populate it in the constructor, and use it in the mid-level methods.

- Per the access discussion earlier, the `getID` and `echoParameter` methods are marked `protected`.

- The `getID` and `echoParameter` methods and the `writeCmdType`, `writeCmdTypeParm`, and `readShort` methods all propagate the unchecked `RuntimeIOException`. See Chapter 7 for more information.

- Per the identity discussion earlier, the method verifyIdentity verifies the device instance ID.

- The nested class CommandTypes models a best practice for consolidating command type codes.

Listing 10-2. Lidar core

```
package org.gaf.lidar;

import static com.diozero.api.SerialConstants.
    BAUD_115200;
import com.diozero.api.SerialDevice;
import com.diozero.api.RuntimeIOException;
import com.diozero.util.SleepUtil;
import java.io.IOException;

public class Lidar implements AutoCloseable {

    public static final int LIDAR_ID = 600;
    private SerialDevice device;

    public Lidar(String deviceFile)
        throws IOException {
        try {
            device =
                SerialDevice.builder(deviceFile).
                setBaud(BAUD_115200).build();
        } catch (RuntimeIOException ex) {
            throw new IOException(ex.getMessage());
        }
    }

    public void close() throws IOException {
        if (device != null) {
```

345

```
            device.close();
            device = null;
        }
    }

public boolean verifyIdentity()
        throws RuntimeIOException {
    return LIDAR_ID == getID();
}

protected short getID()
        throws RuntimeIOException, IOException{
    writeCmdType(CommandTypes.ID.code);

    SleepUtil.sleepMillis(100);
    if (!(device.bytesAvailable() > 1)) {
        throw new IOException(
                "Lidar not powered!");
    }
    return readShort();
}

protected short echoParameter(short parm)
        throws RuntimeIOException {
    writeCmdTypeParm(CommandTypes.ECHO.code,
        parm);
    return readShort();
}

private void writeCmdType(int type)
        throws RuntimeIOException {
    device.writeByte((byte) type);
}
```

```java
    private void writeCmdTypeParm(int type,
        int parm) throws RuntimeIOException {
        device.write((byte) type,
            (byte) (parm >> 8), (byte) parm);
    }

    private short readShort()
            throws RuntimeIOException {
        byte[] res = new byte[2];
        device.read(res);
        short value = (short)(res[0] << 8);
        value = (short) (value |
            (short) Byte.toUnsignedInt(res[1]));
        return value;
    }

    private enum CommandTypes {
        ID(10),
        ECHO(11),
        SERVO_POS(30),
        SERVO_PARMS(32),
        MULTIPLE(50),
        SCAN(52),
        SCAN_RETRIEVE(54),
        WARMUP(60);

        public final int code;

        CommandTypes(int code) {
            this.code = code;
        }
    }
}
```

The readShort and getID methods in Listing 10-2 illustrate an interesting design choice. As discussed in the context of PlayLidar, if the sensor is not powered, a read fails and a program will hang. To detect the condition, we can use a non-blocking read. We could implement a non-blocking read in readShort. However, in actual usage, getID should always be called first (as part of identity verification); further, based on experience with the Unit, if the first read works, all subsequent reads work. So, I decided to make readShort "pure" and do the extra work of a non-blocking read in getID. This design choice follows the advice from Chapter 8; in this case, I don't use a non-blocking read all the time because I don't need it all the time.

Test the Core

You can now test the Lidar core implementation in Listing 10-2. Based on the discussion in Chapter 8, you should create a main class in the package org.gaf.lidar.test; I'll name the class TestLidarCore.

What should TestLidarCore do? Per the identity discussion earlier, it must find the right USB device file; in other words, do USB device identity verification. Clearly it must instantiate a Lidar. It should exercise the two methods, getID and echoParameter. Remember that since getID is used in identity verification, TestLidarCore really only needs to exercise echoParameter.

Identity Verification

Chapter 8 described a utility method that provides two-phased identity verification for the RoboClaw motor controller (see Listing 8-9). Listing 10-3 shows the implementation of the LidarUtil class (in the same package as Lidar) containing a static method findDeviceFile that performs identity verification for the Lidar Unit. The only difference between the utility methods is that the RoboClaw version requires a parameter for the device instance ID, while the Lidar Unit does not. To support identity verification,

you'll have to add the **Utility** project to the **Lidar** project *Libraries* property
(see Chapter 5 for details on how to do so).

Listing 10-3. LidarUtil class

```java
package org.gaf.lidar;

import java.io.IOException;
import java.util.List;
import org.gaf.util.SerialUtil;

public class LidarUtil {

    public static String findDeviceFile(
            String usbVendorId, String usbProductId)
            throws IOException {
        // identity verification - phase 1
        List<String> deviceFles =
                SerialUtil.findDeviceFiles(
                        usbVendorId, usbProductId);
        // identity verification - phase 2
        if (!deviceFles.isEmpty()) {
            for (String deviceFile : deviceFles) {
                System.out.println(deviceFile);
                Lidar lidar = new Lidar(deviceFile);
                boolean verified =
                    lidar.verifyIdentity();
                lidar.close();
                if (verified) return deviceFile;
            }
        }
        return null;
    }
}
```

Note that I've left a `println` statement in phase 2 of verification. It is there strictly to assist testing. It is unneeded in production.

TestLidarCore Implementation

Listing 10-4 shows the test program `TestLidarCore`. `TestLidarCore` represents the general form of any main class intended to use the *protected* methods in `Lidar`. The class must

- Extend the class being tested, in this case, `Lidar`

- Define its own constructor with the proper parameters, in this case, `fileName`

The `main` method in `TestLidarCore` must

- Find the correct device file for the Lidar Unit (doing so verifies the device identity)

- Instantiate the class using the device file for which the USB device identity and device instance ID have been verified

- Call the `echoParameter` method

The Lidar Unit USB device identity comes from Table 7-1 where {usbVendorId, usbProductId} = {1ffb, 2300} for the Pololu A-Star 32U4. The device instance ID is internal to the `Lidar` class (`LIDAR_ID`).

Following the guidelines in Chapter 7, `TestLidarCore` enables the try-with-resources and diozero shutdown safety nets. Since the Lidar Unit cannot cause any problems in the event of abnormal termination, I chose not to use the Java shutdown safety net.

Listing 10-4. TestLidarCore

```java
package org.gaf.lidar.test;

import com.diozero.util.Diozero;
import java.io.IOException;
import org.gaf.lidar.Lidar;
import org.gaf.lidar.LidarUtil;

public class TestLidarCore extends Lidar {

    public TestLidarCore(String fileName)
            throws IOException {
        super(fileName);
    }

    public static void main(String arg[])
            throws IOException {
        final short parm = 1298;
        // identity verification
        String deviceFile =
            LidarUtil.findDeviceFile("1ffb", "2300");
        if (deviceFile == null) {
            throw new
                IOException("No matching device!");
        }

        try (TestLidarCore tester =
                new TestLidarCore(deviceFile)) {
            // issue and check echo command
            short echo = tester.echoParameter(parm);
            if (echo == parm)
                System.out.println("Echo GOOD");
            else
```

```
                System.out.println("Echo BAD");
        } finally {
            Diozero.shutdown();
        }
    }
}
```

To test, I connected the Lidar Unit from this chapter and another Pololu A-Star 32U4 with a different device instance ID (see Appendix A1) to the Raspberry Pi and then powered up the Pi. The result was two USB devices, /dev/ttyACM0 and /dev/ttyACM1, as expected. When I ran TestLidarCore, I got the results shown in Listing 10-5.

Listing 10-5. Output from TestLidarCore execution

```
/dev/ttyACM1
/dev/ttyACM0
ID GOOD!
Echo GOOD
```

As you can see, it turns out the Lidar Unit was the device /dev/ttyACM0. Also, you can see the test succeeded!

Additional Methods

Listing 10-6 shows the *first pass* at the additional methods for Lidar. There are a few aspects worth elaboration:

- As suggested earlier, some interface-level methods have protected access to indicate they should not be used in "production."

- There are methods that don't derive from the Lidar Unit command set. I'll discuss those in the following.

Listing 10-6. Lidar additional methods

```
protected int setServoPosition(int positionHalfDeg)
        throws RuntimeIOException {
    writeCmdTypeParm(CommandTypes.SERVO_POS.code,
        positionHalfDeg);
    return (int) readShort();
}

public short[] getServoParms()
        throws RuntimeIOException {
    writeCmdType(CommandTypes.SERVO_PARMS.code);
    return readNShort(3);
}

protected short[] getRanges(int number)
        throws RuntimeIOException {
    writeCmdTypeParm(CommandTypes.MULTIPLE.code,
        number);
    return readNShort(number);
}

public void scanStart(int delay)
        throws RuntimeIOException {
    writeCmdTypeParm(CommandTypes.SCAN.code, delay);
}

public boolean isTaskDone(boolean wait)
    throws RuntimeIOException {
    if (device.bytesAvailable() > 1) {
        readShort(); // to keep sync
        return true;
    } else {
        if (!wait) {
```

```
                return false;
            } else { // wait
                while (device.bytesAvailable() < 2) {
                    SleepUtil.sleepMillis(1000);
                }
                readShort(); // to keep sync
                return true;
            }
        }
    }

    public short[] scanRetrieve()
            throws RuntimeIOException , IOException {
        writeCmdType(CommandTypes.SCAN_RETRIEVE.code);
        if (readShort() == -1 )
            throw new IOException("No scan
                to retrieve");
        short[] ranges = readNShort(361);
        return ranges;
    }

    public void warmupStart(int period)
            throws RuntimeIOException {
        writeCmdTypeParm(CommandTypes.WARMUP.code,
            period);
    }

    private short[] readNShort(int number)
            throws RuntimeIOException {
        short[] values = new short[number];
        for (int i = 0; i < number; i++) {
```

```
    values [i] = readShort();
    }
    return values;
}
```

The private method readNShort derives from recognition that the interface-level methods getServoParms (implements the command Get Servo Parameters), getRanges (implements the command Get Multiple), and scanRetrieve (implements the command Scan Retrieve) read multiple short values. Thus, it seemed prudent to create a shared method to do so.

The genesis of the public method isTaskDone is far more interesting. The methods scanStart and warmupStart both start tasks that are "long running." At the default servo delay, a Scan finishes and sends its completion code around *30 seconds* after starting the scan. At the minimum warmup period, a Warmup finishes and sends its completion code a *few seconds* after starting; at the maximum warmup period, a Warmup finishes and sends its completion code a *few minutes* after starting. So, to enable efficient multitasking, both methods send the command to the Lidar Unit to initiate the task, but *do not wait* for it to send the completion code. Waiting is the job of isTaskDone. That said, since the completion code for both tasks must be read to maintain synchronized communication, isTaskDone *must* be called at some point *after* a Scan or a Warmup has started and *before* another command gets called so it can read the completion code.

As you can see in Listing 10-6, isTaskDone has a parameter that determines whether to wait for the long-running task to complete or to simply check the current status and return. To support multitasking, while waiting, the method sleeps as much as possible; I chose a relatively long sleep period; it could be shorter or even tailorable via another parameter. An important part of the implementation is reading the completion code after the task finishes to maintain communication synchronization.

Test the Additional Methods

I created a new program to test the complete implementation.
TestLidarAll (see Listing 10-7) allows you to enter the command and
optional parameter. It then calls the appropriate method in Lidar. It is
important to remember that since TestLidarAll takes keyboard input,
you *cannot* successfully run it from NetBeans. You have to push the project
distribution (jar and libraries) to the Raspberry Pi and run it using a secure
shell; see Chapter 5 for details.

Note that for the most part, the cases in the switch statement are
identified by a Lidar Unit command code. The one exception is the case
that calls isTaskDone. I simply chose an unused command code, 55.

Listing 10-7. TestLidarAll

```
package org.gaf.lidar.test;

import com.diozero.util.Diozero;
import java.io.IOException;
import java.util.Scanner;
import org.gaf.lidar.Lidar;
import org.gaf.lidar.LidarUtil;

public class TestLidarAll extends Lidar {

    public TestLidarAll(String fileName)
            throws IOException {
        super(fileName);
    }

    public static void main(String arg[])
            throws IOException, InterruptedException {
        // identity verification
        String deviceFile =
```

```
        LidarUtil.findDeviceFile("1ffb", "2300");

if (deviceFile == null) {
    throw new IOException(
        "No matching device!");
}

try (TestLidarAll tester =
        new TestLidarAll(deviceFile)) {
    // enable keyboard input
    Scanner input = new Scanner(System.in);

    String command = "";
    while (true) {
        System.out.print(
            "Command (type,parm; 'q' is
            quit): ");
        command = input.next();
        System.out.println();
        // parse
        String delims = "[,]";
        String[] tokens =
            command.split(delims);
        if (tokens[0].equalsIgnoreCase("q"))
        {
            tester.close();
            System.exit(0);
        }
        int type =
            Integer.parseInt(tokens[0]);
        int parm = 0;
        if (tokens.length > 1) {
            parm =
```

```java
            Integer.parseInt(tokens[1]);
        }
        System.out.println("type: " + type +
            " parm: " + parm);

        switch (type) {
            case 10:
                int id = tester.getID();
                System.out.println(
                    "ID=" + id);
                break;
            case 11:
                short echo =
                    tester.echoParameter(
                        (short)parm);
                System.out.println("Echo= " +
                    echo);
                break;
            case 30:
                int rc =
                    tester.setServoPosition(
                        parm);
                System.out.println("rc= " +
                    rc);
                break;
            case 32:
                short[] p =
                    tester.getServoParms();
                for (short pv : p) {
                    System.out.println(
                        "pv= " + pv);
                }
```

```
        break;
    case 50:
        short[] ranges =
            tester.getRanges(parm);
        for (short r : ranges) {
            System.out.println(
                "r= " + r);
        }
        break;
    case 52:
        tester.scanStart(parm);
        break;
    case 54:
        ranges =
            tester.scanRetrieve();
        for (short r : ranges) {
            System.out.println(
            "r= " + r);
        }
        break;
    case 55: // fake code
        boolean wait;
        if (parm == 0) wait = false;
        else wait = true;
        boolean status =
            tester.isTaskDone(wait);
        System.out.println(
            "status= " + status);
        break;
    case 60:
        tester.warmupStart(parm);
```

```
                    break;
                default:
                    System.out.println(
                        "BAD Command!");
                }
            }
        } finally {
            Diozero.shutdown();
        }
    }
}
```

I ran `TestLidarAll` and tested all the cases. Everything worked!

You must be careful after starting a scan or a warmup. Those commands return immediately after starting the task, and you'll get another command prompt. The only valid command is 55, which calls `isTaskDone`; otherwise, the Raspberry Pi and Arduino lose communication synchronization. Not good!

Additional Thoughts

During the earlier implementation of `Lidar` and the classes used to test it, some additional design thoughts/questions arose. The following subsections describe them.

Long-Running Tasks

The long-running tasks in Listing 10-6 (Scan and Warmup) in effect have a "start" method and a "wait" method. Both "start" and "wait" must be called to ensure synchronization between the Raspberry Pi and the Lidar Unit. An alternate design for `Lidar` could have a "start and wait" *convenience* method as well as the "start" and "wait" methods. The convenience method could be used when threading is not an issue.

The implementation of the convenience methods is pretty simple. They are shown in Listing 10-8. Note the implication of the methods' names is that they complete the task instead of just starting it.

Listing 10-8. Convenience methods in Lidar

```
public void scan(int delay)
        throws RuntimeIOException,
        InterruptedException {
    writeCmdTypeParm(CommandTypes.SCAN.code, delay);
    isTaskDone(true);
}

public void warmup(int period)
        throws RuntimeIOException,
        InterruptedException {
    writeCmdTypeParm(CommandTypes.WARMUP.code,
        period);
    isTaskDone(true);
}
```

To test the convenience methods, I added the additional cases shown in Listing 10-9 to the switch statement in TestLidarAll.

Listing 10-9. Additional cases in TestLidarAll

```
                case 53:
                    tester.scan(parm);
                    break;
                case 61:
                    tester.warmup(parm);
                    break;
```

I tested the convenience methods, and they worked as expected. In a real project, however, the methods must be used with caution due to their blocking nature.

Read Performance

The readNShort method uses the readShort method, thus interspersing reading two bytes with manipulation to produce a short. A possible performance improvement could result from reading all the bytes from the Lidar Unit and then doing the manipulation to produce all the short values.

I implemented a test reading all the bytes before manipulation. My testing showed basically no difference in performance between the implementation of readNShort shown in Listing 10-6 and the theoretically better performing approach. This suggests the overall processing time is dominated by the serial communication rather than the manipulation or context switching. This experience was a good example of some advice I got long ago: "If it ain't broke, don't fix it."

Raw Range

A range array produced by the Lidar Unit and provided to an application via scanRetrieve is *raw*:

- As indicated in the datasheet, it can contain *error codes* (1 and 5) that could hinder further processing.

- Per the datasheet, a range < 100 suffers from *nonlinearities* in the sensor and should be compensated if such ranges are important to the project.

- A range is simply the *radial* coordinate in a *polar* coordinate system; most processing of lidar information benefits from a *Cartesian* coordinate system.

- It is possible to derive the *angular* coordinate of the polar coordinate from the range array index. A simple division by 2 produces the angular coordinate in 0.5° increments. Alas, that requires a floating-point number, eliminating the use of a simple integer array for the coordinate pair.

- The angular coordinate is not exact due to limitations in the servo and servo controller in the Lidar Unit. While the maximum absolute value of the error is about 0.015°, that may make a difference in some projects.

There are a few ways to deal with this situation. The easiest way is to ignore it for the device library. That said, someone in the project would have to deal with it later. I'll show you an implementation that handles most of the work. There are two major design approaches. One is to inject the necessary processing into Lidar itself; a second is to create an ancillary class. I chose the first for my rover, but I'll show the second in the following.

The ancillary class is LidarPoint, shown in Listing 10-10. From a pure data class perspective, it describes a range reading in terms of its position in the scan array, its polar coordinates, and its Cartesian coordinates.

Listing 10-10. LidarPoint

```
package org.gaf.lidar;

import java.text.DecimalFormat;

public class LidarPoint {
    public int index;
```

```java
public float rho;
public float theta;
public float x;
public float y;

public LidarPoint(int index, float rho) {
    this.index = index;
    this.rho = rho;
}

@Override
public String toString() {
    DecimalFormat df =
            new DecimalFormat("###.00");
    String out = String.format("index = %3d : "
            + "(\u03c1,\u03b8)=(%2$6s,%3$6s) : "
            + "(x,y)= (%4$7s,%5$6s)",
            index,
            df.format(rho), df.format(theta),
            df.format(x), df.format(y));
    return out;
}

private static float servoStepsIn1;
private static boolean configured = false;

public static void setServoParms(short[] parms) {
    configured = true;
    float servoStepsIn180 =
        (parms[2] - parms[0]) * 4;
    servoStepsIn1 = servoStepsIn180 / 180;
}

public static LidarPoint[] processScan(
```

```
      short[] scan) throws RuntimeIOException {

  if (!configured) throw new RuntimeIOException(
    "Servo parameters unset.");

  LidarPoint[] lp =
    new LidarPoint[scan.length];

  for (int i = 0; i < scan.length; i++) {
    // create the point
    lp[i] = new LidarPoint(i, scan[i]);
    // indicate invalid information
    lp[i].rho = (lp[i].rho <= 5) ?
        -1 : lp[i].rho;
    // calculate ideal theta (degrees)
    lp[i].theta = (float)i / 2;

    // calculate exact angle (degrees)
    lp[i].theta = ((int) (lp[i].theta *
      servoStepsIn1 + 0.5)) /
      servoStepsIn1;

    // convert angle to radians
    lp[i].theta = (float)
      Math.toRadians((float) lp[i].theta);
    // calculate Cartesian coordinates
    if (lp[i].rho != -1) {
      lp[i].x = (float)
        Math.cos(lp[i].theta) * lp[i].rho;
      lp[i].y = (float)
        Math.sin(lp[i].theta) * lp[i].rho;
    }
  }
}
```

```
        return lp;
    }
}
```

LidarPoint has two static methods. processScan processes each raw range reading in the scan array to produce a LidarPoint instance. The method addresses the "raw" issues mentioned earlier, except for nonlinearity. It calculates the exact angle for a range reading per the datasheet. Note that the angular coordinate eventually gets represented in radians, as Java (and many other languages) performs trigonometric functions using radians. setServoParms enables the operation of processScan by calculating the important number of servo controller "steps in 1°".

Note   The processScan method is the proper place to address nonlinearity. However, the actual means of doing so is highly dependent on the particular Lidar sensor. In my robot, after much experimentation, I used two different linear equations, one for ranges below 58 cm and a second for ranges between 58 and 100 cm.

To test LidarPoint, I made some slight modifications to TestLidarAll, as shown in Listing 10-11. I added a call to LidarPoint.setServoParms to the case statement for Lidar.getServoParms. I created a new case with an unused command code (57) to retrieve the scan and call LidarPoint. processScan to produce the Cartesian coordinates for the scan.

Listing 10-11. TestLidarAll changes

```
import org.gaf.lidar.LidarPoint;

        case 32:
            short[] p = tester.getServoParms();
            for (short pv : p) {
```

```
        System.out.println("pv= " + pv);
    }
    LidarPoint.setServoParms(p);
    break;

case 57:
    ranges = tester.scanRetrieve();
    LidarPoint[] lps =
        LidarPoint.processScan(ranges);
    for (LidarPoint pt : lps) {
        System.out.println(pt);
    }
```

To do the test, using TestLidarAll, I

1. Ran command 32 to get the servo parameters from the Lidar Unit and set the servo parameters in LidarPoint

2. Ran command 53 to scan

3. Ran command 57 to retrieve and process the scan

Listing 10-12 shows some of the results. The ellipsis indicate lines deleted for brevity.

Listing 10-12. Results of scan processing

```
index =   0 : (ρ,θ)=( 82.00,    .00) : (x,y)= (  82.00,    .00)
index =   1 : (ρ,θ)=( 82.00,    .01) : (x,y)= (  82.00,    .69)
index =   2 : (ρ,θ)=( 81.00,    .02) : (x,y)= (  80.99,   1.42)
index =   3 : (ρ,θ)=( 81.00,    .03) : (x,y)= (  80.97,   2.10)
index =   4 : (ρ,θ)=( 83.00,    .04) : (x,y)= (  82.95,   2.91)
...
index = 356 : (ρ,θ)=(212.00,   3.11) : (x,y)= (-211.87,   7.43)
index = 357 : (ρ,θ)=(230.00,   3.12) : (x,y)= (-229.92,   5.97)
```

```
index = 358 : (ρ,θ)=(242.00,  3.12) : (x,y)= (-241.96,  4.24)
index = 359 : (ρ,θ)=(262.00,  3.13) : (x,y)= (-261.99,  2.22)
index = 360 : (ρ,θ)=(288.00,  3.14) : (x,y)= (-288.00,  -.00)
```

Figure 10-1 shows the kind of "fun" a Lidar Unit provides. I created the plot in a spreadsheet program with the Cartesian coordinates produced by processing a scan (not the scan shown in Listing 10-12). The grid axes are scaled in centimeters. The origin of the grid indicates the position of the Lidar sensor during the scan. To the extent possible, I positioned the Lidar Unit such that it was perpendicular to the surfaces at 0°, 90°, and 180°.

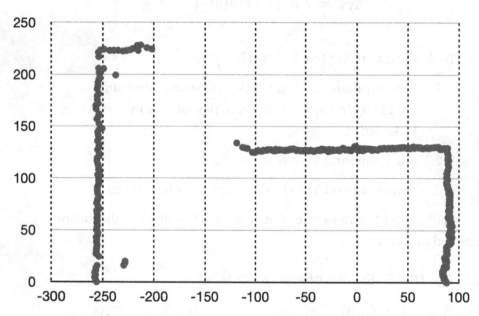

Figure 10-1. *Plot of Lidar Unit scan after processing*

The area scanned is pretty simple, so there is not a lot going on. At the far right, around x=85, you can see a vertical surface which is a combination of a varnished wood door, painted wood trim, and painted sheetrock; some of the irregularity is due to the surface characteristics, and some is due to nonlinearity as the ranges are sometimes less than 100 cm (they were compensated). In the middle, around y=130, you can see an almost horizontal surface, which is a combination of painted wood doors, painted wood trim, and painted sheetrock. On the left, around x=-255, you can see another vertical surface which is painted sheetrock. At the top left, around y=225, you see another horizontal surface which is a combination of painted wood trim and painted sheetrock. The isolated points around (-230, 20) and (-240, 200) represent a table leg and a floor lamp, respectively. The plot demonstrates the fidelity with which the Lidar Unit can represent what it "sees."

What Next?

We've now produced useful information from the Lidar Unit. What next? I'm sure you are tired of hearing this, but what next is up to you. As with the PIMU in Chapter 9, there is a lot more work to do. What we've achieved is actually the easy part! For example, the sensor produces ranges affected by nonlinearity, noise, scanned surface characteristics, and the angle between the sensor and surface; you will almost certainly have to experiment to find the impact in your environment and decide how to address the impact. To actually use the information, you almost certainly have to leverage one or more of the innumerable research papers on using the range data to facilitate localization and navigation.

Summary

In this chapter, you've experienced

- Off-loading tasks from the Raspberry Pi to an Arduino using an extensible client/server pattern

- Analyzing a *moderately complex* "device data sheet" and designing an appropriate Java device library to make that device available to programs in your project

- Implementing the device library using diozero for serial I/O

- Considering *access* issues for methods in the device library, that is, what methods should be public, private, or protected

- Exploring more about determining device identity using diozero support as well as device-specific characteristics

- Considering concurrency issues raised by long-running operations

- Processing raw data to produce more meaningful information

- Recognizing that you often have to iterate a design

Great fun!

CHAPTER 11

An Environmental Sensor

In this chapter, we'll produce a device library for a commonly used IoT device – an environmental sensor. For this book, I chose the Bosch BME280, which measures humidity, pressure, and temperature. The BME280 is a hugely popular sensor, and you can find many breakout boards built with the sensor that make it very easy to include in your project.

In this chapter, I'll discuss

- The joy of finding that diozero supports your device!

- Some of the differences between reading from and writing to a device with I2C and SPI

- The benefits of *playing* with your device, even if you already have a library

Understand the Device

The Bosch BME280 datasheet (`www.bosch-sensortec.com/media/boschsensortec/downloads/datasheets/bst-bme280-ds002.pdf`) shows the device to be moderately complex with different operational modes and configuration options. The following are some interesting highlights:

- The device is *not* 5V tolerant! That isn't a problem since you'll connect to a Raspberry Pi, but you do have to power the device with 3.3V, not 5V.

G. Flurry, *Java on the Raspberry Pi*, https://doi.org/10.1007/978-1-4842-7264-0_11

- The device supports both I2C and SPI interfaces. You must pay particular attention to the details of SPI interaction.

- The I2C interface supports standard, fast, and high-speed modes (see Chapter 7). The maximum SPI clock frequency is 10 MHz.

- Current consumption is measured in µA. This means it is easy to power the device from the Pi.

- There are three modes, *sleep*, *forced*, and *normal*. Forced mode allows the user to drive sampling; normal mode samples continuously. In sleep mode, no sampling occurs.

- Measurement of all three environmental conditions is optional. All three conditions can be oversampled to reduce noise. Pressure and temperature measurements can also be low pass filtered.

- The temperature is used in compensating pressure and humidity, so in effect, it must always be measured to obtain accurate measurements.

- It is important to use burst reads to ensure data integrity.

- Sensor readings must be compensated using parameters stored on the device.

- Three registers control the operational characteristics of the device.

- The "startup time," or time to the first communication after power on, can be as long as two milliseconds (see Table 1 of the datasheet). Part of the "startup time" is copying the compensation parameters to the compensation registers (see Section 5.4.4 of the datasheet).

- A soft reset causes the same behavior as power on (see Section 5.4.2 of the datasheet).

- A device library, called the BME280 API, is available from Bosch (https://github.com/BoschSensortec/BME280_driver).

Looking at the datasheet and thinking about your requirements allows you to understand how you need to configure the BME280 to meet your requirements. This is key to finding a library that supports your needs.

Caution   The BME280 works at 3.3V and *cannot tolerate 5V*. Some breakout boards provide a power regulator and level shifting so you can connect to 5V devices; most don't. Fortunately, the Raspberry Pi is a 3.3V device. The BME280 supports I2C and SPI. Some breakout boards expose both interfaces; most expose only I2C; if you want to connect via SPI, you must acquire an SPI-capable breakout board.

Find a Device Library

To find a device library to use or port, I'll follow the procedure outlined in Chapter 6. The first step is looking at the list of diozero device libraries – there is a BME280 class available! Due diligence requires that you examine the library to ensure it meets your needs. Without going into too much detail, looking at the implementation of BME280 (https://github.com/ mattjlewis/diozero/blob/master/diozero-core/src/main/java/com/ diozero/devices/BME280.java), you can see

- It can use either I2C or SPI to communicate with the device.

- It supports the I2C default device address or a different address.

- It supports setting all the device configuration options, that is, operational modes, oversampling, and low-pass filtering.

- It supports a soft reset. It reads the status register to determine when copying of the compensation data is complete; it uses a two-millisecond delay between status reads.

- It does the compensation using the onboard compensation coefficients.

- It supports reading the status register. Thus, you can determine when data becomes available.

In summary, if you want to use I2C or SPI, the diozero BME280 class almost certainly supports everything you might need to do with the device, and you can use it as is. At worst, it provides a really good starting point for your own library. For example, BME280 always samples, reads, and compensates all three sensors (humidity, pressure, and temperature); if you need to measure only one or two conditions, you could improve performance by modifying your own library to do only what you need.

Note   While it may be difficult to believe, I chose the BME280 for use in the book before I knew diozero existed. While I attribute support for the device in diozero mostly to the popularity of the device, sometimes you just get lucky! Further, in the spirit of full disclosure, I must add that when I started working with diozero, BME280 supported only I2C. I added SPI support.

So, fortune smiled upon you and you found a library for the BME280 in diozero. In the context of a real project, you'd move on. In the context of this book, for the sake of completeness, I'll consider what if that had not been the case. It turns out that because of the popularity of the device, you can find *multiple* device libraries:

- Earlier I mentioned the *Bosch BME280 API*. It supports both I2C and SPI. It is written in C and has implementations for both BSD and Linux systems. The latter might run on a Raspberry Pi. It is specific to the BME280 and has no dependencies on any other libraries.

- Adafruit supplies a C++ library targeting the Arduino. It supports both I2C and SPI (https://github. com/adafruit/Adafruit_BME280_Library). It is dependent on the Adafruit sensor library, but that is not a significant problem for porting. One thing I find curious is that the library uses a ten-millisecond delay between status reads after a soft reset. It also has a few extras beyond just producing compensated data, for example, producing an altitude from the pressure.

- Adafruit supplies a CircuitPython library targeting compatible microcontrollers (`https://github.com/adafruit/Adafruit_CircuitPython_BME280`). It too has some dependencies that seem easy to ignore. You can detect a fair amount of similarity with the Adafruit C++ library.

- A simple search produces several C libraries, a few Python libraries, a Rust library, and others. A popular device indeed!

- The ControlEverythingCommunity provides a Java *test program* (`https://github.com/ControlEverythingCommunity/BME280/blob/master/Java/BME280.java`). It shows the basics of interacting with the device via I2C but cannot be considered a library.

These libraries might prove useful if you require additional insight into device operation, want derivative capabilities, or need some unusual configurations.

Use the diozero BME280

A demonstration of BME280 would be useful. Fortunately, the class is included in the diozero-core jar file in the NetBeans DIOZERO library you created in Chapter 6. For both I2C and SPI, you need to connect Raspberry Pi 3.3V (e.g., header pin 1) to BME280 VIN and Pi ground (e.g., header pin 9) to BME280 GND. I recommend you make *all* connections with the power off.

If you wish to use I2C, you should use Raspberry Pi I2C bus 1. You must also connect Pi SDA (header pin 3) to BME280 SDA/SDI and Pi SCL (header pin 5) to BME280 SCL/SCK; see Figure 11-1.[1]

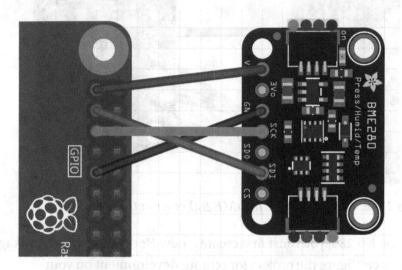

Figure 11-1. *Raspberry Pi to BME280 connections for I2C*

If you wish to use SPI, you should use the Pi SPI bus 0. You must also connect Pi MOSI (header pin 19) to BME280 MOSI/SDA/SDI, Pi MISO (header pin 21) to BME280 MISO/SDO, Pi SCLK (header pin 23) to BME280 SCLK/SCL/SCK, and Pi CE0 (header pin 24) to BME280 CE/CS/CSB; see Figure 11-2.

---

[1] Figures 11-1 and 11-2 were created with Fritzing (https://fritzing.org).

Figure 11-2. *Raspberry Pi to BME280 connections for SPI*

To test BME280, you must first create a new NetBeans project, package, and class; configure the project for remote development on your Raspberry Pi; and configure the project to use diozero (see Chapter 7 for more detail). I named my project **BME280**, my package org.gaf.bme280. test, and my main class TestBME280.

Listing 11-1 shows TestBME280, a modification of the BME280 test programs found among the diozero sample applications (https://github. com/mattjlewis/diozero/tree/master/diozero-sampleapps/src/main/ java/com/diozero/sampleapps). TestBME280 uses either I2C or SPI to read the BME280 once per second a given number of times. It accepts zero, one, or two arguments. The first argument indicates the interface; "i" means I2C and anything else means SPI. The second argument indicates the number of reads. The defaults are I2C and three times.

Following the guidelines in Chapter 7, TestBME280 engages the try-with-resources and diozero shutdown safety nets. Since the BME280 cannot cause any problems in the event of abnormal termination, I chose not to use the Java shutdown safety net.

Listing 11-1. TestBME280 – application to test the diozero
BME280 class

```java
package org.gaf.bme280.test;

import com.diozero.api.SpiConstants;
import com.diozero.devices.BME280;
import com.diozero.util.Diozero;
import com.diozero.util.SleepUtil;
import java.io.IOException;

public class TestBME280 {
    public static void main(String[] args) throws
            InterruptedException, IOException {
        boolean useI2C = true;
        int number = 3;
        switch (args.length) {
            case 2: // set device type AND iterations
                number = Integer.parseInt(args[1]);
            case 1: // set device type
                if (!args[0].toLowerCase().
                    equals("i"))
                    useI2C = false;
                break;
            default: // use defaults
        }

        BME280 bme280;
        if (useI2C)
            bme280 = new BME280();
        else
            bme280 = new BME280(SpiConstants.CE0);
```

```
try (bme280) {
    for (int i = 0; i < number; i++) {
        bme280.waitDataAvailable(10, 5);
        float[] tph = bme280.getValues();
        float tF = tph[0] * (9f/5f) + 32f;
        float pHg = tph[1] * 0.02953f;

        System.out.format(
            "T=%.1f\u00B0C or %.1f\u00B0F "
            + " P=%.1f hPa or %.1f inHg "
            + " RH=%.1f%% %n",
            tph[0], tF, tph[1], pHg, tph[2]);

        SleepUtil.sleepSeconds(1);
    }
} finally {
    Diozero.shutdown();
}
}
}
```

A few things about TestBME280 are worth elaboration:

- It uses the BME280 default configuration parameters. That means no oversampling, no filtering, and normal operation (continuous sampling) with one second between samples.

- BME280 provides values for temperature in Celsius, pressure in hectopascals, and relative humidity in percent. For those of us in a metric-system-challenged country, I've converted Celsius to Fahrenheit and hectopascals to inches of mercury.

- As I mentioned in Chapter 5, the "run remote" feature in NetBeans could not handle the "fancy formatting." Thus, I had to ssh to the Raspberry Pi to run and get proper formatting.

For fun, and some verification of correctness, I downloaded TestBME280 to both the Raspberry Pi 3 Model B+ and the Raspberry Pi Zero W. I placed the 3B+ in my laboratory and the Zero outside on my balcony; I ran the program for 120 seconds, using SPI on the 3B+ and I2C on the Zero. The following lines show results produced toward the end of the period:

> 3B+: T=23.1°C or 73.6°F P=993.9 hPa or 29.4 inHg
> RH=44.9%

> ZW: T=18.5°C or 65.3°F P=998.5 hPa or 29.5 inHg
> RH=52.5%

The results are consistent with expectations. Clearly it was cooler and more humid outside, and the air pressure was almost identical.

Given the success, you could now create an outdoor weather station using the Zero W and a BME280. You could also create a robotic rover using the RoboClaw from Chapter 8, the PIMU from Chapter 9, the Lidar from Chapter 10, and a BME280 to monitor the environmental conditions in accessible areas of your home.

Play with I2C and SPI

While the existence of the diozero BME280 class is good for you in the real world, it is not so great for the virtual world of this book. You've been cheated out of

- Additional experience with I2CDevice (Chapter 9 offered your first experience in this book)

- How to use `SpiDevice`

- And, perhaps more importantly, the differences between I2C and SPI in the same context

The BME280 provides a great opportunity for all three.

As discussed in Chapter 8, it can be very educational to simply *play* with your device. Play can be especially useful if, for example, you're using an unfamiliar I/O capability, you have doubts about what a datasheet is telling you (not an uncommon occurrence), or you just can't wait to work with your shiny new device.

The RoboClaw in Chapter 8 did not qualify for play due to complexity. For the devices in Chapter 10, and Chapter 9 in particular, there was so much work to do we played a bit, but focused on development of the library starting with a useful *core* implementation. The BME280 definitely lends itself to play. So, for the rest of this chapter, we'll *play* with the BME280 using `I2CDevice` and `SpiDevice`. While it is not really necessary, I decided to create a new package for the main classes we'll use to play; I called it `org.gaf.io.test`.

To the Datasheet

Acknowledging redundancy, I state again that the device datasheet (or user manual) is key to understanding how to interact with it. Thus, it is key to playing with it. Section 5 of the Bosch BME280 datasheet describes the *memory* or *register map* and describes the *register usage* independent of communication type. Section 6 in the datasheet discusses the communication via I2C and SPI. Section 5 is the place to start. You can see

- Two blocks of *calibration data* registers; these are read only.

- A block of *sensor data* registers; these are also read only.

- An *ID* register; read only.

- A *reset* register; write only.

- Three *control* registers; read/write.

- A *status* register; read only.

- The I2C controller auto-increments block reads; it *does not* auto-increment block writes.

- The SPI controller auto-increments block reads; it *does not* auto-increment block writes.

From this information, you can determine that to use the BME280, you need the following operations:

- Read a single register.

- Read a register block.

- Write a single register.

I2CDevice

Chapter 7 identified the fundamental read/write methods supported by I2CDevice. Table 11-1 shows the mapping to the operations required to use the BME280 via I2C.

Table 11-1. *I2CDevice methods for BME280 operations*

BME280 operation	I2CDevice method
Read a single register	readByteData
Read a register block	readI2CBlockData
Write a single register	writeByteData

If you want to get more sophisticated, you could use some of
the convenience methods. You can examine the private method
readCoefficients and the public method getValues in BME280 for
example usage of ByteBuffer.

To play, I try to start as simple as possible and then get more
sophisticated if needed. Listing 11-2 shows PlayI2C, a simple program to
test using I2C to access the BME280. It instantiates an I2CDevice instance
on I2C bus 1 with the default BME280 address. It then reads and prints a
register, in this case the ID (or "who am I") register.

Listing 11-2. PlayI2C initial snippet; read a register

```
package org.gaf.io.test;

import com.diozero.api.I2CConstants;
import com.diozero.api.I2CDevice;

public class PlayI2C {

    private static I2CDevice device = null;

    public static void main(String[] args) {
        device = new I2CDevice(
                I2CConstants.CONTROLLER_1, 0x76);

        // 1: test read a register
        byte reg = device.readByteData(0xd0);
        System.out.format("ID=0x%02X%n", reg);

        // close
        device.close();
    }
}
```

```
================================================================
```
Output:
ID=0x60

Running PlayI2C produces the output shown at the bottom of Listing 11-2. The value read is good news, as it is the expected value (see the datasheet).

Listing 11-3 shows an additional snippet of PlayI2C that tests a block read. It reads a block of seven calibration registers and then reads two individual registers as a check.

Listing 11-3. PlayI2C snippet; read a register block

```
// 2: test read register block
byte[] ret = new byte[7];
device.readI2CBlockData(0xe1, ret);
System.out.print("cal");
for (int i = 0; i < 7; i++) {
    System.out.format(" %d=0x%02X ", i, ret[i]);
}
System.out.println();
reg = device.readByteData(0xe1);
System.out.format("cal 0=0x%02X%n", reg);
reg = device.readByteData(0xe7);
System.out.format("cal 6=0x%02X%n", reg);
```

```
================================================================
```
Output:
cal 0=0x87 1=0x01 2=0x00 3=0x0F 4=0x2F 5=0x03 6=0x1E
cal 0=0x87
cal 6=0x1E

Running PlayI2C produces the output for reading the block shown at the bottom of Listing 11-3. The values read as a block are again good news, as the two registers read individually confirm the block values.

Listing 11-4 shows a final snippet of PlayI2C that tests writing a register. It reads a configuration register, writes that register, and then reads the register again to confirm the change. Finally, now that we've confirmed writing a register works, it resets the device to create a known state for later testing.

Listing 11-4. PlayI2C snippet; write a register

```
// 3: test write a register
reg = device.readByteData(0xf4);
System.out.format("reg before=0x%02X%n", reg);
device.writeByteData(0xf4, (byte)0x55);
reg = device.readByteData(0xf4);
System.out.format("reg after=0x%02X%n", reg);

// reset
device.writeByteData(0xe0, (byte)0xb6);
```

===

Output:
reg before=0x00
reg after=0x55

Running PlayI2C produces the output for writing a register shown at the bottom of Listing 11-4. The final value read shows that writing the register worked.

SpiDevice

Chapter 7 identified the fundamental read/write methods supported by SpiDevice. Table 11-2 shows the mapping to the operations required to use the BME280 via SPI.

Table 11-2. SpiDevice methods for BME280 operations

BME280 operation	SpiDevice method
Read a single register	writeAndRead
Read a register block	writeAndRead
Write a single register	write

Unlike the I2CDevice methods, none of the SPI methods have a parameter for a register address. That means it is mandatory to examine Section 6 of the datasheet to understand how to control the BME280 using SPI.

Let's look at reading a single register. It requires two SPI *frames*. In the first SPI frame, you must write a "control byte" that is an eight-bit register address with the most significant bit (MSB) set to "1" (to indicate a read operation). Note that the content of the register appears in the second frame (remember SPI is full duplex). What is not exactly obvious is that you have to make sure that the second frame happens by writing a *second* byte. The content of the second byte written is meaningless. Since we write two frames (bytes), the device returns two frames (bytes). The first byte in the returned two-byte array is garbage, and the second is the content of the desired register.

Reading a register block is not too different from reading a single byte; it requires N+1 frames, where N is the number of bytes you wish to read. You must write the *first* register address (with the MSB set to "1") in the first frame and then write N additional frames to read the desired bytes. Since the device auto-increments on reads, the content of the subsequent bytes written is meaningless. The first byte in the returned byte array is garbage, and the rest are the content of the desired registers.

Writing a single register also requires two SPI frames. In the first SPI frame, you again write a "control byte" that is an eight-bit register address with the MSB set to "0" (to indicate a write operation). In the second frame, you write the desired content of the register.

Listing 11-5 shows PlaySPI, a simple program to test using SPI to access the BME280; it does the same tests as PlayI2C in Listing 11-2. It instantiates an SpiDevice instance using CE0 as the device enable pin. It reads a register, again the "who am I" register. I put PlaySPI in the same package as PlayI2C.

The private method readByte implements the earlier description of how to read a single register. That makes the method analogous to the I2CDevice.readByteData method.

Listing 11-5. PlaySPI initial snippet; read a register

```
import com.diozero.api.SpiDevice;
import com.diozero.api.SpiConstants;

public class PlaySPI {

    private static SpiDevice device = null;

    public static void main(String[] args) {
        device = new SpiDevice(SpiConstants.CE0);

        // 1: test read a register
        byte reg = readByte(0xd0);
        System.out.format("ID=0x%02X%n", reg);

        // close
        device.close();
    }
```

```
private static byte readByte(int address) {
    byte[] tx = {(byte) (address | 0x80), 0};
    byte[] rx = device.writeAndRead(tx);
    return rx[1];
}
}
```

==

Output:
ID=0x60

Running PlaySPI produces the output shown at the bottom of
Listing 11-5. The result shows a successful read.

Listing 11-6 shows additional snippets of PlaySPI that test reading
a register block. The first snippet has several lines inserted into the main
method before the device.close() statement. The second snippet is a
private method added to the class. readByteBlock is analogous to the
I2CDevice.readByteBlock method. It implements the earlier description
of how to read a register block.

Listing 11-6. PlaySPI snippets; read a register block

```
// 2: test read register block [gos in main method]
byte[] ret = readByteBlock(0xe1, 7);
System.out.print("cal");
for (int i = 0; i < 7; i++) {
    System.out.format(" %d=0x%02X ", i, ret[i]);
}
System.out.println();
reg = readByte(0xe1);
System.out.format("cal 0=0x%02X%n", reg);
reg = readByte(0xe7);
```

```
System.out.format("cal 6=0x%02X%n", reg);

private static byte[] readByteBlock(int address,
        int length) {
    byte[] tx = new byte[length + 1];
    tx[0] = (byte) (address | 0x80);
    /* NOTE: array initialized to 0 */

    byte[] rx = device.writeAndRead(tx);

    byte[] data = new byte[length];
    System.arraycopy(rx, 1, data, 0, length);

    return data;
}
```

===

Output:
cal 0=0x76   1=0x01   2=0x00   3=0x12   4=0x22   5=0x03   6=0x1E
cal 0=0x76
cal 6=0x1E

Running PlaySPI produces the output for reading the register block
shown at the bottom of Listing 11-6. The result shows a successful block
read. Note that some of the calibration register values are different from
the I2C test because I used a different BME280 breakout board to test I2C.

Listing 11-7 shows the final snippets of PlaySPI that test writing a
register. Again, there are two snippets. The first snippet has several lines
inserted into the main method before the device.close() statement.
The second snippet is a private method added to the class. writeByte is
analogous to the I2CDevice.writeByteData method. It implements the
earlier description of how to write a single register.

Listing 11-7. PlaySPI snippets; write a register

```
// 3: test write a register [goes in main method]
reg = readByte(0xf4);
System.out.format("reg before=0x%02X%n", reg);

writeByte(0xf4, (byte)0x55);

reg = readByte(0xf4);
System.out.format("reg after=0x%02X%n", reg);

// reset
writeByte(0xe0, (byte)0xb6);

private static void writeByte(int address,
        byte value) {
    byte[] tx = new byte[2];
    tx[0] = (byte) (address & 0x7f); // msb must be 0
    tx[1] = value;

    device.write(tx);
}
```

```
===========================================================
```

Output:
reg before=0x00
reg after=0x55

Running PlaySPI produces the output for writing a register shown at the bottom of Listing 11-7. The result shows a successful write.

A Step Beyond Play

Sometimes you read something about a device that makes you wonder about the impact on your library. If you read the BME280 datasheet highlights earlier, you noticed that power on reset involves copying the compensation parameters from NVM to the registers and that the whole power-on sequence should take a maximum of two milliseconds. If you examine the existing libraries, you will find that after a soft reset, they wait for the NVM data copy to be completed before proceeding. I'd like to know how long it really takes.

Another interesting tidbit is that the BME280 allows an SPI clock frequency up to 10 MHz. I'd like to get some understanding of the performance implications of the higher frequency.

Listing 11-8 shows the program `PlayReal`, in package `org.gaf.io.test`, that lets us investigate both topics. `PlayReal`

- Copies the private methods in `PlaySPI` in Listing 11-7 to read and write bytes.

- Uses the `SpiDevice.Builder` inner class to simplify setting the SPI clock frequency; as shown in Listing 11-8, the frequency is set to 1 MHz initially.

- Resets the device.

- Reads the status register to detect when startup is complete; it increments a counter to track the number of status reads.

- Prints the relevant information.

Listing 11-8. PlayReal

```
package org.gaf.io.test;

import com.diozero.api.SpiConstants;
import com.diozero.api.SpiDevice;

public class PlayReal {

    private static SpiDevice device = null;

    public static void main(String[] args) {
        device = SpiDevice.builder(
                SpiConstants.CE0).
                setFrequency(1_000_000).build();

        // reset
        writeByte(0xe0, (byte)0xb6);
        long tStart = System.nanoTime();

        int cnt = 1;
        while (readByte(0xf3) == 0x01) {
            cnt++;
        }

        long tEnd = System.nanoTime();

        long deltaT = (tEnd  - tStart) / 1000;

        System.out.println("Startup time = " +
            deltaT + "micros." );

        System.out.println(
            "Status read iterations = " + cnt +
                ". Iteration duration = " +
                (deltaT/cnt) + "micros.");
```

393

```java
        // close
        device.close();      }

    private static byte readByte(int address) {
            byte[] tx = {(byte) (address | 0x80), 0};
            byte[] rx = device.writeAndRead(tx);

            return rx[1];
    }

    private static void writeByte(int address,
            byte value) {
        byte[] tx = new byte[2];
        tx[0] = (byte) (address & 0x7f);
        tx[1] = value;

        device.write(tx);
    }
}
```

==

Output:
Startup time = 1553 micros
Status read iterations = 38; Iteration duration = 40 micros

Run PlayReal with an SPI frequency of 1 MHz and you should see results similar to the bottom of Listing 11-8. In the example shown, startup took 1553 μseconds, and the average time for reading the status was 40 μseconds. In several executions, startup took from 1513 to 1633 μseconds, and the average read time ranged from 40 to 44 μseconds.

Now change the SPI clock frequency to 10 MHz and run PlayReal. You should see results similar to Listing 11-9.

Listing 11-9. PlayReal results at 10 MHz

```
Output:
Startup time = 1552 micros
Status read iterations = 63; Iteration duration = 24 micros
```

In several executions at 10 MHz, startup took from 1544 to 1561 μseconds, and the average read time ranged from 24 to 27 μseconds. From these data, we can determine

- Startup time is definitely always less than two milliseconds but does vary a bit.

- Read performance is faster at 10 MHz than 1 MHz but less than a factor of 2X. The performance improvement would likely be better for block reads. I'll leave that test for you!

Summary

In this chapter, you learned

- The benefits of leveraging diozero device libraries when they exist. No work!

- The basics of analyzing the I/O operations required to use the device.

- The basics of using the diozero SpiDevice methods to perform I/O operations required to use the device.

- The differences between I2C and SPI when reading from or writing to the same device.

- It is educational to just *play* with your device.

CHAPTER 12

An Analog-to-Digital Converter

The Raspberry Pi, unlike some of its competitors, does not offer true analog I/O. Analog input is particularly interesting, as IoT projects often need to monitor things that produce analog signals. In this chapter, we'll produce a device library for an analog-to-digital converter, or ADC. For this book, I chose the Microchip MCP3008, a member of an extensive family of ADCs manufactured by the company, for a few reasons:

- It is inexpensive and easy to acquire.

- It is quite easy to use (once you understand it).

- It uses SPI in a different way than many SPI devices.

In this chapter, I'll cover

- The joys of finding that diozero supports your device!

- The benefits of *playing* with your device, even if you already have a library

© Greg Flurry 2021

G. Flurry, *Java on the Raspberry Pi*, https://doi.org/10.1007/978-1-4842-7264-0_12

Understand the Device

As always, you must understand your device. You can find the Microchip
MCP30008 datasheet at `https://ww1.microchip.com/downloads/en/`
`DeviceDoc/21295d.pdf`. It shows the device to be relatively simple to use.
The following are some interesting highlights:

- It supports eight single-ended channels or four pseudo-
  differential pairs.

- It can convert only one channel per SPI interaction.

- It provides values with ten-bit resolution. The values
  reported are in effect the percentage of the input
  voltage with respect to a reference voltage.

- The maximum SPI clock frequency depends on
  the supply voltage, ranging from 3.6 MHz for 5V to
  1.35 MHz for 2.7V. Assuming linearity, for a 3.3V supply,
  the maximum frequency would be about 1.9 MHz.

- The maximum sample rate is the SPI clock frequency
  divided by 18.

- You can read values from the device using different
  approaches; see Sections 5.0 and 6.1 of the datasheet.

Finding a Device Library

To find a device library to use or port, I'll follow the procedure outlined in
Chapter 6. The first step is looking at the list of diozero device libraries, but
you likely won't find it. That said, search the diozero documentation and
you will find an *Expansion Boards* section with a subsection *Microchip*
Analog to Digital Converters. That subsection mentions the corresponding
class (a.k.a. device library) `com.diozero.devices.McpAdc`. The library
supports several members of the MCP3xxx family, including the MCP3008!

Due diligence requires that you examine the library to ensure it meets your needs. Without going into too much detail, looking at the implementation of McpAdc (https://github.com/mattjlewis/diozero/blob/master/diozero-core/src/main/java/com/diozero/devices/McpAdc.java), it exposes only single-ended acquisition. If this is adequate for your project, you can use it immediately. If you need to use differential acquisition or tailor the SPI clock frequency (the default is the maximum frequency for a supply voltage of 2.7V), you'll have to create your own implementation, starting, of course, with the current implementation. I should note that internally, McpAdc does support differential acquisition.

Note   Again, straining credulity, I chose the MCP3008 for use in the book before I realized diozero supported it. Again, I attribute support for the device in diozero mostly to the popularity of the device family.

As with the BME280 discussed in Chapter 11, in the context of a real project, you'd move on. In the context of this book, for the sake of completeness, I'll consider what if I had not found support in diozero. It turns out that again, because of the popularity of the device, you can find multiple device libraries that would facilitate creating your own:

- Adafruit supplies a CircuitPython library targeting the Raspberry Pi (https://github.com/adafruit/Adafruit_CircuitPython_MCP3xxx).

- A search on GitHub produces several Python libraries, at least one JavaScript library, some Android libraries. A popular device indeed!

- A Pi4J "test program" shows how to use the device (see https://nealvs.wordpress.com/2016/02/19/pi4j-adc-mcp3008-spi-sensor-reader-example/).

Even with all the available possibilities, if diozero did not provide support, the MCP3008 (and many in its family) is so simple you might be better off starting from scratch.

Use the diozero McpAdc

A demonstration of McpAdc would be enlightening. The diozero documentation shows an example, including a figure with all the connections. I created a simpler test environment. Figure 12-1 shows a cascade of 1kΩ resistors and the measurement points for channels 0–4 of the MCP3008.

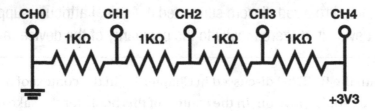

Figure 12-1. *MCP3008 test resistor cascade*

Of course, you must also connect the Raspberry Pi to the MCP3008. See Figure 12-2.[1] First, connect Pi +3.3V (e.g., header pin 1) to MCP3008 V_{DD} and V_{REF} and Pi ground (e.g., header pin 6) to MCP3008 AGND and DGND. You should use Pi SPI bus 0; connect Pi MOSI (header pin 19) to MCP3008 D_{IN}, Pi MISO (header pin 21) to MCP3008 D_{OUT}, Pi SCLK (header pin 23) to MCP3008 CLK, and Pi CE1 (header pin 26) to MCP3008 CS. You must also connect the MCP3008 channels to the resistor cascade as indicated in Figure 12-1.

---

[1] Figure 12-2 was created with Fritzing (https://fritzing.org).

Figure 12-2. *Raspberry Pi to MCP3008 connections*

To get started with the test application, create a new NetBeans project, package, and class; configure the project for remote development on your Raspberry Pi; and configure the project to use diozero (see Chapter 7 for more detail). I named my project **MCP3008**, my package org.gaf.mcp. test, and my class TestMcpAdc, which is derived from diozero McpAdcTest found among the diozero sample applications (https://github.com/ mattjlewis/diozero/tree/master/diozero-sampleapps/src/main/ java/com/diozero/sampleapps).

Listing 12-1 shows the class TestMcpAdc. The implementation constructs an McpAdc for an MCP3008, indicates the use of CE1 for selecting the device, and sets the reference voltage to 3.3V. It then reads channels 0–4 and prints the results. Note that the application follows the safety net guidelines in Chapter 7.

Listing 12-1. TestMcpAdc

```java
package org.gaf.mcp.test;

import static com.diozero.api.SpiConstants.CE1;
import com.diozero.devices.McpAdc;
import com.diozero.devices.McpAdc.Type;
import com.diozero.util.Diozero;

public class TestMcpAdc {

    public static void main(String[] args) {
        try (McpAdc adc = new McpAdc(Type.MCP3008,
                CE1, 3.3f)) {
            for (int i = 0; i < 5; i++) {
                System.out.format("V%1d = %.2f FS%n",
                    i , adc.getValue(i));
            }
        } finally {
            Diozero.shutdown();
        }
    }
}
```

Running `TestMcpAdc` produces the output shown in Listing 12-2. This is what you should expect, given the measurement errors and accuracy of the resistor values.

Listing 12-2. Results from running TestMcpAdc

```
V0 = 0.00 FS
V1 = 0.25 FS
V2 = 0.50 FS
V3 = 0.75 FS
V4 = 1.00 FS
```

> **Caution**   For real-world applications, see Section 6.3 of the
> datasheet regarding buffering and filtering the analog inputs.

Play with SPI

As I mentioned earlier, the MCP3008 provides an example of a different usage of SPI than many other devices. There are no registers to write; there is just data to read that is produced as SPI frames get written to the device. This offers another opportunity to play!

A somewhat painful examination of Sections 5 and 6 of the datasheet shows that the device starts returning valid data bits on the seventh clock after the start bit. Armed with this information, you can place the start bit in a set of SPI frames to position the valid data optimally for your needs. In this section, we'll examine two different ways to retrieve the data from the device:

- The way McpAdc does it (see Section 5 of the datasheet, particularly Figure 5.1).

- The way described in datasheet Section 6.1, in particular, Figure 6.1.

Listing 12-3 shows the class TestMCP (in package org.gaf.mcp.test). It assumes the channel inputs shown in Figure 12-1. First, look at the method getValueD; it implements the sample read approach in datasheet Section 5. The first statement creates a *code* byte with the *channel number* in the 3 least significant bits, a "1" in bit 3 to indicate a *single-ended* read, and the *start* bit (a "1") in bit 4. The next statement creates a three-byte array used to produce a three-frame SPI transaction; the first byte contains the code byte, and the second and third bytes are meaningless but necessary to create the second and third SPI frames. The response from the SpiDevice.writeAndRead

method contains three bytes. The positioning of the start bit means the
first byte is trash, the second byte contains the eight most significant bits of
the ten-bit sample value, and the two most significant bits of the third byte
contain the two least significant bits of the ten-bit value. The last few lines
manipulate the second and third bytes to create the ten-bit value returned.

Listing 12-3. TestMCP

```java
package org.gaf.mcp.test;

import com.diozero.api.SpiConstants;
import com.diozero.api.SpiDevice;

public class TestMCP {

    private static SpiDevice device = null;

    public static void main(String[] args) {
        // use CE1; frequency = 1.35MHz
        device = SpiDevice.builder(SpiConstants.CE1).
                setFrequency(1_350_000).build();

        int[] value = new int[5];
        for (int i = 0; i < 5; i++) {
            value[i] = getValueD(i);
        }
        for (int i = 0; i < 5; i++) {
            System.out.format(
                "C%1d = %4d, %.2f FS, %.2fV %n",
                i, value[i], getFS(value[i]),
                getVoltage(value[i], 3.3f));
        }
        device.close();
    }
```

```java
private static int getValueD(int channel) {
    // create start bit & channel code;
    // assume single-ended
    byte code = (byte) ((channel | 0x18));
    // first byte: start bit, single ended,
    // channel
    // second and third bytes create total
    // of 3 frames
    byte[] tx = {code, 0, 0};
    byte[] rx = device.writeAndRead(tx);

    int lsb = rx[2] & 0xf0;
    int msb = rx[1] << 8;
    int value = ((msb | lsb) >>> 4) & 0x3ff;

    return value;
}

private static int getValueM(int channel) {
    // create channel code; assume single-ended
    byte code = (byte) ((channel << 4) | 0x80);
    // first byte has start bit
    // second byte says single-ended, channel
    // third byte for creating third frame
    byte[] tx = {(byte)0x01, code, 0};
    byte[] rx = device.writeAndRead(tx);

    int lsb = rx[2] & 0xff;
    int msb = rx[1] & 0x03;
    int value = (msb << 8) | lsb;

    return value;
}
```

```
    private static float getFS(int value) {
        float fs = ((float)value / 1024f);
        return fs;
    }

    private static float getVoltage(int value,
        float vRef) {
        float voltage =
            ((float)value / 1024f) * vRef;
        return voltage;
    }
}
```

Next, look at the method getValueM; it implements the sample read approach in datasheet Section 6.1. The first statement creates a *code* byte with a "1" in bit 7 to indicate a *single-ended* read and the *channel number* in bits 4, 5, and 6. The next statement creates a three-byte array where the first byte contains the *start* bit in the least significant bit, the second byte contains the code byte, and the third byte is meaningless but necessary to create the third SPI frame. The response from the SpiDevice. writeAndRead method contains three bytes. The positioning of the start bit means the first byte is trash, the two least significant bits of the second byte contain the two most significant bits of the ten-bit sample value, and the third byte contains the eight least significant bits of the ten-bit value. The last few lines manipulate the second and third bytes to create the ten-bit value returned.

Listing 12-3 shows that TestMCP constructs an SpiDevice instance that uses CE1 for device select and sets the SPI clock frequency to 1.35 MHz (to ensure it is below the maximum frequency for 3.3V). Note that using SpiDevice.Builder allows us to accept the desired defaults for the SPI controller (0) and bit ordering (MSB first). It then reads channels 0–4 using getValueD. Finally, it prints out the raw value, the full-scale value (for comparison with TestMcpAdc), and the voltage calculated using the reference voltage.

Running TestMCP produces the output shown in Listing 12-4. The full-scale results appear identical to that from running TestMcpAdc. That proves a proper implementation of getValueD.

Listing 12-4. Results from TestMCP

```
C0 =    0, 0.00 FS, 0.00V
C1 =  254, 0.25 FS, 0.82V
C2 =  512, 0.50 FS, 1.65V
C3 =  767, 0.75 FS, 2.47V
C4 = 1023, 1.00 FS, 3.30V
```

For fun, in TestMCP, replace the call to getValueD with a call to getValueM and run TestMCP again. You should see results that are very similar to Listing 12-4. That is good and confirms proper understanding of the way the MCP3008 uses SPI (and that there is more than one way to skin a cat).

Tip   During testing of the MCP3008, I initially used 10kΩ resistors. As I shifted the start bit position in the transmitted bytes, I received different values for a channel. That prompted yet another examination of the MCP3008 datasheet. In Section 4, I found the following statement: "larger source impedances increase the offset, gain and integral linearity errors of the conversion." I switched to 1kΩ resistors; I began getting consistent values through a range of start bit positions. Unfortunately, sometimes, you must pay attention to the details!

Turn Play into Reality

If you think about TestMCP in Listing 12-3, you realize it basically does everything that a real device library would do, just very informally. Thus, the play went beyond a core implementation in earlier chapters. Even though not necessary, why not go all the way and create an MCP3008 library?

Of course, to start, we need to create a package and class in the existing **MCP3008** project. I'll call the package org.gaf.mcp3008 and the class MCP3008.

Listing 12-5 shows MCP3008. As you should expect, the class implements AutoCloseable and thus has a close method (see Chapter 7). The class has two constructors to mimic McpAdc. Unlike McpAdc, it has three methods to get information for a channel:

- getRaw provides the unprocessed value for a channel. Note that it is simply a renamed copy of getValueM from TestMCP in Listing 12-3.

- getFSFraction provides the value for a channel as a fraction of full scale.

- getVoltage provides the voltage for a channel.

Listing 12-5. MCP3008

```
package org.gaf.mcp3008;

import com.diozero.api.RuntimeIOException;
import static com.diozero.api.SpiConstants.
    DEFAULT_SPI_CONTROLLER;
import com.diozero.api.SpiDevice;
import java.io.IOException;

public class MCP3008 implements AutoCloseable {
```

```java
private SpiDevice device = null;
private final float vRef;

public MCP3008(int chipSelect, float vRef)
        throws IOException {
    this(DEFAULT_SPI_CONTROLLER,
        chipSelect, vRef);
}

public MCP3008(int controller, int chipSelect,
        float vRef) throws IOException {
    try {
        device = SpiDevice.
            builder(chipSelect).
            setController(controller).
            setFrequency(1_350_000).build();
        this.vRef = vRef;
    } catch (RuntimeIOException ex) {
        throw new IOException(ex.getMessage());
    }
}

@Override
public void close() {
    if (device != null) {
        device.close();
        device = null;
    }
}

public int getRaw(int channel)
        throws RuntimeIOException {
    // create channel code; assume single-ended
```

```
        byte code = (byte) ((channel << 4) | 0x80);
        // first byte has start bit
        // second byte says single-ended, channel
        // third byte for creating third frame
        byte[] tx = {(byte)0x01, code, 0};
        byte[] rx = device.writeAndRead(tx);

        int lsb = rx[2] & 0xff;
        int msb = rx[1] & 0x03;
        int value = (msb << 8) | lsb;
        return value;
    }

    public float getFSFraction(int channel)
            throws RuntimeIOException {
        int raw = getRaw(channel);
        float value = raw / (float) 1024;
        return value;
    }

    public float getVoltage(int channel)
            throws RuntimeIOException {
        return (getFSFraction(channel) * vRef);
    }
}
```

To test, obviously we need a new main class. I'll call mine TestMCP3008 and put it in the existing package org.gaf.mcp.test. Listing 12-6 shows the new main class. Its basic structure is a copy of TestMcpAdc in Listing 12-1, but the formatted output exercises all three data access methods in MCP3008; calling each method is inefficient because the device gets read three times; but this isn't quite the real world!

Listing 12-6. TestMCP3008

```
package org.gaf.mcp.test;

import static com.diozero.api.SpiConstants.CE1;
import com.diozero.util.Diozero;
import java.io.IOException;
import org.gaf.mcp3008.MCP3008;

public class TestMCP3008 {

    public static void main(String[] args)
            throws IOException {
        try (MCP3008 adc = new MCP3008(CE1, 3.3f)) {
            for (int i = 0; i < 5; i++) {
            System.out.format("C%1d = %4d, %.2f FS,
                    %.2fV %n", i, adc.getRaw(i),
                    adc.getRelative(i),
                    adc.getVoltage(i));
            }
        } finally {
            Diozero.shutdown();
        }
    }
}
```

Run TestMCP3008 and you should see some now familiar results, as shown in Listing 12-7. Success!

Listing 12-7. Results from **TestMCP3008**

```
C0 =    2, 0.00 FS, 0.01V
C1 =  256, 0.25 FS, 0.82V
C2 =  512, 0.50 FS, 1.65V
C3 =  769, 0.75 FS, 2.48V
C4 = 1022, 1.00 FS, 3.30V
```

I cannot claim that MCP3008 can replace McpAdc, if for no other reason than it only works for the MCP3008. The former also has little of the sophistication of the latter; for example, it does not inherit much of the diozero framework, nor does it support pseudo-differential sampling. That said, if McpAdc did not exist, MCP3008 would work for many projects.

Summary

In this chapter, you learned

- You should do an exhaustive search for support of your device in diozero; it may be "hiding."

- Once again, sometimes you can find an existing device library in diozero and do little to no work.

- SPI devices can use SPI very differently.

- That sometimes play can approach real code.

- That the devil can hide in the details.

CHAPTER 13

A Stepper Motor Driver

In this chapter, we'll build a device library for a stepper motor driver. Stepper motors get used primarily in robotics projects, but it is not inconceivable they could be used in IOT projects.

There are many ways of driving a stepper motor, including simple drivers such as discrete transistors and H-bridges, which force you to do most of the work, and sophisticated drivers that do most of the work for you. In this book, we'll look at the Watterott SilentStepStick (https://learn.watterott.com/silentstepstick/). It is a driver that I've used in some projects; its primary attraction is *silent* operation. I'd consider it around the middle of the "sophistication spectrum," but it is still very easy to use.

In this chapter, I'll discuss

- Using multiple diozero base I/O devices, specifically GPIO output devices, to construct a single logical device

- Finding, and ignoring, existing device libraries

- Exploring the options and limitations of diozero

Understand the Device

The SilentStepStick breakout board (https://github.com/watterott/SilentStepStick/blob/master/hardware/SilentStepStick-TMC2100_v10.pdf) leverages the Trinamic TMC2100 chip (www.trinamic.com/fileadmin/assets/Products/ICs_Documents/TMC2100_datasheet_Rev1.11.pdf).

© Greg Flurry 2021
G. Flurry, *Java on the Raspberry Pi*, https://doi.org/10.1007/978-1-4842-7264-0_13

That means you get to read and understand *two* datasheets. Lucky you (and me, of course). I suggest browsing the TMC2100 datasheet, then closely reading the SilentStepStick datasheet, then closely reading the TMC2100 datasheet. The following are the most salient TMC2100 features:

- Drives *bipolar* motors at up to 2A per coil, with voltages from 4.75V to 46V.

- Can interpolate steps up to 256 microsteps per step.

- StealthChop mode enables "extremely quiet" operation.

- Enable, direction, and step signals control movement.

- Seven configuration pins (CFG0–CFG6) control operation; one of them, CFG6, is the enable signal.

- Maximum motor current can be controlled internally or externally.

- Logic voltage can be 3.3V or 5V.

The following are the salient features of the SilentStepStick:

- CFG0, CFG4, and CFG5 control "chopper" operation. All three default to the "recommended, most universal choice." CFG4 and CFG5 have *jumpers* that allow change from the default.

- CFG1 and CFG2 control the mode and microstep resolution of the driver. See the table on page 9 of TMC2100 datasheet or the table in Section 3 of the SilentStepStick datasheet for details.

- CFG3 configures the means of setting the maximum motor current. It defaults to "float" for external control. It too has a jumper to allow change from the default.

- A potentiometer on the breakout adjusts maximum motor current; both datasheets provide instructions on how to adjust the current.

In effect, the SilentStepStick establishes a reasonable default configuration that can be changed if you really need to do so. As a result, under the majority of circumstances, you only need to worry about CFG1 and CFG2.

Of course, the SilentStepStick is only interesting if you have a stepper motor attached. Stepper motors are fascinating beasts. See `https://learn.adafruit.com/all-about-stepper-motors/what-is-a-stepper-motor` for a useful introduction. Stepper motors come in many different sizes, require different voltages and currents, exhibit different step sizes, different torque, and so on. And of course, they are used for many different purposes.

That means it is impossible to determine a truly universal set of requirements for the device library or a universal configuration. Thus, I'll simply identify a set of library and configuration requirements based on my past stepper projects.

I have a bipolar stepper motor for which the specifications are 12V, 0.4A, and 200 full steps/revolution (most stepper motors you'll encounter are 200 steps/revolution). Further, I'll require silent operation, but as fast as possible.

I am also going to make some simplifying, but rational, assumptions. First, the default values for CFG0, CFG3, CFG4, and CFG5 are acceptable. Second, the library does not set the configuration of CFG1 and CFG2; instead, it must be told the number of microsteps per step that result from the configuration. These assumptions save GPIO pins but might not be right for all projects.

Find a Device Library

To find a device library to use or port, I'll follow the procedure outlined in Chapter 6. A look at the diozero device libraries shows no stepper motor drivers.

Searching for Java libraries produced nothing for the TMC2100. I did find hints of libraries for its more sophisticated cousins.

Search for Non-Java Libraries

Searching for Python libraries produced nothing for the TMC2100. Again, I found hints of libraries for its more sophisticated cousins.

The SilentStepStick product page has links to an "Arduino Library and Examples," a "General Software Library," and "Arduino Examples." The first two do not offer support for the TMC2100 and so are no help. The last contains a very trivial example that is also not much help. Quite surprising, actually.

I found an Arduino sketch at `https://electropeak.com/learn/` `interfacing-tmc2100-stepper-motor-driver-with-arduino/`. The page contains an interesting summary of the SilentStepStick and TMC2100 datasheets as well as helpful hints. I expected to identify far more Arduino-based candidates.

You may have noticed the SilentStepStick product page says it is compatible with two other stepper motor controllers, the Watterott StepStick and the Pololu A4988 (`www.pololu.com/product/1182`). I'd claim the A4988 is *partly* compatible. It has only three configuration pins, which control the microsteps per step. Fortunately, the available resolutions match those of the SilentStepStick. Also, fortunately, Pololu provides an Arduino library for the A4988 (`https://github.com/laurb9/StepperDriver/blob/master/` `src/A4988.cpp`). The design is actually quite sophisticated in that it allows for "speed profiles," so that the motor is accelerated from stopped up to nominal speed, run at nominal speed, then decelerated down to stopped.

And the Answer Is ...

For better or worse, I will treat this as a "start from scratch" situation because of the anticipated simplicity. I will use the A4988 library for guidance, but ignore its sophisticated aspects, for two reasons. First, my expectations are *low-speed* and *low-torque* requirements. Second, I must leave something for you to do! More on the subject near the end of the chapter.

Device Library Design

Once again, I'll use a top-down approach. We must start with requirements. In very general terms, stepper motors are used in situations that require accurate position control, accurate speed control, or both. For example, a 3D printer requires both. My past stepper motor projects required only speed control, however, and I'll use them as a model to drive requirements. Based on my past projects, I'll summarize the requirements:

- Want to control the direction and speed of rotation.

- Want to start and stop the rotation.

- Anticipate only low speeds.

- Want to enable and disable the driver. It is important to note that when enabled, the driver powers the motor, so the motor produces torque even when stopped. When disabled, the driver does not power the motor, so it does not produce torque; thus, the shaft and anything attached to it can move freely.

- Do *not* want to control the microstepping configuration. Instead, will be *told* the configuration.

417

As hinted earlier, you must use the diozero GPIO digital output devices to control the SilentStepStick. Enable and direction controls are static and should use `DigitalOutputDevice`. The speed is determined by the step control; it could use a `DigitalOutputDevice` or a `PwmOutputDevice`. See Chapter 7 for more information on those diozero devices.

In theory, there could be multiple SilentStepSticks in a project, so there can be multiple instances of the library; in my last stepper project, I in fact used three SilentStepSticks. That means we must allow for multiple instances.

Caution   Raspberry Pi OS is *not* a real-time operating system and Java is not a real-time language. As a result, you *cannot* expect to produce truly accurate stepper motor *speed* control with the SilentStepStick since the Pi generates a step signal that is subject to the vagaries of the OS and Java. That said, you *can* produce truly accurate stepper motor *position* control because position depends only on the number of steps, which the Pi can accurately control.

Interface Design

Based on the earlier requirements, and examination of the A4988 library, the interface needs methods that offer the ability to

- Enable or disable the driver

- Set the direction, either clockwise or counterclockwise

- Set the speed of rotation

- Run or stop

The constructor requires the following parameters:

- The GPIO pins for the enable, direction, and step pins
- The microsteps per step, as determined by the SilentStepStick configuration pins CFG1 and CFG2

Device Library Development

As with any new diozero-based project, you must create a new NetBeans project, package, and class; configure the project for remote development on your Raspberry Pi; and configure the project to use diozero. See Chapter 7 for a summary of the steps. I'll create a project called **SSS** (because SilentStepStick is too long), a package org.gaf.sss, and a class SilentStepStick. However, before creating the library, you should recognize the SilentStepStick presents a perfect opportunity to play. So that's what we'll do.

Play with the Device

Of course, before playing, you must construct the proper circuit for the SilentStepStick. That means connecting the motor, the motor power supply, and the logic power supply (3.3V from the Raspberry Pi). Page 3 of the SilentStepStick datasheet contains a nice circuit diagram you can use as a guide; page 6 contains some pictures I found useful for connecting the motor properly. You must also adjust the maximum motor current (see page 4 of the SilentStepStick datasheet and page 24 of the TMC2100 datasheet).

Since the configuration pins (including the enable pin) default to some reasonable value and direction does not matter, you can drive the motor using only the step pin driven by the Pi. Very nice!

An interesting question is how to drive the step pin. Earlier, I hypothesized using `DigitalOutputDevice` or `PwmOutputDevice`. The `onOffLoop` method of the former supports either a given number of cycles (steps) or an infinite number of cycles at a chosen frequency; good! The latter supports only an infinite number of cycles, though you can change the frequency; also good! Finally, if you read the documentation closely, you'll find that with `PwmOutputDevice`, the desired frequency must be an integer; in contrast, with `DigitalOutputDevice`, you set the on and off periods in floating point, so, effectively, the frequency is in floating point. Thus, while either class works, `DigitalOutputDevice` offers more flexibility, so I'll use it.

An important question is what frequency to use for the PWM signal that will drive the motor. You don't want to go too fast or too slow. The motor has 200 steps per revolution. 1 RPM = 1/60 revolutions/second (RPS), so to produce 1 RPM, you must drive the motor at 200/60 = ~3.333 Hz. If the driver configuration you choose uses microstepping, you have to multiply that result by the number of microsteps per step. For example, if your configuration has 4 microsteps per step, to produce 1 RPM, you must drive the motor at (200/60) * 4 = ~13.333 Hz.

Since I'm after silent operation, I'm going to set CFG1=3.3V and CFG2=open, which turns on StealthChop at 4 microsteps/step. Now, 1 RPM is pretty slow, so let's say the speed should be 4 RPM. Using the earlier formulas, that means a frequency of 4 * (200/60) * 4 = ~53.333 Hz, which produces a period of 18.75 milliseconds and a half period of 9.375 milliseconds.

Now, we'll create a simple program to run the stepper motor. Listing 13-1 shows the program `Step` in package `org.gaf.sss.test`. The program is truly *very* simple; it has just *three* interesting statements. The first creates a `DigitalOutputDevice` instance that drives GPIO pin 17 which is connected to the SilentStepStick *step* pin; the second generates a 53.333 Hz step signal on GPIO pin 17; the third stops the step signal after 5 seconds.

Notice Step enables the diozero safety net. It does so because the DigitalOutputDevice uses a different thread to drive the step pin; that thread must be terminated at shutdown. See Chapter 7.

Listing 13-1. Step

```
package org.gaf.sss.test;

import com.diozero.api.DigitalOutputDevice;
import com.diozero.util.Diozero;

public class Step {

    public static void main(String[] args)
            throws InterruptedException {
        try (DigitalOutputDevice pwm =
                new DigitalOutputDevice(17, true,
                    false)) {

            pwm.onOffLoop(0.009375f, 0.009375f,
                DigitalOutputDevice.
                    INFINITE_ITERATIONS,
                true, null);
            System.out.println("Waiting ...");
            Thread.sleep(5000);

            pwm.stopOnOffLoop();
            System.out.println("Done");
        } finally {
            Diozero.shutdown();
        }
    }
}
```

When you run Step, if everything is connected properly, the stepper motor shaft rotates at roughly 4 RPM for 5 seconds. You can put a piece of tape on the motor shaft to make the rotation easier to detect.

We've confirmed that the initial hardware and software configuration works. You can now begin to play/experiment with different configurations and different PWM frequencies to find a combination that works well for your project. You can also determine the motor direction for different states of the direction pin.

SilentStepStick Implementation

Now, we'll develop SilentStepStick.[1] In earlier chapters, we first developed a core. In the case of SilentStepStick, however, there is little difference between the core and the full library!

Listing 13-2 shows the initial implementation. We know from the interface discussion earlier that we need to set the direction of rotation as either clockwise or counterclockwise; the Direction enum supplies the appropriate constants. We also need to set the configuration in terms of microstep per step; the Resolution enum supplies the appropriate constants. Per Chapter 7, the class implements java.io.AutoCloseable; thus, it also has a close method, which we will complete later.

Listing 13-2. SilentStepStick constants and close method

```
package org.gaf.sss;

public class SilentStepStick implements
        AutoCloseable {

    @Override
    public void close(){
```

---

[1] Again, I'm not including Javadoc or most comments, but you should do so.

```
    }

    public enum Direction {
        CW,
        CCW;
    }

    public enum Resolution {
        Full(1),
        Half(2),
        Quarter(4),
        Eighth(8),
        Sixteenth(16);

        public  final int resolution;

        Resolution(int resolution) {
            this.resolution = resolution;
        }
    }
}
```

Constructor Implementation

Listing 13-3 shows the SilentStepStick constructor. It implements
the requirements discussed earlier. The only parameter not previously
mentioned is stepsPerRev; it specifies the number of steps per revolution
for the stepper motor being driven, necessary for calculating the frequency
of the step signal.

The constructor creates a DigitalOutputDevice to drive the enable
pin (initialized disabled), a second to drive the direction pin (initialized
clockwise), and a third to drive the step pin; the step pin is configured
active high and is initially set low, so no stepping occurs. The constructor

also calculates the number of SilentStepStick microsteps per revolution, which is used later to calculate the frequency of the step signal to achieve a desired speed.

Listing 13-3. SilentStepStick constructor and close method

```
import com.diozero.api.DigitalOutputDevice;
import com.diozero.api.RuntimeIOException;
import com.diozero.util.SleepUtil;
import java.io.IOException;

    private DigitalOutputDevice dir;
    private DigitalOutputDevice enable;
    private DigitalOutputDevice step;

    private final float microstepsPerRev;
    private boolean running = false;

    public SilentStepStick(int enablePin,
            int directionPin, int stepPin,
            int stepsPerRev, Resolution resolution)
            throws IOException {
        try {
            // set up GPIO
            enable = new DigitalOutputDevice(
                enablePin, false, false);
            dir = new DigitalOutputDevice(
                directionPin, true, false);
            step = new DigitalOutputDevice(
                stepPin, true, false);

            // set configuration
            microstepsPerRev = (float)
                (stepsPerRev * resolution.resolution);
```

```java
    } catch (RuntimeIOException ex) {
        throw new IOException(ex.getMessage());
    }
}

@Override
public void close() {
    // disable
    if (enable != null) {
        enable.off();
        enable.close();
        enable = null;
    }
    // stop
    if (step != null) {
        // turn it off
        step.stopOnOffLoop();
        step.close();
        step = null;
    }
    if (dir != null) {
        dir.close();
        dir = null;
    }

}
```

Listing 13-3 also shows the completed close method. It ensures the driver is disabled and the step signal is off, so that the motor stops. The method also closes all the diozero device instances.

Listing 13-4 shows the implementation of the operative methods described earlier. The enable method is self-explanatory, as is the setDirection method.

After further reflection on the interface discussion earlier, it seemed appropriate to provide a *single* method that sets the direction, sets the speed, and turns on the step signal. Thus, the run method has parameters for direction and rotation speed. It uses the parameters to set the direction and determine the frequency of the step signal. The method turns on the step signal at the desired frequency by starting a DigitalOutputDevice infinite on/off loop. The step signal runs until it is turned off by calling the stop method.

Note that I made the decision to run the infinite on/off loop in the background. Further, I decided to ignore the ability to be notified when the loop stops because the loop must be explicitly stopped. These choices seemed reasonable to me. You might make different choices.

Listing 13-4. SilentStepStick operative methods

```
public void enable(boolean enableIt)
        throws RuntimeIOException {
    if (enableIt) {
        enable.on();
    }
    else {
        enable.off();
    }
}

private void setDirection(Direction direction)
        throws RuntimeIOException {
    if (direction == Direction.CW) dir.off();
    else dir.on();
}

public void run(Direction direction, float speedRPM)
        throws RuntimeIOException {
```

```
    if (running) step.stopOnOffLoop();
    // let motor rest (see p.9 of datasheet)
    SleepUtil.sleepMillis(100);

    setDirection(direction);

    float halfPeriod = getHalfPeriod(speedRPM);
    step.onOffLoop(halfPeriod, halfPeriod,
            DigitalOutputDevice.INFINITE_ITERATIONS,
            true, null);
    running = true;
}

public void stop() throws RuntimeIOException {
    step.stopOnOffLoop();
    running = false;
}

private float getHalfPeriod(float speedRPM) {
    float speedRPS = speedRPM/60f;
    float frequency = speedRPS * microstepsPerRev;
    float halfPeriod = 0.5f / frequency;
    return halfPeriod;
}

public int getStepCount() {
    return step.getCycleCount();
}
```

The run method calls the getHalfPeriod method. The latter performs the calculations explained earlier to produce a step signal frequency from the speed parameter (in RPM). It then calculates the half period run uses to set up the DigitalOutputDevice on/off loop.

Finally, note the getStepCount method in Listing 13-4. It is not in the requirements or interface mentioned earlier. I realized after playing with

427

Step (Listing 13-1) and thinking about the implications of the run method in Listing 13-4 that something like getStepCount would be quite useful in understanding stepper motor positioning in the context of a "run then stop" scenario. I requested the developer of diozero insert the necessary logic in DigitalOutputDevice.

Test SilentStepStick

Now, we'll test SilentStepStick. A good first test is to reproduce the effect of the Step program in Listing 13-1. Listing 13-5 shows TestSSS1 that does so.

The "applications" in this chapter of course engage the try-with-resources and diozero shutdown safety nets. They do not engage the Java shutdown safety net since nothing is attached to the stepper motor shaft and thus no damage can result from improper termination.

Listing 13-5. TestSSS1

```java
package org.gaf.sss.test;

import com.diozero.util.Diozero;
import java.io.IOException;
import org.gaf.sss.SilentStepStick;

public class TestSSS1 {

    public static void main(String[] args)
            throws IOException, InterruptedException {

        try (SilentStepStick stepper =
                new SilentStepStick(4, 27, 17, 200,
                SilentStepStick.Resolution.Quarter)) {

            stepper.enable(true);

            System.out.println("Run CW");
```

```
        stepper.run(SilentStepStick.Direction.CW, 4f);
        Thread.sleep(5000);

        System.out.println("Stopping");
        stepper.stop();
        System.out.println("Count = " +
            stepper.getStepCount());

        System.out.println("Disabling");
        stepper.enable(false);

        System.out.println("Closing");
    } finally {
        Diozero.shutdown();
    }
  }
}
```

Run TestSSS1 and you should see motor behavior identical to that when you run Step; you should also see the results shown in Listing 13-6. Note in particular the count of microsteps. With the motor specification, the microstep configuration, and the requested speed, the frequency of the step signal to the SilentStepStick should be 53.333 Hz; thus, a running period of 5 seconds should result in a count of ~267; a count of 275 is a bit disappointing, but not unreasonable. Clearly the loop runs a bit fast.

Listing 13-6. Results of running TestSSS1

```
Run CW
Stopping
Count = 275
Disabling
Closing
```

To have a bit more fun, we can now make the motor run clockwise for a while and then counterclockwise. Listing 13-7 shows `TestSSS2`, which does just that.

Listing 13-7. TestSSS2

```
package org.gaf.sss.test;

import com.diozero.util.Diozero;
import java.io.IOException;
import org.gaf.sss.SilentStepStick;

public class TestSSS2 {

    public static void main(String[] args)
            throws IOException, InterruptedException {

        try (SilentStepStick stepper =
                new SilentStepStick(4, 27, 17, 200,
                SilentStepStick.Resolution.Quarter)) {

            stepper.enable(true);
            System.out.println("Run CW");
            stepper.run(
                SilentStepStick.Direction.CW, 4f);

            Thread.sleep(5000);

            System.out.println("Stopping");
            stepper.stop();
            System.out.println("Count = " +
                stepper.getStepCount());
            System.out.println("Run CCW");
            stepper.run(
                SilentStepStick.Direction.CCW, 2f);
```

```
        Thread.sleep(5000);

        System.out.println("Stopping");
        stepper.stop();
        System.out.println("Count = " +
            stepper.getStepCount());
        stepper.enable(false);

        System.out.println("Closing");
    } finally {
        Diozero.shutdown();
    }

  }
}
```

Run `TestSSS2`, and if everything is wired properly, you should see the motor rotate clockwise for 5 seconds at 4 RPM and then counterclockwise for 5 seconds at 2 RPM. Success!

Listing 13-8 shows the console results of running `TestSSS2`. You can see that again the clockwise count is 275. You can also see that the counterclockwise count is 138, about half of 275, so that count also seems reasonable, if also somewhat higher than expected.

Listing 13-8. Result of running TestSSS2

```
Run CW
Stopping
Count = 275
Run CCW
Stopping
Count = 138
Disabling
Closing
```

What Next?

The implementation of SilentStepStick fulfills one benefit of stepper motors – *speed* control.[2] The clever choice of DigitalOutputDevice allows us to also provide accurate *position* control! The reason is that with a stepping motor, accurate position control translates to moving an accurate number of steps, and DigitalOutputDevice can do that.

Listing 13-9 shows the stepCount method for SilentStepStick that performs position control. It is more complex than the run method (Listing 13-4):

- It does *not* allow termination of any stepping currently running. While a somewhat arbitrary decision, it does help maintain accurate positioning.

- It exposes the ability of the DigitalOutputDevice to run an on/off loop in the foreground or background. The step count could be small enough that running in the foreground makes sense.

- It exposes the ability of the DigitalOutputDevice to call the caller's Action at the termination of the on/off loop. In most background situations, this is a good idea.

- It must intercept the call by the DigitalOutputDevice to an Action in order to maintain internal state.

These design decisions seem reasonable and prudent to me, but you might decide to do something different.

---

[2] With a questionable level of accuracy due to the non-real-time nature of the system.

Listing 13-9. SilentStepStick stepCount method

```
public boolean stepCount(int count,
        Direction direction, float speedRPM,
        boolean background, Action stopAction)
        throws RuntimeIOException {

    if (running) {
        return false;
    } else {

        // let motor rest (see p.9 of datasheet)
        SleepUtil.sleepMillis(100);

        // set up an intercept
        Action intercept = () -> {
            System.out.println("intercept");
            running = false;
        };

        setDirection(direction);

        running = true;
        float halfPeriod = getHalfPeriod(speedRPM);
        if (stopAction != null) {
            step.onOffLoop(halfPeriod, halfPeriod,
                    count, background,
                    intercept.andThen(stopAction));
        } else {
            step.onOffLoop(halfPeriod, halfPeriod,
                    count, background, intercept);
        }
```

```
        return true;
    }
}
```

An explanation of how `stepCount` works could be helpful. First, I'll elaborate on the `Action` mechanism. `stepCount` always defines an internal "intercept" `Action` and provides that in the call to the `onOffLoop` method. Thus, when the on/off loop terminates, the `DigitalOutputDevice` always calls the intercept so it can do any internal housekeeping. If the caller provides a non-null `stopAction`, that `Action` gets called after the internal `Action`.

Next, I'll address the foreground/background option. Assume the caller chooses to run in the foreground. The `running` flag gets set `true` prior to the call to the `onOffLoop` method. The `onOffLoop` method

- Runs until the count is complete

- Calls the internal `Action` which sets the `running` flag `false` (and then calls the caller's `Action` if it exists)

- Returns to the `stepCount` method

The `stepCount` method then returns to the caller with the `running` flag `false`.

Now assume the caller chooses to run in the background. The `running` flag gets set `true` prior to the call to the `onOffLoop` method. The `onOffLoop` method spawns a background thread to run the on/off loop and returns to the `stepCount` method, which in turn returns to the caller with the `running` flag `true`. The caller can perform other tasks while the background thread runs the on/off loop. The background thread

- Runs until the count is complete

- Calls the internal `Action` which sets the `running` flag `false` (and then calls the caller's `Action` if it exists)

At this point, the SilentStepStick instance has the running flag false, and another stepper activity can be initiated.

Now we can test the stepCount method. Listing 13-10 shows the program TestSSS3 that does so. The AtomicBoolean is a Java concurrency construct that enables synchronized communication between two threads; TestSSS3 uses it to know when a step count is finished. As you can see from Listing 13-10, TestSSS3 is similar to TestSSS2, except that it requests a fixed number of steps rather than an infinite number. Further, TestSSS3 identifies an Action (the method whenDone) to take upon count completion; it simply indicates, via the AtomicBoolean, that the count is complete.

Listing 13-10. TestSSS3

```
package org.gaf.sss.test;

import com.diozero.util.Diozero;
import java.io.IOException;
import java.util.concurrent.atomic.AtomicBoolean;
import org.gaf.sss.SilentStepStick;

public class TestSSS3 {

    private static AtomicBoolean done;

    public static void main(String[] args)
            throws IOException, InterruptedException {
        try (SilentStepStick stepper =
                new SilentStepStick(4, 27, 17, 200,
                SilentStepStick.Resolution.Quarter)) {

            done = new AtomicBoolean(false);

            stepper.enable(true);
```

```java
        System.out.println("Run CW");
        done.set(false);
        boolean status = stepper.stepCount(100,
                SilentStepStick.Direction.CW, 4f,
                true, TestSSS3:: whenDone);

        while (!done.get()) {
            Thread.sleep(100);
        }

        System.out.println("DONE");
        System.out.println("Count = " +
            stepper.getStepCount());

        System.out.println("Run CCW");
        done.set(false);
        status = stepper.stepCount(100,
                SilentStepStick.Direction.CCW,
                2f, true, TestSSS3:: whenDone);

        while (!done.get()) {
            Thread.sleep(100);
        }

        System.out.println("DONE");
        System.out.println("Count = " +
            stepper.getStepCount());

        System.out.println("Disabling");
        stepper.enable(false);

        System.out.println("Closing");
    } finally {
        Diozero.shutdown();
    }
```

```
    }

    private static void whenDone () {
        System.out.println("Device done");
        done.set(true);
    }
}
```

Run TestSSS3 and you should see results as in Listing 13-11. It is quite reassuring to see that the microstep counts for both directions of rotation agree with the requested counts.

Listing 13-11. Results of running TestSSS3

```
Run CW
intercept
Device done
DONE
Count = 100
Run CCW
intercept
Device done
DONE
Count = 200
Disabling
Closing
```

Speed Profiles

I mentioned in the section on libraries the notion of "speed profiles" implemented in the Pololu A4988 library. Speed profiles can be extremely important in some stepper motor applications, especially where high speed or high torque are involved. The paper www.ti.com/

```
lit/an/slyt482/slyt482.pdf?ts=1615587700571&ref_
url=https%253A%252F%252Fwww.google.com%252F
```
 explains the concepts and issues.

Fundamentally, the goal of a speed profile is to accelerate the motor from stopped up to a target speed, run for some period at the target speed, and then decelerate down to stopped. A really good question is whether or not it is possible to implement a speed profile using the diozero base I/O API. The answer is a bit complex:

- At the time of writing, the answer is **no**. I base that on an examination of the implementation of `DigitalOutputDevice`.

- That said, with some changes suggested by the Arduino library mentioned earlier, the answer becomes **yes, but**. The "but" has several facets:

  - One form of the changes would impact the performance in ways that might not be palatable for some projects.

  - A second form of the changes would force a potentially unpleasant change in the interface of `DigitalOutputDevice`.

  - Using the revised `DigitalOutputDevice` would require ramping to be done in the foreground or use of Java concurrency constructs or perhaps diozero threading constructs to do it in the background.

I think in reality, the best choice would be to produce a peer or subclass of `DigitalOutputDevice` specifically targeting stepper motor speed profiles. Sadly, both are beyond the scope of the book. That said, if you really need speed profiles and you don't want to create a "speed profile" class, you may be able to find a more sophisticated stepper motor driver that implements profiles, much as the RoboClaw controller does for DC motors (see Chapter 8).

Summary

In this chapter, you've experienced

- Finding existing device libraries and mostly ignoring them

- Creating a device library mostly from scratch

- Using several diozero digital I/O devices to construct a single logical device

- Playing with the device prior to implementing the library

- Realizing that diozero cannot do everything

All good stuff!

CHAPTER 14

A Project

In this chapter, instead of focusing on a *single device*, we shall examine a *project* that requires *multiple devices*. The project I've chosen is what you might consider "the world's most ridiculous metronome." While it is not terribly ambitious, I think it illustrates the sort of steps you must take to complete a project that involves mechanical, electronic, and software components typical of most robotics projects and some IoT projects.

In this chapter, I'll cover

- Identifying project requirements

- Choosing devices for a project

- Experimenting with the devices

- Putting everything together

The Metronome

Before you can identify project requirements, you have to define the project. What is the metronome? In the simplest terms, the metronome waves a "wand" back and forth. To implement it, you could simply wave between two known points, one of which must be a manually established starting point; but that is kind of boring. A more interesting approach is to make the wand start in an arbitrary position and detect the two known points, then wave. Let's go with the interesting approach.

© Greg Flurry 2021
G. Flurry, *Java on the Raspberry Pi*, https://doi.org/10.1007/978-1-4842-7264-0_14

So, we now must address some design decisions around the fundamental elements of the metronomes. How do we

- Move the wand?

- Detect the known points?

In this book, we've discussed two devices that move things: the RoboClaw for DC motors (Chapter 8) and the SilentStepStick for stepper motors (Chapter 13). At this point, either would suffice for the metronome.[1]

We've not discussed any devices in this book that detect position or presence on the scale required for the metronome. The first two devices that come to my mind are photodetectors and limit switches, probably because I've used both in past projects. That said, I only had "crash" (a.k.a. limit) switches available at the time of writing, so I used them (see `www.dfrobot.com/product-762.html` and `www.dfrobot.com/product-763.html`).

Mechanical Design

Now we know we can use one of the two motor types to move the wand back and forth and that we'll use limit switches to detect when the wand reaches the two known points. This leads to some mechanical design questions. How do we

- Mount the wand to the motor?

- Align the wand and the switches so the wand activates the switches to establish the known points?

---

[1] An attractive option would be a servo; however, the servo mentioned in this book was encapsulated by the Lidar Unit in Chapter 10 and not connected to a Raspberry Pi.

In the era of 3D printing, you might decide to design and 3D print the custom parts to build the proper mechanical structure. At the time of writing, I, however, happened to have a collection of Actobotics® parts (see www.servocity.com) laying around from previous projects. They allowed me to design and build a mechanical structure quickly from standard parts.

Based on the parts I had at the time, I had to use a stepper motor rather than a DC motor. Given that constraint, I did an initial mechanical design for the metronome using Fusion360 (see www.autodesk.com/products/fusion-360). Figure 14-1 shows the major elements of the mechanical design.

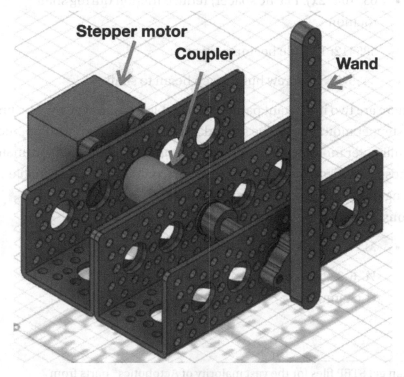

Figure 14-1. Metronome mechanical design

The design uses the following Actobotics® parts,[2] some of which are not visible in Figure 14-1:

- 585444 (2x): 5-hole U-channel; for base structural support

- 555156: NEMA 14 stepper motor mount; attaches the motor to U-channel

- 634076: 2.75″ x ¼″ D-shaft; drive shaft for wand

- 535198 (2x): Flanged ball bearing; shaft support

- 625302 (2x): Set-screw collar; lock shaft in place

- 633104 (2x): Plastic spacer; reduce friction during shaft rotation

- 585412: 13-hole beam; the *wand*

- 545548: Set-screw hub; attach beam to shaft

There are two important parts not available from ServoCity. The first is the stepper motor itself. The second is a flexible coupler[3] to adapt the five-millimeter motor shaft to the ¼″ Actobotics® drive shaft. I fortunately had those parts from previous projects; you could use any reasonable stepping motor and a corresponding coupler.

Construction also required

- M3 screw (4x): Attach stepper motor to mount

- ¼″ 6-32 truss head screw (4x): Attach mount to U-channel

---

[2] You can get STEP files for the vast majority of Actobotics® parts from www.servocity.com/step-files/ and use them in 3D CAD programs.

[3] A flexible coupler reduces mechanical strain due to misalignment between the motor shaft and the drive shaft.

- 5/16″ 6-32 screw (4x): Attach U-channel to U-channel

- 6-32 nut (4x): Attach U-channel to U-channel

As you can tell, the Actobotics® parts use the imperial measurement system. The switches use the metric system, so I could not use Actobotics® parts to mount the limit switches. I happened to have some M3 standoffs and screws and was able to mount the switches in acceptable positions using them.

Figure 14-2 shows the metronome mechanical implementation, including the mounted switches. You might notice a minor difference between Figures 14-1 and 14-2. I found that to ensure the wand contacted the switches, I had to put plastic spacers between the wand and set-screw hub.

Figure 14-2. *Metronome mechanical implementation*

In the spirit of honesty, I admit the construction in Figure 14-2 is not ideal because it is prone to mechanical damage. The switches are designed so that an object can move by, close the switch, and keep on moving by, with no damage to the switch. Unfortunately, I did not have the parts to mount the switches in a position enabling that behavior. If you examine the position of the switches, you'll recognize that the wand moves directly toward a switch so that if it keeps going, it hits the switch body and something will likely break! The unfortunate mechanical design limitation requires extra caution in the software design and test.

Electronic Design

Obviously, we will use a Raspberry Pi to provide overall control for the metronome. The choice of a stepper motor for driving the metronome means we use the SilentStepStick from Chapter 13 to drive the motor; that requires three GPIO pins on the Pi. We have two limit switches, each of which must be monitored by the Pi; each requires a single GPIO pin.

We can duplicate, from Chapter 13

- The connections from the stepper motor to the SilentStepStick

- The power and signal connections from the SilentStepStick to the Pi

- The motor power connections to the SilentStepStick

- The SilentStepStick microstep configuration

The limit/crash switches are a bit more complex than most switches (see `http://image.dfrobot.com/image/data/SENO138-L/Crash%20sensor%20Sch.pdf` for a schematic). The switches are normally open and have a built-in pull-up resistor and an LED that lights when the switch closes. Thus, each switch requires connections to power (I used 3.3V rather than 5V to be Pi safe), ground, and to a GPIO pin to detect when the switch closes.

Software Design

There is a difference between this chapter and earlier chapters. We are not creating a *device library*; instead, we are creating a complete *project*. Thus, our main goal is to create a Java *application*, not a Java *library*. By now, you should remember the setup for developing a library using diozero. Developing an application is slightly different (see Chapter 5). In this case, you create a new project (I'll call mine **Metronome**), a package (org.gaf.metronome), and a new main class (Metronome).

We established in the previous section that we will use the SilentStepStick via its library from Chapter 13. But what about the switches? How do we detect switch closure as quickly as possible, to minimize the possibility of a crash? Examining the diozero Javadoc, the only candidate at the time of writing was DigitalInputDevice. See Chapter 7.

Looking in detail at the capabilities of DigitalInputDevice, it seems there are three approaches to detect a switch closing:

- waitForActive: Waits until the GPIO pin detects the active state, which would be *low* for a normally open switch

- whenActivated: Calls an "interrupt handler" each time the GPIO pin detects the active state

- addListener: Calls an "interrupt handler" each time the GPIO pin detects the desired edge(s), which would be *falling* for a normally open switch

In multi-device projects, you generally need to test each device individually and then test combinations. We in effect did a lot of testing of the SilentStepStick and its library in Chapter 13. As part of the switch

447

testing, it would be a good idea to test all three approaches to determine which produces the fastest detection. This sounds like playing (and fun) to me!

Project Component Testing

As mentioned earlier, we've already tested the SilentStepStick, but we do need to test the switches. To do it, I'll create another package in **Metronome** called org.gaf.metronome.test to contain the test programs.

Test waitForActive

We will first test waitForActive using the program TestWait, shown in Listing 14-1. The idea is to detect the switch closing using waitForActive and generate a pulse using a DigitalOutputDevice. In theory, this allows us to measure the delay between switch closure and being able to do something about it. In Chapter 9, we used whenActivated to catch interrupts and experienced some anomalous timing on the first and possibly second interrupts. Thus, TestWait exercises waitForActive multiple times to see if the same timing anomalies occur.

Because of the threading used by DigitalOutputDevice, TestWait enables the try-with-resources and diozero safety nets. See Chapter 7.

Listing 14-1. TestWait

```
package org.gaf.metronome.test;

import com.diozero.api.DigitalInputDevice;
import com.diozero.api.DigitalOutputDevice;
import com.diozero.api.GpioPullUpDown;
import com.diozero.util.Diozero;
```

```java
public class TestWait {

    public static void main(String[] args)
            throws InterruptedException {
        try (
        DigitalInputDevice did =
            DigitalInputDevice.Builder.
            builder(20).
            setPullUpDown(GpioPullUpDown.NONE).
            setActiveHigh(false).build();
        DigitalOutputDevice dod =
            new DigitalOutputDevice(21,
            true, false)) {

            int num = 3;
            for (int i = 0; i < num; i++) {

                System.out.println("Waiting ...");
                boolean status =
                    did.waitForActive(5000);
                dod.on();
                if (status) {
                    System.out.println("Got it");
                }
                Thread.sleep(5);
                dod.off();

                System.out.println("Killing time");
                if (i < (num - 1))
                    Thread.sleep(4000);
            }
            System.out.println("Done");
        } finally {
```

```
        Diozero.shutdown();
    }
  }
}
```

As you can see in Listing 14-1, TestWait loops. Each iteration waits for switch closure and then produces a pulse. It then "kills some time" to allow you to prepare for a new switch closure.

Figure 14-3 shows the results captured by my oscilloscope for the *first* of three switch closures. The top trace shows the GPIO pin monitoring the switch. The bottom trace shows the GPIO pin producing the output pulse. You can see that the time from the first visible edge of the switch signal to the leading edge of the pulse is approximately 1.8 milliseconds.

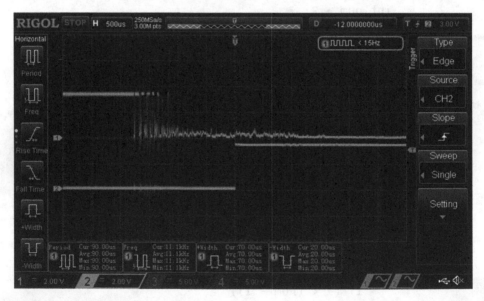

Figure 14-3. *TestWait first interrupt*

You can also see in Figure 14-3 the sad reality of dealing with mechanical switches. The switch contacts "bounce" for a while but eventually stabilize. This is a classic problem with mechanical switches – when is the switch *really* activated? For the switch I'm using, the bounce period appears to be somewhere between 500 microseconds and several milliseconds depending on the voltages the Raspberry PI GPIO uses to define low and high and for how long the voltage must be stable. That said, a very common expectation for a debounce period is up to 50 milliseconds.

Tip   As you can see in Figure 14-3, mechanical switches "bounce." You can find lots of information on the subject online. The following references offer some insight into why switches bounce, the implications, and how to handle bounce: www. labbookpages.co.uk/electronics/debounce.html, www. allaboutcircuits.com/technical-articles/switch-bounce-how-to-deal-with-it/, and www.eejournal.com/ article/ultimate-guide-to-switch-debounce-part-9. diozero includes com.diozero.api.DebouncedDigitalDevice that successfully debounces some switches I tested, but not others (e.g., the switches in this chapter). You should be prepared to test your switches and even implement your own debounce approach.

Figure 14-4 shows the results for the *third* of three switch closures. You can see that the time from the first visible edge of the switch signal to the leading edge of the pulse is approximately 800 microseconds. This is a definite improvement. I speculate the difference is due to JVM class loading and possibly JITC[4] completion.

---

[4] JITC is the just-in-time compiler that is part of the JVM.

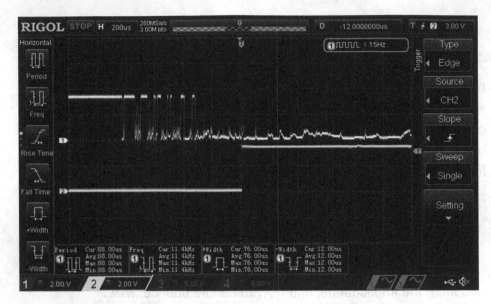

Figure 14-4. *TestWait third interrupt*

Test whenActivated

Now we'll test whenActivated using the program TestWhen, shown in Listing 14-2. TestWhen is quite different from TestWait. As in Chapter 9, we must create an "interrupt handler" (method when) to catch the interrupt generated by the switch and of course identify the interrupt handler using whenActivated. The interrupt handler generates the pulse and also keeps count of the number of events produced by the switch closure.

Listing 14-2. TestWhen

```
package org.gaf.metronome.test;

import com.diozero.api.DigitalInputDevice;
import com.diozero.api.DigitalOutputDevice;
import com.diozero.api.GpioPullUpDown;
import com.diozero.util.Diozero;
```

```
public class TestWhen {

    private static int cnt;
    private static DigitalOutputDevice dodP;

    public static void main(String[] args)
            throws InterruptedException {
        try (
            DigitalInputDevice did =
                DigitalInputDevice.
                Builder.builder(20).
                setPullUpDown(GpioPullUpDown.NONE).
                setActiveHigh(false).build();
            DigitalOutputDevice dod =
                new DigitalOutputDevice(21,
                true, false)) {

            did.whenActivated(TestWhen::when);

            dodP = dod;

            cnt = 0;

            System.out.println("Waiting ...");
            Thread.sleep(10000);

            System.out.println("Count = " + cnt);
        } finally {
            Diozero.shutdown();
        }
    }
```

```
private static void when(long ts) {
    cnt++;
    dodP.on();
    dodP.off();
}
}
```

Figure 14-5 shows the results of running TestWhen. The scope trace shows some interesting aspects:

- The switch closure is on the left; the bouncing is nearly undetectable due to the horizontal scale for the oscilloscope.

- The first pulse occurs about two milliseconds after switch closure.

- There are *four* pulses generated from *one* switch closure; there is a cluster of three, including the first, starting around 2 milliseconds after switch closure and spaced about 2 milliseconds apart; the last of the four is about 34 milliseconds from switch closure.

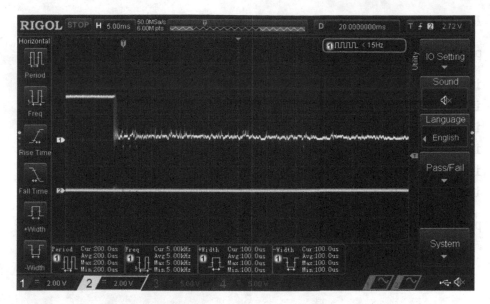

Figure 14-5. *TestWhen results*

Fundamentally, the results are a good demonstration of the impact of switch bounce. In the spirit of full disclosure, during testing, the pulse count printed by TestWhen ranged from 1 to 12, with 4 being the most common.

Bottom line: I assert that whenActivated is as good as waitForActive in terms of the delay between switch closure and the ability to take action. However, whenActivated could be harder to use because of multiple events from switch bounce.

Test addListener

Now we'll test addListener using the program TestListen, shown in Listing 14-3. TestListen is nearly identical to TestWhen, but of course uses addListener instead of whenActivated.

Listing 14-3. TestListen

```java
package org.gaf.metronome.test;

import com.diozero.api.DigitalInputDevice;
import com.diozero.api.DigitalInputEvent;
import com.diozero.api.DigitalOutputDevice;
import com.diozero.api.GpioEventTrigger;
import com.diozero.api.GpioPullUpDown;
import com.diozero.util.Diozero;

public class TestListen {

    private static int cnt;
    private static DigitalOutputDevice dodP;

    public static void main(String[] args)
            throws InterruptedException {
        try (
            DigitalInputDevice did =
                DigitalInputDevice.Builder.
                builder(20).
                setPullUpDown(GpioPullUpDown.NONE).
                setActiveHigh(false).
                setTrigger(
                GpioEventTrigger.FALLING).build();
            DigitalOutputDevice dod =
                new DigitalOutputDevice(21,
                true, false)) {

            did.addListener(TestListen::listen);

            dodP = dod;

            cnt = 0;
```

```
        System.out.println("Waiting ...");
        Thread.sleep(10000);
        System.out.println("Count = " + cnt);
    } finally {
        Diozero.shutdown();
    }
}

private static void listen(
        DigitalInputEvent event) {
    cnt++;
    dodP.on();
    dodP.off();
}
}
```

I ran TestListen and observed quite different results compared
to TestWhen. The first output pulse produced was always around 15
milliseconds after the first burst of switch closures. However, the closure
count was roughly the same. I assert that addListener is not as good as
waitForActive because of the much longer delay and the multiple events
from switch bounce.

It appears that either waitForActive or whenActivated can work well
for detecting switch closure as fast as possible. waitForActive appears to
be a bit easier to use, so we'll use it. Now we can move forward with the
development of Metronome.

Caution   In Chapter 9, and in this chapter, we experienced anomalous GPIO timing. It is important to understand the limitations of a system built using Raspberry Pi OS and Java. Raspberry Pi OS *is* a multitasking operating system and *is not* a real-time operating system. These characteristics place limitations on the timeliness of producing output and reacting to input. Java Virtual Machine features such as lazy class loading, garbage collection, and just-in-time compiling can exacerbate the limitations imposed by Raspberry Pi OS. In most cases, the limitations will not cause problems, but you must always recognize the limitations exist. In some cases, it is easy to work around them, as in Chapter 9. In some cases, you may have to simply accept them, as in this chapter. In cases with extreme real-time requirements, you may have to off-load some tasks to subsystems that can better accommodate real-time requirements, as in Chapter 8 and Chapter 10.

Metronome Development

Based on the loosely defined goals early in the chapter, we know we require SilentStepStick to drive the stepper motor. To make it available in the **Metronome** project, you must add the **SSS** project to the **Metronome** classpath property; see Chapter 5. We also know that we need a DigitalInputDevice for each switch. The previous section concluded that we should use waitForActive to detect switch closure.

Further, we can copy code snippets from TestSSS1 (Listing 13-5) and from TestWait (Listing 14-1) to seed Metronome development. Listing 14-4 shows an initial skeleton for Metronome. It creates an instance of SilentStepStick using the parameters from Chapter 13 and an instance of DigitalInputDevice, using the parameters from Listing 14-1, for the switches encountered when the wand travels clockwise (swCW) and

counterclockwise (swCCW). As you can see from the listing, the skeleton
doesn't do anything else, except enable the try-with-resources and diozero
safety nets, plus the Java shutdown safety net; Metronome enables the
latter because the stepper could continue to run and crash the wand into a
switch under abnormal termination.

Listing 14-4. Metronome skeleton

```
package org.gaf.metronome;

import com.diozero.api.DigitalInputDevice;
import com.diozero.api.GpioPullUpDown;
import com.diozero.util.Diozero;
import java.io.IOException;
import org.gaf.sss.SilentStepStick;

public class Metronome {

    public static void main(String[] args)
            throws IOException {
        try (
        SilentStepStick stepper =
            new SilentStepStick(4, 27, 17, 200,
            SilentStepStick.Resolution.Quarter);
        DigitalInputDevice swCW =
            DigitalInputDevice.Builder.
            builder(20).
            setPullUpDown(GpioPullUpDown.NONE).
            setActiveHigh(false).build();
        DigitalInputDevice swCCW =
            DigitalInputDevice.Builder.
            builder(21).
```

```
                setPullUpDown(GpioPullUpDown.NONE).
                setActiveHigh(false).build()
        ) {

            // engage Java shutdown safety net
            Diozero.registerForShutdown(stepper);

        } finally {
            Diozero.shutdown();
        }

    }
}
```

We'll now develop `Metronome` iteratively, add function and test, add function and test, and so on. The first thing to add is the ability to detect both switch closures. Thinking ahead, we should probably assume that you have to manually position the wand prior to running the program so that it isn't closing a switch prior to running the program. Further, it is probably a good idea to wait for an indication everything is ready to go.

Listing 14-5 shows the code snippet for the switch test implementation; it gets placed before the `finally` statement in Listing 14-4. Running this version of `Metronome` produces the output at the bottom of the listing when you first close the clockwise switch and then close the counterclockwise switch. If you see that, success!

Listing 14-5. Metronome switch test

```
// wait for start
System.out.println(
    "Waiting to start .... Press CW switch.");
boolean status = swCW.waitForActive(10000);
if (status) {
    System.out.println("Starting");
} else {
```

```
    System.out.println("Failure to start!");
    System.exit(1);
}
// check for CCW
System.out.println(
    "Waiting for CCW .... Press CCW switch.");
status = swCCW.waitForActive(10000);
if (status) System.out.println("Got CCW");
```

Output ----------------------

Waiting to start .... Press CW switch.
Starting
Waiting for CCW .... Press CCW switch.
Got CCW

Next, we can try running the stepper motor clockwise and counterclockwise, slowly, changing directions as the switches get pressed. Listing 14-6 shows the revised Metronome. After waiting for the start switch, we first enable the stepper, then start it moving clockwise at 1 RPM. At that point, we wait for the clockwise switch to close, and stop the stepper when it does. Then we start the stepper moving counterclockwise at 1 RPM and wait for the counterclockwise switch to close and stop the stepper when it does.

Listing 14-6. Metronome motor test

```
// wait for start
System.out.println("Waiting to start .... Press CW switch.");
boolean status = swCW.waitForActive(10000);
if (status) {
    System.out.println("Starting");
} else {
    System.out.println("Failure to start!");
```

```
    System.exit(1);
}
// make sure switch not bouncing
Thread.sleep(100);

// run to CW switch
stepper.enable(true);
System.out.println("Run CW");
stepper.run(SilentStepStick.Direction.CW, 1f);
System.out.println("Waiting to hit switch ...");
status = swCW.waitForActive(20000);
stepper.stop();
if (status) {
    System.out.println("Got it");
} else {
    System.out.println("Motor not running");
    System.exit(1);
}
// run to CCW switch
System.out.println("Run CCW");
stepper.run(SilentStepStick.Direction.CCW, 1f);
System.out.println("Waiting to hit switch ...");
status = swCCW.waitForActive(20000);
stepper.stop();
if (status) {
    System.out.println("Got it");
} else {
    System.out.println("Motor not running");
    System.exit(1);
}

stepper.enable(false);
```

To test `Metronome`, now you obviously have to connect the SilentStepStick to the Raspberry Pi, the stepper motor, and motor power (see Chapter 13). I suggest first testing without the wand attached to prevent any unpleasant surprises; you will of course have to hit the switches yourself to simulate wand movement. Once you hit the clockwise switch to start, the motor should rotate clockwise and should continue to do so until you hit the clockwise switch. Then the motor should stop and start rotating counterclockwise and should continue to do so until you hit the counterclockwise switch. Then the motor should stop. If you see this behavior, declare success!

Assuming the manual test works, attach the wand and run `Metronome` again. Once you hit the start switch, the wand should rotate clockwise and should continue to do so until it hits the clockwise switch. Then the wand should stop and start rotating counterclockwise and should continue to do so until it hits the counterclockwise switch. Then the wand should stop. If you see this behavior, declare success again!

Go Beyond Initial Requirements

Now all the pieces are in place to create the metronome behavior described early in the chapter. It would be pretty trivial to place the code segments that drive the stepper and test a switch in a loop so that the wand waves between the switches. However, I think it would be far more interesting to wave *without* hitting the switches. This is possible because `SilentStepStick` can move a requested number of steps and can report how many steps it has taken however it moves.

We now need to do some more design. To start, look at Figure 14-6, which shows the position of the wand when it closes the *clockwise* switch; this *clockwise closure* position (CWC) is marked by the *solid* line through the wand. The *solid* line on the left shows the *counterclockwise closure* position (CCWC).

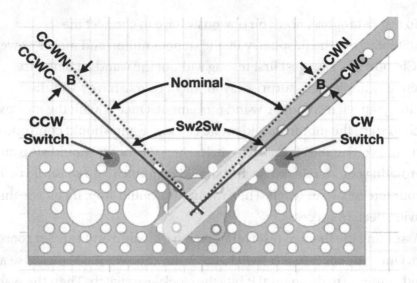

Figure 14-6. *Wand position at switch closure*

With the `Metronome` version of Listing 14-6, the wand first moves from its arbitrary starting position to CWC. We don't care how many steps that takes. The wand then moves from CWC to CCWC. That requires some number of steps, labeled Sw2Sw in Figure 14-6. So, Sw2Sw is the number of steps to move the wand from CWC to CCWC, or from switch closure to switch closure. But we want to move the wand back and forth *without* switch closure. We should be able to achieve that by moving fewer steps, that is, between the *dotted* lines in the figure; those dotted lines represent a *clockwise non-closure* position (CWN) and a *counterclockwise non-closure* position (CCWN). Basically, we need to define a buffer number of steps ("B" in the figure) between a switch closure position (e.g., CWC) and a switch non-closure position (e.g., CWN). With these concepts in place, we can determine that the number of steps required to move from

- CWC to CCWC = Sw2Sw

- CCWC to CWN = Sw2Sw − B

- CWN to CCWN ("Nominal" in Figure 14-6) = Sw2Sw – (2 x B)

- CCWN to CWN = Sw2Sw – (2 x B)

- CWN to "middle" = (Sw2Sw / 2) – B

Listing 14-7 shows the updates to Metronome to achieve the new goal, waving back and forth without hitting the switches, then leaving the wand position in the "middle," between CCWN and CWN. The code shown must be inserted before the last statement in Listing 14-6 (stepper.enable(false)).

Listing 14-7. Metronome final snippet

```
// get step count; calculate moves
int sw2sw = stepper.getStepCount();
System.out.println("Step Count = " + sw2sw);
int buffer = 15;
int first = sw2sw - buffer;
int nominal = sw2sw - (2 * buffer);
int middle = sw2sw/2 - buffer;

// move to CW
stepper.stepCount(first,
    SilentStepStick.Direction.CW, 4f, false, null);

// move back and forth
for (int i = 0; i < 4; i++) {
    // move to CCW
    stepper.stepCount(nominal,
            SilentStepStick.Direction.CCW, 4f,
            false, null);
    // move to CW
    stepper.stepCount(nominal,
```

```
        SilentStepStick.Direction.CW, 4f,
        false, null);
}

// move to middle
stepper.stepCount(middle,
        SilentStepStick.Direction.CCW, 4f,
        false, null);
```

A few interesting points about the updates:

- All stepper movements during waving run at *4* RPM instead of the *1* RPM during the search for the switches. There is no reason to be cautious because the wand will not hit a switch!

- I chose an arbitrary number of wave cycles. You can certainly parameterize it or maybe make it infinite, perhaps terminated when *you* hit a switch.

- I thought it interesting to leave the wand in the middle of the wave area when finished, but you could stop it anywhere.

If you run `Metronome` with the updates, you should see the now-familiar slow rotation clockwise to close the CW switch and then the slow rotation counterclockwise to close the CCW switch. Then you should see fast movement to move clockwise, followed by fast movement for four cycles of moving counterclockwise then clockwise, and finally fast movement counterclockwise to the middle of the wave area. Congratulations!

Note   If you want to see the metronome in action, you can view a video in the book's code repository.

Get Closer to the Real World

There is another way to go beyond the initial requirements. In the previous implementation (Listings 14-6 and 14-7), we used the limit switches to calibrate the wand movement, so the wand doesn't activate the switches while waving. In the real world, we'd also use the limit switches to guard against crashes that might occur for various reasons, for example, bad coding or a mechanical problem.

How would we do that? We must monitor the switches while controlling the stepper. Based on the tests we made early in the chapter, we can't use the `waitForActive` method on `DigitalInputDevice` since it prevents us from doing anything else. However, those tests suggest that `whenActivated` would be a good choice for monitoring the switches while doing something else simultaneously. The associated interrupt handler called when the switch activates can stop the stepper. But you can see in Listing 14-7 that there are several statements that start the stepper, and so we must guard against starting the stepper again after it is stopped. We can synchronize everything using an `AtomicBoolean` (see Listing 13-10 for more information).

Listing 14-8 shows `Metronome` with the modifications needed to detect crashes (I've left out the import statements). You can see the following differences from the first implementation:

- Early in the listing: The declaration of the `AtomicBoolean` called `emergency`.

- At the end of the listing: The interrupt handler, `limitHit`, that stops the stepper and sets `emergency` true when a switch is activated.

- After the clockwise move following intentionally hitting both switches: Set up `limitHit` to be called if either switch gets activated.

- Finally, where waving takes place: Each move gets guarded by a check of emergency.

Listing 14-8. Metronome with crash detection

```
public class Metronome {
    private static SilentStepStick eStop;
    private static final AtomicBoolean emergency =
            new AtomicBoolean(false);

    public static void main(String[] args)
            throws IOException,InterruptedException {
        try (
            SilentStepStick stepper =
                new SilentStepStick(4, 27, 17, 200,
                SilentStepStick.Resolution.Quarter);
            DigitalInputDevice swCW =
                DigitalInputDevice.Builder.
                builder(20).
                setPullUpDown(GpioPullUpDown.NONE).
                setActiveHigh(false).build();
            DigitalInputDevice swCCW =
                DigitalInputDevice.Builder.
                builder(21).
                setPullUpDown(GpioPullUpDown.NONE).
                setActiveHigh(false).build()
        ) {

            // set up for emergency stop
            eStop = stepper;

            // engage Java shutdown safety net
            Diozero.registerForShutdown(stepper);
```

```java
// wait for start
System.out.println(
    "Waiting to start ....
    Press CW switch.");
boolean status =
    swCW.waitForActive(10000);
if (status) {
    System.out.println("Starting");
} else {
    System.out.println(
        "Failure to start!");
    System.exit(1);
}
// make sure switch not bouncing
Thread.sleep(100);

// run to CW switch
stepper.enable(true);
System.out.println("Run CW");
stepper.run(SilentStepStick.Direction.
    CW, 1f);
System.out.println(
    "Waiting to hit switch ...");
status = swCW.waitForActive(20000);
stepper.stop();
if (status) {
    System.out.println("Got it");
} else {
    System.out.println(
        "Motor not running");
    System.exit(1);
}
```

```
// run to CCW switch
System.out.println("Run CCW");
stepper.run(
    SilentStepStick.Direction.CCW, 1f);
System.out.println("Waiting to
    hit switch ...");
status = swCCW.waitForActive(20000);
stepper.stop();
if (status) {
    System.out.println("Got it");
} else {
    System.out.println(
        "Motor not running");
    System.exit(1);
}

// get step count; calculate moves
int sw2sw = stepper.getStepCount();
System.out.println(
    "Step Count = " + sw2sw);
int buffer = 15;
int first = sw2sw - buffer;
int nominal = sw2sw - (2 * buffer);
int middle = sw2sw/2 - buffer;

// move to CW
stepper.stepCount(first,
        SilentStepStick.Direction.CW, 4f,
        false, null);

// set up limit switches for emergency
swCW.whenActivated(Metronome::limitHit);
swCCW.whenActivated(Metronome::limitHit);
```

```
        // move back and forth
        for (int i = 0; i < 4; i++) {
            // move to CCW
            stepper.stepCount(nominal,
                SilentStepStick.Direction.CCW,
                4f, false, null);
            if (emergency.get()) break;
            // move to CW
            stepper.stepCount(nominal,
                SilentStepStick.Direction.CW,
                4f, false, null);
            if (emergency.get()) break;
        }

        // move to middle
        if (!emergency.get())
            stepper.stepCount(middle,
                SilentStepStick.Direction.CCW, 4f,
                false, null);

        stepper.enable(false);
    } finally {
        Diozero.shutdown();
    }
}

private static void limitHit(long ts) {
    emergency.set(true);
    eStop.stop();
}
}
```

If you run the updated `Metronome`, you should see the behavior of the previous version. But if you hit either of the switches while the wand is waving, the stepper stops, and `Metronome` terminates. Congratulations again!

Summary

In this chapter, you've learned how to

- Analyze a project and identify the requirements

- Identify the proper devices to implement the project

- Experiment with devices to choose the proper usage

- Evolve project requirements to fully utilize device capabilities

I hope you enjoyed this exercise in "putting it all together" to define and implement a complete project using diozero.

APPENDIX A1

Arduino Command Server

Why discuss the Arduino microcontroller in the context of a book about the Raspberry Pi? In robotics projects, it is common to off-load tasks from the Pi to an Arduino, achieving parallel processing. There are general benefits to parallel processing, but perhaps the most important benefit is that tasks can get much closer to "real-time" behavior running on an Arduino than running on a Pi. The Pi's multitasking operating system has to allocate resources to your task *and* numerous system tasks. The Arduino has no OS and so devotes all resources to your task, and an Arduino task has very good control over the timing of actions.

In some cases, there is another good reason to leverage an Arduino. Due to the prevalence of device libraries written for the Arduino (see Chapter 6), you can let the Arduino control the device via an existing library and then let the Pi control the Arduino. Thus, you can avoid porting one or more device libraries!

Enabling task off-load to an Arduino is the purpose of this appendix. I'll show you an Arduino *framework* I call the *command server* that performs tasks on behalf of an application running on a Raspberry Pi. In Appendix A2, I'll use the framework to create a real device, specifically a Lidar Unit.

© Greg Flurry 2021
G. Flurry, *Java on the Raspberry Pi*, https://doi.org/10.1007/978-1-4842-7264-0

Tip   Even if you don't need to off-load tasks, an Arduino can prove beneficial as a *tool*. You can load an Arduino C++ device library and experiment with it to help you understand how the device and the device library work. This can greatly aid you in developing your own device library in Java.

Some Arduino Background

Since this book features the Raspberry Pi, I don't think it is appropriate to dig too deeply into the Arduino ecosystem. In this section, however, I hope to provide enough context to help you understand this appendix.

Arduino per se refers to an open source electronics microcontroller (see www.arduino.cc/en/Guide/Introduction). You can buy *official* Arduino products from the Arduino organization (see www.arduino.cc/en/Main/Products). Since Arduino is open source, you can buy *Arduino-compatible* products from many other manufacturers. This vast array of products comes with different levels of function, in different sizes, and at different costs.

All Arduino products have base I/O capabilities similar to the Raspberry Pi, offering some or all of GPIO, serial, I2C, and SPI, plus true analog input. The I/O capabilities make the Arduino a capable and very popular microcontroller.

The Arduino organization offers an IDE specifically targeting Arduino-compatible microcontrollers (see www.arduino.cc/en/software and https://create.arduino.cc/projecthub/Arduino_Genuino/getting-started-with-the-arduino-desktop-ide-623be4). The IDE runs on many workstation platforms, including macOS and Windows. Using the IDE, you can write C/C++ programs, called *sketches*, compile them, download them from the workstation to the Arduino over a serial connection (sometimes specialized just for download), and run them from the workstation using the *Serial Monitor* feature built into the IDE (see `www.seeedstudio.com/blog/2019/12/16/how-to-use-arduino-serial-monitor-and-alternatives-to-try/`). As hinted earlier, while writing sketches, you can leverage literally hundreds of existing device libraries; in fact, library management is another important feature of the IDE.

Choose an Arduino

The best way to connect most Arduinos to a Raspberry Pi is via a serial port (there are advanced, and expensive, Arduinos that have Wi-Fi or Bluetooth). All Arduinos have one or more serial ports (see `www.arduino.cc/en/pmwiki.php?n=Reference/serial`), generally accessed via RX/TX pins on the IO header. Basically, you can connect *any* Arduino to a Raspberry Pi using serial I/O. Thus, you can choose an Arduino that suits the other functional, size, and cost requirements of your project.

An important consideration in connecting a Pi and an Arduino via the RX/TX pins is *level shifting*. The Pi uses 3.3V logic levels, while most Arduinos use 5V logic levels (some do use 3.3V); connecting 3.3V devices to 5V devices can create disaster. The official Arduino Leonardo and MICRO products, based on the ATmega32u4, support serial communication to a workstation or other systems via a USB micro-B-connector. The USB port eliminates worries about level shifting and makes it very easy to connect to a Pi via a common USB-A to micro-B cable. The USB port makes it very easy to download programs to an Arduino from your workstation and even provides an easy way to power the Arduino. Most such products have a second serial port on the GPIO RX/TX pins, which allows the Arduino to communicate not only with the Pi but with another serial device.

Because of all these advantages, I recommend an ATmega32u4-based Arduino. You can find many Arduino-compatible boards built with the ATmega32u4. For this book, I'll use the Pololu A-Star Micro (`www.pololu.com/product/3101`). That said, the content of this appendix applies to other Arduinos as well.

Once you've chosen your Arduino, you may have to install a board manager for it. To do so for the A-Star Micro, see `www.pololu.com/docs/0J61/6.2`.

Tip   If you decide to use an Arduino that requires level shifting, you can find ways to build your own or buy them. For example, see `https://randomnerdtutorials.com/how-to-level-shift-5v-to-3-3v/` and `https://oscarliang.com/raspberry-pi-and-arduino-connected-serial-gpio/`.

The Command Server Pattern

The Arduino *command server* is a *client/server pattern* I created for one of my robots. Since the goal is off-loading work from the Raspberry Pi to the Arduino, the Pi is the client and the Arduino is the server. Generally, the pattern works as follows:

- The Pi writes *commands* to the Arduino.

- The Arduino *performs the tasks* implied by the commands and returns any *results*.

- The Pi reads any *results*.

The command_server Sketch

The command server implementation described in this appendix is just a basic skeleton. The implementation assumes that a command from the client consists of a *command type* (a single byte) and a single optional *command parameter* (a two-byte integer). Any task performing a command can return zero or more two-byte integers.

The implementation includes only two very simple commands that together confirm the minimal functioning of the command server. One command returns what can be considered an ID or version number, and the second returns the parameter received.

Commands and results get communicated serially. An Arduino sketch communicates serially by reading or writing information via the *primary* Arduino serial port using the Serial interface (see www.arduino. cc/reference/en/language/functions/communication/serial/). An Arduino uses that port to communicate with the IDE's Serial Monitor. With an ATmega32u4-based product, that is also the port used by the Arduino to communicate with a Raspberry Pi via its USB serial port. An important aspect of the command server sketch is that it makes it easy to switch between

- Sending commands from the Serial Monitor and seeing the results from task execution *and* seeing all debug information produced by the sketch

- Sending commands from the Pi and reading only the results of task execution by the Pi

You can find the **command_server** sketch in the book's code repository. While I could have implemented the sketch as a single file, instead I organized it into three files to make the code more understandable, more maintainable, and more extensible. The three files are

1. command_server.ino contains the setup and loop functions always present in Arduino sketches and contains the serial communications functions used to interact with the client.

2. cmd_executor.h contains various constants shared among the files.

3. cmd_executor.ino contains an implementation of the executeCommand function that acts as the dispatcher for commands.

Figure A1-1 shows the **command_server**[1] sketch in the Arduino IDE. You can see that the IDE shows each of the three files in the sketch in its own *tab*. This makes it easy to move from file to file simply by clicking the tab.

---

[1] An Arduino sketch requires that one file has the same name as the sketch.

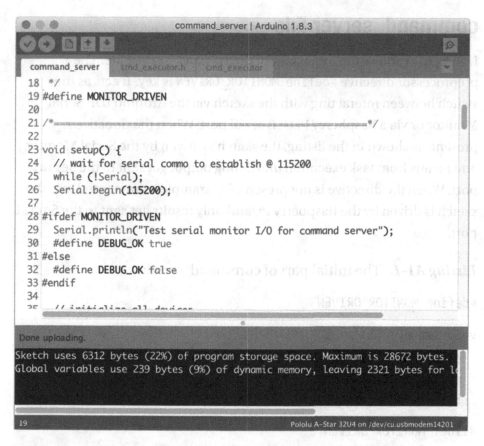

```
● ● ●                    command_server | Arduino 1.8.3

✓  →  ▢  ▲  ▼                                                    🔎

command_server    cmd_executor.h    cmd_executor                    ▼

18  */
19  #define MONITOR_DRIVEN
20
21  /*═══════════════════════════════════════════════*/
22
23  void setup() {
24    // wait for serial commo to establish @ 115200
25    while (!Serial);
26    Serial.begin(115200);
27
28  #ifdef MONITOR_DRIVEN
29    Serial.println("Test serial monitor I/O for command server");
30    #define DEBUG_OK true
31  #else
32    #define DEBUG_OK false
33  #endif
34
35    // initialize all devices

                                    ●

Done uploading.

Sketch uses 6312 bytes (22%) of program storage space. Maximum is 28672 bytes.
Global variables use 239 bytes (9%) of dynamic memory, leaving 2321 bytes for l

19                              Pololu A-Star 32U4 on /dev/cu.usbmodem14201
```

Figure A1-1. *Arduino IDE with command_server sketch*

Tip   If you want to load the command_server sketch into the
Arduino IDE, you can do so in at least two ways. You can navigate
to the "sketch repository" (in macOS, by default ~/Documents/
Arduino/), create a folder named command_server, and place the
three files from the book's code repository in that folder (you may
have to restart the IDE). You also simply create a new sketch named
command_server, create the three files (tabs), and copy the content
for each file.

---

command_server File

Listing A1-1 shows the initial part of the command_server file. The preprocessor directive #define MONITOR_DRIVEN is key. It acts as the switch between interacting with the sketch via the Arduino IDE Serial Monitor or via a Raspberry Pi USB serial port. When the directive is present, as shown in the listing, the sketch is driven by the Serial Monitor, and results from task execution *and* debug output get sent to the Serial port. When the directive is not present, for example, commented out, the sketch is driven by the Raspberry Pi, and only results get sent to the Serial port.

Listing A1-1. The initial part of command_server

```
#define MONITOR_DRIVEN

void setup() {
  // wait for serial commo to establish @ 115200
  while (!Serial);
  Serial.begin(115200);

#ifdef MONITOR_DRIVEN
  Serial.println("Test serial monitor I/O
      for command server");
  #define DEBUG_OK true
#else
  #define DEBUG_OK false
#endif

  // initialize all devices
  setUpCommandExecutor();
}
```

```
void loop() {
  // get command type
  int commandType = getCommandType();

  // execute the command
  executeCommand(commandType);
}
```

The setup function shown in Listing A1-1 does several things:

- Waits for the USB serial connection to open on the Serial port at 115200 baud

- Uses additional preprocessor directives to test MONITOR_DRIVEN; if defined (Serial Monitor connected), it outputs text to the Serial Monitor and sets the value of DEBUG_OK to true, allowing debug output; if not defined (Pi connected), it sets the value of DEBUG_OK to false, preventing debug output.

- Calls setUpCommandExecutor to initialize any devices used to perform the tasks implied by the commands.

The loop function shown in Listing A1-1 simply waits for an incoming command using the function getCommandType and calls executeCommand to dispatch the task to the proper function.

Listing A1-2 shows the rest of the command_server file. You can see different implementations of the getCommandType, getParameter, and returnInt functions used for interaction with the Serial Monitor (first set) and for interaction with the Raspberry Pi (second set). The preprocessor directive #ifdef causes the first set of functions in the listing to be used only if MONITOR_DRIVEN is *defined*. The preprocessor directive #else causes the second set of functions in the listing to be used only if MONITOR_DRIVEN is *not defined*.

In the Serial Monitor-oriented set of functions, based on exchanging *character strings*, the getCommandType function reads a character string typed into the Serial Monitor and parses it to produce an integer value that is the command type, and an optional second integer value that is the command parameter. The getParameter function simply returns the parameter to the calling function. The returnInt function writes a character string representing the integer result to the Serial Monitor.

Listing A1-2. Serial Monitor functions in command_server

```
#ifdef MONITOR_DRIVEN // use strings

int cmd[2]; // command type [0] & parameter [1]

int getCommandType() {
  while (Serial.available() < 1) {
  }
  String inputString =
    Serial.readStringUntil('\r\n');

  // parse the input command, as cmdtype[,parameter]
  char buf[inputString.length()];
  inputString.toCharArray(buf, sizeof(buf));
  char *p = buf;
  char *str;
  int i = 0;
  while ((str = strtok_r(p, ",", &p)) != NULL) {
    String str2 = String(str);
    cmd[i] = str2.toInt();
    i++;
  }
  return cmd[0];
}
```

```
int getParameter() {
    return cmd[1];
}

void returnInt(int res) {
    Serial.println(res);
}

#else // use bytes

int getCommandType() {
  while ((Serial.available() < 1)) {}
  return Serial.read();
}

int getParameter() {
  int parm;
  while ((Serial.available() < 2)) {
  }
  byte buf[2];
  Serial.readBytes(buf, 2);
  parm = buf[0] << 8;
  parm = parm + buf[1];
  return parm;
}

void returnInt(int data) {
  byte buf[2];
  buf[0] = data >> 8;
  buf[1] = 0x00ff & data;
  Serial.write(buf, 2);
}

#endif
```

483

In the Raspberry Pi-oriented set of functions, based on exchanging *bytes*, the getCommandType function reads a *single byte* from the Pi to produce an integer value that is the command type. The getParameter function reads *two bytes* from the Pi to produce the optional two-byte integer parameter for the command. The returnInt function takes the integer parameter and produces two bytes representing that integer and writes those bytes so they can be read by the Pi.

cmd_executor.h File

Listing A1-3 shows the content of the cmd_executor.h file. The preprocessor directive #define DEBUG_CMDEXEC true indicates that debug output is allowed in the executeCommand function defined in cmd_executor, if, of course, debug output is allowed at all. CS_ID indicates the identity or perhaps version number for a particular implementation of the command server.

The rest of the file defines the allowed command types. As said earlier, for the skeleton command server, there are only two commands:

- ID returns CS_ID which is useful for ensuring that the client and server agree on the identity of the command server, as well as available commands and task implementations.

- ECHO returns the incoming parameter. This is only for testing the basic command server operation.

Listing A1-3. cmd_executor.h

```
#ifndef _cmd_exec_h
#define _cmd_exec_h

#define DEBUG_CMDEXEC true

const int CS_ID = 100;
```

```
/* Command types */
const int ID = 10; // identify "command executor"
const int ECHO = 11; // echo input parameter

#endif
```

cmd_executor file

Listing A1-4 shows the content of the cmd_executor file. The setUpCommandExecutor function in general calls other functions (possibly in other files) to initialize any capabilities (e.g., devices) needed to execute commands. In this framework-only implementation, there are no such initializer functions.

setUpCommandExecutor shows how to structure debug output. The preprocessor directive #if DEBUG_OK && DEBUG_CMDEXEC means that *both* DEBUG_OK and DEBUG_CMDEXEC must be true for the Serial.println statement to be included in the compiled program. Fundamentally, DEBUG_OK, set in command_server, controls debug for the entire sketch, while DEBUG_CMDEXEC, set in cmd_executor.h, controls debug only in cmd_executor (really in any file that tests against DEBUG_CMDEXEC). If you want to inject debug output in functions in other files, you should #define related identifiers and use the same technique to "guard" debug Serial. println statements in those files.

The executeCommand function can execute some commands, as shown in Listing A1-4. The expectation for the framework, however, is that most command execution gets delegated to functions implemented in additional files.

Listing A1-4. cmd_executor

```
#include "cmd_executor.h"

void setUpCommandExecutor(void) {
  #if DEBUG_OK && DEBUG_CMDEXEC
    Serial.println("setUpCommandExecutor");
  #endif
}

void executeCommand(byte cmdType) {
  switch (cmdType) {

    case ID:
      #if DEBUG_OK && DEBUG_CMDEXEC
        Serial.println("ID");
      #endif
      returnInt(CS_ID);
      break;

    case ECHO:
      #if DEBUG_OK && DEBUG_CMDEXEC
        Serial.println("Echo");
      #endif
      returnInt(getParameter());
      break;
  }
}
```

Test the Command Server

With the understanding of how the command server works, you can test it. First, you must connect your workstation to the Arduino; for an ATmega32u4-compatible product, you use a micro-B cable appropriate for your workstation. Next, you must configure the Arduino IDE with a board manager that understands your particular Arduino board; then, you have to select your board as the target; finally, you must identify the workstation port used to communicate with the board. For the Pololu A-Star 32U4 Micro, www.pololu.com/docs/0J61/6.2 shows the details. For other boards, the overall process would be similar.

Once you have everything set up, make sure the preprocessor directive MONITOR_DRIVEN in the command_server file is *defined*. Compile and download the sketch to the Arduino (click the right-pointing arrow in the menu bar). If all is well, the status bar below the code will stay green and say "Done uploading" (see Figure A1-1). If something went wrong, the status bar will turn orange and give some indication of the error; the pane below the status bar will contain details.

Now start the Serial Monitor (click the magnifying glass on the right of the menu bar). At the bottom of the Serial Monitor window, set the baud rate to 115200. You should see the first two lines shown in the Serial Monitor output pane, as shown in Figure A1-2.

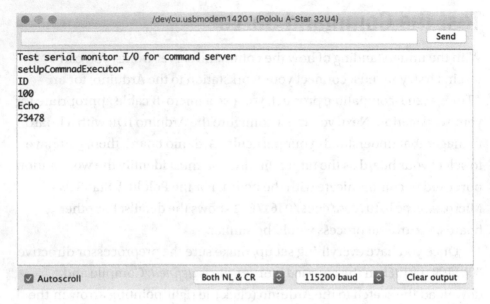

Figure A1-2. *Arduino IDE Serial Monitor testing command_server*

Now type "10" (just the digits, not the quotes) and hit Enter. This initiates the "ID" task; you should see the third and fourth lines in the output pane in Figure A1-2. Next, type "11,23478" and hit Enter. This initiates the "ECHO" task; you should see the last two lines in the output pane in Figure A1-2. Success!

Now that you've verified the skeleton command server functions properly, you need to configure it to communicate with the Raspberry Pi instead of the Serial Monitor. You know what to do – make the preprocessor directive MONITOR_DRIVEN undefined (I just commented the line containing the directive), and then download the code to the Arduino.

The Command Server As a "Device"

Recognize that the **command_server** sketch, downloaded with MONITOR_ DRIVEN in the command_server file *undefined*, in effect turns the Arduino into a "device" that can be connected to the Raspberry Pi via a USB serial port. The skeleton framework implementation described earlier has a very simple "datasheet":

> The "device" communicates via its USB port. It expects the following: baud rate=115200; 8 data bits per character; no parity bits; 1 stop bit.

> The "device" accepts commands that have a command type (a single byte) and a single optional command parameter (a two-byte integer). A command can return zero or more two-byte integers.

> The "device" exposes two commands:

> **ID** (10) has no parameter and returns the ID of the "device" (= 100).

> **Echo** (11) has one parameter and returns that parameter.

Test the "Device" from Raspberry Pi

Now you can create a Java device library to test the command server "device" from the Raspberry Pi. You must first connect the Raspberry Pi to the Arduino using a USB-A to micro-B cable. See Chapter 5 for how to use NetBeans, Chapter 6 for how to use diozero in NetBeans, and Chapter 7 for how to use the diozero SerialDevice to communicate serially.

I created a project called **CommandServer**, a package called `org.gaf.test` and a main class called `TestCmdServer`. Listing A1-5 shows the implementation of `TestCmdServer`.

The application first creates a diozero `SerialDevice` with the proper characteristics for communication with the command server. Next the application sends the single-byte command (type only) for the "ID" task, reads the two-byte response, formats the response as a Java `int`, and prints the response. Then the application sends a multi-byte command with the single-byte command type for the "ECHO" task and the two bytes of the Java `short` parameter, reads the two-byte response, formats, and prints the response.

Listing A1-5. TestCmdServer

```
package org.gaf.test;

import static com.diozero.api.SerialConstants.*;
import com.diozero.api.SerialDevice;

public class TestCmdServer {

    public static void main(String[] args)
            throws InterruptedException {
        SerialDevice device = new SerialDevice(
            "/dev/ttyACM0", BAUD_115200,
            DEFAULT_DATA_BITS,
            DEFAULT_STOP_BITS, DEFAULT_PARITY);

        // get the ID
        device.writeByte((byte) 10);
        byte[] res = new byte[2];
        // read the response byte array
        device.read(res);
        // construct response as short
```

```
short value = (short)(res[0] << 8);
value = (short) (value | (short)
    Byte.toUnsignedInt(res[1]));
System.out.println("ID= " + value);

// echo a parameter
short parameter = 12345;
device.write((byte) 11, (byte)
    (parameter >> 8), (byte) parameter);
// read the response byte array
device.read(res);
// construct response as short
value = (short)(res[0] << 8);
value = (short) (value | (short)
    Byte.toUnsignedInt(res[1]));
System.out.println("Parameter= " + value);
   }
}
```

When you run `TestCmdServer`, you should see the following output in the NetBeans Output pane:

    ID= 100
    Parameter= 12345

Note   To ensure that I could hard code /dev/ttyACM0 as the device file, the "device" was the only thing plugged into a Raspberry Pi USB port when I ran the test. See Chapter 7 for more detail.

Summary

In this appendix, you

- Learned about a client/server pattern called the command server that allows you to use an Arduino to off-load tasks from a Raspberry Pi

- Learned a bit about the Arduino ecosystem

- Built and tested the command server using features of the Arduino IDE running on a workstation

- Built a Java application using NetBeans to test the command server connected to a Raspberry Pi

You must remember, however, the command server framework described in this appendix is really only a *model*. *It does nothing useful*. The real power comes from extending it. It is specifically designed to make it easy to extend the command set, by implementing additional commands, in additional files, or in the executeCommand function. It is also possible to extend the command syntax; the command type could be a two- or even a four-byte integer, as could the command parameter; similarly, the returned values could be a four-byte integer, or even a character string. By extending the framework, *you* can create a "device" to do what *you* need it to do. See Appendix A2 for an example.

APPENDIX A2

Custom Lidar Unit

This appendix describes a custom Lidar Unit of the sort used in mobile robots for localization. I think you might find it interesting for a number of reasons:

- It provides a real-life example of off-loading tasks from the Raspberry Pi.

- It leverages the command server framework described in Appendix A1.

- It demonstrates the use of multiple physical devices to produce a single logical device.

- It leverages existing device libraries (no porting!).

The Hardware Design

Why build a custom Lidar Unit? There are a few reasons:

- *Cost*: At the time I needed a Lidar device, the cost of off-the-shelf "real" units *started at* a few hundred US$.

- *Function*: The "real" units provided a 360° scan multiple times per second, and I convinced myself that my requirements could be met with a 180° scan at intervals of many seconds.

- *Mindset*: The notion of building from scratch sounded challenging, but interesting and fun as well.

© Greg Flurry 2021
G. Flurry, *Java on the Raspberry Pi*, https://doi.org/10.1007/978-1-4842-7264-0

After a bit of research on Lidar sensors, I chose the Garmin LIDAR-Lite v3 "Optical Distance Measurement Sensor" (https://buy.garmin.com/en-US/US/p/557294). It has a great range (up to 40 meters), great resolution, decent accuracy, is reasonably low power, and runs off 5V. It is still sold, but there are now newer, and maybe better, models available.

Since all the Garmin LIDAR-Lite v3 (LLv3) does is measure distance, I needed something to rotate it through 180°. A servo seemed like the perfect answer. I had some inexpensive standard (*analog*) servos already, so I didn't need to purchase one!

Of course, I also needed something to control *and synchronize* the LLv3 and the servo. Synchronization I felt was key, and another reason, besides parallelism, I decided to off-load from the Raspberry Pi to an Arduino (specifically the Pololu A-Star Micro mentioned in Appendix A1). Figure A2-1 shows the resulting hardware design. In this design, a 5V power bank supplied power to the Pi, the LLv3, and the servo; the USB connection from the Pi powered the A-Star.

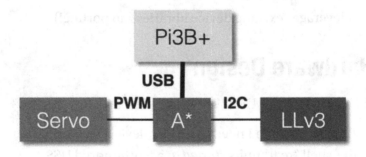

Figure A2-1. *Initial Lidar Unit hardware design*

As you can see in Figure A2-1, I chose to use I2C to communicate with the LLv3 (using an existing C++ library; more on that later). At a high level, the Pi sends commands to the Arduino. The Arduino takes a range reading from the LLv3 using I2C, and it positions the servo using the built-in Arduino `Servo` class.

The design worked, but the results were disappointing. After analysis, I concluded that

- The servo was *too* inexpensive. It did not position consistently given the same input. Its positioning over 180° was nonlinear. It was very slow to stabilize at a position.

- The Arduino Servo class could not produce the servo control signal with enough precision (microsecond at best) and possibly with not enough accuracy.

To address the deficiencies, I

- Purchased a *digital* servo, with higher speed, higher torque, metal gears, linear positioning, and a smaller dead band.

- Injected into the design a Pololu Micro Maestro Servo Controller (www.pololu.com/product/1350). It provides a number of interesting features, but the most important is an accurate servo control signal with 0.25 microsecond precision.

Figure A2-2 shows the improved hardware design. In this design, a 5V power bank supplied power to all components but the A-Star; the USB connection from the Pi powered the A-Star. The Maestro can be controlled via USB or TTY serial. Since the Raspberry Pi uses the Arduino USB port, the new design required use of the serial capability via the RX/TX pins on the Arduino.

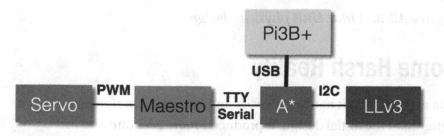

Figure A2-2. Improved Lidar Unit design

With the improved design, the Pi sends commands to the Arduino. The Arduino takes a range reading from the LLv3 using I2C and positions the servo by sending a command to the Maestro (using an existing C++ library; more on that later) that then generates the control signal to position the servo.

Figure A2-3 shows the actual Lidar Unit with the components in the design labeled.

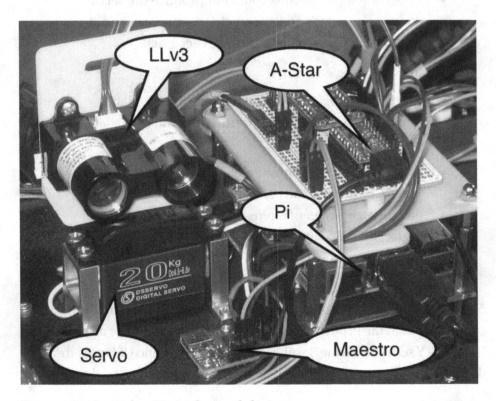

Figure A2-3. *Lidar Unit physical design*

Some Harsh Reality

The new Lidar Unit hardware design in Figure A2-2 performed much better than the initial design. It produced more accurate and more consistent results. That said, the new design exhibited two problems.

I found the LLv3 produced inaccurate ranges until it "warmed up." After extensive experimentation, I found that from initial power on to the expected accuracy for range readings, it could require taking more than 20,000 range readings. In addition, after an initial warmup period followed by a period of inactivity, the LLv3 again produced inaccurate ranges. Fortunately, after an initial warmup, a few hundred range readings appeared sufficient to produce the expected accuracy.

I also found the design appeared to require almost 80 milliseconds to stabilize its position enough to assure accurate range readings. I suspect the reason was mechanical (e.g., flexing between the servo gear and horn, flexing between the servo horn and the 3D printed mount for the LLv3, flexing between the mount and the LLv3) rather than electronic, but I have no definitive proof.

You will see these two problems reflected in the software design described in the following.

The Lidar Unit Sketch

As mentioned earlier, the Arduino sketch for Lidar Unit leverages

- The command server framework described in Appendix A1.

- An existing device library for the LLv3. See https:// github.com/garmin/LIDARLite_Arduino_Library.

- An existing library for the Maestro. See https:// github.com/pololu/maestro-arduino.

To get started, in the Arduino IDE (see Appendix A1 for some IDE basics) I copied the **command_server** sketch and named it **lidar_command_server**. I then used the IDE *Library Manager* to download the proper libraries; I searched for the phrases "LIDAR Lite" and "Maestro" to find them. See www.arduino.cc/en/Guide/Libraries for more detail.

497

After all that, the Arduino IDE contains three tabs for the three files from the original **command_server** sketch:

- `lidar_command_server` (main): The only change I needed to make in the file was uncomment the preprocessor directive #define MONITOR_DRIVEN. This allowed me to debug using the IDE Serial Monitor. For operation with the Raspberry Pi, I simply commented the directive again.

- `cmd_executor.h`: I changed the value of the identifier CS_ID and added constants for the new commands. See the following.

- `cmd_executor`: Added code to implement the new commands. See the following.

There are four additional files (and tabs):

- `lidar.h`: Contains constants and variables for the LLv3 commands

- `lidar`: Contains the implementation of LLv3 functions

- `servo.h`: Contains constants and variables for the Maestro commands

- `servo`: Contains the implementation of the Maestro functions

Tip   Once you've loaded the device libraries for the LLv3 and the Maestro, you can use some of the example sketches that get downloaded with the libraries. The examples help you get familiar with the devices. You can find the examples in *File* ➤ *Examples* ➤ *LIDAR-Lite V3* and *File* ➤ *Examples* ➤ *PololuMaestro*.

---

cmd_executor.h

Listing A2-1 shows the meaningful content of cmd_executor.h for **lidar_command_server**. Compare Listing A2-1 to Listing A1-4 and you'll see a different CS_ID and new commands. I'll explain the new commands in the next subsection.

Listing A2-1. cmd_executor.h snippet

```
const int CS_ID = 600;

const int ID = 10;
const int ECHO = 11;

/* Command types for a Lidar Unit */
const int LIDAR_SERVO_POS = 30;
const int LIDAR_SERVO_PARMS = 32;
const int LIDAR_MULTIPLE = 50;
const int LIDAR_SCAN_START = 52;
const int LIDAR_SCAN_RETRIEVE = 54;
const int LIDAR_WARMUP = 60;
```

cmd_executor

Listing A2-2 shows the content of cmd_executor. The setUpCommandExecutor function calls functions defined in other files to initialize the Maestro and the LLv3.

The ID and ECHO commands work exactly as in the generic command server described in Appendix A1, except ID now returns a theoretically unique ID.

Listing A2-2. cmd_executor

```
#include "cmd_executor.h"
#include "lidar.h"
#include "servo.h"

void setUpCommandExecutor(void) {
  #if DEBUG_OK && DEBUG_CMDEXEC
    Serial.println("setUpCommandExecutor");
  #endif

  setUpServos();
  setUpLidar();
}

void executeCommand(int cmdType) {
  // execute command
  switch (cmdType) {

    case ID:
      #if DEBUG_OK && DEBUG_CMDEXEC
        Serial.println("ID");
      #endif
      returnInt(CS_ID);
      break;

    case ECHO:
      #if DEBUG_OK && DEBUG_CMDEXEC
        Serial.println("Echo");
      #endif
      returnInt(getParameter());
      break;
```

```
case LIDAR_MULTIPLE:
  #if DEBUG_OK && DEBUG_CMDEXEC
    Serial.println("Lidar multiple");
  #endif
  lidarMultiple(getParameter(), true);
  break;

case LIDAR_SERVO_PARMS:
  #if DEBUG_OK && DEBUG_CMDEXEC
    Serial.println("Lidar servo parms");
  #endif
  // return the parameters
  for (int i = 0; i < 3; i++) {
    returnInt(servoParm[i]);
  }
  break;

case LIDAR_SCAN_START:
  #if DEBUG_OK && DEBUG_CMDEXEC
    Serial.println("Lidar scan start");
  #endif
  // do the scan
  scan(getParameter());
  returnInt(1);
  break;

case LIDAR_SCAN_RETRIEVE:
  #if DEBUG_OK && DEBUG_CMDEXEC
    Serial.println("Lidar scan retrieve");
  #endif
  // check for data completed
  if (rangeTotal == 361) { // return the data
    returnInt(361);
```

```
    for (int i = 0; i < 361; i++) {
      returnInt(rangeBuffer[i]);
    }
  } else {
    returnInt(-1);
  }
  break;

case LIDAR_SERVO_POS:
  #if DEBUG_OK && DEBUG_CMDEXEC
    Serial.println("Lidar Half");
  #endif
  {
  int parm = getParameter();
  int retCode;
  if ((parm >= L_SERVO_POS_MIN * 2) &&
      (parm <= L_SERVO_POS_MAX * 2)) {
    lidarHalf(parm);
    retCode = parm; // return success
  }  else {
    retCode = -1; // return failure
  }
  returnInt(retCode);
  break;
  }

case LIDAR_WARMUP:
  #if DEBUG_OK && DEBUG_CMDEXEC
    Serial.println("Lidar warmup");
  #endif
  {
  int num = getParameter();
```

```
    if (num < 0) num = 0;
    else if (num > 5) num = 5;
    num = 1000 + (num * 4000);
    // warm up lidar
    lidarMultiple(num, false);
    // let user know it is done
    returnInt(1);
    break;
    }
  }
}
```

I'll describe the Lidar command specifics briefly here and offer more detail in the "datasheet" later.

- LIDAR_MULTIPLE takes the desired number of range readings from the LLv3 and returns each immediately.

- LIDAR_SERVO_PARMS returns the values sent to the Maestro to produce positions at 0°, 90°, and 180°.

- LIDAR_SCAN_START starts a cycle of LLv3 range readings followed by a servo movement; the ranges are stored in memory.

- LIDAR_SCAN_RETRIEVE returns the range readings stored in memory.

- LIDAR_SERVO_POS moves the servo to the desired position.

- LIDAR_WARMUP takes a number of range readings and "dumps" them.

lidar.h

Listing A2-3 shows `lidar.h`. Notice the statement `#include "LIDARLite.h"`. It in effect loads the LLv3 library. The statement `LIDARLite lidar` instantiates the library for use in `lidar`. You can also see variables for the buffer that contains the ranges from a scan and the total number of ranges acquired.

Listing A2-3. lidar.h

```
#ifndef LIDAR_CMD_H
#define LIDAR_CMD_H

#define DEBUG_LIDAR true

#include "LIDARLite.h"

const int LIDAR_PRE_WARMUP_CNT = 200;

// Lidar object
LIDARLite lidar;

// buffer for ranges from scan
int rangeBuffer[361]; // the buffer
int rangeTotal; // the number acquired

#endif
```

Warning   The Garmin library version 3.0.6 that I downloaded into the Arduino IDE **is not compatible with the command server design**! If you examine `LIDARLite.cpp`, you will find that in the event of errors, the `write` and `read` methods write to `Serial`. This will of course disrupt communication between the Arduino and the Raspberry Pi. My experience suggests that since the methods retry on errors, such writes to Serial are quite rare, but do happen. In such situations, it would be possible to "live with it" or copy the LIDARLite.cpp file into your sketch and guard against such writes using preprocessor directives as done elsewhere in lidar_command_server. I chose the latter approach for my robot, but obviously chose the former approach for this book.

lidar

Listing A2-4 shows lidar. A description of the functions:

- setUpLidar sets the I2C speed to 400 KHz and configures the LLv3 library to use its default settings.

- lidarMultiple takes the number of range readings indicated by a parameter; it can return or "dump" a reading based on a second parameter.

- scan sweeps the servo in 0.5° increments (as closely as possible) from 0° to 180°, producing 361 range readings. A parameter indicates the delay in milliseconds after servo movements to allow for settling before taking a range reading; 0 means the default delay of 80 milliseconds.

Listing A2-4. Lidar

```
#include "lidar.h"

void setUpLidar(void) {
  lidar.begin(0, true);
  lidar.configure(0);
}
```

```
void lidarMultiple(int number, boolean send) {
  for (int i = 0; i < number; i++) {
    int range = lidar.distance(true);
    if (send) returnInt(range);
  }
}

void scan(int pause) {
  int servoDelay;
  // determine delay for servo to stop
  if (pause == 0) {
    servoDelay = L_SERVO_HALF_DELAY;
  } else {
    servoDelay = pause;
  }

  lidarHalfSlow(0, true);
  setSpeedAccel(LIDAR_PAN, 0, 0);
  rangeTotal = 0;

  lidarMultiple(LIDAR_PRE_WARMUP_CNT, false);

  for (int angleX2 = 0; angleX2 < 361; angleX2++) {
    rangeBuffer[angleX2] = lidar.distance(true);
    rangeTotal++;
    if ((angleX2 + 1) <= 360) {
      lidarHalf(angleX2);
      #if DEBUG_OK && DEBUG_LIDAR
        Serial.println(" Lidar Servo move");
      #endif
    }
    delay(servoDelay);
  }
}
```

servo.h

Listing A2-5 shows `servo.h`. The statement `#include <PololuMaestro.h>` loads the Maestro library. The preprocessor directives regarding the Maestro ensure that the RX/TX hardware gets used. The constants define

- The Maestro channel used for the servo.

- The minimum angle (in degrees) achievable (maximum clockwise rotation), the maximum angle achievable (maximum counterclockwise rotation), and the "middle" angle in between the minimum and maximum. In terms of a mobile robot orientation, those angles correspond to right, left, and forward.

- The value in microseconds to achieve the minimum, maximum, and "middle" angles using the Maestro. These values were empirically derived using the *Maestro Control Center* application (see `www.pololu.com/docs/0J40/4`). They will be different for a different servo.

- The calculations produce the value in 0.25 microseconds for

  - The 0° position

  - The delta from 0° to 180°

  - The delta for 1°

- The value for the speed and acceleration for some servo movements using the Maestro

- The default delay between servo movements during a Lidar scan

Listing A2-5. servo.h

```
#ifndef SERVO_CMD_H
#define SERVO_CMD_H

#define DEBUG_SERVO false

#include <PololuMaestro.h>

/* For Micro Maestro */
#ifdef SERIAL_PORT_HARDWARE_OPEN
  #define maestroSerial SERIAL_PORT_HARDWARE_OPEN
#else
  #include <SoftwareSerial.h>
  SoftwareSerial maestroSerial(10, 11);
#endif
MicroMaestro maestro(maestroSerial);

// Maestro constants
const int LIDAR_PAN = 2; // Maestro servo channel

const int L_SERVO_POS_MIN = 0;
const int L_SERVO_POS_DEFAULT = 90;
const int L_SERVO_POS_MAX = 180;

const int L_SERVO_POS_0_US = 830; // in microsec
const int L_SERVO_POS_90_US = 1480;
const int L_SERVO_POS_180_US = 2130;

const int servoParm[] = {L_SERVO_POS_0_US,
  L_SERVO_POS_90_US, L_SERVO_POS_180_US};

// used in mapping deg to 0.25 microsec "steps"
const int L_SERVO_STEPS_AT_0 = L_SERVO_POS_0_US * 4;
const float L_SERVO_STEPS_IN_180 =
  ((float)(L_SERVO_POS_180_US - L_SERVO_POS_0_US)) * 4;
```

```
const float L_SERVO_STEPS_IN_1 =
  L_SERVO_STEPS_IN_180 / 180.0; // for one degree

// speed and acceleration constant for slow movement
const int SPEED_ACCEL = 20;

// millisecond delay for traveling 0.5 degree
const int L_SERVO_HALF_DELAY = 80;

#endif
```

servo

Listing A2-6 shows servo. A description of the functions:

- setUpServoControl configures the Maestro to use the maximum serial baud rate.

- setUpServos calls setUpServoControl and then positions the servo at 180° (I found that this helps to ensure consistency of scans that start at 0°; hysteresis is likely involved).

- setSpeedAccel sets the speed and acceleration for the Maestro for the Maestro channel indicated by a parameter. Any non-scan movement is constrained using this method.

- mapHD2QM maps a position value in 0.5° to a value in 0.25 microseconds that can be sent to the Maestro.

- lidarHalf sends the servo to a position defined in 0.5° increments.

- lidarHalfSlow sends the servo to a position defined in 0.5° increments with speed and acceleration controlled by the Maestro; it also waits for the end of the movement to return to the caller.

- lidarServoWait waits for a controlled servo movement to end; it uses a script stored in the Maestro; see the Maestro User's Guide (www.pololu.com/docs/0J40) for details.

Listing A2-6. Servo

```
#include "servo.h"

void setUpServoControl() {
  // Set the serial baud rate.
  maestroSerial.begin(200000);
}

void setUpServos(void) {
  setUpServoControl();

  // initialize lidar servo position
  lidarHalfSlow(L_SERVO_POS_MAX * 2, true);
}

void setSpeedAccel(uint8_t channel, uint16_t speed,
  uint16_t acceleration) {
  #if DEBUG_OK && DEBUG_SERVO
    Serial.println("set speed, accel for channel "
      + (String) channel);
  #endif
  maestro.setSpeed(channel, speed);
  maestro.setAcceleration(channel, acceleration);
}
```

```
int mapHD2QM(int halfDeg) {
  int target;
  float fTarget;
  float fAngle = ((float)halfDeg / 2);

  // map from degrees to 0.25 microseconds
  fTarget = (fAngle * L_SERVO_STEPS_IN_1);
  target = L_SERVO_STEPS_AT_0 +
    (int) (fTarget + 0.5);
  return target;
}

void lidarHalf(int angleX2) {
  int mapped = mapHD2QM(angleX2);
  #if DEBUG_OK && DEBUG_SERVO
    Serial.println(
      " 0.25 microsec mapping at setTarget: "
      + (String) mapped);
  #endif
  maestro.setTarget(LIDAR_PAN, mapped);
}

void lidarHalfSlow(int angleX2, boolean wait) {
  setSpeedAccel(LIDAR_PAN, SPEED_ACCEL, SPEED_ACCEL);
  lidarHalf(angleX2);
  if (wait) {
    lidarServoWait();
  }
}

void lidarServoWait() {
  // wait till (almost) done
  #if DEBUG_OK && DEBUG_SERVO
```

```
    Serial.println("waiting on target");
  #endif
  maestro.restartScript(0);
  while (!maestro.getScriptStatus()) {
  }
  #if DEBUG_OK && DEBUG_SERVO
    Serial.println("hit target");
  #endif
}
```

Test

The best way to "unit test" **lidar_command_server** is to uncomment
the preprocessor directive #define MONITOR_DRIVEN in lidar_command_
server, download the sketch to the Arduino, and start the Arduino IDE
Serial Monitor. Listing A2-7 shows the output produced for the commands
entered in the order 10, 11, 30, 32, 50, 60, 52, 54 (the ellipses denote
removed output).

   Everything appears to work as expected. The only thing worthy of note is
some of the range reports, which equal 1. These readings make sense as the
Lidar sensor was pointed at my workstation monitor at a very acute angle.

Listing A2-7. Serial Monitor output

```
Test serial monitor I/O for command
setUpCommandExecutor
ID          |-- 10
600         |
Echo        |-- 11
2468        |
Lidar Half  |-- 30 -> Lidar moves to 90°
180         |
```

```
Lidar servo parms      |-- 32
830                    |
1480                   |
2130                   |
Lidar multiple   |-- 50
248              |
...              |
248              |
Lidar warmup   |-- 60
1              |
Lidar scan start      |-- 52
 Lidar Servo move     |
...             |
 Lidar Servo move     |
1              |
Lidar scan retrieve   |-- 54
361            |
83             |
...            |
47             |
45             |
...            |
60             |
1              |
1              |
...            |
22             |
...            |
119            |
1              |
```

273		
279		
...		
300		
297		

Tip   Don't forget to comment the preprocessor directive `#define`
`MONITOR_DRIVEN` in the `lidar_command_server` tab before
connecting the Lidar Unit to a Raspberry Pi.

Lidar Unit "Datasheet"

The Lidar Unit described in this appendix delivers a 180° scan at
increments of approximately 0.5°, for a total of 361 ranges. The Lidar
sensor used to detect ranges has the following characteristics (see
`https://static.garmin.com/pumac/LIDAR_Lite_v3_Operation_Manual_`
`and_Technical_Specifications.pdf` for details):

- *Range*: 5 cm to 40 meters

- *Resolution*: 1 cm

- *Accuracy*: +/- 2.5 cm at distances greater than 1 meter.
  Nonlinear below 1 meter.

Power

The Lidar Unit derives power for the control electronics from the USB
connector. The remaining components require a separate supply of 5V and
at least 1A.

Reset is achieved by disconnecting the USB cable between the client system and the Lidar Unit.

Interface

The Lidar Unit has a USB Micro-B connector. The serial characteristics are

- Baud rate = 115200

- 8 data bits per character

- No parity bits

- 1 stop bit

The Lidar Unit is command based. A Lidar Unit command has a command type (single byte) and an optional parameter (two-byte integer). A command returns one or more two-byte integers. The Lidar Unit offers commands to scan and retrieve the results as well as commands for testing and calibrating range readings. The commands are described in the following list:

Get ID (type = 10)

No parameters. Returns an identifier for the Lidar Unit (= 600). Intended for device identification, as well as functional verification.

Echo Parameter (type = 11)

Parameter meaningless. Returns the parameter. Intended for functional verification.

Set Servo Position (type = 30)

Parameter indicates a desired servo position in 0.5° increments (e.g., for 90° the parameter = 180). Drives the servo to the desired position. Returns the parameter on success and -1 on failure. Intended for functional verification.

Get Servo Parameters (type = 32)

No parameters. Returns the values (in microseconds) used to position the servo to 0°, 90°, and 180°. Used for calculation of the theoretical position at which ranges get taken during a scan (see **Scan Retrieve** below).

Ideally, the servo could position the Lidar sensor with a resolution of 0.5°. The resolution of the servo controller in the Lidar Unit is 0.25 microseconds, so it is generally not possible to position the servo at the *ideal* angle.

The servo parameters can be used to calculate the exact angle at which range value in a scan gets taken; the calculated angle is *theoretical* because the servo may not actually be able to achieve that angle (e.g., due to dead band). With the servo parameters for the Lidar system at the time of writing, the maximum absolute value of the difference between ideal and theoretical angles is about 0.015°.

For many situations, the difference between the ideal angle and theoretical angle is likely small enough to not matter. The following paragraphs describe the algorithm to calculate the theoretical angle.

Given the resolution of the servo controller is 0.25 microseconds, there are four "steps" per microsecond. Using the servo parameters, it is possible to calculate the number of "steps" per degree. Assume pos180 is the value returned for 180° and pos0 is the value returned for 0°; the following equation shows the calculation for the number of "steps" in 180° (note that all the following calculations *must* be done in floating point unless otherwise indicated):

```
stepsIn180 = (pos180 - pos0) * 4
```

From that value, it is easy to find the number of steps in 1° as follows:

```
stepsIn1 = stepsIn180 / 180
```

Once a Lidar scan of 361 ranges is retrieved, the *ideal* angle for a range is calculated from its index in the range array:

```
idealAngle = ((float) index) / 2
```

Because the servo controller can only accept an integral number of "steps," the next calculation, the number of steps to produce the ideal angle, must result in an *integer*:

```
stepsInAngle = (int) (idealAngle * servoStepsIn1 + 0.5)
```

The *theoretical* angle can be calculated as follows:

```
exactAngle = ((float)stepsInAngle) / stepsIn1
```

Note   You might wonder why the servo parameter for 90° is not used in the preceding calculations. The initial analog servo in the design exhibited nonlinear positioning and required different compensation between 0° and 90° than between 90° and 180°. The final digital servo exhibited linear positioning from 0° to 180°, so only those two parameters are required. I left 90° in the parameter set "just in case."

Get Ranges (type = 50)

Parameter specifies the number of range readings desired. It takes the desired number of range readings and returns them as taken. Intended for functional verification and for range calibration.

Scan (type = 52)

Parameter indicates the delay (in milliseconds) between a servo movement and a range reading; 0 implies the default delay of 80 milliseconds, which is the smallest delay that provides accurate ranges; values under 10 milliseconds are not recommended. It starts a cycle of a range reading followed by a servo movement followed by the delay specified; the ranges are *stored in memory*. When all 361 ranges are acquired, the command returns 1.

Note that a default delay results in an overall scan time of approximately 29 seconds! It is advisable not to do a hard wait for the return value.

Scan Retrieve (type = 54)

No parameters. Returns -1 if the scan did not finish; otherwise, returns the number of ranges available (=361), and then the 361 range readings.

Do not issue this command until a Lidar scan completes (see **Scan**). Doing so will likely disrupt communications between the client and the Lidar Unit and force a reset of the latter to recover.

Range readings are in centimeters. Some ranges indicate errors:

- A range = 1 indicates "no return signal"; that typically means a range > 40 meters or a "troublesome" surface such as glass or other highly polished surfaces (usually associated with acute scan angles).

- A range = 5 indicates an "invalid measurement condition" that can occur for "a variety of reasons" according to Garmin technical support.

- A range >= 6 is valid, but a range < 100 is inaccurate due to nonlinearity in the Lidar sensor; if important, a range < 100 requires compensation to approximate the actual range.

Warmup (type = 60)

Parameter represents a warmup period length; the values can be 0–5, indicating a period of several seconds (0) to a few minutes (5). Warmup consists of a number of range readings that are discarded. Returns a 1 when complete. Due to the time required to complete warmup, it is advisable not to do a hard wait for the return value.

Summary

In this appendix, you learned

- How to extend the command server framework from Appendix A1 to create a new device

- How to use the new device to off-load tasks from the Raspberry Pi

- How to define and implement an abstract interface that makes multiple physical devices appear as a single logical device

Chapter 10 showed how to create a Java device library to use the Lidar Unit from the Raspberry Pi.

APPENDIX A3

NetBeans and Maven

Note One hundred percent of the methodology described in this appendix and seventy-five percent of the text used to describe it came from the developer of diozero, Matt Lewis. My profuse thanks to him for patiently promoting Maven as a modern alternative to Ant, and especially for taking the time to develop and document the methodology. It is an important contribution to the "Java for the Raspberry Pi" community.

The choice of an IDE build automation tool is a very subjective topic. An alternative approach to Ant, used in the bulk of the book, is a tool that aims to eliminate as much of the up-front work as possible by providing an opinionated, templated approach based on convention over configuration. Apache Maven (`https://maven.apache.org`) is one such tool and is a very popular choice. All major Java IDEs support Maven, NetBeans included. This appendix describes how to create diozero-based projects using NetBeans and Maven without requiring much Maven knowledge.

© Greg Flurry 2021

G. Flurry, *Java on the Raspberry Pi*, https://doi.org/10.1007/978-1-4842-7264-0

Caution   This appendix describes the Maven "how to" at a level of detail necessary only to accomplish the overall task. It does not necessarily describe the "why" or the underlying details of any subtask. If you want a broader understanding, you'll have to do your own searching. You have been warned.

In addition to the templated approach and convention-based defaults, one of the great benefits of Maven is that it supports *versioned dependencies*. This means that you only need to specify your application's dependencies and Maven does the hard work of downloading all those dependencies for you – including transitive dependencies, that is, dependencies of dependencies, and so on. Doing this manually can be difficult, especially when maintaining version-specific dependencies and subsequent upgrades.

To make life even easier, Maven has the concept of project template toolkits, called *archetypes*, that can get you up and running with a new project very quickly. While there are generic Java project archetypes, it is even better when the library that you want to use provides its own specialized Maven archetype. Fortunately, diozero provides one – the *diozero-application* archetype.

In this appendix, we'll develop a diozero-based device library and an application that uses that library. Since the emphasis is on using Maven rather than on using diozero, we are going to develop a very simple device library for an LED. We won't perform any of the precursor steps in development as in the bulk of the book. Instead, we will jump immediately into developing a device library in NetBeans using Maven. With the library in place, we'll then develop an application that uses the library, again using Maven. We'll also investigate various approaches for running and debugging the application.

Create a NetBeans Project Using Maven and diozero

To start a new NetBeans project using Maven and diozero, select **New Project**. In the *Choose Project* dialog shown in Figure A3-1, select **Java with Maven** in *Categories*, and then in *Projects* select **Project from Archetype**.

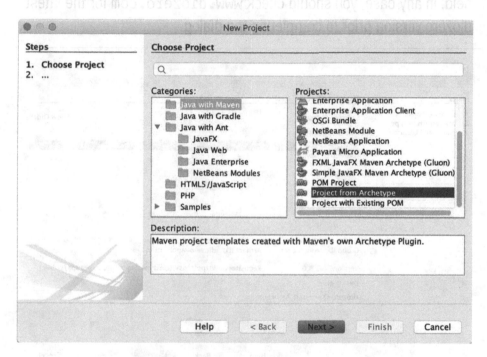

Figure A3-1. *Choose Project dialog*

Click **Next** to proceed to the *Maven Archetype* dialog shown in Figure A3-2. You must first enter "diozero" in the *Search* field. Then, in the *Known Archetypes* field, select **diozero-application**. The dialog automatically fills the rest of the fields, including the latest version of diozero.[1]

---

[1] If you wish to use an older version of diozero, select the **Show Older** box. Then you can select whatever version you wish.

523

Tip   While testing the methodology in this appendix, diozero moved from version 1.2.2 to version 1.3.0. For unknown reasons, the NetBeans dialog in Figure A3-2 continued to suggest version 1.2.2 after 1.3.0 became available. This may or may not happen to you. I worked around the possible bug simply by typing 1.3.0 in the *Version* field. In any case, you should check `www.diozero.com` for the latest diozero version prior to completing the dialog.

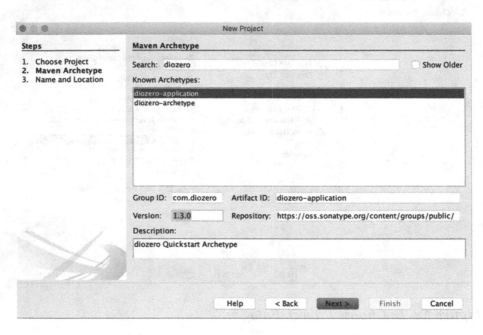

Figure A3-2.   *Maven Archetype dialog*

Click **Next** to proceed to the *Name and Location* dialog shown in Figure A3-3. You now must enter information specific to your project.

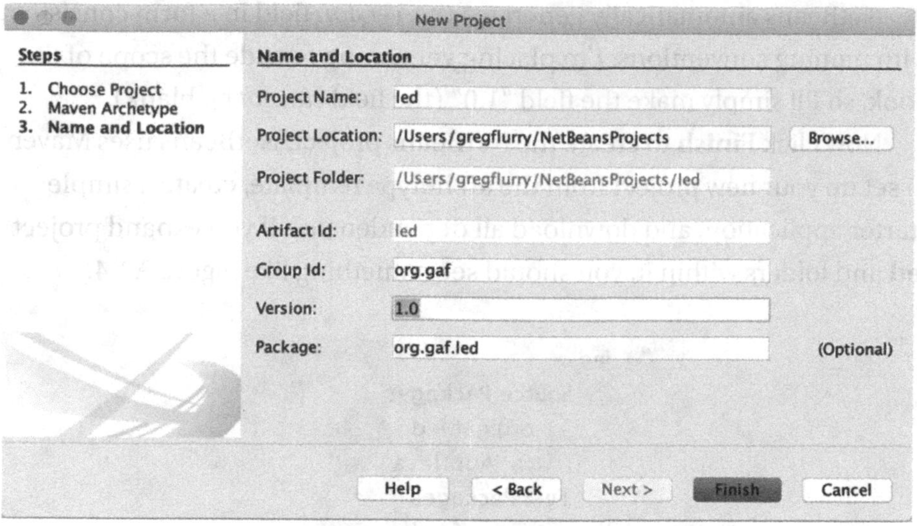

Figure A3-3. *Name and Location dialog*

There are two key bits of information that you must provide:

- *Project Name,* which NetBeans automatically uses as the Maven *Artifact Id*

- *Group Id,* which is a unique identifier for your organization

Maven defines naming conventions for the information (see `https://maven.apache.org/guides/mini/guide-naming-conventions.html`). In keeping with those conventions, the *Artifact Id* for this example is "led." The NetBeans *New Project* wizard forces the *Project Name* to be the same as the *Artifact Id.*[2] The *Group Id* in my case is "org.gaf", but of course yours would be different.

---

[2] If you want a project name consistent with the rest of the book, you can change the content of the <project>/<name> element in the pom.xml file to "LED." You can find pom.xml in the *Project Files* folder of the **led** project.

NetBeans automatically generates the *Version* field in a form consistent with naming conventions. I'm placing versioning outside the scope of the book, so I'll simply make the field "1.0" (the field *cannot* be blank).

Now click **Finish** to create the NetBeans project. NetBeans uses Maven to set up your new project from the archetype template, create a simple starter application, and download all dependencies. If you expand project **led** and folders within it, you should see something like Figure A3-4.

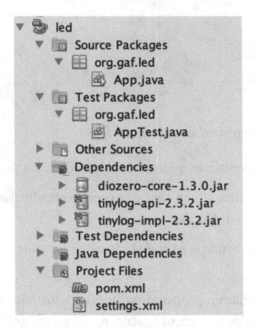

Figure A3-4. *Project led*

Develop a Device Library

Now we will build on the basics in the previous section to develop a device library. As you should expect, the approach differs a bit from that in Chapter 5 and later chapters since we are using Maven.

First, delete the App and AppTest classes Maven created based on the archetype. Next, create a new Java class called LED in the existing *Source* package org.gaf.led.

Obviously, before proceeding, we need some definition of the function and interface for LED. For a constructor, we'll need to know what GPIO pin drives the LED. To keep things very simple, we'll just include methods to turn the LED on and off; this is a subset of the existing diozero LED interface.

We will use the diozero DigitalOutputDevice to drive the LED; see Chapter 7. Its simplest possible constructor mandates an LED circuit like that shown in Figure A3-5. With that circuit, after the DigitalOutputDevice gets created, the LED is off; when it is "on," the LED is on; when it is "off," the LED is off. Note that I used GPIO pin 18, but you can use any GPIO pin you wish.

Figure A3-5. LED circuit

Listing A3-1 shows the complete implementation of LED. See Chapter 7 for the reason LED implements AutoCloseable.

Listing A3-1. LED class

```
package org.gaf.led;

import com.diozero.api.DigitalOutputDevice;

public class LED implements AutoCloseable {

    private final DigitalOutputDevice led;
```

```
    public LED(int pin) {
        led = new DigitalOutputDevice(pin);
    }

    @Override
    public void close() {
        led.close();
    }

    public void on() {
        led.on();
    }

    public void off() {
        led.off();
    }
}
```

Now that the device has been implemented, you can install it into your *local Maven repository* so it can be used by applications you develop locally. Right-click the **led** project, and select **Run Maven ➤ Goals**. In the resulting *Run Maven* dialog (see Figure A3-6), enter "install" in the *Goals* field. To save some time later, select *Remember as* and enter a meaningful name in the text field, for example, "Install" (you can actually use any phrase you want). If you make a change to the library, you can reinstall it by right-clicking **led** and selecting **Run Maven ➤ Install**.

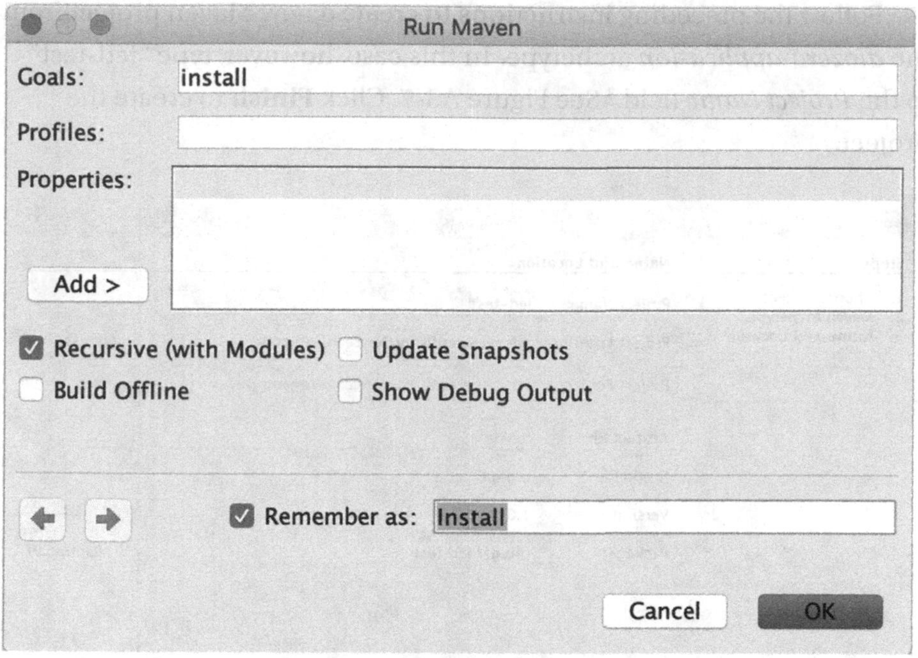

Figure A3-6. Run Maven dialog (install)

Click **OK** in the dialog to run the Maven *install* goal. Check the *Output* panel in NetBeans; you should see "BUILD SUCCESS" once it has successfully completed.

Test the Device Library

Now we can test the **led** library. As discussed in Chapter 8, there are five options for the location of the test code. When doing remote development with Maven, the best option (a different NetBeans project) is also the preferred option. Thus, we will create another project to contain the test application. These instructions also apply for any application that uses a device library.

Follow the preceding instructions to create a new Maven project from the *diozero-application* archetype. In this case, however, type "led-test" in the *Project Name* field.[3] See Figure A3-7. Click **Finish** to create the project.

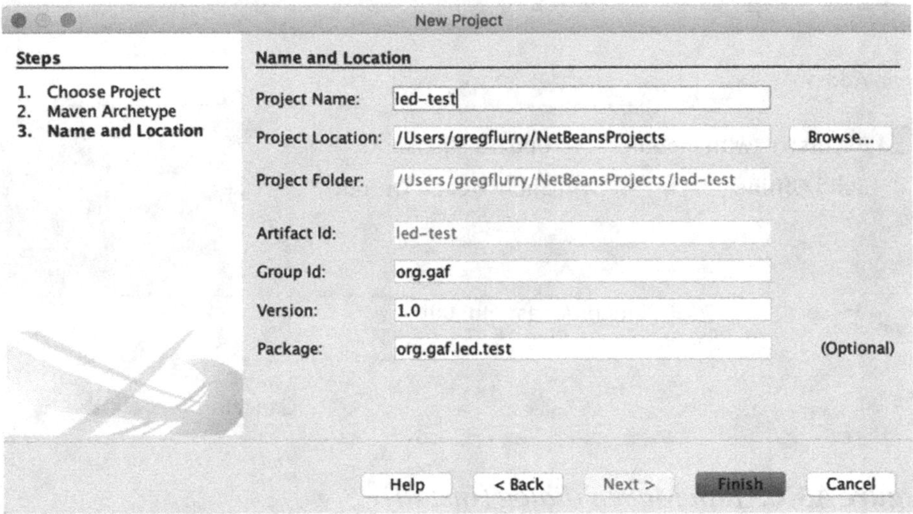

Figure A3-7. *Maven Name and Location dialog for testing*

You now need to tell Maven that the project uses the **led** library you developed earlier. To do so, you must add a *dependency* on the **led** library. Open pom.xml under *Project Files* in the **led-test** project, and add the <dependency> element for the library after the diozero-core <dependency> element in the <dependencies> element, as shown in Listing A3-2. Note that the values for the <groupId>, <artifactId>, and <version> elements in the added <dependency> element must match those used to create the **led** library.

---

[3] As before, you can change the project name by changing the content of the <project>/<name> element in pom.xml.

Listing A3-2. pom.xml \<dependencies\> element

```xml
<dependencies>
  <dependency> <!-- existing -->
    <groupId>com.diozero</groupId>
    <artifactId>diozero-core</artifactId>
  </dependency>
  <dependency> <!-- added -->
    <groupId>org.gaf</groupId>
    <artifactId>led</artifactId>
    <version>1.0</version>
  </dependency>
</dependencies>
```

Once again, delete the App and AppTest classes Maven created. Create a new main class in the *Source* package org.gaf.led.test, and name it TestLED. Listing A3-3 shows the implementation. TestLED simply toggles the LED on and off a few times. Consult Chapter 7 for the reasons underlying the usage of the *try-with-resources* statement and Diozero.

Listing A3-3. TestLED

```java
package org.gaf.led.test;

import com.diozero.util.Diozero;
import org.gaf.led.LED;

public class TestLED {

    public static void main(String[] args)
            throws InterruptedException {
        try (LED led = new LED(18)) {
```

```
        for (int i = 0; i < 5; i++) {
            led.on();
            Thread.sleep(500);
            led.off();
            Thread.sleep(500);
        }
    } finally {
        Diozero.shutdown();
    }
  }
}
```

Run TestLED with a diozero Remote Provider

As mentioned in Chapter 6, diozero includes two *remote* providers that allow your application to run in NetBeans on your workstation yet exercise a remote Raspberry Pi's base I/O capabilities to control an attached device. The beauty of this remote development approach is that you can rapidly make and test changes to the device library and the application entirely within NetBeans with no need to copy anything to the Pi or log in to the Pi to run the application. And of course, you can debug as well. That said, the approach cannot be used when a timely response to sensor input is critical, nor to make realistic performance measurements for an application intended to run completely on the Pi.

Note   Changes to the device library require that you reinstall the library locally. Changes to the application require only that you rerun the application.

The remote magic in this appendix derives from the *pigpio-remote* provider. It has a feature that supports remote communication over a network using sockets. To use it, you must have pigpio on your Raspberry Pi. If you are running Raspberry Pi OS **Recommended** or **Full,** you have it! If you are running **Lite**, you must install it. To do so, in a terminal with a ssh session to your Pi, run the commands:

```
sudo apt update
sudo apt -y install pigpio pigpiod
```

Next, you must enable remote access to base I/O (e.g., GPIO) by running the raspi-config tool in your ssh terminal (remember to preface the command with sudo). Navigate to **5 Interfacing Options ➤ P8 Remote GPIO Enable/Disable**, and select **Yes** to *Would you like the GPIO server to be accessible over the network?* Then select **OK** and then select **Finish**.

Next, you must make sure the *pigpiod daemon* is running. Depending on your circumstances, you can use the following commands:

- sudo systemctl start pigpiod to start the daemon once

- sudo systemctl enable pigpiod to enable the daemon to start at boot time

You might also need the following commands:

- sudo systemctl stop pigpiod to stop the daemon

- sudo systemctl disable pigpiod to disable the daemon from starting at boot time

Now you need to add an application dependency on the pigpio provider. Simply add the "diozero-provider-pigpio" <dependency> element shown in Listing A3-4 to the <dependencies> element in pom.xml for **led-test**.

Listing A3-4. pigpio <dependency> element

```
<dependency>
    <groupId>com.diozero</groupId>
    <artifactId>diozero-provider-pigpio</artifactId>
    <version>${diozero.version}</version>
</dependency>
```

Once you've added the dependency, right-click **led-test** and select **Build**. When the build finishes, look at the **led-test** *Dependencies* folder to see one way Maven shows its worth. It automatically handles all transitive dependencies that are required by the diozero pigpio provider, that is, dependencies of dependencies and so on. As a result, you will see *three* new libraries in *Dependencies*:

- diozero-provider-pigpio-1.3.0.jar, which depends on pigpio-java

- pigpio-java-2.5.10.jar, which depends on netty-all

- netty-all-4.1.65.Final.jar

Think of the work saved!

Finally, you must set the main class to run for **led-test** and configure the pigpiod hostname. Bring up the **led-test** *Properties*, and click the **Run** category. As instructed in Chapter 5, set the *Main Class* field to `org.gaf.led.test.TestLED`. Add the following to the *VM Options* field (replace "pi3b4book.local" with the hostname or IP address of your Raspberry Pi, e.g., 192.168.1.42):

-DPIGPIOD_HOST=pi3b4book.local

Figure A3-8 shows the results. Click **OK** to save the properties.

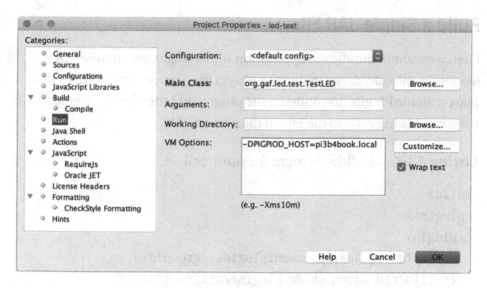

Figure A3-8. *Run properties for led-test project*

If you want to see proof of success, connect an LED to your Raspberry Pi as shown in Figure A3-5. Run `TestLED` by clicking the **Run** icon. When you run `TestLED`, you should see the LED blink. Success!

Run TestLED on a Raspberry Pi

Running `TestLED` on the Raspberry Pi from NetBeans, as supported out of the box by Ant, is a bit more complicated as the required class files must be copied to the Pi, and the application must be run remotely. As always, there are options; however, the goal is to automate things as much as possible. There are several aspects involved; the following subsections explain them.

Build a Single JAR File

First, we want to bundle the application into a single, executable JAR file for download. Maven includes a plugin that can do exactly that – the Maven Shade Plugin. To configure the plugin, add the <build> element shown in Listing A3-5 to the end of the pom.xml file.

Listing A3-5. <build> element for pom.xml

```
<build>
 <plugins>
  <plugin>
   <groupId>org.apache.maven.plugins</groupId>
   <artifactId>maven-shade-plugin</artifactId>
   <executions>
    <execution>
     <phase>package</phase>
     <goals>
      <goal>shade</goal>
     </goals>
     <configuration>
      <transformers>
       <transformer implementation=
         "org.apache.maven.plugins.shade.
          resource.ManifestResourceTransformer">
        <mainClass>
         org.gaf.led.test.TestLED
        </mainClass>
       </transformer>
      </transformers>
```

```
    <artifactSet>
      <!--
      | Exclude the pigpio provider
      | and dependencies from
      | the single JAR as we will run
      | this on the Pi itself
      | using the default built-in provider.
      |-->
      <excludes>
        <exclude>
          com.diozero:diozero-provider-pigpio
        </exclude>
        <exclude>
          uk.pigpioj:pigpioj-java
        </exclude>
        <exclude>io.netty:netty-all</exclude>
      </excludes>
    </artifactSet>
   </configuration>
  </execution>
 </executions>
 </plugin>
</plugins>
</build>
```

Caution   The single-line <transformer> element in Listing A3-5 is split into multiple lines for formatting purposes. The split breaks a build. Ideally you should copy the pom.xml snippets from the book's code repository.

As you can see from Listing A3-5, the <build> element is mostly "boilerplate," but it contains application-specific elements. The <mainClass> element identifies the main class you want to run; for TestLED, the element content is `org.gaf.led.test.TestLED`. The <excludes> element excludes all artifacts related to diozero-provider-pigpio. This is because we will run directly on the Raspberry Pi itself and can rely on the diozero built-in provider rather than use pigpio. For a different application, the <mainClass> content would be different; the <excludes> element might not exist, or its content could be different.

Caution   Once you've added this <plugin>, you can no longer run with the remote provider (started via the **Run** icon).

Now you can create the JAR file. Right-click the **led-test** project, and select **Run Maven ➤ Goals**. You'll see the *Run Maven* dialog shown in Figure A3-9. In the *Goals* field, type "package". Select *Remember as* and enter "Package" in the field to make it easier to recreate the JAR later. Click **OK** to run the goal and generate the JAR file.

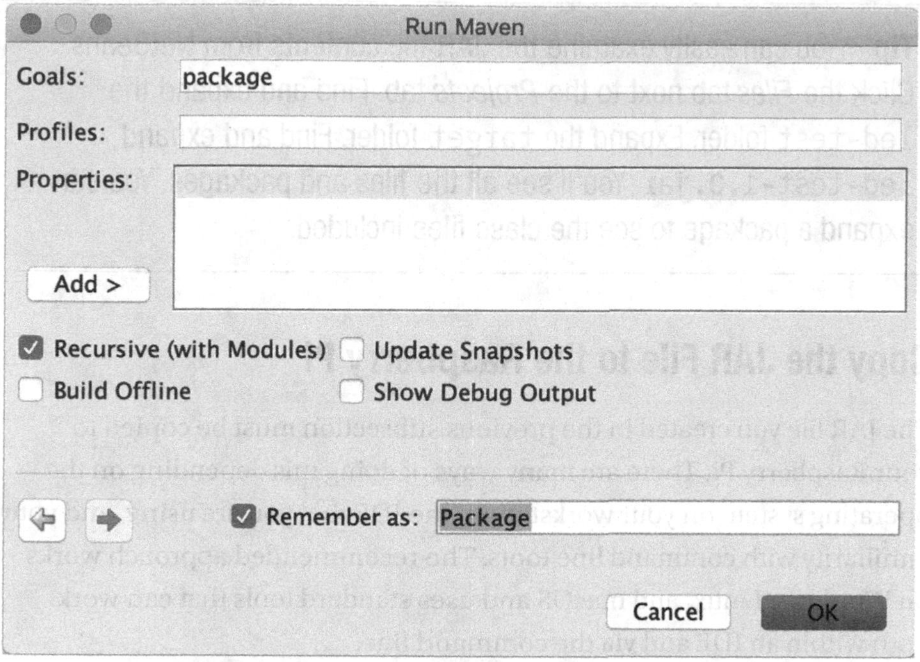

Figure A3-9. *Run Maven (package)*

You can find the generated JAR file in the project's `target` folder. If you inspect the contents, you will see that it contains the project's classes (in this case, `org.gaf.led.test.TestLED`) as well as all the dependencies (in this case, `org.gaf.led.LED`, `com.diozero.*`, and `org.tinylog.*`). Additionally, if you inspect the MANIFEST.MF file (in the `META-INF` folder), you will see that Maven set the Main-Class. This allows you to run Java applications with the command `java -jar <jarfile>` rather than the more complex command `java -cp <jarfile> <main class>` (see Chapter 5).

Tip   You can easily examine the JAR file contents from NetBeans. Click the *Files* tab next to the *Projects* tab. Find and expand the `led-test` folder. Expand the `target` folder. Find and expand `led-test-1.0.jar`. You'll see all the files and packages. You can expand a package to see the class files included.

Copy the JAR File to the Raspberry Pi

The JAR file you created in the previous subsection must be copied to your Raspberry Pi. There are many ways of doing this depending on the operating system on your workstation, the IDE that you are using, and your familiarity with command line tools. The recommended approach works on Windows, Linux, and macOS and uses standard tools that can work both within an IDE and via the command line.

The approach is based on ssh (Secure Shell Protocol) and scp (Secure Copy Protocol). These tools are standard on all UNIX®-like operating systems, including Linux and macOS; however, these are not available by default on Windows. Fortunately, the tools are available on Windows via Cygwin (`www.cygwin.com`) or Windows Subsystem for Linux (`https://docs.microsoft.com/en-us/windows/wsl/about`). This appendix assumes Cygwin (make sure that the openssh package is installed).

First, confirm you have a *ssh key* on your workstation. Look at the content of the folder `~/.ssh`. You'll almost certainly see a file named `known_hosts`. If you also see files named `id_rsa` and `id_rsa.pub`, you have a ssh key (these are the default names for a private/public key pair). If not, you can create a key pair using the command `ssh-keygen`. The rest of the instructions assume the default names, so when prompted by `ssh-keygen` for a file name, just hit enter to accept the default. Further, for convenience, when prompted for a passphrase, leave it empty by simply hitting enter (this is somewhat less secure than having a passphrase).

The public key must be copied to your Raspberry Pi. Use the following command:

```
ssh-copy-id pi@host
```

where *host* is the hostname or IP address of your Pi. You will be prompted for the password for the user pi. Once successful, you can then safely copy files and remote login to your Pi without typing a password.

To copy the project's JAR file to the Pi, in a terminal on your workstation, you must first navigate to the project's top-level folder. For NetBeans and **led-test**, that would be the folder <your_base>/NetBeanProjects/led-test. Then, you must run the following command:

```
scp target/led-test-1.0.jar pi@host:/home/pi/.
```

You should be prompted to enter user pi's password the first time you copy. Once you've run the command, ssh to your Pi as user pi, and look in the home folder. You should see led-test-1.0.jar. Note that you don't have to copy the JAR to the home folder; however, the folder to which you copy must exist.

Run TestLED on the Raspberry Pi

Once you've copied the JAR file to your Raspberry Pi, you can run TestLED from a terminal on your workstation. Enter the following command:

```
ssh pi@host java -jar led-test-1.0.jar
```

When you run the command, you should see the LED blink. If your application does any console output, it will show up in the terminal. Wonderful!

Automate Build, Download, Run

At this point, you can create a single JAR file for a project using NetBeans and Maven. You must then manually copy the JAR file to the target Raspberry Pi. You can then manually run the application. Wouldn't it be nice to fully automate the entire sequence using NetBeans and Maven? Good news – Maven provides the *exec* plugin to support automation. There are several actions involved in enabling the behavior.

First, at the end of the <build>/<plugins> element in `pom.xml`, add the <plugin> element shown in Listing A3-6 to configure the exec-maven-plugin. The configuration tells Maven to run the UNIX® Shell script `remote_run.sh` as part of the Maven exec:exec life cycle phase. Most of the <plugin> element is boilerplate, except for the last two of the <argument> elements. The next-to-last element contains the username and the hostname or IP address for the target Raspberry Pi. The last element contains the folder into which the JAR file gets copied; you can use any folder you wish, but again, the folder must exist.

Listing A3-6. exec-maven-plugin configuration

```
<plugin>
  <groupId>org.codehaus.mojo</groupId>
  <artifactId>exec-maven-plugin</artifactId>
  <executions>
    <execution>
      <goals>
        <goal>exec</goal>
      </goals>
    </execution>
  </executions>
```

```
<configuration>
  <executable>sh</executable>
  <arguments>
    <argument>
      ${project.basedir}/remote_run.sh
    </argument>
    <argument>
      ${project.artifactId}-${project.version}.jar
    </argument>
    <argument>pi@host</argument>
    <argument>/home/pi</argument>
  </arguments>
</configuration>
</plugin>
```

Next, you must create the shell script remote_run.sh in the root
folder of the project (for NetBeans and **test-led**, that would be the folder
<your_base>/NetBeanProjects/led-test). remote_run.sh, shown in
Listing A3-7, simply wraps the scp and ssh commands demonstrated
earlier into a parameterized executable that runs natively on macOS and
Linux systems as well as within Cygwin on Windows systems.

Listing A3-7. remote_run.sh

```
#!/bin/sh

# Assign variables from command line arguments
jar_file=$1
scp_target=$2
target_dir=$3
source_file=target/$jar_file
destination_file=$scp_target:$target_dir/.
```

```
# Copy the JAR file to the remote server
echo "Copying $source_file to $destination_file ..."
scp $source_file $destination_file
if [ $? -ne 0 ]; then
        echo "Error copying $source_file to
        $destination_file"
        exit -1
fi

# SSH to the remote server, change directory
# into the target directory and
# run the Java application
echo "Running the application on the remote server $scp_
target..."
ssh $scp_target "cd $target_dir && java -jar $jar_file"
exit $?
```

Caution   I found that copying Listing A3-8 to create
`remote_run.sh` is not a good idea. The shell is very sensitive
to formatting characters and generally cannot execute with even
one errant "return," for example. Ideally you should copy `remote_`
`run.sh` from the book's code repository.

Now you can run the TestLED application *remotely* from NetBeans.
Right-click the **led-test** project, and select **Run Maven ➤ Goals**. You'll
see the *Run Maven* dialog as shown in Figure A3-10. In the *Goals* field,
type "exec:exec". Click *Remember as* and enter "Exec" in the field to make
it easier to rerun the application. Click **OK** to run the goal that executes
TestLED.

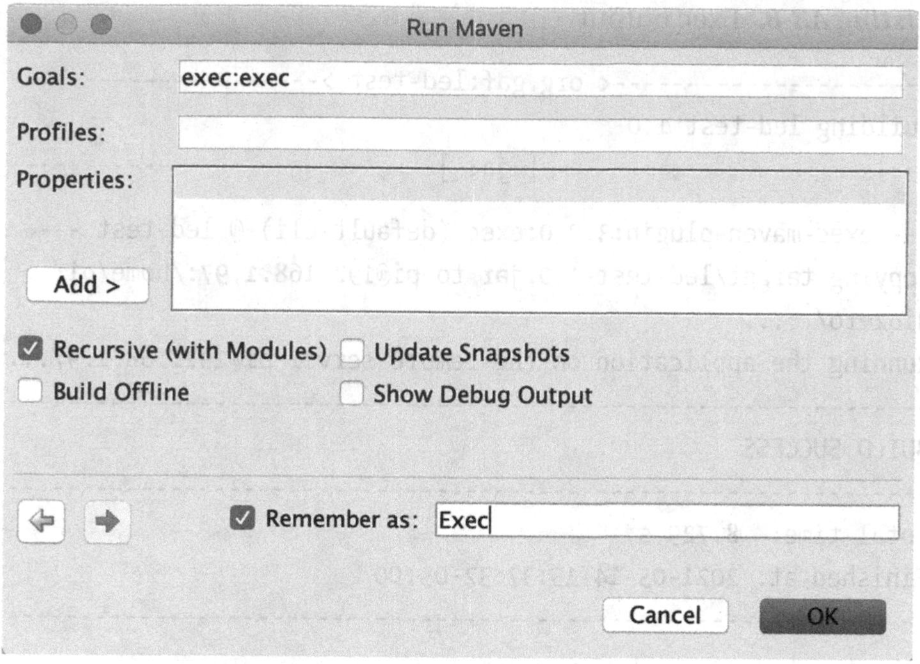

Figure A3-10. Run Maven (exec:exec)

When you run `TestLED` via Maven successfully, you should see results like those shown in Listing A3-8 in the NetBeans *Output* pane. The results indicate that Maven built the single JAR file, called `remote_run.sh,` which downloaded the JAR to the Raspberry Pi and ran `TestLED` on the Pi. In addition, you should also see the LED blink. Success!

Listing A3-8. Exec output

```
--------------------< org.gaf:led-test >--------------------
Building led-test 1.0
-------------------------[ jar ]----------------------------

--- exec-maven-plugin:3.0.0:exec (default-cli) @ led-test ---
Copying target/led-test-1.0.jar to pi@192.168.1.97:/home/pi/
diozero/. ...
Running the application on the remote server pi@192.168.1.97...
------------------------------------------------------------
BUILD SUCCESS
------------------------------------------------------------
Total time:  8.729 s
Finished at: 2021-05-14T15:37:32-05:00
------------------------------------------------------------
```

Summary

In this appendix, we've covered a lot of ground. You've learned how to use NetBeans, Maven, and UNIX® shell commands and scripts to

- Create a diozero-based NetBeans project from a Maven archetype

- Create and install (locally) a new device library

- Create an application that uses the new device library

- Run the application "remotely" using the diozero remote provider

- Create a single JAR file for the application and its dependencies

- Copy the JAR file to a remote Raspberry Pi using ssh

- Execute the application on a remote Raspberry Pi
  using `ssh`

- Create and copy the JAR file, and *remotely* execute the
  application from NetBeans

Congratulations! You can now do remote development with NetBeans using Maven as the build tool.

Index

A

B

© Greg Flurry 2021
G. Flurry, *Java on the Raspberry Pi*, https://doi.org/10.1007/978-1-4842-7264-0

U

V

W, X, Y

Z

Printed in the United States
by Baker & Taylor Publisher Services

Printed in the United States
by Baker & Taylor Publisher Services